To
John
Something to help
fill your bookcases.
Lots of hugs

Xmas 94

MALCOLM HAMER

THE RYDER CUP

THE PLAYERS

Dedication

To: Jill

First published in 1992 by
The Kingswood Press
81 Fulham Road
London SW3 6RB

A product of FORSTER Books

Designed by Bob Bickerton

A catalogue record for this book is available from the British Library

Typeset by Tradespools.
Printed and bound in Great Britain by
BPCC Hazells Ltd
Member of BPCC Ltd

ISBN 0–413–35891–7

The 1927 British team, about to sail to the USA

CONTENTS

The 1933 British team

ACKNOWLEDGEMENTS

I would like to thank all the people who helped me in the preparation of this book.

The following Ryder Cup players who gave generously of their time: Peter Alliss, Severiano Ballesteros, Brian Barnes, Ken Bousfield, Hugh Boyle, Neil Coles, Ben Crenshaw, Max Faulkner, Bernard Gallacher, Brian Huggett, Bernard Hunt, Tony Jacklin, Sam King, Peter Oosterhuis and Lee Trevino.

The following organizations who provided essential information: the Professional Golfers' Association, United States Golf Association, PGA European Tour, US PGA Tour, *Golf Illustrated*, *Golf Monthly*, the Royal and Ancient Golf Club of St Andrews and the British Golf Museum.

Finally, my thanks to Alison Finch, who typed the manuscript.

The Great Britain and American teams who contested the 1929 Ryder Cup matches at Moortown.

INTRODUCTION

Some explanations are necessary about the way in which the information on the players is presented. Where 'GB' appears after a golfer's name, it signifies one who played for Britain in the years before 1979, including the Irish players, since the nomenclature 'GB and Ireland' was too cumbersome. In the text, I also refer to 'British' players. From 1979 onwards all European golfers became eligible for the Ryder Cup and all are named as having represented Europe. When a player such as Bernard Gallacher has played both before and after 1979, he is described as having represented GB and Europe.

All the players who were selected for the Ryder Cup matches which actually took place have been included in this book. A handful of them on the British side (Laurie Ayton, Stewart Burns, Allan Dailey, George Gadd, Eric Green, Jack Hargreaves and Reg Horne) were unlucky enough not to get a game, but are included. The US GA picked their Ryder Cup teams for the 1939 and 1941 matches, which did not take place, and such honorary selections have been ignored.

I have not annotated the different methods of selection, which have varied over the years from nominations by a committee (the 1927 team was picked by the great triumvirate of Vardon, Braid and Taylor) to systems based partly or wholly on the Order of Merit. The recent European system of taking the leading nine players from the Order of Merit, with the addition of three selected by the captain, seems likely to prevail for the foreseeable future. The Americans have used similar methods, though sometimes spread over two years.

The original format for the Ryder Cup of ten players contesting four foursomes and eight singles games over 36 holes remained until 1961, when the number of games was increased to eight foursomes and sixteen singles, all played over 18 holes. Fourball matches were introduced in 1963 and the teams were increased to 12 members in 1971. In 1977, the format was changed once more, to include five foursomes, five fourballs and ten singles. It was unpopular, especially with the spectators, who had too few matches to watch. Two years later, the present arrangement was agreed: eight foursomes and eight fourballs on the first two days, followed by twelve singles on the final day.

Through all the changes, the Ryder Cup has remained one of the most compelling of all sporting contests. Matchplay, the essence of golf, ensures drama; and none more powerful than the climaxes of the matches in 1933 at Southport, 1953 at Wentworth, 1969 at Birkdale and, finally, in 1991 at Kiawah Island, when millions of television viewers around the world watched an extraordinary golfing tale reach its conclusion.

It is always diverting to argue the merits of sportsmen from different generations. Was Denis Compton a better batsman that Graham Gooch or George Best a better footballer than Stanley Matthews? The conclusions are even hazier when golfers of different eras are compared. Suffice to say that, if one were able to assume divine powers and convene the ultimate Ryder Cup match, the selectors would be able to choose from most of the finest golfers in the game's history. The match would be played on a great course, such as Birkdale, Muirfield or Royal St George's; Pinehurst, Oakmont or Pebble Beach. The golfers called to the colours would all be in their prime and transposed by magic to the same era. For the sake of argument the teams would be as follows: Europe – Severiano Ballesteros, Eric Brown, Henry Cotton, Nick Faldo, Bernard Gallacher, Tony Jacklin, Bernhard Langer, Sandy Lyle, Abe Mitchell, Jose Maria Olazabal, Peter Oosterhuis and Dai Rees; USA – Billy Casper, Jimmy Demaret, Walter Hagen, Ben Hogan, Lloyd Mangrum, Byron Nelson, Jack Nicklaus, Arnold Palmer, Gene Sarazen, Sam Snead, Lee Trevino and Tom Watson.

Divine dispensation would allow the captain to play in the match and it is difficult to imagine whether Hagen or Hogan would stand aside for the other; whether Rees, Cotton, Jacklin or perhaps Ballesteros would be the wisest choice for Europe. Whoever was at the helm, it would be an epic battle on the course, with matches in plenty to savour: Ballesteros against Hogan, Brown against Hagen, Cotton against Watson, Faldo against Nelson, Mitchell against Nicklaus, Jacklin against Sarazen . . .

The two captains of 1933, J H Taylor (on the left) and Walter Hagen, with Sam Ryder

A HISTORY OF THE RYDER

The idea of a regular match between the golf professionals of America and Britain had often been mooted, especially by Walter Hagen. It became a reality when a patron appeared in the shape of Samuel Ryder.

There had been two informal contests between the professionals of the two countries. In 1921, at Gleneagles, a British team captained by J H Taylor defeated an American side which included Walter Hagen. In 1926, another match took place, this time at Wentworth, mainly to occupy the leading professionals during the gap between the qualifying rounds for the Open Championship and the tournament proper. The British team defeated the Americans by the decisive margin of 12 points.

By this time, Samuel Ryder had become an important figure in British professional golf circles. His company, founded in the last years of the previous century in St Albans, had made a fortune from his revolutionary idea of selling penny packets of seeds to the enthusiastic gardening public. Ryder had joined Verulam Golf Club in 1910 and had become besotted with the game, although he was into his fifties. In 1923, he put his marketing flair and his love of golf together and decided to sponsor a professional tournament, identified with his company's name. All the leading professionals played in the Heath and Heather tournament over 36 holes at Verulam; they each received a guarantee of £5 plus expenses and Arthur Havers won the first prize of £50.

Such was Ryder's fanatical interest in golf that he also decided to employ his own professional. It was another form of sponsorship which anticipated the endorsements enjoyed by modern professionals, and Ryder's choice was Abe Mitchell. Ryder gave him a salary of £500, plus expenses of £250, in the hope that this would free him from the chores of a club professional's job and enable him to devote himself to winning tournaments, in particular the Open Championship.

Samuel Ryder was an obvious choice as a benefactor when the idea of a regular match between British and American professionals was suggested. It is possible that Ryder had already agreed to donate a cup when the 1926 match took place. But the basic rules of the contest had not been agreed and the first official match was to take place a year later, in Worcester, Massachusetts. *Golf Illustrated*, whose editor, George Philpot, was to manage the British team, took the initiative in trying to cover the team's anticipated expenses of £3,000 through donations from golf clubs. But, to the magazine's annoyance, strongly expressed in their columns, only 216 golf clubs out of a total of 1,750 made contributions. Samuel Ryder made up the difference and the team, captained by Abe Mitchell, prepared to sail for New York on the *Aquitania*.

It was sad that Mitchell, who was the model for the effigy of the golfer on the top of the Ryder Cup itself, was taken ill with appendicitis before the ship sailed. Ted Ray stepped in as captain and Herbert Jolly was hurriedly summoned to make up the numbers.

It had been agreed that the event would comprise four foursomes and eight singles, all to be played over 36 holes – which was to remain the format until 1961. It was also agreed that only 'home-bred' professionals could represent their countries: that is, those golfers born and residing in their respective countries. Thus, players such as Tommy Armour, Jim Barnes and Macdonald Smith were excluded from the American team on grounds of birth; in later years, Henry Cotton, Percy Alliss and Aubrey Boomer were not selected for Britain because they were attached to clubs in Europe.

Several of the British players were known to American golf enthusiasts: for example, Ted Ray, who had won the US Open in 1920, and the team received a very enthusiastic welcome. Arthur Havers remarked that the team was 'submerged by hospitality and kindness ... in a world of luxury and plenty'. But this generosity did not extend to the golf course, where the British were soon in trouble.

Ted Ray and Fred Robson, regarded as the grand old men of the British team, led the way in

The scene at Worcester, Massachusetts, in 1927

the foursomes against Walter Hagen and Johnny Golden. After 11 holes, the British were three up, but the Americans took the next four holes to go ahead. It remained a very close tussle, but the American pair won on the 35th green. Havers and Jolly were four down at lunch and played poorly to lose comfortably to Gene Sarazen and Al Watrous. George Duncan and Archie Compston, judged to be the best British pair, were five down at lunch and were sunk soon afterwards by Johnny Farrell and Joe Turnesa. Only Aubrey Boomer and Charles Whitcombe kept the flag flying; they played beautifully, to score level fours for the 31 holes they needed to vanquish Leo Diegel and Bill Mehlhorn.

The American team, who were supposedly unfamiliar with 'Scotch foursomes', had already assumed a two-point lead after the first day. Nor did they relinquish their grip on the second day; when Leo Diegel beat Ted Ray by seven and five, the Americans won their seventh point – and the Ryder Cup. Although Charles Whitcombe halved his game with Sarazen, who won the final hole with a par four, only George Duncan, playing last, recorded a full point: he beat Joe Turnesa on the final green with a birdie.

The *Golf Illustrated* reporter wrote that 'the British rout was complete' and, in what was to become a familiar tale over the years, the observers noted how much better were the Americans at putting. The *Times* wrote of the visiting team's marked inferiority in this department of the game and Ted Ray, the British captain, summed up the match as follows: 'Our opponents beat us fairly and squarely, and almost entirely through their astonishing work on the putting greens. I consider that we can never hope to beat the Americans unless we learn to putt.'

But Samuel Ryder's cup had taken its first tentative steps on the way to becoming one of the great sporting spectacles. A few years later, Ryder spoke these words in a radio broadcast: 'I trust that the effect of this match will be to influence a cordial, friendly and peaceful feeling throughout the whole civilized world . . . I look upon the Royal and Ancient game as being a powerful moral force that influences the best things in humanity.'

At Kiawah Island in 1991, multi-millionaire golfers battled away to win the little golden trophy; NBC gave the event 21 hours of coverage and sent their pictures around the world for hundreds of millions to see; chauffeurs drove the players in huge limousines, escorted by police; the world's golfing media, television and radio and the Press were there in force; the fixture was heavily sponsored; and the crowds were large and demonstrative. Even if the hype surrounding the fixture has become excessive and the confrontational posturing of some of the players at Kiawah Island was distasteful, the games were mostly played in the best of sporting spirits. If he looked down on the scene from his celestial resting place, would Samuel Ryder have been pleased? One hopes so.

1957 – LINDRICK

The face of British golf in the Fifties was as austere as the decade itself; the Open Championship was dominated by the overseas players, Bobby Locke and Peter Thomson, and only Max Faulkner disturbed their dominance, when he won the great event at Portrush in 1951. The Ryder Cup had been in the firm grasp of the Americans since 1933, even if the British had tugged at it presumptuously in 1953, at Wentworth, before losing by the odd point.

Even though the American team for Lindrick did not include such stars as Sam Snead, Ben Hogan, Jimmy Demaret and Cary Middlecoff, the pundits considered that it was more than good enough to vanquish the British. Leonard Crawley was loud in his praise of the opposition: 'The golden age of the Twenties has returned to American golf . . . the utterly beautiful swinger has come back to replace the less graceful, hard-hitting slugger.' He singled out the American captain, Jackie Burke, as the finest stylist in the world and Doug Ford as 'one of the boldest putters on earth'.

If Lindrick seemed a curious course on which to stage the Ryder Cup, the explanation was simple: money. Sir Stuart Goodwin, a Yorkshire industrialist, put up £10,000 to sponsor the fixture and was given the right to nominate the venue. There was some criticism of his choice, since a main road crosses the course at two points; and it was rather short and, therefore, favoured the Americans, with their mastery of the wedge shot. Henry Longhurst also criticized the accommodation provided for the American team: a commercial hotel in the middle of Sheffield was hardly suitable, in his opinion.

A familiar pattern was imposed on the match by the Americans, as the foursomes began on the first morning. Doug Ford and Dow Finsterwald opened with two birdies against Peter Alliss and Bernard Hunt, as did Art Wall and Fred Hawkins behind them. Not that the golf of Ford and Finsterwald was faultless, since they were in the rough six times in the first nine holes, but always seemed to find a good lie; at the seventh hole, the ball lay so well in the rough that Finsterwald hit a wood on to the green. The Americans were one hole up at lunch, started the afternoon round by playing the first six holes in 20 strokes, but only overcame the sterling resistance of Hunt and Alliss on the 35th green.

Max Faulkner and Harry Weetman played some 'lamentably poor' shots and were easily beaten by Ted Kroll and Jack Burke; Christy O'Connor and Eric Brown were woefully inaccurate from the tee and could not cope with the brilliant golf of Dick Mayer and Tommy Bolt, who had a morning round of 67, went to the turn after lunch in 32 shots and won easily by seven and five. It was left to the captain, Dai Rees,and Ken Bousfield to save the British team's blushes. Unperturbed by the American pair's start (Art Wall and Fred Hawkins began with 3s at the first three holes), Rees and Bousfield levelled the match after 18 holes and then pulled away to win in the afternoon. Leonard Crawley opined that it was 'abundantly clear that the Americans were equipped with an altogether superior short game and that an old, old story was again about to raise its grisly head.'

If the rest of the British team was subdued by failure, the captain, Dai Rees, as implacable in his determination as ever, was not. His main problem was to decide on the players to omit from the singles; but the solution was made easy for him by Faulkner and Weetman, who both made it clear that they had played badly and offered to stand down from the following day's matches. But, in the half hour or so that it took Rees to exchange his order of play with that of Jack Burke, Weetman changed his stance. He made an inflammatory statement to the Press that he would never play in a team captained by Rees again. The captain was convinced that the sad business was orchestrated by Weetman's wife, Freda, and by some of his misguided friends.

Such an incident might have cast the British team down even more, but it had the opposite effect: their resolution was already hardening in the fire kindled by Dai Rees, as inspirational as ever. He felt

confident that it was his destiny to retrieve the Ryder Cup after 24 years. He was even more sure when his instinct to put Eric Brown at the top of the order, where he might encounter the brilliant but erratic Tommy Bolt, proved correct.

Above all, a change in the weather heartened Rees. The wind had altered direction and freshened and had made the course two or three shots harder. The greens had been properly cut and were much faster; a story later went around that the greenkeeper had not realised that the Ryder Cup was due to start on the preceding day and, therefore, had not cut the grass to tournament length.

The Fates were clearly with the British players from the start. Six of the Americans took three putts on the first green and, after five holes, the British were ahead in seven of the eight games and level in the other. In contrast to the day before, it was the British who were holing the putts and the Americans who were missing them. By lunchtime, Peter Mills was five holes up on Jack Burke, who was substituting for a sick Ted Kroll; Brown was four up on Bolt and relishing every moment of the battle; Bousfield was five up on Hebert and Rees, 'prancing around as if he had springs in his boots' as Leonard Crawley put it, four up on Furgol. Only Alliss and Bradshaw were in arrears, both by one hole.

In the afternoon, the British players ran away from their opponents. Brown, jaw jutting and teeth clenched, saw Tommy Bolt off; Mills disposed of Burke in fine style; Rees demolished Ed Furgol, and no golfer in the world would have withstood the tigerish British captain on that day. The moods of the preceding day were reversed; the possibility of victory inspired the British players, whereas the unexpected prospect of defeat caused the Americans to collapse. As *The Times* correspondent wrote: 'Frankly, you could have knocked us all down with a feather.'

The cheers were rolling across the Lindrick course. Max Faulkner was charging around from match to match, acting both as chief cheer-leader and motivator and as scorer, since there were very few scoreboards on the course in those days. He remembers going head over heels down one slippery bank, much to the delight of the spectators, and crawling through the legs of the crowd to tell Dai Rees how his other players were faring.

The vital point was finally won by Ken Bousfield, who beat Lionel Hebert on the 33rd hole. The Ryder Cup had at last returned to British keeping and no player more deserved to hold the slender gold trophy aloft in triumph than Dai Rees.

The triumphant British captain, Dai Rees, in 1957

Jack Nicklaus made a supreme sporting gesture . . .

1969 – ROYAL

In 1969, the British golfing public gave a rapturous welcome to the champion they had craved for two decades. Tony Jacklin won the Open Championship at Lytham and registered the first British victory since Max Faulkner's in 1951. Jacklin was young, confident and aggressive and had no fear of tangling with the dominant American stars of golf, such as Jack Nicklaus, Lee Trevino and Billy Casper. In his preview of the Ryder cup, Leonard Crawley presciently wrote: 'His presence . . . could be the spark that will light another bonfire such as the one that consumed the United States at Lindrick in 1957.' There were other young golfers in the British team who were also savouring the thought of the battle to come: Bernard Gallacher, Peter Townsend, Maurice Bembridge and Brian Barnes. At their head was Eric Brown, as flinty a competitor as any in the Ryder Cup, a man who had won all his singles matches in the biennial event. Neil Coles still considers that Brown was the best captain for whom he played, but the Scot's abrasive approach got him into trouble before a ball had been hit. Brown apparently told his players not to look for American balls in the rough; his reason was that if a British player trod on an American ball, this would result in the loss of the hole. This was incorrect and seemed churlish, and was rightly ignored when battle commenced.

The rival captain, the incomparable Sam Snead, had ten newcomers in his side. Only Gene Littler and Billy Casper had appeared before in the American colours, but the 'new boys' had long ago shed their golfing innocence. In Jack Nicklaus, Lee Trevino, Tommy Aaron, Dave Hill, Raymond Floyd and Frank Beard, the American team had six of the most accomplished players in the world.

The home team could not have made a better start in the foursomes. The experienced pair of Brian Huggett and Neil Coles always had the measure of Miller Barber and Ray Floyd, while Gallacher and Bembridge won a narrow victory over Trevino and Ken Still. The latter player showed early signs that the occasion was perhaps too much for him. Bembridge had to ask him to move out of his line of vision on the 13th tee and Still reacted in an exaggerated way; on the same hole the American tried to explode a shot from under the lip of a bunker and was hit by the rebound. But it was only on Trevino's instruction that the hole was conceded.

It was the manner of the victory by Jacklin and Townsend over Hill and Aaron that caught the imagination of the crowds and fired the confidence of the British team. They began with three birdies and were seven under par when they won in spectacular style on the 17th green. Townsend, who could see that the Americans' ball was just short of the putting surface, hit a soaring 3-wood to within a few feet of the pin and Jacklin rolled the ball home for an eagle. With the old firm of Alliss and O'Connor wresting a half from Casper and Beard, the British team were three points ahead at lunchtime.

Whatever Sam Snead said to the American team during the interval, it worked. They came roaring out in the second series of foursomes and won three of them by the thin margin of one hole. Jacklin and Townsend sustained Britain's fortunes by beating Beard and Casper; the British pair went ahead for the first time at the 17th hole and won the match by dint of Townsend's beautifully judged pitch over a bunker at the 18th.

The competitive quality of the play and the high tension with which it was imbued combined to produce a second day of great drama: seven of the eight games went to the final green. The British captain, Eric Brown, made the daring decision to split his winning combination of Jacklin and Townsend on the grounds that the Open champion could match anyone in the four-balls on his own. His plan succeeded in the morning, since both players, with different partners, won their games. Huggett and Alex Caygill managed a half against Floyd and Barber and so the British team

BIRKDALE

went into lunch two points ahead of the Americans. By nightfall, the score had been levelled at eight points apiece, with the American pairs unbeaten during the afternoon.

The second series of four-balls was marred by some rancorous disputes between Huggett and Gallacher on the one side, and Dave Hill and Ken Still on the other. Leonard Crawley went to the heart of the matter when he wrote: 'All four are born fighters who are not prepared to bow the knee to anyone.' The problem was exacerbated, in Gallacher's opinion, by an indecisive referee and by the Americans' lack of knowledge of the rules of matchplay. Ill-feeling, mainly orchestrated by Still, was apparent from the start and it all came to a head on the seventh green, where Still putted up short of the hole and holed out. He had played out of turn and the British pair protested; the correct procedure was for Still to replace his ball without penalty. In the very highest of dudgeon, Still grabbed Gallacher's marker and conceded the hole; he added some remarks which reinforced his displeasure. There was a further quarrel on the next green, but by that time the two captains, supported by Lord Derby, the President of the PGA, arrived to calm both the players and the crowd. Dave Hill got on with the game in the best possible way by playing superlative golf to win the game.

At eight points to each team, the scene was set for a bravura finish on the final day, when two series of eight singles matches were played. The Americans were fast out of the stalls as Trevino beat Peter Alliss and Hill accounted for Townsend. Alliss asked to be dropped from the afternoon matches, since he had putted so poorly; it was his final Ryder Cup appearance. Although Brian Barnes lost to Casper on the final green, the British won all the other five encounters; Jacklin defeated Nicklaus comfortably by four and three.

At lunchtime, Eric Brown was glowing with excitement, and with the knowledge that Britain needed only three and a half points to win Sam Ryder's golden trophy. Gallacher played superb golf to defeat Trevino (a Monday headline was to read 'Gallacher's lion heart typifies British spirit') and Peter Butler gathered the second point, with a win over Douglass. But both Coles and O'Connor lost and, with two games left on the course, the whole match was tied.

Jacklin, one hole down to Nicklaus, was sizing up his long putt on the 17th green, just as Brian Huggett, level with Casper, was assessing his own putt of around four feet on the final green. A huge roar of excitement and joy went up to the heavens as Jacklin holed his putt for an eagle three to level matters with Nicklaus. Huggett thought it was 'a winning cheer' and that Jacklin had beaten Nicklaus, so his putt to halve with Casper was the one that would win the Ryder Cup. In it went, one of the bravest of strokes, and Huggett collapsed in tears. But the game was still on, with the two pre-eminent golfers of their respective countries, Jacklin and Nicklaus, fighting it out down the final hole.

The exchanges between the two champions have been variously recalled down the years but, as they walked towards their drive, they certainly agreed that they were both petrified. Nicklaus played first and hit the centre of the green; Jacklin went for the flag but rolled to the back. His putt was short by 18 inches. In typical style, Nicklaus gave his putt every chance and it rolled about four feet past. In terminal silence, he holed out calmly, and then picked up Jacklin's marker to signal a halved game and a tie in the Ryder cup for the first time. His words to Jacklin were: 'I was sure that you would hole the putt, but I was not prepared to see you miss.'

It was a supreme gesture by a supreme sportsman, an encapsulation of the spirit of the Ryder Cup. If the shade of Sam Ryder were looking, he would no doubt have wept a celestial tear.

... to the relief of Tony Jacklin

THE JACKLIN Y

No one was more surprised by the offer of the captaincy of the European Ryder Cup team than Tony Jacklin. His exclusion from the 1981 side, in favour of Mark James, whose behaviour at The Greenbrier two years earlier was eccentric, had been a bitter disappointment; so much so that he had even refused the invitation to be present at Walton Heath as an official.

The choice of Jacklin as captain was both imaginative and courageous and, after some thought, he accepted the proposal made by Ken Schofield, the executive director of the PGA. Jacklin made various demands, the main motivation being that his team should have the best of everything, in particular, first-class travel and equipment and the company of their wives and girl friends. The captain was determined that the players would step on to the first tee without any feelings of inferiority. He got everything for which he asked.

Jacklin was keenly aware that the one man he needed in his team was the brilliant and charismatic Spaniard, Severiano Ballesteros. Not only was he one of the best players in the world, but he was an inspiring personality. He would be the talisman of the team, just as Jacklin himself had been in 1969. But Ballesteros was as disenchanted with the men who ran European golf as Jacklin had been. He had also been excluded from the team in 1981 because of his dispute with the European tour administrators over appearance money. There is no more stubborn a man than Ballesteros if he feels he has been wronged. But Jacklin, respected by the Spaniard as a great champion, set out to get his man. He knew that Ballesteros would relish any opportunity to take the Americans on at matchplay golf, and he was also able to argue that if he gave himself fully to the Ryder Cup cause, the British fans would take him to their hearts. So it proved and Ballesteros was to become the most influential figure in the Ryder Cup over the next decade.

The 1983 European team was chosen straight off the money list; this was to change in later years when the captain had the freedom to choose three of the twelve players. As he prepared for the encounter at the PGA National course in Florida, Jacklin no doubt savoured the idea of confronting again his old rival, Jack Nicklaus, who was the American captain. Jacklin nearly whisked the Cup away at his first attempt, as the Europeans led the Americans by one point after the first day and the teams were level at the end of the second.

One of Jacklin's shrewdest moves was to pair Ballesteros with the young newcomer, Paul Way. They lost their first game, a foursomes, to Tom Kite and Calvin Peete, and the Spaniard expressed his doubts about the partnership. But Jacklin persisted with the idea that Ballesteros, as mentor, would bring the best out of Way. He was right: they won two and a half points from their next three outings. In addition, Faldo and Langer won three points out of four together and the lightweight pair of Brian Waites and Ken Brown wrested an unexpected point from Gil

EARS – 1983-89

Morgan and Fuzzy Zoeller in the first series of fourballs.

On the final day, the first European disappointment was Ballesteros's failure to defeat Zoeller, who was suffering from a bad back. At the final hole, the Spaniard was on the brink of disaster and needed a remarkable shot to escape with a half; from a fairway bunker, he hit a 3-wood on to the edge of the green, a carry of well over 200 yards. Behind him, Faldo and Langer won their matches, but it was the American middle order of Gilder, Crenshaw and Peete which put the impetus back into the American team. Paul Way won another point, but Woosnam lost and with two games left on the course, the match was tied at 13 points.

At the final hole, the combative Lanny Wadkins hit a brilliant pitch to within inches of the hole, to gain a half with Canizares. The whole affair now depended on Bernard Gallacher and Tom Watson. Both played the 17th hole poorly, but Watson one stroke less poorly than Gallacher and the Ryder Cup was left in American hands again.

Nevertheless, Jacklin's team had shocked the Americans, who had only just survived to record their narrowest ever win at home. But the Europeans had shown themselves to be unafraid of their opponents and Jacklin had a springboard which would enable his players to soar to success at the Belfry two years later. The Europeans felt even more confident of their ability, since Langer had won the Masters earlier that year and Sandy Lyle the Open Championship. Jacklin's wildcard selections were Faldo, Ken Brown and Jose Rivero. Once again Jacklin was pitted against an American captain with a dazzling playing record: Lee Trevino, who had been his nemesis in the early Seventies.

On the first day of the contest, the Americans began in a confident mood and won the foursomes series by three games to one. Calvin Peete and Tom Kite, straight hitters both, justified Trevino's claim that they were his strongest pair by easily accounting for Faldo and Langer. The Spaniards, Ballesteros and Pinero, saved Europe's day by winning twice. At lunchtime on the second day, there occurred one of those cock-eyed incidents that occasionally changes the whole pattern of a sporting contest. On the 18th green, Craig Stadler had a tiny putt of less than two feet to win his match, in partnership with Strange, against Lyle and Langer. He could have knocked it in one-handed, but he pulled the putt past the hole and allowed the Europeans to gain an unlikely half. Stadler's moment of madness tilted the whole match to the Europeans; in the afternoon, the Americans seemed to have been shocked out of their usual efficiency and they lost three of the four foursomes by wide margins.

As in 1957 at Lindrick, the crowd on the final day seemed to sense that Europe's hour had at last come. The tough Spaniard, Manuel Pinero, was delighted when he was drawn to meet the ultra-competitive Lanny Wadkins and beat him on the 17th green. Woosnam lost to Stadler, but Way continued his fine sequence with a win over Raymond Floyd. Ballesteros had the worst of the exchanges with the accomplished Kite and was three down with five to play; but his incandescent will to win never showed brighter and he snatched a half from a seemingly

Tony Jacklin and his team celebrate their 1985 victory at the Belfry

Tony Jacklin, one of the prime influences on the Ryder Cup

hopeless position. 'He hit shots I never even dream about,' said Kite resignedly. Lyle and Langer won their games and the scene was set for Sam Torrance to put himself firmly in the focus of Ryder Cup history. At the 18th, his opponent, Andy North, made things easy for him by skying his tee shot into the water, but Torrance siezed his great opportunity with aplomb. A crashing drive, a short iron and one putt gave him a birdie and returned the great trophy to Europe after a gap of 28 years.

It was appropriate that Tony Jacklin should continue as the captain, his sights set on defeating the American on their own turf for the first time. Once again, they were to be in the charge of Jack Nicklaus, whose team had narrowly thwarted the Europeans in 1983, and the 1987 match was to be played at his own course, Muirfield Village in Columbus, Ohio.

The Americans made a formidable start to the tie and, early on the first morning, were leading in all the foursomes. Faldo and Woosnam, judged to be Europe's strongest combination, were four down to Wadkins and Mize. But the British pair led the fight-back. Woosnam's thrilling 1-iron into the 15th green levelled the game and the Britons went on to win by two holes. In the meantime, Ballesteros was at his inventive best in covering the mistakes of his young compatriot, Olazabal, and they defeated Larry Nelson and Payne Stewart at the final hole, after Ballesteros had found the green with a long iron from a distant bunker. In the afternoon, the European team whitewashed the Americans in the fourball games; although the results were apparently quite close, the European dominance was emphasized by the statistic that the Americans won only ten of the 68 holes which were played. On the following morning, the Europeans increased their lead to five points and the margin was the same after the second series of fourballs, during which some remarkable golf was played by both sides. Faldo and Woosnam had five birdies between them in their first five holes against Kite and Strange and won all of them; they went to the turn with a better ball score of 29, as did Andy Bean and Payne Stewart on their way to victory over Brand and Darcy.

With 12 singles to come on the final day, Europe needed only four points to retain the Ryder Cup. As the Americans fought back vehemently, it seemed at one stage that the points would not be forthcoming. The Europeans were behind in almost every game and their bankers, Langer and Lyle,were three and four down respectively. Several games went all the way to the final hole and it was there that the Europeans proved mentally stronger. Both Howard Clark and Torrance won the 18th hole, the former to defeat Pohl and the latter to halve with Mize. Then Darcy holed a slippery putt to beat Crenshaw, whose putter had snapped early in the round, and Langer wrested a crucial half point from Larry Nelson. Finally, Ballesteros accounted for Strange on the 17th green and it was fitting that the inspiring Spaniard, who had given everything to Europe's cause, should contribute the point that ensured Europe's first victory on American soil.

Two years later at the Belfry, the Americans made their usual fast start in the foursomes and took them by three matches to one. But the European retaliation was swift and sure when they made a clean sweep of the afternoon fourballs. Ballesteros and Olazabal, who had halved their foursomes game against Watson and Beck, won the first five holes against Watson and O'Meara. When the Spanish pair seemed to falter in the middle of the round, Ballesteros made victory certain with an eagle at the tenth hole, followed by birdies at the next three holes. One hope that he did not say 'Elementary my dear Watson' to the great American golfer.

Honours were shared on the second day, with four points to each team. The most accomplished golf came in the game between Beck and Azinger and Faldo and Woosnam, with 18 birdies recorded when the Americans won on the 17th green. As the singles began, the European side needed five points to retain the Ryder Cup and another half a point to win it. The Americans began with verve and determination; at one time, only one European, Mark James, was in the lead. Tom Kite crushed Clark by the record score of eight and seven; Ballesteros suffered a rare defeat at the hands of Azinger; and Olazabal and Rafferty gained Europe's first points as their opponents, Stewart and Calcavecchia both drove into the water at the final hole. But the tide turned in Europe's favour as James beat O'Meara, Christy O'Connor flew his unforgettable 2-iron shot on to the final green to defeat Couples, and Canizares snatched a final-hole victory over Ken Green. The Ryder Cup had been retained by Europe, but the half point needed for outright victory did not materialize. The Americans dug into their reserves of determination to win the last four games and ensure the second tie in the Ryder Cup. The American captain, Raymond Floyd, rightly said: 'The one winner was the game of golf.'

Tony Jacklin knew that it was the time to stand aside as captain. In the four matches from 1983 to 1989 he had achieved more than anyone had hoped. He had been fortunate to have several of the best golfers in the world to call upon: Ballesteros, Faldo, Lyle, Langer and Woosnam. But Jacklin's supreme achievement had first been to win their confidence and then to weld a collection of disparate individuals from different countries and cultures into a formidable golfing entity. In so doing, he had maintained the tradition of the Ryder Cup and had presided over its renaissance as the pre-eminent team event in golf.

A

AARON, TOMMY

USA

Born: 22.2.37

Appearances: 1969, 1973

Record: P6 W1 L4 H1

Although he won very few tournaments, Tommy Aaron was a very consistent golfer on the American tour. His first important win was in the Canadian Open of 1969 when he finished with a memorable round of 64 to tie with Sam Snead, whom he beat in the play-off. Apart from the Atlanta Classic in 1979, Aaron's only other win was in the 1973 Masters.

His victory would perhaps have soothed his unpleasant memories of the 1968 Masters tournament, when he wrote down the wrong figure for Roberto de Vincenzo's score at the 71st hole. The Argentinian scored a birdie three, but Aaron recorded a four and the higher score had to stand. De Vincenzo lost by one stroke to Bob Goalby.

Tommy Aaron's consistent golf earned him a place in the American team which tied the Ryder Cup match at Birkdale in 1969. In his four games he gathered one and a half points: his full point came in a foursomes victory with Dave Hill over Neil Coles and Brian Huggett. At Muirfield four years later, despite his win in the Masters earlier that year, his swing was out of sorts. One vividly remembers him trying, on the practice ground, to retrieve his game with the help of Jack Nicklaus. As the gloom descended, we spectators sought the comforts of bars and restaurants, but Aaron soldiered on. He lost both his games, although the Americans retained the Ryder Cup.

ADAMS, JIMMY

GB

Born: 21.10.10

Appearances: 1947, 1949, 1951, 1953

Record: P7 W2 L5 H0

With his very long swing, the shaft way beyond the horizontal, Jimmy Adams was a reminder of the methods of an earlier golfing age. As a boy at Troon he had caddied for the Open champion of 1883, Willie Fernie, who had clearly influenced Adams's swing. Because it was so smooth and rhythmic, it served him well throughout his career, allied as it was to a beautifully controlled putting stroke.

Adams came very close to winning the Open twice before the war. He was runner-up to Alf Padgham in 1936 at Hoylake and had a tense contest with Reg Whitcombe in 1938 to finish second again.

He was selected for the 1939 Ryder Cup, which was cancelled owing to the Second World War, and had to wait until 1947 to make his debut in the match in which Britain garnered only one point. In the foursomes Adams and Faulkner were two up at lunch on the dreadnought American pair of Ben Hogan and Jimmy Demaret, but eventually went down by two holes.

In the next match, at Ganton in 1949, Adams had the distinction of winning both his matches. He played superbly in the foursomes, in partnership with an irrepressible Max Faulkner, to defeat 'Dutch' Harrison and Johnny Palmer and he beat Palmer again in the singles. His results in his last two appearances were less than glorious as he suffered the irresistible force of Sam Snead and Lloyd Mangrum in 1951 and then lost to Jack Burke. His last match, in the very close encounter of 1953, was an anti-climax as he lost heavily, with the newcomer, Bernard Hunt, to Jack Burke and Ted Kroll.

Adams won several tournaments after the war, including the Dunlop Masters and the Opens of Belgium, Holland and Italy; and he was runner-up in the PGA Matchplay tournament on three occasions.

ALEXANDER, STEWART

USA

Born: 6.8.18

Appearances: 1949, 1951

Record: P2 W1 L1 H0

Skip Alexander had a useful career as a professional in the late Forties, when he won two tournaments, one of which was the Tucson Open in 1948.

 Percy and Peter Alliss remain the only father and son to have played in the Ryder Cup

He made his first appearance in the Ryder Cup in the following year, at Ganton, and lost his foursomes match to Fred Daly and Ken Bousfield. He won another tournament in 1950, but in September of that year he broke both his ankles and was badly burned in a tragic air crash, of which he was the only survivor.

He made a remarkable recovery and was able, just over a year later, to play again in the Ryder Cup at Pinehurst; he beat John Panton with great ease by eight and seven.

Alexander won a further event, the Skyway Open in 1954, and then became a club professional. In 1959 he was awarded the Ben Hogan Trophy for his courage in overcoming injury to continue his golf career.

ALLISS, PERCY

GB

Born: 8.1.97

Appearances: 1929, 1933, 1935, 1937

Record: P6 W3 L2 H1

Although he made an unhappy start to his Ryder Cup career, Percy Alliss had an excellent record, with three wins and a half out of six games. In 1929, the captain of the side, George Duncan, did not give him a match because he was adjudged 'short of practice', a euphemism for out of form.

Percy Alliss had a number of tournament wins to his credit during the 1920s and 1930s. For several years he was the professional at the Wannsee Club in Berlin and won the German Open on five occasions and the Italian Open twice. He won the Penfold twice and the *News of the World* Matchplay championship twice, when it was second only to the Open in prestige.

Alliss was a remarkably consistent player in the Open. In the years from 1928 to 1939 he finished in the top five no less than five times. He came closest to winning in 1931, when he was third behind Tommy Armour and had the misfortune to hit a ball out of bounds on the 72nd hole.

Alliss's first game in the Ryder Cup, in 1933 at Southport, was a baptism of fire against Gene Sarazen and Walter Hagen. But, in harness with Reg Whitcombe, he halved the match and then beat Paul Runyan in the singles. He and Alf Padgham were heavily defeated by Henry Picard and Johnny Revolta in 1935, but Alliss got his revenge two years later over the same pair. In 1935 he was Britain's only winner in the singles, when he beat Craig Wood after being three down after 18 holes.

Henry Cotton rated Alliss as one of the most consistent strikers of a golf ball in the game: a man who rarely missed a fairway or a green. He felt that Alliss's clean striking and great control made him capable of winning any tournament. His woods and long irons were superb and his one weakness was his inconsistent putting; only this prevented him from being regarded as one of the very best players of his time.

ALLISS, PETER

GB

Born: 28.2.31

Appearances: 1953, 1957, 1959, 1961, 1963, 1965, 1967, 1969

Record: P30 W10 L15 H5

It was pre-ordained that Peter Alliss, the son of Percy, would become a professional golfer and he duly became one at the age of 15. He inherited from his father a beautifully simple and orthodox style which, allied to his strong physique, enabled him to hit the ball long and far.

In 1953, aged 22, he became the youngest player to be selected for the Ryder Cup, although he had not yet won an important professional tournament. He was also the first son to follow his father into a Ryder Cup team – a distinction which still remains. Fate had reserved the cruellest of examinations for Alliss and another young golfer who was making his debut, Bernard Hunt. Theirs were the last matches on the course on the final day and, if both of them had managed a par five down the 18th at Wentworth, the Ryder Cup would have been won for Britain. Each player took six and the match was lost by one point. Peter Alliss experienced the misery of taking four shots when only about 40 yards from the hole.

He has never forgotten the experience, one which was made more bitter by the hammering the two youngsters received from the Press. Alliss is convinced that he was passed over for the 1955 match (as was Hunt) as a sort of punishment for the ill fortune of 1953. The team was partly selected in those days and Alliss had won the 1955 Dunlop Masters, the last tournament before the final choice was made. Alliss played in the victorious team of 1957, but lost both his matches. He had to wait until the 1959 tie in California for his first Ryder Cup win in company with Christy O'Connor in the foursomes. He halved his singles with Jay Herbert and was the only unbeaten British player.

Alliss was to be one of the most prominent British golfers from the late Fifties to the end of the Sixties. In three successive weeks in 1958 he won the Spanish, Italian and Portugese Opens; he won the Dunlop Masters twice (1955 and 1959), the PGA Close Championship on three occasions and the Martini. He won the Vardon Trophy for the lowest stroke average in 1964 and 1966.

It was surprising that Alliss, despite his great golfing gifts, never came close to winning a major championship. His best finish in the Open was eighth; and one of the answers to this conundrum was that his putting was rather suspect.

In the middle period of his Ryder Cup career, he played golf of a very high standard; in the four matches from 1959 to 1965, he won nine and halved four of his 18 games in a period when Britain lost every tie. His victims included Arnold Palmer, who never beat him in a singles, Billy Casper and Ken Venturi. He vividly remembers his first battle with Palmer in 1961 at Lytham. It ended in a halved match after some superb shot-making by both players. They were applauded all down the last fairway, as if it were the Open Championship. In foursomes and fourball matches, he was particularly successful with Christy O'Connor, for whom Alliss has the highest regard.

In 1965, Alliss won five points out of six; his only defeat was in a fourball match at the hands of Arnold Palmer and Dave Marr. In 1967 the British team were heavily defeated and Peter Alliss's final appearance was in the epic drawn match, two years later, at Royal Birkdale. He recalls how he was beaten in the morning singles by Lee Trevino, mainly because he had become very shaky on the greens. He felt that he outplayed the American and was inside his ball on eight or nine of the greens, but lost two and one. He asked to be omitted from the afternoon matches.

It was time to follow new paths and television brought a fresh bloom to Alliss's career in golf. He succeeded Henry Longhurst, a supremely hard act to follow, on BBC Television. His urbane and knowledgeable, and often quirky, comments have brought him a deserved success in this field. He has published many books (including a novel) and videos and is an excellent after-dinner speaker.

He has been involved in golf-course architecture for many years, initially with Dave Thomas, and now with Clive Clark. If he has one regret it is that he was never asked to captain the Ryder Cup team, even though he was the captain of the Professional Golfers' Association in 1962 and again in 1987.

Peter Alliss has had a long and honourable career in professional golf and to many he is, through the power of television, the voice of the modern game.

AYTON, LAURENCE

GB

Born: 25.2.14

Appearances: 1949

Although he was selected for the match at Ganton in 1949, which was won narrowly by the USA, Laurie Ayton did not play a game. He won his place by reaching the final of the *News of the World* Matchplay tournament in the previous year, when he lost to Fred Daly. This was his best finish in an important professional tournament.

AZINGER, PAUL

USA

Born: 6.1.60

Appearances: 1989, 1991

Record: P9 W5 L4 H0

Paul Azinger should have won the Open Championship at Muirfield in 1987. After two opening rounds of 68, he led the field and, with nine holes to play on the final day, was three shots clear of Nick Faldo. While the Englishman churned out the pars, Azinger let his lead dribble away; the final indignity was to drop shots at the last two holes and finish in a tie for second place.

Azinger had to attend the qualifying school three times before establishing himself on the American tour. His first good year was in 1986 and he played brilliantly in the following year to finish second in the money list; he won the Phoenix Open, the Las Vegas Invitational and the Greater Hartford Open. With a victory in each of the next two seasons, he easily secured his place in the 1989 Ryder Cup team.

Although Azinger lost his opening fourball match at the Belfry to Sam Torrance and Gordon Brand Jr, he won his other three encounters. He and Chip Beck revenged themselves on Torrance and Brand in the foursomes and the American pair just prevailed in a dazzling fourball against Nick Faldo and Ian Woosnam. In total, the players scored 18 birdies, of which seven were recorded by Azinger. He went on to defeat Severiano Ballesteros in the singles. He defended a one hole lead stoutly for most of the round and, at the final hole, despite hitting his drive into the water, conjured up a five to hold off the Spaniard.

Azinger's great consistency kept him in the top ten of the American money list for the next two years and, at Kiawah Island, he came up against his old adversary, Ballesteros, again. A distinct chill pervades the relationship of these two golfers, made even more frigid by a dispute in their opening foursomes. Azinger and Beck had used golf balls of differing compressions at some of the opening holes, which was a breach of the rules. It seemed to harden the resolve of Ballesteros and Olazabal, who were three down at the time, and they forged on to win the game. Azinger and Beck lost to them again in the fourballs, but Azinger and O'Meara crushed Faldo and Gilford in the foursomes.

Azinger was drawn to meet Olazabal in the singles. It was a fierce battle, marked by courageous golf played in a generous spirit. Azinger finally went ahead at the 17th hole and made the point safe for his team at the final hole.

B

BALLESTEROS, SEVERIANO

Europe

Born: 9.4.57

Appearances: 1979, 1983, 1985, 1987, 1989, 1991

Record: P30 W17 L8 H5

One poet wrote of another: 'His like is seldom born, being admitted through the ivory gates where most must enter through the gates of horn.' A suitable introduction also for Seve Ballesteros, who was blessed with an abundance of those talents essential to a champion golfer. He first gave full reign to his extravagant and precocious gifts at the 1976 Open Championship, when he was only 19 years old. At the end of the third round he led the championship and had showed that he was totally unafraid of the course or the occasion. He was there to win (although on this occasion he had to give best to Johnny Miller) and in the process intended to pound Birkdale into submission.

He could hit the ball huge distances and if he was in trouble off the fairway, he simply sent his ball flying on its way along with any adjacent obstructions. His strength, packed though it was in a well-proportioned frame, was reminiscent of Arnold Palmer's. His play from bunkers was superb and his putting was nerveless; above all, his inventiveness with his short irons was unparalleled. He showed this at the final hole of the championship, when he needed a birdie four to tie with Jack Nicklaus for second place. After two shots, his ball lay in a horribly difficult spot at the side of the green; the pin was close to that edge and guarded by bunkers. Somehow Ballesteros threaded his ball between the bunkers to within a few feet of the hole and made his birdie. The eminent golf teacher, John Jacobs, said: 'That shot alone convinced me that Seve was a genius.'

The young Spaniard not only had a beautiful swing, full of rhythm and grace, but also had the looks and bearing of a Hollywood star. While some were waxing lyrical about his golf, others were captivated by his flashing, dark-eyed smile.

Ballesteros was born in a modest farmhouse overlooking the fishing village of Pedrena. From an early age he hit shots with a makeshift 3-iron, with pebbles as golf balls, on the beach. Occasionally he sneaked out to play a few holes on the adjoining Royal Pedrena golfcourse, where he worked as a caddie. Ballesteros's uncle, Ramon Sota, was the best-known golfer in Spain and all his brothers became professionals, so it was no surprise when he followed suit at the age of 16.

After his astonishing display in the 1976 Open Championship, Ballesteros won his first tournaments, the Dutch Open and the Lancome Trophy. In the latter, he overtook Arnold Palmer with a score of 31 over the final nine holes. He finished as the leader of the Order of Merit and remained on top for the next two years, during which time he won the French Open, the Swiss Open (twice), the German and Scandinavian Opens and the Martini. With an international outlook which was unusual in one so young, he had also won the Japanese Open twice, the Otago Classic in New Zealand and the Kenya Open; in 1978 he won his first tournament in the USA, the Greater Greensboro Open. It was then that the American tour commissioner, Deane Beman, offered Ballesteros membership of the American tour without the formality of his attending the qualifying school. But the Spaniard turned the offer down, and this snub planted the seeds of a later conflict between the two men.

In 1979 at Lytham, Ballesteros won the first of his Open Championships and became the youngest champion in this century. His magnificent second round of 65, which equalled the course record, kept him in touch with Hale Irwin, who led the field after three rounds. It is said that Ballesteros hit very few fairways during his final two rounds, but his strategy was to put his ball into the positions which gave him the easiest approaches into the greens. With powers of inventiveness that amounted to witchcraft, he had no fear of the rough. Under the brilliant

onslaught, Hale Irwin withered away and the final salvo was Ballesteros's play at the 16th hole during the fourth round. He carved a huge drive right of the fairway into a temporary car-park; his ball had gone so far that he only needed a sand-wedge for his second shot and he holed the putt for a birdie. He won the Open by three shots from Nicklaus and Crenshaw. Some American pundits sarcastically called him the 'carpark champion', but Ballesteros put them in their place a year later at the Masters.

After two rounds at Augusta in 1980, Ballesteros led the way by three shots; after three rounds by seven. On the final day he was ahead at one point by ten shots. Despite some dropped shots over the final holes, he won by four strokes to become the youngest golfer to wear the green jacket. At the press conference afterwards, Ballesteros, never a person to forget a slight, made ironic references to 'how lucky' he had been.

In 1979, after considerable pressure from the Americans, the Ryder Cup team was opened to European golfers and Ballesteros, along with his compatriot, Antonio Garrido, was selected. It was an unhappy debut at The Greenbrier, since he lost four matches to Larry Nelson, who was in scintillating form. The two Spaniards managed to win just one game, a foursomes against Zoeller and Green.

But Ballesteros did not rejoin the team for the match in 1981, when he became embroiled in a bitter dispute over appearance money., The European tour administrators had decreed a limit of $10,000 as guarantees for European stars like Ballesteros. The Spaniard, fiercely protective of his status as an Open and a Masters champion, would not accept such a limit, especially since it was not applied to American golfers. He took the ruling as a direct personal affront and went off the play in Australia, where in won the PGA Championship; in Japan, where he won the Dunlop Phoenix event, and anywhere else where the appearance money was good. Up to August of that year, he only played in Europe in the French Open, the Open Championship at Sandwich and the Scottish Open. As a result he did not qualify for the Ryder Cup team and the captain, John Jacobs, did not offer him a place as a 'wild card'. Europe were heavily defeated at Walton Heath and there was undoubtedly some extra impetus to Ballesteros's efforts in the World Matchplay Championship at Wentworth; he beat Langer, Irwin and Crenshaw on the way to victory.

In the following year Ballesteros retained his matchplay title and also won the Madrid and the French Opens. It was a prelude to his second victory at the Masters, and he made it possible with a blitzkrieg beginning to his final round. He was four under par after four holes and eventually cruised home by four shots.

By this time Ballesteros was the most dynamic golfer in the world. He had an unmatched weight and variety of shot and a vibrant will to win; when the force was with him, no other golfer in the world could compete. He brought colour and audacity to the golf-courses of the world; amid the tournament journeymen he was all dash and drama, a charismatic buccaneer who could outface any risks: the spectators loved him wherever he played.

When Tony Jacklin agreed to take on the captaincy of the Ryder Cup team in 1983, he knew that he needed Ballesteros, not only for his supreme skill but as a rallying point for the European team. At first Ballesteros professed to have no interest in the Ryder Cup, but Jacklin's powers of persuasion eventually won the day. In the very close match at the PGA National, which went to the Americans by a single point, Ballesteros played his expected important part. In partnership with the inexperienced Paul Way, he gathered two and a half points from four games and then halved his singles with Fuzzy Zoeller. At the 18th hole of that match, Ballesteros was in a bunker, 240 yards from the green, after two strokes. His shot with a 3-wood to the fringe of the green is still remembered as one of the epic shots in Ryder Cup history, daring in conception and supreme in execution. It enabled him to halve the match.

A second Open Championship victory came to Ballesteros in 1984 at St. Andrews. His flair for a dramatic finish saw him wrest a vital par four from the forbidding 'road hole', the 17th, in his final round. From left of the fairway he had a margin of error of only a few feet but his 6-iron was flawlessly hit. As Tom Watson wrecked his chances at the same hole by

taking five shots, Ballesteros secured his second Open Championship with a birdie at the final hole.

Despite winning nearly 20 tournaments around the world in the next few years, Ballesteros had to wait until 1988 to win another major championship. He dominated the European tour, especially in 1985 and 1986, when he won 11 events, and improved his bank balance by winning the Million Dollar Challenge in South Africa two years in succession. Ballesteros played regularly on the American tour in 1984 but only appeared in nine events in 1985,well short of the number prescribed for tour members, and his uneasy relationship with the autocratic Deane Beman flared into an open feud. The commissioner childishly ordered that Ballesteros's name be struck off the 1985 money list and that he be banned from the 1986 tour except for the major championships and five other tournaments to which sponsors could invite him. Never able to resist a tilt at a windmill, Ballesteros maintained that he was a special case, and the less xenophobic American golfers, such as Jack Nicklaus, Tom Watson and Raymond Floyd, supported his cause. The real problem was that Beman, with the mentality of an insurance salesman, could not cope with a genius like Ballesteros, arrogant though he was.

In those circumstances, Europe's long-awaited victory in the Ryder Cup at the Belfry in 1985 must have delighted Ballesteros, who took three points out of our in harness with Manuel Pinero and then halved with Tom Kite in the singles. With five holes to play, Ballesteros was three holes in arrears, but three birdies saved the day. 'He hit shots I never even dream about', said Kite.

Ballesteros should have won the Masters again in 1986 but, in the final round, he hit a glaringly bad iron shot into the water at the 15th hole. A second failure a year later, at Augusta, when he, together with Greg Norman, lost a play-off to Larry Mize, sent him into a golfing depression. The dark and brooding side of Ballesteros's personality was more often seen.The dazzling smile was replaced by a frown as he peered suspiciously at the world from eyes shadowed by his beetling brows.

But he roused himself for the Ryder Cup encounter at Muirfield Village in 1987. Here began his brilliant partnership with the youthful Jose Maria Olazabal. So far they have played 12 matches together and have won nine and lost only one. At Muirfield Village they began with three wins and were only defeated, in a four ball match, by Hal Sutton and Larry Mize. It was appropriate that Ballesteros holed the putt which gave Europe its first victory in the USA, when he beat Curtis Strange on the 17th green.

Perhaps the tonic of winning the Ryder Cup in America had its effect, since Ballesteros began to win tournaments again in 1988. At Lytham,where he had triumphed in 1979, he produced a spectacular last round of 65 to relegate Nick Price to runner-up and to win his third Open title. The sparkle was back in Ballesteros's smile and he went on to lead the Order of Merit for the fifth time; he also won the Westchester Classic in America. If 1989 was a relatively quiet year for Ballesteros, he was in his usual dominant form in the Ryder Cup at the Belfry. He and Olazabal were unbeaten and they handed out severe thrashings to Tom Watson and Mark O'Meara and to Mark Calcavecchia and Ken Green in the fourballs. But Ballesteros lost his singles to Azinger at the 18th hole, when both players were in the water; Azinger made a remarkable five to hold the Spaniard off.

In the following year it seemed that all the Ballesteros magic had fled him. He won one tournament, the Balearic Open, but failed to qualify for the final rounds of six tournaments, including the Open and the US PGA Championship. However a victory in Japan early in 1991 rekindled the flame and the great Spaniard won the PGA Championship, the British Masters and the World Matchplay Championship for the fifth time. In the desperately close encounter at Kiawah Island Ballesteros's will to win was a glittering example to the rest of the European team. He was unbeaten in his five games and only Payne Stewart and Fred Couples managed to prise half a point from his ebullient partnership with Olazabal.

Early in 1992 Ballesteros won two European tour events to take his world-wide tally to over 70 victories, including five major championships. Still only in his mid-thirties, he will be a force in the major tournaments for many years to come. No player since

Arnold Palmer has had the same electrifying effect on the game. As well as the inherent grace of his swing, he lives every shot of every round and engages the spectators in his emotions. They identify with him as with no other player. This ability to give himself heart and soul to the task has made Ballesteros the inspirational figure in golf in the last decade or so; and never more so than in the Ryder Cup matches, in which his commitment is intense. As Tony Jacklin said of him: 'As a golfer, as a striker of the ball, Seve is supreme. It's his balance, his poise. The game lives in him.'

BANNERMAN, HARRY

GB

Born: 5.3.42

Appearances: 1971

Record: P5 W2 L2 H1

Harry Bannerman did not gain a tournament victory of any note outside his native Scotland, whose professional championship he won in 1967 and 1972. In the same years he played in the World Cup.

His best finish in the Open was equal 11th in 1971, the year of his one appearance in the Ryder Cup at St. Louis. The USA team included four of the best golfers in the world, in Arnold Palmer, Jack Nicklaus, Billy Casper and Lee Trevino, but this was Britain's best result so far in America. The margin of defeat was only five points.

Bannerman played an important part in the tough contest and showed his fine qualities as a matchplayer. With Bernard Gallacher, he won his foursomes against Casper and Miller Barber and went out twice in the fourball matches on the next day with Peter Townsend. They lost narrowly to Jack Nicklaus and Gene Littler in the morning and had a furious battle with the mighty pair of Nicklaus and Palmer in the afternoon. The quality of golf was superb: the latter pair's better ball score to the turn was 30, but they were one down. It took a birdie putt by Jack Nicklaus of around 15 feet on the final hole to win the game.

Harry Bannerman was in his element in the singles matches. With a cigar clamped between his teeth, he strode jauntily down the fairways and was not at all overawed by his opponents. He halved with Arnold Palmer in the morning and inflicted a defeat on Gardner Dickinson for the one and only time in Ryder Cup matches – until then he had played nine and won nine. The match was played in virtual silence from the seventh hole onwards, where Bannerman was awarded the hole following an infringement of the rules by Dickinson's caddie.

BARBER, JERRY

USA

Born: 25.4.16

Appearances: 1955, 1961

Record: P5 W1 L4 H0

Although Jerry Barber played for two victorious American sides, he had a rather poor record in the Ryder Cup. His solitary win was in a foursomes game in 1961, when he was captain and when the matches were played over 18 holes for the first time. He and Dow Finsterwald beat Tom Haliburton and Neil Coles on the final green.

Barber was a slight, bespectacled man, whose short game was unrivalled in professional golf. He made the utmost of his talents because he practised more assiduously than any contemporary. As Gary Player was later to say: "The more I practise, the luckier I get."

He won seven American tournaments, including the Tournament of Champions in 1960 and the US PGA at Olympia Fields in 1961. On each of the final three holes, he holed putts from between 20 and 60 feet to tie with Don January; and he won the play-off by a shot.

BARBER, MILLER

USA

Born: 31.3.31

Appearances: 1969, 1971

Record: P7 W1 L4 H2

With his contorted, looping backswing, Miller Barber looks anything but an accomplished golfer. Ben Crenshaw said rather unkindly of him that when he swings 'it looks as if his golf club gets caught in a clothesline.' But at impact everything is perfectly in position and he swings through the ball and sends it on a very long journey. He turned professional quite late after service in the US Air Force and had his first success at the Cajun Classic in 1964. He had 11 victories on the American tour during a career that lasted until the early Eighties, but his best period was from 1967 to 1974, when he won an event every year and finished in the top 20 in most tournaments.

In 1969 Barber finished in the top ten in the four major championships and had excellent chances to win both the Masters and the US Open. In the latter tournament he was three strokes ahead of the field after three rounds, but his final round of 78 left him seven shots behind the winner, Orville Moody. In 1973 he won the first World Open at Pinehurst and pocketed a record prize of $100,000.

He made his first appearance in the Ryder Cup at Birkdale in 1969 and lost his foursomes with Raymond Floyd. But he redeemed himself with two halved fourball matches and then hammered an off-form Maurice Bembridge in his one singles game. His form in 1971 was not so good and he lost his three matches, although the Americans retained the Cup.

Barber, who used to be known as 'Mr X' because of the dark glasses he always wears and his withdrawn demeanour, owns a golfcourse in Texas and has found a new lease of golfing life on the Seniors tour. He has won over 20 tournaments, including the Seniors Open on three occasions; by the end of 1991, when he finished 20th in the Order of Merit, he had won nearly $3 million on the Seniors tour.

BARNES, BRIAN

GB & Europe

Born: 3.6.45

Appearances: 1969, 1971, 1973, 1975, 1977, 1979

Record: P25 W10 L14 H1

For nearly two decades the commanding figure of Brian Barnes was easily spotted as he strode along the fairways. His height and large frame enabled him to generate enormous power from a smooth and controlled swing and this alone would have assured his popularity with the spectators. But his affable personality reinforced his appeal, since he has always been aware that golf is also an entertainment, and that a jocular exchange with the gallery wins many friends: it also helps to pass the time between shots, because no golfer alive can concentrate for a whole round.

Barnes has his unconventional side, too, and in warm weather might be seen playing in a pair of shorts; he might drink a can of beer or two on the way round and often has a pipe on the go. To the great delight of American spectators at the Masters, he was even seen to play shots out of the bunkers with his pipe still clenched in his teeth. His outspokeness has also endeared him to the fans, if not to golf's administrators; especially when his criticisms of slow play led him to make the practical protest of taking a folding chair to one tournament so that he could rest between shots. If he had taken a table, a silver service and a buffet lunch with him, nobody would have been surprised.

Golf needs players like Brian Barnes. Apart from his formidable skills, he enlivened the tournament scene; and to the delight of many of his supporters he has returned to the European circuit after a gap of several years.

Barnes was blessed with considerable gifts as a sportsman, and they were nurtured at Millfield School, among whose other notable pupils were Gareth Edwards and Mary Rand. After leaving school, he won several amateur events, including the British Youths' Championship, and then became a professional. His first successes came in 1969, when he won the Young Professionals Championship and the Agfacolour tournament. Other good results ensured his appearance in the 1969 Ryder Cup at Birkdale.

This was a remarkable match in which to make one's debut and, although Barnes lost his three games, his distinguished career in the biennial fixture was under way. Two years later, the British team lost by no great margin in St Louis; Barnes lost his one fourball match but made a major contribution by winning both his singles, the first against Mason Rudolph and the second against Miller Barber.

In 1970 Barnes had followed Tony Jacklin's example by playing in the USA. He won his player's card and his game was ideally suited to American conditions. His great power enabled him to fly his shots into the yielding greens with confidence. He stayed for several weeks, was close to winning tournaments on several occasions and then sprained his ankle and had to return to Britain. His wife, with a young child to care for, felt she could not commit herself to a life in America and the experiment was abandoned. But later that year Barnes won an important tournament, the Australian Masters.

During the Seventies he won tournaments in Europe at regular intervals. They included the Opens of France, Holland, Spain, Italy and Portugal, the Martini International and the PGA Matchplay Championship. He was also a popular figure on the Safari Circuit in Africa.

In 1973, at Muirfield, he and Bernard Gallacher teamed up for the first time in the Ryder Cup, a partnership which was to bring great success during a period when the British were largely dominated by the brilliant

American teams. In ten matches together, Barnes and Gallacher won five times and halved once.

Their skills dovetailed perfectly. Barnes's great strength and powers of recovery complemented Gallacher's wonderfully adept short game. Above all, they had great faith in each other and were united in their determination to 'get out there and beat the Americans'. Neither of them were in awe of their opponents, although Barnes remembers that he was in a torment of nerves before each match; it was much worse than playing in an ordinary tournament:

'You're playing not only for the team but millions of Brits throughout the world. If you make a mistake, you feel you've let them down'. He also recalls that on Gallacher's insistence, he always had to hit the first drive in the foursomes and every time he was quite convinced that he would miss the ball. Such are the intense pressures of the Ryder Cup.

On the first day at Muirfield, he and Gallacher gave the British team a huge surge of confidence by winning both their matches. They beat Lee Trevino and Billy Casper on the last green and then destroyed Tommy Aaron and Gay Brewer with some magnificent golf.

Britain led by three points, but during the night Gallacher went down with food poisoning and much of the British self-confidence was dissipated. The Americans closed the gap on the next day and pulled away to win the match with ease on the final day.

At Laurel Valley in 1975, the Americans defeated the British team again without difficulty, but Barnes stole the show on the final day by defeating Jack Nicklaus twice. The great American had won five tournaments in that year, including the Masters and the US PGA Championship. Barnes modestly plays down his extraordinary feat by saying that, in a match over 18 holes, the result can hinge on a couple of putts or a bit of luck. Nevertheless, Nicklaus engineered a second match in the afternoon. A blind eye was turned to this manipulation of the draw since the Americans had won the Ryder Cup by lunchtime and Nicklaus rightly thought that a return match would interest the fans. The resolute Barnes won again by two and one and he remembers that the two opponents discussed a common interest, fishing, most of the way round.

At Lytham two years later, Barnes lost his foursomes and his fourball matches, but beat yet another US Open champion, Hale Irwin, in his singles. His final appearance was as a member of the first European Ryder Cup team, at The Greenbrier in 1979. He finished in great style by winning three of his four games in partnership with Gallacher, even though he lost his singles to John Mahaffey on the final green.

In 1981 John Jacobs, the captain, was keen to pick Barnes again, but he was just outside the acceptable ranking in the Order of Merit. It was ironic that, a couple of weeks after the team was picked, he won the Tournament Players Championship at Dalmahoy. His final round of 62 included a nine-hole score of 28, which equalled the British tournament record.

A couple of years later, Barnes withdrew from the circuit. He had had enough of living out of a suitcase. For several years he occupied himself by doing promotional work, helped his father-in-law, Max Faulkner, to set up West Chiltington Golf Club, and went fishing. He returned to the European tour fully in 1991 and finished in 79th position in the Order of Merit. He is as popular as ever and intends to play on until he is eligible for the American Seniors tour in 1995.

BARRON, HERMAN

USA

Born: 23.12.09

Appearances: 1947

Record: P1 W1 L0 H0

Herman Barron was born in New York and was involved in golf from the age of 10, when he began work as a caddie and helped out in the professional's shop.

He showed up well in the US Open on several occasions in the 1930s and finished in fifth place in 1941 at the Colonial Club in Texas. In the following year he won the Western Open and was the runner-up in the Canadian Open in 1945.

In 1946 Barron had a real chance to win the US Open: pars at the last two holes were required for victory. He dropped a shot at both and did not even get into the play-off. However, he owed his place in the 1947 Ryder Cup side to that performance, allied to his winning two tournaments.

He was not at his best in his one match, a foursomes against Dai Rees and Sam King. The brilliance of his partner, Byron Nelson, pulled them through to a narrow victory, even though the American pair were three down shortly after lunch.

BEAN, ANDY

USA

Born: 13.3.53

Appearances: 1979, 1987

Record: P6 W4 L2 H0

One might say that Andy Bean was born with a silver putter in his hands, because his father owned a golf course in Florida and the young Bean could play to his heart's content. He became a professional in 1975, by which time he was a formidably strong man of 6′ 4″. His first tournament win was in 1977 and he has won 11 events on the American tour, including the Doral Open (three times), the Kemper and Western Opens and the Byron Nelson Golf Classic.

Bean qualified for the Ryder Cup match at The Greenbrier, Virginia, in 1979 and experienced mixed fortunes. In his fourball match against Nick Faldo and Peter Oosterhuis, he and Lee Elder were eight under par when they won; but in his foursomes match, with Tom Kite, the same European pair were six holes up at the turn and never let that lead diminish.

At Muirfield village, Ohio, in 1987, Bean once again showed his gift for sustained bursts of brilliant scoring. He and Payne Stewart were eight under par and six holes up after ten holes of their fourball match against Eamonn Darcy and Gordon Brand Jr; and in the singles Bean bet Ian Woosnam partly because he scored three 2s during the match.

In 1991 Bean had a poor season by his high standards. He finished in 88th position in the money list, with less than $200,000.

BEARD, FRANK

USA

Born: 1.5.39

Appearances: 1969, 1971

Record: P8 W2 L3 H3

Frank Beard is best described as a journeyman professional. He was a very consistent golfer, particularly skilful with his putter, and he deliberately cultivated an anonymous persona. A tall and solid figure, who wore spectacles, he said of himself: 'I'm a colourless guy who just plays.' He was seriously ill in 1964 and, when he recovered, refused his nomination for the Ben Hogan Award on the grounds that he 'hadn't done anything, just got well.'

Beard came of good sporting stock, since his father was also a golf professional and his brother was an All-American basketball player. He won 11 tournaments in the years between 1963 and 1971, including the Texas Open, the Tournament of Champions on two occasions and the American Golf Classic. He was leader of the Order of Merit in 1969 without winning a tournament and is said to have observed: 'I can't win anything but money.'

In the tied fixture at Birkdale in 1969, he played three games in partnership with Billy Casper and came out level with one win, one defeat and one half, but he was heavily defeated in the singles by Christy O'Connor. In 1971 at St. Louis, after losing his foursomes and winning his first fourball, he had a see-saw game, with Charles Coody, against Neil Coles and Christy O'Connor. The American pair were four up after five holes, but were pegged back to level by four successive birdies from the Britons. The match ended in a half after two more brilliant birdies by Neil Coles at the 16th and 17th holes.

Beard was a member of the US PGA Tournament Committee and now plays on the Seniors circuit.

BECK, CHARLES HENRY

USA

Born: 12.9.56

Appearances: 1989, 1991

Record: P7 W4 L2 H1

Chip Beck showed what a determined and dependable golfer he is at the Belfry in 1989, when he was the only unbeaten American in the Ryder Cup. He had the rare distinction of wresting a half, in partnership with Tom Watson, from the dynamic Spanish pair, Severiano Ballesteros and Jose Maria Olazabal and then he and Paul Azinger won two further points together. In beating Faldo and Woosnam, the quality of the golf was such that the Americans, despite reaching the turn with a better ball score of 30, were only one up. The four players recorded 18 birdies in their 17 holes. Beck continued to play splendidly as he beat Bernhard Langer, the latter's first defeat in a Ryder cup singles game.

Beck is no stranger to the traumas of overwhelming defeat. Ballesteros crushed him in an early round of the World Matchplay Championship at Wentworth, when he referred to the ordeal as going through 'the crucible of humiliation'. Such a phrase gives a clue to the subject in which he graduated: journalism at the University of Georgia. However, the typewriter had to wait when he joined the American tour in 1979. He found it very hard going until the mid-Eighties, when his consistent game began to bring success. His best year was 1988, when he won the Los Angeles Open and finished second in the money list with nearly $1 million.

Although he won the Buick Open in 1990, Beck did not qualify automatically for the Ryder Cup team at Kiawah Island, but Dave Stockton picked him on the basis of his record at the Belfry in the previous fixture. His partnership with Azinger did not bring the anticipated success, since they were twice defeated by Ballesteros and Olazabal and had to parry a complaint about a breach of the rules in their foursomes match into the bargain. Beck was rested on the second day of the match, which paid dividends when he bounced back to defeat Ian Woosnam in the singles.

Two weeks after the American victory at Kiawah Island, Beck put his name into the record books by scoring 59 in the third round of the Las Vegas Invitational tournament. This equalled Al Geiberger's 1977 record and earned him a bonus of half a million dollars.

BEMBRIDGE, MAURICE

GB

Born: 21.2.45

Appearances: 1969, 1971, 1973, 1975

Record: P16 W5 L8 H3

Maurice Bembridge was one of the most assiduous of golf professionals. He travelled the world to play in tournaments, to Australia and New Zealand, the USA, the Far East and Africa. He scored several successes: for example he won the Caltex event in New Zealand, the Lusaka Open, and the Kenya Open three years in succession.

With his cheerful and bouncy demeanour, Bembridge was a most determined competitor with an excellent all-round game which enabled him to win a succession of important events. He beat Dai Rees in the final of the PGA Matchplay Championship in 1969, its last year as a matchplay tournament, and won the Sumrie in the same year. Two years later, he won the Dunlop Masters. In 1974 he had a brilliant run, with victories in the Piccadilly Medal, the PGA Championship and the Double Diamond Tournament.

Bembridge played in the 1974 Masters at Augusta and finished in ninth position, mainly due to a wonderful final round of 64, which equalled the record for the lowest round.

He made his first Ryder Cup appearance at Birkdale in 1969 and won two and a half points out of five. Two years later, in St Louis, he only played two matches, but at Muirfield in 1973 his pugnacious spirit was invaluable, as he won three points out of six. It was admirable golf against such daunting opponents as Palmer and Nicklaus. He drew the latter twice in the singles, secured a half in the morning but was narrowly defeated in the afternoon. His final appearance at Laurel Valley, in 1975, was disappointing, since he lost all three matches.

Bembridge's appearances at European tournaments grew less frequent during the Eighties, mainly because he moved to the USA.

BLANCAS, HOMERO

USA

Born: 7.3.38

Appearances: 1973

Record: P4 W2 L1 H1

The son of a greenkeeper at the River Oaks Country Club in Houston, Homero Blancas grew up with golf; and his brilliance, while playing for the University of Houston team, marked him out as a future star. Although he won four tournaments on the American tour, including the Phoenix Open and the Monsanto Open, he did not quite live up to his early promise.

He made his one appearance in the Ryder Cup at Muirfield in 1973 and acquitted himself well with two and a half points out of four. He was paired with another American of Mexican descent, Lee Trevino, and they beat Christy O'Connor and Neil Coles in the first series of fourballs; in the second series they halved with Maurice Bembridge and Brian Huggett. On the final day, Blancas comfortably defeated Peter Butler but fell victim to Brian Huggett in the afternoon.

Blancas now plays on the Seniors tour in the USA.

BOLT, TOMMY

USA

Born: 31.3.18

Appearances: 1955, 1957

Record: P4 W3 L1 H0

It is a shame that the catalogue of stories about 'Thunder' Bolt's legendary bad temper have outweighed his considerable reputation as a golfer. He not only had a magnificent golf swing but also applied a finesse and imagination which made him one of the best shot-makers of his day; no less a judge than Lee Trevino rated him as one of the most inventive of all golfers.

Bolt's problem was that he was a perfectionist and golf is not a game that lends itself to such a philosophy. It is more a game in which 'a good bad 'un' should be welcomed; the wise player moves on and plans his next shot. But from Bolt it often evoked a colourful string of oaths and the hurling of a club up the fairway. On one famous occasion, at the 1960 US Open at Cherry Hills, his driver found a resting-place in the lake to the left of the 18th tee, from where Bolt had just snap-hooked his ball into watery oblivion. He said wryly: 'I guess at one time or another I probably held distance records for every club in the bag.' Despite the brilliance of his stroke making, Bolt was very fallible on the putting green and this was a dreadful provocation to a man of such unstable temperament. Jimmy Demaret reckoned that his putter had spent 'more time in the air than Lindberg'.

All the stories obscured Bolt's great talent. He did not join the American golf tour until 1950, when he was in his thirties, but won his first tournament, the prestigious North and South Open, in the following year. During the next decade he won 15 tournaments, including the US Open in 1958 at Southern Hills. On a blisteringly hot final day, Bolt played the final two rounds in a brilliant 69 and 72 to hold off the young Gary Player. In 1952 he had been in a position to mount a challenge for the Masters at Augusta. With four holes to play, he was level with Sam Snead, the eventual winner; but his putting nerves got the better of him and he took three putts on three of the greens to finish equal third.

Despite his putting troubles, Tommy Bolt had a swing that was made to last and he won the World Seniors tournament in 1969 and was third in the US PGA Championship in 1971. At the end of the Seventies, he was still winning Seniors events.

Bolt relished matchplay and was a considerable success in his two Ryder Cup appearances. At Thunderbird Ranch in 1955, he and Jack Burke had a titanic battle with Arthur Lees and Harry Weetman. The British pair scored a 68 in the morning round and were only ahead by one hole; after lunch they went to the turn in 34 shots and had not improved their position. Bolt and Burke ground away until they were one up, with the final hole to play. Weetman holed out for a birdie but Burke followed him in for a birdie to win the game in wonderful style. Bolt had an easy victory over Christy O'Connor in the singles.

In the match at Lindrick in 1957, won by Britain, the infamous Bolt temper tarnished his reputation. After an easy win with Dick Mayer in the foursomes, Bolt was drawn to meet the fiercely competitive Eric Brown. It was a potentially explosive confrontation and so it proved. As the teeing-off time approached and there was no sign of the combatants, the light-hearted Jimmy Demaret opined: 'They're out on the practice ground throwing clubs at each other at fifty paces.'

Eric Brown, who was never to lose a Ryder Cup singles, beat Bolt by four and three and the words which were exchanged at the end of the match put the American into a rage. In the locker-room, he snapped a wedge in two; later he stated that the British crowd was the most unsporting he had ever experienced; and he declined to attend the prize-giving ceremony.

For all his tantrums, some of which were exaggerated and quite a few of the others stage-managed by himself, 'Thunder' Bolt was in the very highest class as a golfer. He was a colourful character who added some much-needed panache to the golfing scene. If he had been able to master his temper and the art of putting, he would certainly have added to his tally of major championships.

BOOMER, AUBREY

GB

Born: 1.11.97

Appearances: 1927, 1929

Record: P4 W2 L2 H0

The rule that Ryder Cup players must be resident in their own country restricted Aubrey Boomer's appearances for Britain. He spent much of his career in Europe, at St Cloud and later at the Royal Golf Club de Belgique; he won 11 continental Open championships and was runner-up on seven other occasions. He also travelled to Argentina and won the Mar del Plata Open in 1927.

Boomer played in the forerunner of the Ryder Cup at Wentworth in 1926 and won both his matches, but he was only a late replacement for Herbert Jolly in the following year. The *Aquitania* picked him up at Cherbourg *en route* to New York.

He won his foursomes match with Charles Whitcombe, but lost his singles to Johnny Farrell. Two years later he reversed the results, and when he beat Joe Turnesa on the final afternoon, Britain took the lead in the match for the first time. The young Henry Cotton made victory sure shortly afterwards.

Boomer had a fine run at the Open Championship in 1927, when he tied for second place with Fred Robson at St Andrews. They were both unfortunate to find Bobby Jones in irresistible mood, as he won with a record score of 285.

His contemporaries recalled him as a charming man, with a fast and flowing swing which sometimes made his golf unpredictable. He was capable of brilliant bursts of scoring: as in the 1929 French Open, when he had a round of 61.

BOROS, JULIUS

USA

Born: 3.3.20

Appearances: 1959, 1963, 1965, 1967

Record: P16 W9 L3 H4

Julius Boros was an unmistakable figure on the golf course. At over six feet in height and tipping the scales at over 200 pounds, he was an impressive sight as he ambled nonchalently along the fairways, almost as if in a dream. Not that he wasted any time over the ball; his long, relaxed and rhythmic swing was just a quiet and effective interruption to his progress. He was affectionately nicknamed 'The Moose'.

He was a late entrant to professional golf at the age of 30, after renouncing his job in accountancy. But within three years he had scaled the heights of his new career. In 1952 he won the US Open by four shots from 'Porky' Oliver and followed this up by taking the huge first prize in the World championship of Golf. Boros was the 'Player of the Year' and the leading money winner.

Over the next 15 years, Boros won 18 tournaments and he was particularly successful in the US Open. He finished in the top ten on nine occasions and was the runner-up twice. In 1963, at Brookline, Massachusetts, he won the great championship again, after a play-off with Jacky Cupit and Arnold Palmer. He had won the World Championship of Golf again in 1955 and not many years passed without his winning a tournament. In 1967, when he might have been regarded as more of an elder statesman than a serious contender for the winner's cheque, Boros came first in the Phoenix, Florida Citrus and Buick Opens.

In the following year, he became the oldest player to win the US PGA championship and followed this with a victory in the Westchester Classic.

Boros was 40 years old when he made his debut in the Ryder Cup in 1959, although a broken leg had prevented him from appearing at Lindrick two years earlier. During his four appearances, he demonstrated the great quality of his golf by winning nine and losing only three of his games.

At Eldorado in 1959, he only played once but he and Dow Finsterwald beat the formidable British foursomes pair of Rees and Bousfield. He played again in 1963 and, after being unbeaten in the foursomes and fourballs, won one and lost one against Harry Weetman. At Birkdale two years later, he won four points out of five. In 1967 the American team thrashed the British and once again Boros was very much to the fore. In five games he lost only once, to Brian Huggett in the first series of singles. One highly impressed spectator was heard to remark of Boros that the only time he went off the fairway was 'to get a Coke.' Boros played on the American tour through the Seventies and then on the Seniors tour up to the end of the Eighties. With his victories in the three majors, his other tournament wins and his wonderful record in the Ryder Cup, he must be regarded as one of the very best of American golfers.

BOUSFIELD, KEN

GB

Born: 2.10.19

Appearances: 1949, 1951, 1955, 1957, 1959, 1961

Record: P10 W5 L5 H0

The son of a stationmaster, Ken Bousfield became an assistant to Archie Compston at Coombe Hill at the age of 15. It was not until after the Second World War, during which he served in the Royal Marines, that Bousfield began to play the main professional events and his first notable victory was in the *News Chronicle* tournament in 1951.

By that time, he had been selected for the 1949 Ryder Cup team which was narrowly defeated by the Americans at Ganton. He won his only match, a foursomes in partnership with Fred Daly, against Bob Hamilton and Skip Alexander. The British pair raced to the turn in 33 shots, were two ahead at lunchtime and won by four and two. Bousfield was in action again at Pinehurst two years later, but he and Daly met the toughest of all American pairings, Ben Hogan and Jimmy Demaret, and were defeated.

He had his most successful year in golf in 1955, when he won the German Open and both the PGA Close and the PGA Matchplay Championships. He beat the renowned matchplayer, Eric Brown, in the final of the latter event. In the morning round Bousfield scored 68, to be three holes up, but lost them all immediately after lunch. He showed his own brand of calm resolution by fighting back to win.

Although he was in the Ryder Cup team at Thunderbird Ranch, California, in 1955, he was unable to play because of illness. But consolation for his bad luck was assured in 1957, when the British won their famous victory at Lindrick. Bousfield teamed up with the captain, Dai Rees, to prevent the Americans from a making a clean sweep of the foursomes. They beat Art Wall and Fred Hawkins, but the Americans looked the

favourites to retain the Cup until the great rally began on the second day. It was led by Dai Rees and Eric Brown, with fierce support from Mills, Hunt and O"Connor. But it was Ken Bousfield who won the decisive point, when he beat Lionel Hebert on the 33rd green. Hebert confessed that his opponent had 'putted me off the course'.

Putting was one of Bousfield's great strengths, as was his short game; he was a masterly player of all types of wedge shots, especially the pitch and run. The Open champion of 1939, Dick Burton, said of him: 'Within 100 yards of the hole I have never seen anyone better.' This deft touch made up for his lack of length and he was always at his best on fast-running courses when subtlety and control, rather than power, were necessary. In 1957 he won a Dunlop tournament at Southport and Ainsdale with a wonderful display of golf; over five rounds he did not take more than five shots for any hole. Bousfield also has fond memories of his final round of 66 in the 1958 Swiss Open at Crans-sur-Sierre. He won by one shot from Flory Van Donck after completing the last nine holes in 30 strokes. He also won the Belgian Open in that year and the German Open, for the second time, in 1959.

At the Eldorado Country Club in 1959, Bousfield lost both his Ryder Cup matches; in his singles he could not withstand the power of Mike Souchak, despite covering the first nine holes after lunch in 32 shots, to go from five down to two down. In 1961, with his usual partner, Dai Rees, he won one foursomes and lost the other; in the singles he lost to Billy Casper, but beat Jerry Barber.

His determination and coolness under extreme pressure had earned him a splendid record in the Ryder Cup of five wins and five defeats. His career on the British circuit went on. He won the Portuguese Open twice and the Swallow-Penfold tournament in 1961. He gained the British Seniors title in 1972, but lost the World Seniors play-off to Sam Snead.

Bousfield has remained at Coombe Hill all his career and his steadfast qualities were neatly summarised by Pat Ward-Thomas: 'It is refreshing sometimes to walk a few holes with him, for no other reason than to absorb a little of the soothing quality of his play and his company.'

BOYLE, HUGH

GB

Born: 28.1.36

Appearances: 1967

Record: P3 W0 L3 H0

Hugh Boyle began his career as a caddie in the Midlands and turned professional in 1953. He began to play the main professional tournaments in the early Sixties, in between teaching engagements in places as distant as Hong Kong and Pakistan.

The first sign that he was a player of quality came in 1965, when he finished second in the Senior Service Tournament in a field which included some top American players; and in the top 20 in the Open. In the following year he won the Daks Tournament, the Yomiuri International Open (he was the first British player to win a Japanese event) and was runner-up in the Indian Open.

Boyle's *annus mirabilis* was 1967, when he won five tournaments, including the Schweppes and the Martini, and represented Ireland in the World Cup.

He easily qualified for the British team, which was handsomely defeated in Houston, Texas, by an American team led by Ben Hogan, and with such brilliant golfers as Casper, Palmer and Littler in the vanguard.

Hugh Boyle had the misfortune to be drawn out of the hat twice against Arnold Palmer, the superstar of golf, who was still at the height of his golfing powers. In the second series of foursomes, Boyle and Gregson were demolished by Palmer and Dickinson (who won five points out of five in the match). On the following afternoon, the formidable presences of Palmer and Julius Boros awaited Boyle and George Will on the tee in a fourball match. When Will eagled the ninth, the Britons were four up, but they subsided to defeat by one hole.Hugh Boyle was out first on the next day and lost to Gay Brewer.

Boyle is now the professional at the Royal Wimbledon Golf Club and plays the Seniors' events in Britain with some success.

BRADSHAW, HARRY

GB

Born: 9.10.13

Appearances: 1953, 1955, 1957

Record: P5 W2 L2 H1

At the age of 40, it was a relatively late debut in the Ryder Cup for Harry Bradshaw and he was the first golfer from southern Ireland to be selected. In the tense match at Wentworth in 1953, he won both his matches. His foursomes win over Walter Burkemo and Cary Middlecoff could not have been closer, as his partner, Fred Daly, had to hole a putt of around four feet on the final green to win the match.

Although Britain lost by one point, Bradshaw won his singles against Fred Haas.

In the Forties and Fifties, Harry Bradshaw had something of a monopoly in the Irish Professional Championship: he won it ten times between 1941 and 1957 and also won the Irish Open in 1947 and 1949. But it was several years before he was able to win a tournament in Britain.

Before that happened, he was to come very close to winning the Open Championship at Royal St George's in 1949. He was deprived of his triumph by a bizarre incident at the fifth hole during the second round. From his drive, his ball finished in a broken beer bottle. He was unsure of the ruling (in those days he would not have been given a free drop) and played the ball as it lay; with his eyes firmly shut, he smashed into the bottle but only moved the ball about 30 yards. Clearly unsettled by his bad luck, he went on to score a round of 77. His other three rounds were 68, 69 and 70 and it is arguable that he would have won the championship. As it was, he tied with Bobby Locke, but was soundly beaten in the play-off.

Bradshaw grew up with his own highly individual swing. It was natural and free of inhibition and was marked by a lovely rhythm, but it was certainly not graceful. He had a peculiar grip, with three fingers of his right land overlapping his left; and he also had a loop in his swing and a pronounced sway. Nevertheless, he was an admirably consistent player who invariably kept his ball in play. Above all, he had a remarkable touch on and around the greens; his chipping was superb and he hit his putts with a very firm rap and kept his head down until he heard the ball rattle into the cup.

He ws also a very brisk player, as Henry Longhurst noted: 'He can size up a shot, choose his club, hit the ball on to the green and be walking after it, all in the time that it takes an American to test the direction of the wind.'

Bradshaw at last won a major British event in 1953, the Dunlop Masters at Sunningdale. He played the last six holes on the Old Course in 120 shots to hold Max Faulkner at bay and won the tournament again two years later.

After his sparkling debut in the Ryder Cup, Bradshaw was in the firing-line again at the Thunderbird Club, in California, in 1955. On this occasion he and Dai Rees lost to Sam Snead and Cary Middlecoff and he and Jack Burke fought a dazzling battle in the singles. In the morning round, Bradshaw played six successive holes in three shots apiece, recorded a score of 65 and was merely on level terms with his opponent. The afternoon exchanges were finely balanced but Burke finally edged away to win a memorable game. The referee said afterwards that Bradshaw did not hit a single bad shot, which highlights how well Jack Burke played.

Harry Bradshaw had the consolation of playing in the winning British side at Lindrick in 1957 and he halved his singles with Dick Mayer.

In the following year, Bradshaw had one of his greatest triumphs when he won the Canada Cup with Christy O'Connor as his partner. The event (now the World Cup) was played in Mexico City at a height of over 7,000 feet. The physical strain on the players was considerable and especially on a man like Bradshaw, who was in his late forties and who weighed in at around 15 stone. Not only did the Irish pair win the team event against the likes of Snead and Hogan, Brown and Panton, Player and Henning, but Bradshaw tied for the individual prize with Angel Miguel of Spain, but he lost the play-off.

In his later years Harry Bradshaw was the professional at the famous Portmarnock Club near Dublin.

BRAND, GORDON J

Europe

Born: 6.8.55

Appearances: 1983

Record: P1 W0 L1 H0

Such was his success on the 'Safari Circuit' during the Eighties that Gordon J Brand was nicknamed the 'African King'. He topped the Order of Merit there on three occasions, but it was not until 1989 that he won a European tour event, the Belgian Open at Royal Waterloo.

Brand's pronounced pause at the top of his swing makes him a distinctive figure on t he course, and his golf was good enough to give him second place behind Greg Norman in the 1986 Open at Turnberry.

He played in one of the most exciting Ryder Cup matches of all, in 1983, in Florida, when America won by one point. Tony Jacklin, the captain, did not call upon him until the singles matches on the final day (when every player must participate) and he lost to Bob Gilder by two holes.

Perhaps it was some consolation that he played for England when the team won the Dunhill Cup in 1987. He is still a regular player on the European Tour, although he missed the 1991 season through injury.

BRAND JR, GORDON

Europe

Born: 19.8.58

Appearances: 1987, 1989

Record: P7 W2 L4 H1

With his white cap and jaunty walk, Gordon Brand Jr is a familiar figure on the fairways of Europe. The son of a professional golfer, he had a distinguished career as an amateur. He won both the English and the Scottish Amateur Strokeplay Championships and the Golf Illustrated Gold Vase, and played in the 1979 Walker Cup; he then became a professional and won the 1981 qualifying school tournament. Rarely has a golfer made the transition to the professional game with such ease. He won two tournaments in 1982, his first year on the circuit and finished seventh in the Order of Merit. In his ten years on the circuit, he has finished in the top dozen of the Order of Merit on seven occasions and has passed the £1 million mark in prize money.

Brand has won several prestigious events, including the European Open, Dutch Open, Benson & Hedges International and the South Australian Open. He had a particularly good season in 1987 and qualified for the Ryder Cup team to play at Muirfield Village, Ohio. It was Europe's first victory in America and Brand, partnered with Jose Rivero, began with a win over Ben Crenshaw and Scott Simpson in his first fourball match. Two defeats followed, but he played his part in the singles by finishing all square with Hal Sutton.

In the tied match two years later, Brand and Torrance won their fourball match over Strange and Azinger by dint of a lovely bunker shot from Brand at the final hole. The same pair lost their foursomes game and Brand lost a tight singles match to Mark McCumber by one hole.

BREWER, GAY

USA

Born: 19.3.32

Appearances: 1967, 1973

Record: P9 W5 L3 H1

The pronounced loop in Gay Brewer's swing, the result of a broken elbow at the age of 7, did not hinder his progress to the top tier of American golf. He was the son of a railway worker and one of seven children, but he took to golf at an early age and won the US PGA Junior Championship at the age of 17, when he beat Mason Rudolph in the final. He became a professional in 1956 but his most prolific years were during the late Sixties.

Brewer should have won the Masters in 1966 when, at the 72nd hole, his ball came to rest at the back of the green and a long way from the flag. His first putt seemed good, but meandered on down the slippery green and came to rest over six feet away. He just missed the putt back and found himself in a play-off with Tommy Jacobs and Jack Nicklaus, which the latter won. But Brewer's regrets over a golden opportunity missed only lasted to the following year: he putted superbly across the frightening greens of Augusta to win the Masters title by one shot from Bobby Nichols.

In the same year, Brewer played in the Ryder Cup at Houston and lost his first match, a foursomes in company with Doug Sanders, to the young and ebullient Tony Jacklin and Dave Thomas. But he won his next three games and then finished with a defeat at the hands of Peter Alliss. Brewer was selected again for the fixture at Muirfield in 1973 and scored two and a half points out of four. This included a half in the singles against Neil Coles and a win over Bernard Gallacher.

Gay Brewer won ten tournaments in the USA, including the Canadian Open, and also took the title of Alcan Golfer of the Year in 1967 and 1968 when the event was played at St Andrews and Royal Birkdale.

He continued to play on the American tour until the early Eighties and then found renewed success on the Seniors tour.

BROADHURST, PAUL

Europe

Born: 14.8.65

Appearances: 1991

Record: P2 W2 L0 H0

Hindsight, so comfortable because of its infallibility, decrees that the European captain at Kiawah Island, Bernard Gallacher, made a grave error in not using Paul Broadhurst until the second series of fourball matches on the second afternoon. It was said that he was a streaky player, a birdies-and-bogeys man who was best suited to fourball play. But he took to Ryder Cup play in exemplary style, as he and Ian Woosnam defeated the stern American pair of Paul Azinger and Hale Irwin. In the singles, Broadhurst was always in command against the accomplished Mark O'Meara; he was four ahead after eight holes and won quite easily.

Broadhurst first made his mark as an amateur by winning the Lytham Trophy in 1988 and was the leading amateur in the Open Championship in the same year. He turned professional and won the Cannes Open in his first season and won a second tournament in 1990. He showed his great potential in the Open Championship at St Andrews by scoring a record 63 in the third round; he amassed eight birdies in the first ten holes.

He qualified for the 1991 team in wonderful style by finishing with a victory and two second places in the last three events before the team was selected. It is typical of Broadhurst's determination and common-sense that he went to the USA the week before the Ryder Cup in order to get used to the conditions. He finished in a meritorious ninth position in the BC Open. His progress after Kiawah Island was notable: he was unbeaten both in the Dunhill Cup and the Four Tours Championship in Australia. With his excellent, if unorthodox, swing and wonderful short game, Broadhurst has the talent to reach the very top ranks of golf.

Gay Brewer (left)

BROWN, ERIC

GB

Born: 15.2.25

Appearances: 1953, 1955, 1957, 1959
Captain 1969, 1971

Record: P8 W4 L4 H0

Eric Brown came out of the blue to win the Scottish Amateur Championship in 1946 and turned professional soon afterwards. Shackled by the restrictive rule that decreed that a professional had to wait for five years before being allowed to enter a major PGA tournament, he was confined to local and European events. When the shackles were struck, he was a force in British tournaments and won the Dunlop Masters in 1957 and the British Matchplay Championship in 1960 and 1962. He won several European Opens, including the Swiss, Italian and Portuguese. He was even the runner-up in the Los Angeles Open of 1960 and was winning tournaments in the late Sixties. He also finished third in the Opens of 1957 and 1958. In the latter year, he took six down the final hole at Lytham, when a par four might have won him the title.

Together with John Panton he dominated Scottish golf. He won the professional championship seven times between 1956 and 1968 and represented his country in the Canada Cup every year from 1954 to 1962 and in 1966 and 1967.

Brown was a tough as he looked on the golf course and his qualities were seen at their best in the rough and tumble of Ryder Cup matchplay. His temperament was suited to head-to-head encounters because he was an inspirational player whose golf could burst into sudden and brilliant life. His record in the singles was remarkable, with four wins in four matches: against Lloyd Mangrum, Jerry Barber, Tommy Bolt and Cary Middlecoff. There was not a dud among them; between them they had won four US Open championships, one US PGA Championship and one Masters title.

Brown's Ryder Cup career began in 1953 at Wentworth and he must have wondered what had hit him. He and John Panton were seven holes down at the ninth to Sam Snead and Lloyd Mangrum and were sunk without trace. But Brown was as buoyant as ever in the singles and beat the hard-boiled Mangrum partly by dint of superb birdies at the final two holes.

The pattern continued in 1955 at the Thunderbird Club, when Brown lost his foursomes easily but beat the diminutive Jerry Barber. In the famous British win at Lindrick, he and O'Connor were hammered by Dick Mayer and Tommy Bolt and the captain, Dai Rees, put Brown out first in the singles in the hope that he would meet the highly volatile and aggressive Tommy Bolt. He guessed right and the American was just the opponent for Brown to savour. He beat him by four and three and the following exchange was reported. Bolt: 'You won, Eric, but I didn't enjoy the game.' Brown: 'No, of course you didn't enjoy it because you were ******* licked.'

In the locker room Bolt apparently broke a club in his anger (he was a renowned breaker of clubs) and refused to attend the closing ceremony.

Eric Brown's heroics in the biennial fixture were not over. As usual, he lost his foursomes in 1959 at the Eldorado Club but demolished Cary Middlecoff by four and three.

Despite his volatile temperament, Brown was very much a natural choice as captain of the Ryder Cup team and became so in 1969. This was the occasion of the famous tied match at Lytham and St Anne's and Brown did not endear himself to the Americans by some of his comments in the days before the match. The Press reported that he had ordered the British team not to help the Americans look for their balls in the rough. Brown was ungracious, especially in a game in which it is gentlemanly to help your opponent in such a way. But the awkwardness was smoothed away by explaining that Brown did not want a British player to run the risk of treading on an American ball and thereby losing a hole.

The result at Lytham was a great fillip to British golf, which was in a highly charged state of anticipation after Tony Jacklin's victory in the Open Championship earlier that summer.

Brown was asked to soldier on and, although Britain lost the fixture at St Louis in 1971, it was only by a margin of five points out of a possible 32. It was the best result by a British team in the USA so far and confirmed Eric Brown as a formidable captain. Neil Coles, who has played more Ryder Cup matches than any other European, picked him out as the best leader in his experience.

With his outstanding record in the Ryder Cup singles and his success as a captain, Eric Brown must be singled out as a major influence on the famous fixture.

BROWN, KEN

GB & Europe

Born: 9.1.57

Appearances: 1977, 1979, 1983, 1985, 1987

Record: P13 W4 L9 H0

Tall and lean, with a gangling gait, Ken Brown was dubbed 'the walking 1-iron' by Lee Trevino. It was no surprise that he took to golf since, in his boyhood, his bedroom window overlooked Harpenden Common Golf Club; he won his first notable victory in the Carris Trophy at the age of 17. A year later he became a professional and spent a year and a half as an assistant at Verulam Golf Club, which was where Sam Ryder played his golf.

Brown's first tournament success was a victory in the Irish Open in 1978. Although he finished in the top ten in the Order of Merit in 1978, 1979 and 1980, a further victory eluded him until the Dutch Open in 1983. Brown won his way into the Ryder Cup at Lytham in 1977, but only played once. He and Mark James lost their fourball game to Hale Irwin and Lou Graham; but Brown was within inches of holing a chip shot from behind the final green to save the match.

Two years later, at The Greenbrier, Brown and James caused great problems for the team by their immature behaviour. They would not attend team meetings; they refused to be photographed and tried to avoid wearing the team clothing. Perhaps they had been reading the existentialists and were in a state of alienation. They lost their opening fourball match to Lee Trevino and Fuzzy Zoeller and James was then declared unfit. Brown made it clear that he would not partner anyone except James, but was sent out in a foursomes match with Des Smyth, to whom he hardly addressed a word. Not surprisingly, Hale Irwin and Tom Kite trounced the European pair by seven and six. It was ironic that Brown was one of the few European winners in the singles matches on the final day. He was later fined £1,000 and banned from international team golf for a year.

Brown attracted another fine, for slow play, in 1980. His play is at times agonizingly laboured,

particularly as he prowls about the greens to assess his putts. Nevertheless, his putting is one of the great strengths of his game and for many years he used a hickory-shafted blade putter to considerable effect.

Brown was a part of Tony Jacklin's highly successful Ryder Cup teams of the Eighties and was one of his special selections in 1985 and 1987, by which time he was playing in the USA. He played a useful part in Europe's great battle at the PGA National course in Florida in 1983. He and Brian Waites gained an unexpected victory over Morgan and Zoeller in a fourball game and Brown went on to beat Ray Floyd in his singles. In the next two encounters, when Europe won the Ryder Cup at the Belfry in 1985 and at Muirfield Village in 1987, Brown's contribution of one point from five matches was disappointing.

Brown committed himself to the American tour in 1985 and won the Southern Open in 1987. After a further season in the USA, he returned to play on the European circuit and continues to do so. He commentates on golf occasionally for BBC Radio and is involved in golf course design.

BURKE, BILLY

USA

Born: 14.12.02

Appearances: 1931, 1933

Record: P3 W3 L0 H0

Billy Burke was one of that select band of golfers who won all his matches in the Ryder Cup. In his 1931 singles match, he outplayed one of the fiercest competitors among the British players, Archie Compston, when he beat him seven and six.

Burke's finest golfing year was 1931. He won the US Open, the first man to do so with steel-shafted clubs. He showed his mettle in that championship since the 36 hole play-off with George von Elm did not decide matters and they played another 36 on the following day. Billy Burke got home by a solitary stroke.

In the same year he reached the semi-final of the US PGA Championship. Burke won 13 events in the USA, over a span of 14 years, and played on until the late Forties.

BURKE, JACK

USA

Born: 29.1.23

Appearances: 1951, 1953, 1955, 1957, 1959
Captain 1957, 1973

Record: P8 W7 L1 H0

If Ted Kroll had not been taken ill on the final day of the 1957 tie, Jack Burke would have recorded seven wins out of seven in the Ryder Cup. He was the captain in that year, had to step in against Peter Mills and was soundly defeated. Nevertheless, Burke's was a magnificent record in the series and he was appointed as the non-playing captain in 1973, when the USA won the match at Muirfield.

Jack Burke was steeped in golf from a very early age. His father, Jack senior, was a professional golfer who was good enough to reach second place in the US Open of 1920 and to win several tournaments. He was a notable teacher who helped great players, such as Craig Wood, Henry Picard and Babe Zaharias.

It was no surprise that Jack junior grew up to be a golfer of the very highest class. His great years were in the Fifties, although he won a couple of tournaments early in the next decade. In 1952 he won four tournaments in succession. He confessed that it was his best putting streak ever; and he was a brilliant putter: 'I could hit any side of the hole from any distance at any time. It wasn't a question of whether I was going to putt good, but how good I was going to putt.' In the same year he even survived the ordeal of being voted 'the handsomest athlete in America'. He was clearly a man of great character.

Jack Burke was one of the best 'bad weather' players in the game, as he demonstrated in the 1952 Masters, when he was runner-up to Sam Snead. The winds were violent and his closing round of 69 was the only score under 70 during the last two days.

He came of age as a golfer in 1956, when he won two major championships. The weather at the Masters was again troublesome and Burke made up eight shots in the final round over the amateur, Ken Venturi. He went on to win the US PGA Championship as well and felt that he had at last lived up to his promise, that the burden of his father's expectancy had been lifted. Burke won a total of 17 tournaments on the American tour.

During the Fifties, he was a member of four winning Ryder Cup sides for the USA and, together with Sam Snead, was their most successful player. He played brilliant golf on many occasions. In his foursomes match with Ted Kroll in 1953, the pair did the morning round in 66 strokes and were seven up on Jimmy Adams and Bernard Hunt; and his 1955 match, partnered by Tommy Bolt against Arthur Lees and Harry Weetman, was one of the most exciting ever played. The British pair scored 68 in the morning and were only one up; after lunch they went out in 34 shots and were still only one up. The Americans slipped ahead during the closing holes and held Lees and Weetman off with a birdie on the final green. It is curious that he was picked for the 1959 match in California but was not given a game by the captain, Sam Snead.

In partnership with Jimmy Demaret he built the Champions Golf Club at Houston, Texas, where the 1967 Ryder Cup and the 1969 US Open were played.

BURKEMO, WALTER

USA

Born: 9.10.18

Appearances: 1953

Record: P1 W0 L1 H0

Burkemo was a particularly good matchplayer, as was shown by his record in the US PGA Championship. He won it in 1953, and was a runner-up twice and a semi-finalist in the 1950s.

He only won one other tournament but earned a consistent living as a professional. For example, he showed good form in the US Open and finished in a tie for fourth place in 1957 and in fifth place a year later.

His only appearance in the Ryder Cup was at Wentworth in 1953. Paired with Cary Middlecoff, he lost his foursomes on the final green to Fred Daly and Harry Bradshaw.

BURNS, STEWART

GB

Born: 1899

Appearances: 1929

Stewart Burns was selected for the match at Moortown in 1929 but was not offered a game by the captain, George Duncan. His main golfing achievements were to win the Scottish Professional Championship three times between 1925 and 1928 and the Middlesex Championship in 1929.

BURTON, RICHARD

GB

Born: 11.10.07

Appearances: 1939, 1937, 1949

Record: P5 W2 L3 H0

In many respects Dick Burton was the forgotten Open champion. He won at St Andrews in 1939 but the Second World War precluded his enjoying either the limelight or the rewards of holding the famous championship. He had won the event in fine attacking style, hitting the ball great distances and putting brilliantly. On the 72nd hole, his huge drive left him just a pitch on to the green and he holed the putt for a birdie.

He played twice in the Ryder Cup before the war and lost both his singles games: to the short-game expert, Paul Runyan, in 1935 and then to Sam Snead two years later at Southport. The weather was appalling and the great American player looked outlandish in a long white mackintosh which he donned between shots. But he consistently outdrove Dick Burton, who was reckoned to be a long hitter, and beat him easily by five and four. Burton was sometimes a victim of his reputation as a big hitter when he tried too hard for extra length and put himself into trouble.

In 1949 Dick Burton was in fine form and won the *News Chronicle* tournament with a record total of 266 shots. This was more than enough to book his place in the Ryder Cup side and in company with Arthur Lees, he won a riveting match against the American 'bankers', Lloyd Mangrum and Sam Snead, by one hole. Britain had a wonderful chance to win the match, since the team only required three and a half points from the eight singles matches. But the American team took six of the available points, to win with something to spare. Dick Burton lost his singles match to Clayton Heafner.

On his retirement from tournament golf, Burton became the professional at Coombe Hill.

BUSSON, JACK

GB

Born: 2.11.11

Appearances: 1935

Record: P2 W0 L2 H0

It must have been a daunting introduction to Ryder Cup golf for Jack Busson when he went to the first tee, in the company of Alf Perry, for his first match at Ridgwood, New Jersey, in 1935. Waiting for the British pair were Walter Hagen and Gene Sarazen, the most accomplished American golfers of their time, who had won 18 major championships between them.

In contrast, Jack Busson had, in the previous year, won the Yorkshire Open, the Leeds Challenge Cup and the *News of the World* Matchplay tournament and that was to be his best ever year in professional golf.

The Americans won at a canter, by eight and seven, but on the following day Busson, to his great credit, gave Sarazen a very stern match. He was one up after 18 holes, but finally lost on the 34th green.

Busson's best finish in the Open Championship was at Sandwich in 1938, when he was the joint leader after 36 holes. The gales arrived on the final day but he fought pugnaciously on to finish in joint fourth position.

BUTLER, PETER

GB

Born: 25.3.32

Appearances: 1965, 1969, 1973

Record: P14 W3 L9 H2

For two decades Peter Butler was a familiar figure on the British scene. He dressed conservatively and played conservatively, but he was good enough to win a string of tournaments in the Sixties and early Seventies.

After several wins in events in the Midlands, Butler's breakthrough came with his victory in the 1959 Swallow-Penfold tournament. He won £1000, which was a considerable sum for those days. In the next decade he was one of the most consistent British golfers, and won the PGA Close, Bowmaker, Martini, Piccadilly, Penfold, Wills and Sumrie tournaments. He travelled extensively overseas and won the Colombian Open, as well as the French Open in 1968 at St Cloud; he became the St Cloud professional for the next four years. He was one of the few British players to appear regularly in the Masters at Augusta. He played every year from 1964 to 1971 and his best finish was on his first appearance, when he was 11th. Two years later, he led the field after two rounds and eventually finished in 13th place.

Although his game assured him of an excellent livelihood on the British circuit, Butler was just short of the highest class, as his Ryder Cup record shows. He first played at Birkdale in 1965 when he and Lionel Platts, after losing the first three holes of their foursomes to Julius Boros and Tony Lema, did very well to keep the margin of defeat down to one hole. But worse was to follow in a fourball match against two former US Open champions, Billy Casper and Gene Littler. The British pair were four holes up with four to play and allowed the Americans to escape with a half. On the 15th green, Butler needed two putts to win the game, but contrived to take three. He and Platts halved their second fourball game, but Butler lost both his singles, to Tony Lema and Arnold Palmer.

It was a harsh baptism and emphasized the gulf between the best American and the best British players – a gulf which was nearly bridged four years later at Birkdale, when the match was tied. Although Butler lost both his foursomes and his fourball match, he played a vital part on the final day by defeating Ray Floyd and Dale Douglass to secure two points for Britain. Two years later at Old Warson, St Louis, he won one point from two matches and his final appearance was at Muirfield in

1973 when he lost all three of his games. This was the year that Bernard Gallacher became ill after the first day and Butler had to step forward unexpectedly to partner Brian Barnes. They lost their foursomes on the final green to Jack Nicklaus and Tom Weiskopf, but Peter Butler had the distinction of holing in one at the 16th. It is still the only hole in one in the history of the Ryder Cup.

In 1977 Butler became the professional at the RAC Club at Epsom and he is also on the committee of the British Seniors tour.

Peter Butler celebrates his hole in one in the 1973 Ryder Cup at Muirfield

CALCAVECCHIA, MARK

USA

Born: 12.6.60

Appearances: 1987, 1989, 1991

Record: P11 W5 L5 H1

If Mark Calcavecchia were a ship's captain, nobody would want to sail with him, such is his propensity for ending up in the water at crucial moments. However many Ryder Cup matches he plays, and wins, he will be haunted by his tee shot on the final day at the 17th hole at Kiawah Island. His seemingly iron-clad position of four holes up with four to play against Colin Montgomerie had already been eroded to two holes up, not by any brilliance from his opponent but by his own poor play. At the tantalizing 17th hole Montgomerie's tee shot found the water and Calcavecchia, when any sort of a shot on to dry land would have sufficed, followed him into the lake. He compounded his misery by taking three putts and then lost the last hole too. So, Britain grabbed a very unlikely half from the throes of defeat. Such are the nerve-twanging pressures of the Ryder Cup.

Up to that point, Calcavecchia had been having a successful Ryder Cup. He and Payne Stewart had clung on determinedly to register two narrow victories in the foursomes matches, even if he and Corey Pavin had been easily beaten in the fourballs by Steve Richardson and Mark Jones.

Calcavecchia became a professional golfer in 1981, but he found little success on the American tour until his first victory in 1986 in the Southwest Golf Classic. In the next four years he won four more events and was always in the top ten in the money list. His greatest triumph, however, was to win the Open Championship at Troon in 1989, when he won a play-off against Greg Norman and Wayne Grady.

Calcavecchia made his first

appearance in the Ryder Cup at Muirfield village in 1987. He only played two matches and, although he lost his fourball, he defeated Nick Faldo in the singles on the final green. In 1989 at the Belfry he played in all five series; he won both his foursomes matches in partnership with Ken Green but lost both his fourballs. In his singles against Ronan Rafferty, water was yet again to bring about his demise. With the match level, he hit his ball into the water at the 18th hole not once, but twice and conceded the match to his opponent.

With his ungainly swing, Calcavecchia hits the ball powerfully with a pronounced fade; under extreme pressure that fade can become a disastrous slice, as seen at Kiawah Island. But those were exceptional circumstances and he has the game to win many more tournaments, as he showed in the 1992 Phoenix Open: a brilliant last round of 63 brought him a victory by five shots.

CANIZARES, JOSE MARIA

Europe

Born: 18.2.47

Appearances: 1981, 1983, 1985, 1989

Record: P11, W5 L4 H2

With his accurate iron play and gifted short game, Canizares has been one of the most consistent players in Europe during the last two decades. During the first half of the Eighties his worst position in the Order of Merit was 11th and he won the World Cup team event twice during that time and the individual prize once.

During his first two Ryder Cup appearances, at Walton Heath in 1981 and at the PGA National, Florida, two years later, he experienced some mixed fortune. In his very first game, he and his partner, Des Smyth, belaboured Bill Rogers and Bruce Lietzke six and five, in a fourball match and he also started with a victory in 1983, over Floyd and Gilder in the foursomes. But he and Sam Torrance then met humiliating defeat, by seven and five, in the second series of foursomes at the hands of Lanny Wadkins and Gil Morgan. Fate decreed that in the singles, with the tie poised at 13 points each, and only two matches left on the course, Canizares should arrive at the final hole one up on Wadkins. Both players were short of the green in two shots at the long final hole; but whereas Canizares pitched up well short of the pin, Wadkins hit a dazzling shot to within a few inches of the hole. The match was halved and behind them Tom Watson defeated Bernard Gallacher for the USA to win by one point.

But in 1985 at the Belfry the European side was at last to regain the Cup and Canizares played an important role by winning two of his three matches and halving the other. When he did not qualify for the 1987 match, it might have been supposed that the Spaniard, now past his fortieth year, had drawn the line under his Ryder Cup career. But two years later his high finish in the German Open, the last qualifying event before the team was selected, ensured his return. Although he lost his fourball match, his typically

Canizares, joyfully on the move after beating Ken Green in 1989

resolute victory over Ken Green on the final green secured the point that Europe needed to retain the Ryder Cup. Behind him the Americans won all four points and the match was tied, as in 1969.

Canizares is the professional at La Duquesa, in southern Spain, and continues to play on the European golf tour.

CASPER, BILLY

USA

Born: 24.6.31

Appearances: 1961, 1963, 1965, 1967, 1969, 1971, 1973, 1975
Captain 1979

Record: P37 W20 L10 H7

Billy Casper's tally of 51 tournament wins in the USA, including two victories in the Open and one in the Masters, was only surpassed by five players: Sam Snead, Jack Nicklaus, Arnold Palmer, Ben Hogan and Byron Nelson. Even though they all won more major tournaments than Casper, it is surprising that he is rarely assessed as being in the same 'superstar' category. Even during his long and brilliantly successful career, he stayed in the shadow of the big three: Palmer, Nicklaus and Gary Player.

One of the reasons for his rather anodyne golfing image was the way he played the game. He was very cautious, very much in the mould of Peter Thomson, as he plotted his way carefully around the course; his objective was to get the ball to the place where the real golf began, on the putting green. The characteristics which excited the fans – the muscular attack of Palmer, the chilling efficiency and power of Nicklaus or the unparalleled will to win of Player – were not for Casper.

Perhaps he made the game look too easy. He had the great virtue of being a very quick and unfussy player; by the time he got to the ball, he knew what sort of shot he wanted to play and with which club. A look, a waggle and away went the ball. Where Walter Hagen exacted the last ounce of drama from the easiest shot, Casper made the most difficult of shots look simple.

Nor did Casper look anything like an athlete. In his early days he was a rotund man of around 230 pounds, although he later slimmed down on a diet designed to combat his many allergies. He was an undemonstrative person and also dressed for the part; his habitual colours were sombre, with a preference for blue, grey and black. In his later years he confessed that he should have eschewed the soberness of a Ben Hogan and adopted more of a 'show business' persona. There was little of interest for the fans in his private life either; he was a convert to the Mormon Church and adhered faithfully to their strict principles.

So there was not a great deal in Casper's personality upon which the Press and the public could seize, except his golf which, during his best years from 1957 to 1970, was as good as anyone's. He had an unvarying routine as he set himself up to the ball, an unhurried, rounded swing, and a superb rhythm. Not that Casper was orthodox, since his body slid laterally on the downswing and he dragged his right foot forward in pursuit. But any errors in his long game were annulled by his wonderful touch with his wedges and his supreme skill with his putter. With an unusually wristy stroke and a firm rap of the blade, he holed out as well as anyone in the history of the game.

Casper won his first tournament, the Labatt Open, in 1956 and five more events in the succeeding two years. He won the US Open at Winged Foot in 1959 by one shot from Bob Rosburg, and his artistry with his putter was the crucial factor: over the four rounds, he took only 112 putts. He kept on winning tournaments, over 20 in the next six years, until the Open title came his way again in 1966 at the Olympic Club, San Francisco.

It was Casper's ill luck that the event was described as 'the Open that Arnold Palmer lost' rather than 'the Open that Casper won'. It is true that Palmer should certainly have taken his second US Open. With only nine holes to play he led Casper by seven shots but rather than conserve his lead, Palmer had another grander design: he was determined to beat Ben Hogan's Open record of 276, set at the Riviera Club, Los Angeles, in 1948. In his anxiety he frittered away shots, while Casper plodded on in his undramatic way. On the 18th green, Palmer had to hole a tricky putt to force a play-off, which Casper won, despite being two strokes adrift at the turn.

Billy Casper was to win one more major tournament, the Masters in 1970. The Augusta course seemed to inhibit him because he could not bring himself to go for the carries over water at the par 5s. But he should have won the 'green jacket' in 1969 when he led after each of the first three rounds, but in the final one took 40 shots to the turn. However, in 1970 his nerve held as he was involved in another play-off, this time with Gene Littler, and he won by five shots.

Casper made his first appearance in the Ryder Cup at Lytham in 1961, the beginning of a wonderful unbroken run in the fixture, in which he played eight times in succession to compile a total of 37 games, a record for an American. He was unbeaten in the first two fixtures, with seven wins and one halved game. The half was at East Lake in 1963 and Neil Coles only held Casper off by dint of a number of remarkable putts, not the least of which was on the 18th green. Casper drily commended the Englishman for 'a nice putting round'.

He was by no means as successful at Birkdale in 1965. He and Gene Littler lost their second foursomes game to Peter Alliss and Christy O'Connor. The standard of the golf was such that the British pair went to the turn in 31 shots and were only one hole up. He and Littler went on to halve two fourball matches with Lionel Platts and Peter Butler, but Casper lost both his singles, to Peter Alliss and then to his old adversary, Neil Coles.

But Casper was back to his winning ways two years later at Houston, with four and a half points out of five. Only Alliss held him at bay in a singles. In the famous tied match at Birkdale in 1969, Casper was playing in the penultimate singles against Brian Huggett who, when he holed a tricky putt for a halved game, thought wrongly that he had won the Ryder Cup for Britain.

Although he lost all three of his games at St Louis in 1971, Casper bounced back at Muirfield two years later and, now in his forties, played all six matches to win four points, which included singles Victories over Brian Barnes and Tony Jacklin. Neither did he waver at Laurel Valley in 1975, with another two wins and a half from his four matches.

Billy Casper played on to the end of the seventies and his last victory on the US tour was in the New Orleans Open in 1975. He was a regular visitor to Britain, although he did not win a tournament. In Europe, however, he won the Lancome Trophy and the Italian Open in the mid-Seventies. He played with

success on the American Seniors circuit and will be remembered for his wonderfully easy and effective style and as one of the greatest of all putters.

CAYGILL, ALEX

GB

Born: 22.8.40

Appearances: 1969

Record: P1 W0 L0 H1

Alex Caygill had the distinction, despite playing only one match in the Ryder Cup, of having both an unbeaten record as an individual and of playing in an unbeaten team.

In his only match, at Birkdale in 1969, he partnered Brian Huggett in the first series of fourballs and halved against Ray Floyd and Miller Barber. This was the great tie which ended all square, with 13 points to each team.

Caygill's best year was in 1969 when he won the Penfold and the Martini tournaments and was ninth in the Order of Merit.

CLARK, CLIVE

GB

Born: 27.6.45

Appearances: 1973

Record: P1 W0 L1 H0

Clark's distinguished career as an amateur culminated in his being runner-up to Michael Bonallack in both the British and the English Amateur Championships of 1965. In the same year, he tied for first place in the Lytham Trophy and the English Open Amateur Strokeplay Championship, and he played in the Walker Cup match in Baltimore.

His success persuaded him to abandon his study of architecture and turn professional. In his first round as a professional, he broke the course record at Saunton and continued his fast start with a tie for third place in the Open of 1967; only Roberto de Vicenzo and Jack Nicklaus were ahead of him. His victories as a professional included the Bowmaker, Agfa-Gevaert, John Player and Sumrie tournaments.

In his one game in the 1973 Ryder Cup, he and Eddie Polland lost three and two to the juggernaut pair of Jack Nicklaus and Tom Weiskopf.

Clark's is now the voice you hear at the trouble spots 'down on the course' at televised golf tournaments. He also designs golf courses with Peter Alliss.

CLARK, HOWARD

GB & Europe

Born: 26.8.54

Appearances: 1977, 1981, 1987, 1989

Record: P13 W6 L6 H1

Howard Clark first made his mark in golf by winning the British Boys Championship; his father was able to give him some financial support while he played on the amateur circuit. He was chosen for the Walker Cup in 1973 and turned professional later that year.

His breakthrough came in 1978, when he won the Portuguese Open and finished fifth in the Order of Merit. In the previous year, he had done well enough to earn his place in the Ryder Cup at Lytham, but was disappointed when he only played one game. He was sent out first in the singles, probably as a sacrificial lamb; so it proved since he was beaten by Lanny Wadkins. He next played at Walton Heath in 1981 and, after halving his fourball match, took the considerable scalp of Tom Watson in the singles. Clark had six birdies and an eagle in his victory by four and three. Clark is a powerful player with an uncertain temperament and the most successful period of his career was in the mid-Eighties. From 1984 to 1987, he was always in the top ten of the Order of Merit and won several tournaments, including the PGA Championship. He seems to have a liking for sunny climes: he won the Madrid Open on three occasions, the Spanish Open and the individual title in the World Cup, which was played in California.

Clark also played a sterling part in the three Ryder Cups, from 1985 to 1989, in which Europe were unbeaten. In his ten matches, he came out even, with five wins and five defeats. His victories included a vital one, at the final hole, over Dan Pohl at Muirfield Village in 1987; and he and Mark James won their two fourball matches in the tied match at the Belfry two years later. Unfortunately, Clark was routed by Tom Kite in the singles; the eight and seven

margin was a record for the Ryder Cup.

In the last two years, Clark has dropped down the Order of Merit, possibly as a result of his efforts to modify his swing. In 1991 he ended in the disappointing position of 68th, with prize money of less than £60,000.

COLES, NEIL

GB

Born: 26.9.34

Appearances: 1961, 19963, 1965, 1967, 1969, 1971, 1973, 1977 P40 W12 L21 H7

During the Sixties and Seventies Neil Coles was one of the most consistent and successful British golfers. From 1961 to 1982 he won 28 European tournaments and was always in the top 20 in the Order of Merit; in 18 of those 22 years, he was in the top ten and he won the Vardon Trophy in 1963 and 1970.

Coles began to play golf at the age of 15 and just over a year later decided to become a professional. His handicap was not even in single figures at that time but his father was able to provide enough financial support for him to devote all his time to golf. At the age of 21, he won the Hertfordshire Championship against a strong field, which included Dai Rees. His first important win was in the Ballantine tournament in 1961 and he also finished equal third in the Open Championship at Birkdale.

In 1961 Coles qualified for the Ryder Cup match at Lytham and his first two foursomes games, which he lost, emphasized the forbidding nature of the fixture. The first shot by the powerful American, Mike Souchak, was a 1-iron to within nine inches of the hole; Coles's partner, Tom Haliburton, had to try to match him, but with a 2-wood. Although in the singles Coles broke 70 in his match against Gene Littler, the US Open champion, to his annoyance he only halved. But Littler needed a birdie three at the last to save himself. In his second game, Coles again broke 70 and beat Dow Finsterwald.

In the following years he won the Senior Service, Daks and Martini tournaments and

faced the American team once again at East Lake, Atlanta. He and Bernard Hunt fought back magnificently in their first foursomes match to gain a half against the powerful American pair of Julius Boros and Tony Lema. Their self-confidence was punctured by the captain, John Fallon, who decided to split them up for the afternoon foursomes. Coles was astonished by the decision and the British lost every game after lunch. In the fourballs on the next day, Coles and O'Connor won their match against Bob Goalby and Dave Ragan by dint of O'Connor's birdie two at the final hole, but in his two singles matches, Coles only gathered half a point. This was against Billy Casper and Coles confesses that he played very badly but putted embarrassingly well. He won the last hole with a long putt for a birdie two and, as they shook hands, Casper said drily, 'Good putting round, Neil', and strode away.

The result at Birkdale in 1965 was somewhat closer, although the American team won by seven points. Coles played all six games and won three points, including a win over Casper. Two years later, in the heavy defeat at Houston, he beat Doug Sanders twice in the singles. Late in the second game, Coles's ball was plugged in a bunker and the cheerful Sanders remarked that a win for himself in the afternoon would be fair. Coles replied that it was not yet over and got his ball out to within a foot of the pin, while Sanders took three putts.

During the mid-Sixties, Coles kept winning tournaments, including such prestigious events as the PGA Matchplay Championship (1964 and 1965) and the Dunlop Masters. He also reached the final of the first World Matchplay Championship at Wentworth, but lost narrowly two and one to the intimidating Arnold Palmer, who was then at the height of his powers.

In the tense 1969 Ryder Cup match at Birkdale, which ended in a tie, Coles finished with three and a half points out of six. He has a vivid memory of his victory, in partnership with Tony Jacklin, over Jack Nicklaus and Dan Sikes in the first series of fourballs. At the 17th, Coles was the only player who could get a four. He was some distance from the hole but he could afford to take two putts. As he surveyed the first putt, the enthusiastic Jacklin advised him 'not to leave it short'. The last thing Coles needed was advice but, to his credit, he putted up dead. Although he beat Tommy Aaron in the first singles, he lost to Sikes in the afternoon and thinks that Eric Brown ('the best captain I played for; he didn't give a damn about the Americans and that rubbed off on the team') made a mistake in picking him. He was tired and Hunt, who had not played in the morning, would have been a better choice.

With an outstanding sequence of victories in the early Seventies, including the Daks, Bowmaker, Carrolls, Sumrie and Wills tournaments, the Italian, German and Spanish Opens and the PGA Matchplay Championship, Coles was always in the top ten of the Order of Merit and was an integral part of the Ryder Cup team.

In 1971 at Old Warson, St Louis, he remembers his foursomes win with Christy O'Connor over Billy Casper and Jerry Barber. Time after time he asked O'Connor who should hit the first drive and, just as often, the Irishman evaded the question. Eventually, to the astonishment of their opponents, their strategy amounted to tossing a coin on the first tee. The pair also halved a fourball against Frank Beard and Charles Coody. Two years later at Muirfield they played three matches together but gathered only one point. One of the defeats was by Lee Trevino and Homero Blancas, who chattered away in Spanish throughout the game. Coles disliked playing Trevino and was unlucky enough to draw him in the singles. Coles lost heavily and recalled that he had had 'a basinful of Trevino that week.'

Coles's final appearance was at Lytham in 1977 when he lost his three games. He has played more games in the Ryder Cup (40) than anyone else and recorded twelve wins and seven halves.

Neil Coles's last major victory was in the Sanyo Open in 1982, in Spain at the age of 48. But even in 1987 he was able to win over £50,000 with a very limited schedule. He made a formidable impact on the Senior events; he has won the PGA Seniors title four times and the Seniors British Open once (1987).

Coles was always a distinctive figure on the golf-course. With his bare and suntanned pate encircled by a shock of crinkly white hair, he looked more like a benign academic than a golfer. He looked imperturbable too, but confesses that he only kept his fierce tensions under control by a great effort of will.

His method was his own, instilled by his long hours of practice and experiment as a youth. His clubhead, its heel close to the ball, was hooded in the address position and at the top of the swing the club was shut. But he schooled himself to repeat his swing, which was marked by an excellent rhythm and a lovely long finish. His short game was superb and one remembers a wonderfully deft shot, played with his 'persuader' from a very bare lie, during the Open at Birkdale in 1976: the ball came to rest within inches of the hole.

It is surprising that he did not fare better in the Open. His best results were equal third in 1961 and equal second in 1973 at Troon. But Coles does not like links golf. He said of St Andrews: 'I hate its arrogant lumps and bumps and the times you must play shots with one leg up in the air'. He might also have made a greater impact in other countries, especially the USA, if he had not had an aversion to flying. This greatly restricted his golfing horizons; for example, he insisted on travelling by sea to the Ryder Cup matches in the USA.

Neil Coles was a key figure, in concert with John Jacobs, Peter Alliss and Bernard Hunt, in forming a separate tournament players' division of the PGA and is now chairman of the PGA European tour's board of directors.

COLLINS, BILL

USA

Born: 23.9.28

Appearances: 1961

Record: P3 W1 L2 H0

Although he turned professional in 1951, Bill Collins did not play the American tour on a full-time basis until 1958. He was a strong and somewhat portly ex-Marine who won several tournaments, including the New Orleans Open in 1959, the Houston and the Hot Springs Opens in the following year, and the Buick Open in 1962.

His one success in the 1961 match was with the big-hitting Mike Souchak against Tom Haliburton and Neil Coles, who were both making their debuts.

COMPSTON, ARCHIE

GB

Born: 14.1.93

Appearances: 1927, 1929, 1931

Record: P6 W1 L4 H1

For such a formidable matchplayer, Archie Compston had a poor Ryder Cup record. In the inaugural tie of 1927 he lost both matches, though he went down only by one hole to Bill Mehlhorn in the singles. However, in Britain's victory two years later, he was unbeaten and had a comprehensive win over the great Gene Sarazen.

Compston's abilities were signalled by his second place, tied with Ted Ray, in the 1925 Open Championship at Prestwick, which was won by Jim Barnes. He won the PGA Championship in the same year and again in 1927. In 1928 he thrashed Walter Hagen (18 and 17) over 72 holes for a stake of £500. It is said that Hagen had not regained his 'land legs' after crossing the Atlantic; but he was at the peak of his powers, and would have beaten most opponents on one leg. In his autobiography, Hagen recalled,

Archie Compston with Walter Hagen

with wry humour, how in the following week a newspaper had two pages of advertisements listing the many products which had enabled Compston to beat him.

Compston had his best chance of winning the Open in 1930, when his remarkable third round score of 68 enabled him to make up six strokes on Bobby Jones and lead him and the rest of the field by one shot. Jones described Compston on that day as an awesome figure, 'striding after the ball as though he could not wait to vent his fury on it.' But in the afternoon he collapsed in disastrous fashion, scored an 82 and Bobby Jones won the Open, the second major of his Grand Slam year.

Archie Compston was one of the great characters of golf. He was very tall and immensely strong, and had a forceful presence to go with his prominent stature. His bluntness was often construed as rudeness and his informality, which was encouraged on his frequent trips to the more liberal climate of America, did not always suit the stiffer atmosphere of British

golfing circles. But Henry Longhurst called him a genial giant, and he was known as an inspiring teacher.

He was an inspired gambler, too, and made so much money on bets with the members of Coombe Hill Golf Club that the tax man became interested and tried to claim a share. The dispute went to court and, to general delight, Compston won his case. Longhurst recalled how the cunning professional challenged him and two other Cambridge undergraduates to a match with high stakes. Compston took them all to the cleaners and Henry had to sell his car to meet his obligations.

After the disappointment of his collapse in the 1930 Open, Compston never got close to winning it again. But he was one of the most personable of golfers, a showman like Walter Hagen or Lee Trevino. Beneath the extrovert, there was a complicated personality. As Longhurst wrote: 'He was a lonely and lovable man, ever searching for something he never quite found.'

COODY, CHARLES

USA

Born: 13.7.37

Appearances: 1971

Record: P3 W0 L2 H1

Charles Coody had a very successful amateur record, especially in his native Texas, where he was based as a lieutenant in the US Air Force; he reached the semi-final of the US Amateur Championship in 1962.

He turned professional soon afterwards but, while he consistently finished in the money, he did not win many tournaments. His rare victories included the Dallas Open in 1964 and the Cleveland Open in 1969. However, in 1971 he reached the pinnacle of his career when he won the Masters; two birdies in the last four holes kept him ahead of Jack Nicklaus and Johnny Miller.

In his one appearance in the Ryder Cup, at St Louis in 1971, his best result was a half in his fourball with Frank Beard, against Neil Coles and Christy O'Connor.

In the 1970s, it was the fashion for major British sponsors to import American golfing stars and pay them handsome sums of appearance money. Coody made two profitable forays in 1973 when he won the Wills Open and the John Player Classic at Turnberry.

In the latter event, Coody, a tall and solid player, who was used to playing in windy conditions in Texas, needed all his strength in weather which was so bad that the tented village was blown away and when last seen was heading for Ireland.

Coody joined the Seniors tour in 1987 and has played with great success to win nearly $2 million in prize money.

COTTON, HENRY

GB

Born: 26.1.07

Appearances: 1929, 1937, 1947
Captain 1947, 1953

Record: P6 W2 L4 H0

Henry Cotton was the most influential British professional golfer of the modern age. He had brilliant success as a player at a time when the Americans were the dominant force in professional golf; his victories in the Open Championship in 1934, 1937 and 1948 stemmed the transatlantic tide. No British player has since recorded three victories in the Open. But he also had a radical influence on the role and status of the professional golfer.

It was unusual for a man with Cotton's background to become a professional golfer. He was born into a solid middle-class milieu and was educated at a public school, Alleyns. In his day, the pro golfer came up from the ranks of the caddies and eventually attained 'non-commissioned' status as a club professional. The great players, such as Harry Vardon, J H Taylor and James Braid attained some distinction and celebrity by their victories, especially in the Open, but they had to remember to doff their caps to the amateurs, the gentlemen golfers.

By tradition, Cotton should have been one of the latter, but he ignored the regimented social barriers and became a professional at the age of 17. His ambition and enterprise was shiningly apparent, since he became an assistant at Mougins Golf Club, near Cannes, at 19 and the professional at Langley Park a few months later.

At this very early stage in his career, he already had the refreshing outlook that urged him to 'have a go at anything', as he later wrote in *This Game of Golf*. He was blessed with great intelligence, and with a restless, intensely enquiring mind, his greatest ally in his long pursuit of golfing excellence.

Cotton announced himself as a golfer of great potential by finishing ninth behind Bobby Jones in the Open of 1927, at St Andrews. In the following year,

Henry Cotton, the captain, with the 1947 team. Fred Daly is on his right and Dai Rees on his left.

he was runner-up to Charles Whitcombe in the *News of the World* Matchplay Championship.

In that year he decided to further his education by playing in America. Such a decision was a sign of his ambition and courage, as he set off for uncharted golfing waters with £300 in his pocket. He started well by finishing third in his first American tournament, the Sacramento Open, which was won by Tommy Armour. His success thereafter was moderate, although he returned to Britain a few months later with his £300 intact. Much more important, he had realised that his upright swing, which produced a faded shot, was inadequate if he were to win major championships. He knew he had to mimic the American style and learn to draw the ball in order to hit it further.

In 1929, at the age of 22, the young lion played his first Ryder Cup at Moortown (Leeds) in a victorious British side, captained by George Duncan. Although Cotton lost his foursomes, he beat Al Watrous in the penultimate singles to secure the point which Britain required to win the match. He recalled the tension and excitement which surrounded his game. There were 10,000 spectators on the course and in those days they roamed freely on the fairways; there were no ropes to keep them back. It was a great test for a young golfer.

It is curious and irritating to record that Cotton did not play in the match again until 1937. In 1931 Cotton wanted to stay on in the USA, after the Ryder Cup, to play a few tournaments and was told by the PGA that he must return to Britain with the team. Attitudes were struck and attempts at compromise rejected. Not for the last time, Cotton demonstrated that he was not to be browbeaten by amateur officials.

During the time of the next two matches Cotton was the professional at Royal Waterloo in Belgium and was ineligible because each team, by this time, had to comprise natives of and residents of the country represented. Both Percy Alliss and Aubrey Boomer were excluded for the same reason.

Cotton's departure to Belgium coincided with the flowering of his great talent. American players had dominated the Open Championship throughout the Twenties and early Thirties and Cotton's sternest ambition was to win the greatest title in golf. He had to endure great disappointment in 1933 at St Andrews. After three rounds he was tied for the lead and threw it all away with a final round of 79.

But in 1934 he led the field all the way at Royal St George's. His second round of 65 decimated the other competitors and it was commemorated by the best-selling Dunlop golf ball. Cotton won again in 1937, at Carnoustie, against opposition

which could not have been more formidable, since the whole American Ryder Cup team was present. The last round was played in such appalling conditions of soaking rain and fierce winds that play was nearly abandoned. Henry Longhurst wrote later that the rain was so heavy on the roof of the Press tent that it drowned out the clatter of the typewriters. Cotton's score of 71 was one of the greatest rounds played in the Open.

Immediately afterwards, he played the American PGA champion, Densmore Shute, over 72 holes and beat him six and five. It confirmed Cotton's status at the top of professional golf.

The Ryder Cup of 1937 had gone to the Americans by a convincing margin at Southport. Halfway through the singles matches on the final afternoon, the two teams were tied with four points each, but the Americans won all the last four matches. Cotton lost his foursomes match, but beat Tony Manero, the US Open champion, easily in the singles.

Cotton, now at the peak of his ability, was chosen to captain the 1939 Ryder Cup team but the onset of war put paid to these and all other golfing plans. He was invalided out of the RAF and spent much of the war raising money for the Red Cross. He was awarded the MBE for his work.

Ryder Cup hostilities resumed in 1947, when Britain, captained by Cotton, were crushed eleven matches to one in Portland, Oregon. It was Cotton's last appearance as a player, but he re-established some of Britain's golfing dignity by winning the Open for the third time at Muirfield in the following year. The foundation of his victory was a brilliantly accomplished second round of 66, with King George VI supporting him in the gallery. His consistency can be measured by his play from the tee: he hit the fairway 52 times out of 56 attempts with his driver.

After 1948, Cotton restricted his appearances and did not even enter the Open for some years. He declined to offer himself for the 1949 Ryder Cup team, but captained it again in 1953, when Britain lost by one point at Wentworth. Peter Alliss recalls that Cotton demanded the best of everything for his team in those depressing days of post-war austerity. The team were accommodated at the dormie house at Sunningdale Golf Club, were fed on steaks accompanied by a glass of wine, and were taken to see *Guys 'n' Dolls* in London.

Henry Cotton was still the brightest star of British golf. He had a house in Eaton Square, spoke French and drove expensive cars. To some extent he had carried on where Walter Hagen had left off. Like Hagen, his self-belief enabled him to remove the barriers put up to keep professional golfers in their place.

Cotton knew his value as one of the pre-eminent golfers in the world and as far and away the best British golfer. With his keen and restless intelligence, he set out to secure the rewards which he deserved. This undoubtedly riled many members of the golfing establishment, but Cotton pursued his goals with dignity and great style. There was no point in their waving their 'old school ties' at him, because he could wave his own back. He was a dedicated traveller, who won many overseas tournaments: The Mar del Plata Open in Argentina; the Belgian, Italian, French and German Opens on many occasions; even the Czechoslovakian Open in 1939. Although he never made any impact in America, this was a carefully considered omission. His first preoccupation was to secure his own territory, Britain, and this he did with great ease. He was immensely enterprising and innovative. As Gene Sarazen noted, he was one of the first professionals to experiment with the new sand-wedge and became an expert in its use. He poured forth a flood of ideas on all aspects of the game and was always ready to try something different.

Who but Cotton could have devised a driving range from which you hit floating golf balls into the sea, as he did in Monte Carlo in 1946? Who but Cotton could have done a golfing act with fluorescent golf balls on a darkened stage, at the Coliseum? He played to packed houses in 1938 but plans to tour the provincial theatres in the following year were thwarted by the imminence of war.

Gene Sarazen called him 'the hero of modern British golf ... unhurrying Henry, sleek as Noel Coward'. Cotton got to that eminence by working harder than any other contemporary golfer; only Hogan equalled his intensity. As a consequence, he had a deep knowledge of the dynamics of the golf swing and very few golfers have ever equalled his power and effortless authority. In Henry Longhurst's opinion, Cotton refined, or 'cleaned up', the golf swing and noone hit the ball with quite his directness and economy of movement. His three-quarter swing was always under perfect control, powerful and rhythmic, and Dai Rees maintained that no golfer, not even Jack Nicklaus or Arnold Palmer, could hit long irons and fairways woods as far as Cotton. He stressed the dominant role of the hands in the golf swing, accompanied by good balance and a free swing of the club head.

In his early fifties, Cotton was still good enough to finish in the top ten in the Open on three occasions. He was a source of great encouragement to younger players, as his work with the Golf Foundation and 'Rookie of the Year' award showed. He paid for the latter with his own money and it was typical of his directness that it was not awarded if he could not find a worthy recipient. He remained a great communicator to the end of his days. He wrote many books and articles, designed and built courses (including his beloved Penina, in Portugal), was a dedicated teacher and above all a supreme enthusiast about the game he adorned.

Cotton's knighthood was conferred on him only a few days before his death, and no one in sport had ever deserved such an honour more.

COUPLES, FRED

USA

Born: 3.10.59

Appearances: 1989, 1991

Record: P7 W3 L3 H1

In 1992, Fred Couples emphatically answered his critics by winning the Masters at Augusta in splendid style. It was his third victory of the year, following his successes in the Los Angeles Open and the Nestle Invitational.

In the late Eighties, Jack Nicklaus had songled out Fred Couples as the epitome of everything that was wrong with American golf. In his opinion, it was too comfortable a life when well over a hundred players could make more than $100,000 in a season. that was why American golfers had forgotten how to win; and Fred Couples, loaded with natural talent, was one of the worst offenders.

The criticism at that time was harsh but justifiable. Couples had been on the circuit since 1981 and had won only two tournaments, the Kemper Open and the Tournament Players Championship. In 1987, he won another event, the Byron Nelson Classic and was consistent enough in the next two years to win his place in the 1989 Ryder Cup team for the Belfry.

Couples made a miserable debut in the tied match. He and Lanny Wadkins lost their fourball game to Mark James and Howard Clark and he was not called upon again until the singles. Couples stood on the 18th tee level with Christy O'Connor Jr and hit a huge drive about 70 yards past his opponent's ball. But the Irishman hit one of the shots of his career, to within a few yards of the hole. Couples, clearly unnerved, hit his 9-iron weakly to the right of the green, left his chip some way from the pin and conceded the game to O'Connor.

The incident was a neat encapsulation of Couples the golfer. He has a languid and very powerful swing; his relaxed and cheerful manner make him popular wherever he goes; but does he have the gravitas to become a champion? That question was partly answered at the 1991 Ryder Cup match at Kiawah Island. The American captain, Dave Stockton, had the astute idea of pairing Couples with the veteran Raymond Floyd, who could be counted upon to act as a mentor to the younger man. The tactic worked superbly, as they won their first two games together and only lost to the European juggernauts, Ballesteros and Olazabal. Couples went on to halve his second fourball match and to defeat Sam Torrance in the singles.

Couples's experiences at the Ryder Cup may well turn out to have been a golfing 'road to Damascus' and his conversion has begun triumphantly with his first success in a major championship. He has had high finishes before in the major events; equal fourth in the Open in 1984 and 1988; equal third in the US PGA Championship in 1982 and second in 1990; and third in the US Open in 1991. Fred Couples may now go on to realise his great talent by winning several more of those major championships.

COX, BILL

GB

Born: 18.3.10

Appearances: 1935, 1937

Record: P3 W0 L2 H1

It is hardly surprising that Bill Cox became one of Britain's leading golf teachers. He worked for Henry Cotton at both Langley Park and Royal Waterloo and was no doubt influenced by 'the Master's' profound knowledge and great enthusiasm.

Although he never won an important tournament, Cox was a very consistent performer. But in his first Ryder Cup appearance, in 1935 at Ridgewood, New Jersey, he and Edward Jarman were hammered in the foursomes by Paul Runyan and Horton Smith. In the singles, Cox was five down after 18 holes to Smith but won six holes in the next nine to be one up. He finally halved the match, a proper reward for his great determination.

In the 1937 match, Cox played excellent golf in a narrow foursomes defeat at the hands of Ralph Guldahl and Tony Manero and should certainly not have been omitted from the singles matches by the captain, Charles Whitcombe.

Bill Cox was the professional at Fulwell after the war and was awarded an OBE in 1967.

COX, WILFRED

USA

Born: 27.10.97

Appearances: 1931

Record: P2 W2 L0 H0

Wilfred Cox is one of the select band of players to have a perfect record in the Ryder Cup. In a comprehensive defeat of the British side in the fierce heat of Columbus, Ohio, 'Wiffy' Cox was one of several Americans to win both their matches. He beat the formidable Abe Mitchell in the singles.

With his simple three-quarter swing, played from a wide stance, Cox won several tournaments during the 1930s; he also had an excellent record in the US Open. He was much to the fore in PGA matters and served on the national PGA tournament committee.

CRENSHAW, BEN

USA

Born: 11.1.52

Appearances: 1981, 1983, 1987

Record: P9 W3 L5 H1

After a brilliant amateur career, during which he was the outstanding college player in America, Ben Crenshaw entered the 1973 qualifying school for the PGA tour. He finished 12 strokes ahead of his nearest rival and in his first tournament as a professional, the Texas Open, he took first place. At this time, the pundits were not asking whether Crenshaw had the stuff of greatness, but how soon he would surpass Hogan, Palmer or even Nicklaus. He was a handsome figure, with his long blond hair, and soon had his own army of supporters, embarrassingly called 'Ben's bunnies'.

But predictions of his future greatness were premature and he did not win another tournament until the Bing Crosby in 1976. In that year he won two other events and finished second in the money list. Over the next eight years, he won half-a-dozen tournaments, including the Irish Open. But the major championships to which he aspired eluded him. He was a runner-up in the Open Championship in 1978 and 1979 and third in 1980; he was third in the US Open in 1975 and second in the US PGA championship in 1979 after a play-off with David Graham; in the Masters at Augusta, he was the runner-up in 1976 and 1983.

Crenshaw played some of his most scintillating golf in 1979. When he won the Phoenix Open, his scores included a second round of 61; his partner, Bill Rogers, spoke of it as 'the easiest 61 imaginable'. But a victory in a major championship did not seem to be a part of Crenshaw's destiny. Some commentators considered that his uncertain play off the tee would never allow him one of the greatest prizes; while others declared that his brilliant putting more than offset the errors of his long game. At last, in 1984, golf fans all over the world watched with delight as he won the Masters by two shots from Tom Watson. Crenshaw's putting had been magnificently assured on the terrifyingly slick Augusta greens.

By then, he had played in two Ryder Cups and he remembers his battles with affection; he 'never had anything but a high-spirited match.' At Walton Heath in 1981 he lost his fourball match but demolished Des Smyth in the singles by six and four. Two years later, at the PGA National course, he played an important part in the narrowest of American victories by winning two and a half points out of four, including a victory in

the singles over Sandy Lyle. During 1986 and 1987 Crenshaw was in excellent form; he won three more events in America and was third in the money list in the latter year. But he lost all of his three matches at Muirfield village. His encounter in the singles with Eammon Darcy was a curious affair, in that Crenshaw broke his putter after going two down to Darcy at the sixth hole. He recalls that the shaft of the putter had rusted away from the inside; he had rapped other putters much harder without breaking them. Despite his reputation as 'Gentle Ben' there is a fiercer side to his nature. For the rest of the round, he improvised his putts with the leading edge of this sand-iron, and then used his 1-iron to such good effect on the greens that he was actually one hole up at the 16th. A birdie from Darcy levelled the match at the next hole and the Irishman sank a nasty downhill putt on the final green to win the match.

Crenshaw has won two more events in the USA since then and invariably plays well at the Masters; during the period 1987 to 1991, he has finished in the top four on four occasions. He is a regular and very welcome visitor to Britain for the Open Championship and intends to play over 20 events in 1992. He has qualms about the excessive hype which now surrounds the Ryder Cup and decided reservations about the atmosphere at American tournaments, where the spectators are becoming 'a little too vocal'. Crenshaw has begun to design golf courses, but will only take on commissions which he can supervise himself. He is an admirer of the work of such designers as Harry Colt, Tom Simpson and Mackenzie Ross and there is no doubt that Crenshaw's courses will be built with a due regard for the classic principles of golf architecture.

D

DAILEY, ALLAN

GB

Born: 8.5.08

Appearances: 1933

Allan Dailey was born not far from St Andrews, but spent most of his career in England, and particularly at the Berkshire Golf Club, where he was the professional for many years.

He probably owed his selection for the Ryder Cup team to his performance in the Roehampton tournament of 1933, when he beat three international players on his way to victory. But the captain, J H Taylor, did not give him a game.

Dailey was a member of the British team which toured South Africa in 1936 and was joint fourth in the Open of 1938.

DALY, FRED

GB

Born: 11.10.11

Appearances: 1947, 1949, 1951, 1953

Record: P8 W3 L4 H1

With his jaunty walk and engaging personality, Fred Daly looked the archetypal Irishman, especially with his habit of whistling quietly to himself as he rolled along the fairways. For a few years after the Second World War he was second in reputation as a golfer only to Henry Cotton. He had two important firsts to his name: the first Irishman to win the Open Championship, and the first Irishman to play for Britain in the Ryder Cup.

At the age of 9, Daly was already caddying at Portrush, which is where he learned to hit the ball long and straight through the wind. He was the professional at Mahee Golf Club at the age of 17 and by 1946 had won the Ulster Championship on seven occasions, as well as the Irish Open and the Irish Dunlop Tournament.

Daly was at the height of his considerable powers in 1947, when he won the Open at Hoylake by one shot. A long putt on the 72nd hole kept him in the lead from Reg Horne and the American amateur, Frank Stranahan. Daly went on to win the PGA Matchplay Championship: the first golfer since James Braid in 1905 to win the two most prominent British events in the same year. He won again in the following year but came second to Henry Cotton in the Open.

In his first Ryder Cup match, in 1947, Daly had a draw in the foursomes anyone would have dreaded: Sam Snead and Lloyd Mangrum. He and Charlie Ward were six down after 18 holes and never recovered. His first win in the contest came two years later, when he and Ken Bousfield played some sterling golf to beat Bob Hamilton and Skip Alexander in the foursomes.

The tense match of 1953, won by one point by the USA, saw Daly at his best. With his fellow Irishman, Harry Bradshaw, he scored Britain's only point on the first day. He was renowned for his ability to

Fred Daly

hole out under pressure and needed all his resolve to coax in a putt of four feet (the captain, Henry Cotton, convinced himself that the putt was nearer four yards) to win the match on the 36th hole. As was his habit, Daly made at least a dozen passes above the ball, accompanied by sidelong glances at the hole, almost as if he were trying to catch it off its guard. On the following day, Daly's game, and especially his putting, was far too good for Ted Kroll, whom he hammered nine and seven.

Fred Daly won his third Matchplay title in 1952. He never lost his zest for the game and made his final appearance in the Open in 1973. He partnered Gene Sarazen, who holed in one at the eighth, the famous 'postage stamp' at Troon. He was the professional at the Balmoral Club in Belfast for 30 years.

DARCY, EAMONN

GB & Europe

Born: 7.8.52

Appearances: 1975, 1977, 1981, 1987

Record: P11 W1 L8 H2

A very unkind television commentator once said that Eamonn Darcy's swing resembled an octopus falling out of a tree. It is certainly idiosyncratic at the top , with his elbows pointing in directions not recommended by the coaching manuals. But at the point of impact, everything is back in place and his swing has been effective enough to earn him over £1 million in prize money over the last two decades. In the 1991 Open Championship Darcy tied for fifth place and was the leading European golfer.

Darcy made his Ryder Cup debut in 1975, at Laurel Valley, in a fourball, partnered by Christy O'Connor Jr. He must have wondered what had hit him, as Tom Weiskopf went to the turn in 30 shots with his own ball; the American pair won easily. His Ryder Cup career has covered a long span and his first victory was a long time in coming. But, by his defeat of Ben Crenshaw at Muirfield Village in 1987, Darcy won the point that secured Europe's first ever win on American soil. He had to hole a slippery downhill putt and did so with aplomb. Up to that point, all that Darcy had to show for his efforts in the Ryder Cup were a couple of halved matches.

The genial Darcy is a native of Delgany, County Wicklow, and had ambitions to be a jockey. When he grew too heavy, he turned his attentions to golf and became a professional in 1969. By the mid-Seventies, he was in the top ten of the Order of Merit and began to travel the world to play golf. His victories have included the Desert Classic, and the New Zealand, Spanish and Kenyan Opens.

Darcy finished 18th in the Order of Merit in 1991 and missed selection for the Ryder Cup match at Kiawah Island by the thin margin of £58. It must have been particularly galling, because he decided not to compete in the final qualifying tournament, the German Open, when some place money would have ensured his selection. He has represented Ireland in the World Cup seven times and was a member of the Irish team which won the Dunhill Cup in 1988.

DAVIES, WILLIAM

GB

Born: 5.1.92

Appearances: 1931, 1933

Record: P4 W2 L2 H0

Bill Davies's most notable victories were in the Northern Championship in 1931 and 1935 and the Leeds challenge Cup in 1931 and 1939. But he often showed strongly in the Open Championship and finished in the top ten four times between 1925 and 1932.

Davies was known as a fighter and he proved this in 1931. He and Archie Compston were hammered in the foursomes by Gene Sarazen and Johnny Farrell, but in the singles he bounced back to beat the latter, to garner one of Britain's meagre three points.

In the exciting battle at Southport two years later he helped Syd Easterbrook to the narrowest of wins, by one hole, over Craig Wood and Paul Runyan in the foursomes. Although he lost his singles to Wood, Britain won the Ryder Cup by a single point.

DAWSON, PETER

GB

Born: 9.5.50

Appearances: 1977

Record: P3 W1 L2 H0

Dawson won his way into the Ryder Cup team by some consistent play in 1977, without winning a tournament. He also represented England in the World Cup in the same year.

The fixture was played at Lytham in 1977 and had a new format of five foursomes on the first day, five fourballs on the second and ten singles on the final day. Nobody liked it, least of all the spectators, who did not have enough matches to watch.

In his foursomes, Dawson was paired with the experienced Neil Coles and, although they were two holes up with three to play, they contrived to lose to Dave Stockton and Jerry McGee. The British pair took on Ed Sneed and Lanny Wadkins in the fourballs and were easily beaten, but Dawson had the consolation of defeating Don January in the singles.

Dawson has the distinction of being the only left-hander to have played in the Ryder Cup. he is currently the professional at Hardelot, in northern France.

DEMARET, JIMMY

USA

Born: 24.5.10

Appearances: 1947, 1949, 1951

Record: P6 W6 L0 H0

It is surprising that Jimmy Demaret, a flamboyant, wise-cracking character, was such a close friend of the stern and relentless Ben Hogan. It was quite a contrast but they had at least one thing common: a perfect record in the Ryder Cup. In Demaret's case, his tally of six wins from six matches showed that exceptional skills underlay his carefree manner.

Demaret's 31 victories on the American tour spanned the 20 years from 1938 to 1958 and included six wins in 1940 and another six in 1947. In 1961 he won the Canada Cup (now the World Cup) with Sam Snead and, at the age of 54, he finished equal first with Tommy Jacobs in the Bob Hope Desert Classic but lost the play-off.

He certainly had a swing which was built to last. He played all his shots with a narrow, open stance and hit the ball with a controlled fade. He was accurate and consistent and won the Masters on three occasions. His first victory at August, in 1940, was his sixth tournament win in succession and the foundation was a first round of 67. He played the back nine in 30 strokes, a record which was later equalled by Gene Littler and Ben Hogan.

In the 1930s Jimmy Demaret was sponsored by a bandleader and a night-club owner from Galveston and, whenever he could, he used to do some crooning for his sponsors. He was a very personable and gregarious character and one of his grumbles about the tournaments was that the clothes the professionals wore 'made the place look like a funeral parlour'. In the late 1930s, he found what he wanted in the garment area of New York, roll after roll of bright, light-weight cloth. He had

Jimmy Demaret, one of the most colourful dressers in golf

his own shirts and slacks made and put his own distinctive mark on the sartorial traditions of the game. One of the correspondents of *Golf Illustrated* commented on his attire for the 1949 Ryder Cup matches: 'a scarlet cap, salmon pink sweater and cerise slacks'. That was a rather sombre outfit for Jimmy Demaret.

Someone wrote that Demaret practised less and had more fun than any other great player but he rarely looked like losing a game in the Ryder Cup. In his first game, he was partnered by Hogan in the foursomes and they had some initial uneasy moments against Jimmy Adams and Max Faulkner. But the American pair, despite being four down after nine holes, ground out a victory which thereafter rarely seemed in doubt. Hogan, after his car crash, was unable to play in 1949, at Ganton, but was made captain. His insistence on a strict regime of practice did not suit Demaret well; he said that he practised twice as much as he wanted and half as much as Hogan wanted. But it brought results because the USA won a close match.

In 1951, Demaret was back in partnership with Ben Hogan and they won their foursomes easily against Fred Daly and Ken Bousfield. In the singles Demaret had a fierce encounter with Dai Rees but won by two holes. A crucial factor was his remarkable play from the sand. Rees calculated that he was in 11 bunkers but got up and down in two shots from ten of them. No doubt the Welshman exaggerated a bit but it is true that he holed a shot direct from a bunker on the 35th hole, when Rees thought he would claw a hole back for the British team. With typical generosity, Demaret gave his sand-wedge to Rees after the match.

After his retirement from tournament play, Jimmy Demaret commentated on golf for American television, presented Shell's *Wonderful World of Golf* and, with Jackie Burke, built the Champions Club at Houston, where the 1967 Ryder Cup and the 1969 US Open were played.

DICKINSON, GARDNER

USA

Born: 14.9.27

Appearances: 1967, 1971

Record: P10 W9 L1 H0

A protege of Ben Hogan, on whom he modelled himself in every way, even down to the flat white cap and the impassive face, Gardner Dickinson had one of the best records in the Ryder Cup. On his debut at Houston in 1967, he won both his foursomes with Arnold Palmer, both four-balls with Doug Sanders and then defeated a young Tony Jacklin in the singles.

Four years later, Dickinson was in action again at St Louis and, with Palmer as his partner again, won his first three matches and then beat Christy O'Connor emphatically in the singles. His final match was against Harry Bannerman, a fine matchplayer but not one of Britain's top golfers. Ironically, Dickinson managed to lost and thereby spoil his perfect record.

Dickinson had turned professional in 1952 and played on the American tour until the mid-Seventies. He won seven tournaments between 1956 and 1971, including the Doral Open, the Cleveland Open and the Atlanta Golf Classic. Dickinson has an excellent reputation as a golf teacher and played on the Seniors tour until the end of the Eighties.

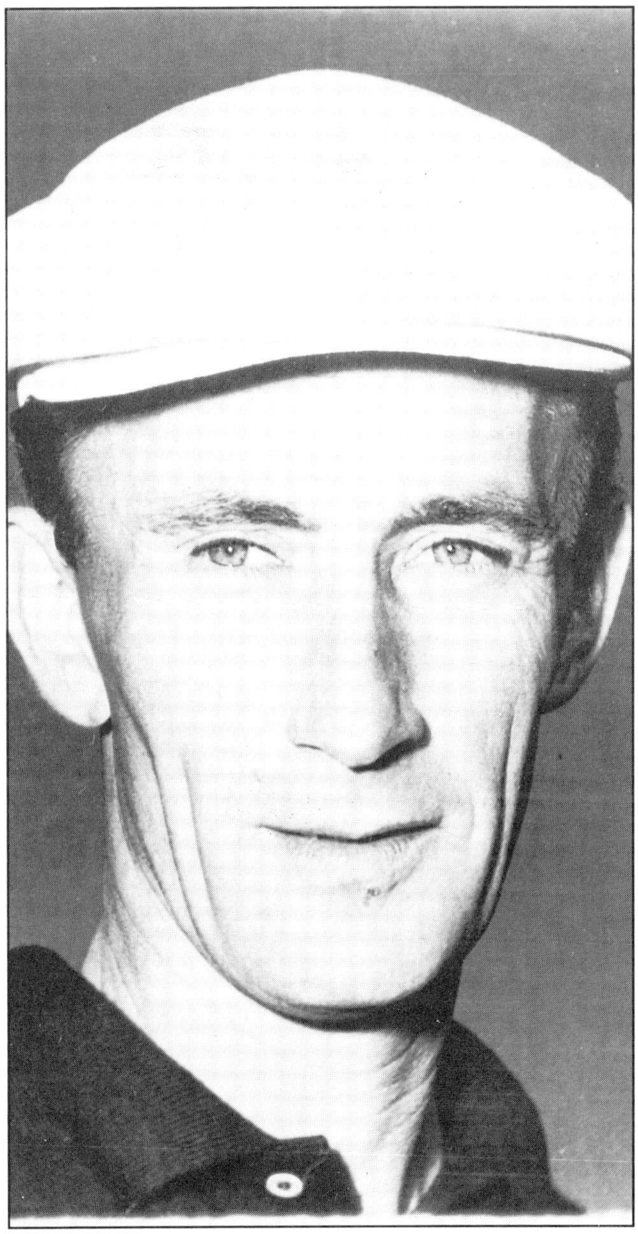

Gardner Dickinson, one of the most successful Ryder Cup players

DIEGEL, LEO

USA

Born: 27.4.99

Appearances: 1927, 1929, 1931, 1933

Record: P6 W3 L3 H0

A highly original thinker about the game, Leo Diegel's name was adopted to describe his eccentric mode of putting. His crouched posture, with his forearms jutting out almost horizontal and the top of the shaft nearly touching his chin, was called 'Diegeling'. Gene Sarazen said he putted 'like a man seized with cramps', but it was Diegel's solution to his putting nerves. He would have been the first golfer to try the broom-handle putter if he were playing today.

Diegel was a very intense and highly strung man, to whom golf was a consuming passion. His friend, Gene Sarazen, recalled that he would get up from the dinner table and try different types of swing between courses. He always had a new theory to explore but, as Henry Cotton pointed out, he had a remarkable freshness in his approach to golf and was always ready to experiment with new shots.

He had a thoroughly depressing record in the Open Championships of Britain and America. Often he trembled on the brink of success, only to experience failure. At the age of 20, in 1920, he should have won

the US Open at Inverness. The veteran British golfer, Ted Ray, had set a target of 295 and Diegel only had to finish the last five holes in par to win by three shots. He perpetrated a series of dreadful errors and finished tied for second place. Gene Sarazen thought that this early failure blighted the rest of his career.

In 1929, Diegel led the Open at Muirfield after two rounds but scored a third round 82, admittedly in bad weather, and Hagen won. Once again, in the Open at St Andrews in 1933, victory beckoned to him. On the final hole he had a putt to win; he not only missed it but also the one back and so failed even to get into the play-off with Densmore Shute and Craig Wood.

Nevertheless, Diegel won around 30 tournaments in his career, which was a lengthy one; he turned professional in 1916 and was still playing in 1939. He won the Canadian Open four times in the Twenties and his most successful years were at the end of that decade. He won the US PGA Championship in 1928 and 1929 and on the first occasion interrupted Walter Hagen's domination of the event. Hagen had won it four years running and had beaten 22 opponents in the process. But Diegel beat him in the quarter-final, hammered Sarazen nine and eight in the semi-final and then disposed easily of Al Espinosa to become champion.

Diegel's defeat of Hagen must have been sweet revenge, since 'Sir Walter' had beaten him in the final of 1926. At lunchtime, half-way through the 36 holes, Hagen had a three-course meal served to him with champagne. Opposite him, the nerve-racked Diegel, hardly able to face his tea and toast, rushed from the table, ran into a glass door and duly lost the match by a wide margin.

Hagen selected him for the inaugural Ryder Cup match in 1927, at Worcester, Massachusetts. He went out in the foursomes with his friend Bill Mehlhorn (they were bridge partners and were good enough to play in the national championships) and they were the only American pair to lose a match – heavily at that, to Charles Whitcombe and Aubrey Boomer. But Diegel restored his reputation by demolishing Ted Ray in the singles. He won both his matches at Moortown in 1929, when the Americans lost the tie. In the process, he got his revenge on Boomer in the foursomes and thrashed Abe Mitchell by nine and eight. Mitchell played excellent golf, with a morning round of 70, but was five down. His opponent was 'Diegeling' the putts in from all angles and all distances.

Leo Diegel was a terrible worrier on the golf-course and that lay behind his fallibility as a putter; but he was intelligent enough to devise solutions to his many golfing problems, whether real or imagined. He was so often a brilliant player and it was less than just that he failed to win an Open championship. As he ruefully said: 'They keep trying to give me a championship but I won't take it'.

DOUGLAS, DAVE

USA

Born: 1.1.18

Appearances: 1953

Record: P2 W1 L0 H1

The grandfather of Dave Douglas worked at a golfcourse near Edinburgh and his father emigrated to America at the age of 20. Although Douglas won eight tournaments in America, his best year was in 1953, when he won the Canadian Open and was chosen for the Ryder Cup team to play at Wentworth.

In partnership with 'Porky' Oliver, he won his foursomes game against Peter Alliss and Henry Weetman, when the latter's erratic play cost the British pair the crucial 35th hole. On the next day, the tall, slim and reserved Douglas found himself in the match that was to decide the destiny of the Ryder Cup.

As he stood on the 36th tee, one down to his opponent, Bernard Hunt, the drama which so often enlivens the Ryder Cup was reaching its climax. The tie was level at five points to each country and, ahead by the green, Peter Alliss looked certain to get at least a half to ensure that Britain would, at the very worst, tie the match. Although he contrived to lose his game to Joe Turnesa, the betting was still firmly on a win for Hunt and a tie overall for the cup. 'All he had to do was get par down the last'. These words have no doubt haunted Alliss and Hunt down the years.

It was Dave Douglas who got his par down the last and he must have watched in disbelief, and sympathy, as Bernard Hunt three-putted the final green to hand the Ryder Cup to the USA.

DOUGLASS, DALE

USA

Born: 5.3.36

Appearances: 1969

Record: P2 W0 L2 H0

The most successful year for Dale Douglass was certainly 1969, when he won both the Azalea Open and the Kemper Open. Although he was a player of great stamina, who used to average 35 tournaments a year, he only won one other event on the PGA tour, the Phoenix Open in 1970.

Douglass earned his selection for the 1969 fixture at Royal Birkdale but lost both matches. With Dave Hill, he narrowly lost a fourball against Christy O'Connor and Peter Townsend and was easily beaten in the second series of singles by Peter Butler. He has been one of the leading lights of the Seniors tour since 1986 and has won over $2 million.

DREW, NORMAN

GB

Born: 25.5.32

Appearances: 1959

Record: P1 W0 L0 H1

As a result of winning the Irish Amateur Championship in 1952 and 1953, Norman Drew forced himself into the Walker Cup side in the latter year. After turning professional he had a wonderful year in 1959, when he won the Irish Championship, the Irish Dunlop Tournament and the *Yorkshire Evening News* Tournament and was runner-up in the Dunlop Masters.

Drew had certainly earned his place in the team to play the USA at Eldorado Country Club, and he became the first golfer to represent Britain in both the Walker Cup and the Ryder Cup.

In the singles, he was put out as a sacrificial lamb against Doug Ford, who had won the Masters in 1957. Although Drew was four down early on, he cut the deficit to one hole by lunchtime. On the 36th tee he was still one down. The par-five hole is one of the best on the course and has a lake right in front of the green. Ford played for safety and was just short of the lake in two shots. Drew, advised by his great friend, Peter Mills, went for the carry and hit a superlative 3-wood shot to within a few inches of the hole to halve his match.

In the Sixties, Drew lost his putting stroke and his uncertainties on the greens adversely affected his whole game; he eventually withdrew from tournament golf.

DUDLEY, ED

USA

Born: 10.2.01

Appearances: 1929, 1933, 1937

Record: P4 W3 L1 H0

A tall, handsome and well-dressed man, Dudley was thought by Henry Cotton to have one of the best-looking swings he had ever seen. It was smooth, unhurried and powerful; but perhaps the game came too easily to him, because he never showed that extra dimension of talent that might have brought him a major title. He led the US Open after three rounds in 1937, but subsided to fifth place; and he finished third in the Masters in the same year. His best finish in the Open was seventh place, in 1933 at St Andrews.

Nevertheless, he won many tournaments in the 1930s, including the Philadelphia Open on three occasions. He reached the quarter-finals of the US PGA Championship no less than six times, and the semi-final in 1932.

Dudley had an excellent record in the Ryder Cup. Although he lost his first match, a foursomes with Gene Sarazen in 1929, he managed three points from the three matches in his other two appearances.

He was the professional at the Augusta National Club for over 20 years and the President of the PGA of America from 1942 to 1948.

DUNCAN, GEORGE

GB

Born: 16.9.83

Appearances: 1927, 1929, 1931

Record: P5 W2 L3 H0

The modern professional golfer, if taken back in a time machine to the first two decades of this century, would be astonished by the speed at which the game was then played. George Duncan was the quickest player of them all, so much so that James Braid remarked that he played so fast that he looked as if he didn't care. He was called 'Miss 'em quick' Duncan and entitled his autobiography *Golf at the Gallop*.

George Duncan began his golf as a caddie at the Old Links, Aberdeen, and became the professional at Stonehaven at the age of 17. Along the way, he turned down an offer to play professional football for Aberdeen. He had a beautifully natural golf swing, fast and flowing, but orthodox. He was a long hitter, especially off the tee; a clean hitter of his irons and an exceptionally good putter. He had been much influenced by Harry Vardon, whose philosophy was to take the 'all air route', by dint of which the golfer would eliminate the vagaries of the bounce of the ball. Duncan was an inspirational player and relished the challenge of a difficult shot; it was not in his character to play safe. But he was also a temperamental player and, according to that acute observer, Henry Cotton, if he started well he could easily score below 70; but if he started badly he found it difficult to fight back to post a respectable score.

Duncan's first important win was in the British Professional Matchplay Championship of 1913 and he won the French Open in the same year. He had a marvellous record in the Open Championship; between 1906 and 1914 he was in the top ten on six occasions. When one reflects on his outstanding skills, it is surprising that he only won the Open once, in 1920. But he did so with his own typical brilliance. After two mediocre rounds of 80 at Deal, he was 13 shots behind Abe Mitchell. He spotted a driver he fancied in the exhibition tent, bought it and used it throughout the 36 holes which were played on the final day. His round of 71 in the morning made up all the leeway on Mitchell, who scored a disastrous 84 and Duncan followed this with a 72 to win by two shots from Alex Herd.

Duncan had always been a notably good matchplayer and had played several challenge matches before the First World War against James Braid, Harry Vardon and Ted Ray and it was natural that he should play in the forerunner of the Ryder Cup in 1926. He beat Walter Hagen by the margin of six and five.

In the Ryder Cup proper, Duncan won his singles matches but managed to lose all his foursomes, invariably by very wide margins. He was the captain of the British team in 1929 and proved to be an excellent leader. He and Aubrey Boomer lost their foursomes to Leo Diegel and Al Espinosa, but the American pair were in superb form; in the morning they went round in 68 shots and were seven holes up. The American captain, Walter Hagen, is said to have engineered the draw for the singles matches so that he would play Duncan, the opposing captain, and told the American team that they already 'had a point in the bag'. On the contrary, Duncan had a score of 68 in the morning, to be five holes in the lead, and after lunch went to the turn in 31 to beat 'the Haig' by ten and eight. It was Hagen's only defeat in ten Ryder Cup matches and, in his usual sporting manner, he admitted that

Duncan had given him 'a terrific shellacking'.

With his very dark hair parted just off-centre, his good looks and his smart clothing, which often included a bow tie, George Duncan was an instantly recognizable and very popular figure at golf tournaments between the wars. He should have forced a play-off with Walter Hagen in the 1922 Open at Sandwich but, at the end of a brilliant final round, he missed a putt of around eight feet. He won the Belgian Open, the French Open for the second time in 1927 and the Irish Open. He had a long career as a leading golfer; he first played for Scotland against England in 1906 and his ninth and final appearance was in 1936. In his latter years he was the professional at Mere.

DUTRA, OLIN

USA

Born: 17.1.01

Appearances: 1933, 1935

Record: P4 W1 L3 H0

The family of Olin Dutra originally came from Spain, and he was an exceptionally tall and heavy man who hit the ball with great ease and had a lovely touch with his putter.

He entered professional golf the hard way. As a teenager he worked in a hardware store but used to get out of bed at dawn to put in his quota of practice. His persistence and determination were rewarded when he won the USPGA Championship in 1932 and he ensured his place in the history of golf by winning the US Open at Merion in 1934. His last two rounds of 71 and 72 thwarted Gene Sarazen.

Dutra made an unrewarding debut in the Ryder Cup in 1933. He lost his foursomes but on the next day seemed to be heading for an easy win over the veteran, Abe Mitchell. Dutra was three up after nine holes, but then lost the next eight and Mitchell hammered him to the tune of nine and eight. Two years later, he and Ky Laffoon lost their foursomes to the Whitcombe brothers but Dutra defeated Alf Padgham in the singles.

Olin Dutra was a notable influence on American golf in the 1930s and was Chairman of the USPGA Tournament committee in 1935.

E

EASTERBROOK SYD

GB

Born: 22.1.05

Appearances: 1931, 1933

Record: P3 W2 L1 H0

For a man who never won an important tournament, Syd Easterbrook had a splendid record in the Ryder Cup, which culminated in his holing the decisive putt to win the tie at Southport in 1933.

On the previous day Easterbrook had, with Bill Davies, won a very tight foursomes match against the formidable pairing of Craig Wood and Paul Runyan. Although the British pair got to two holes up with two to play, they lost the 35th hole and Easterbrook had to hole an unpleasant short putt on the final green for victory.

The ebb and flow of the singles matches finally left Easterbrook and Densmore Shute as the only game on the course, with the teams level at five and a half points each. The British player had had a depressing start by losing the first three holes, but the game was level as both players put their balls to within 20 feet of the final hole. Shute putted too strongly and missed the return, to leave Easterbrook with a difficult putt of around four feet with a left-to-right borrow. He holed out manfully to give Britain the closest of victories.

Easterbrook might have won the Open at St Andrews shortly afterwards but he took an unfortunate seven shots at the 14th to end in a tie for third place. His old rival, Densmore Shute, finished ahead of him in a tie with Craig Wood and won the play-off.

Syd Easterbrook, who holed the putt that won the Ryder Cup in 1933

ELDER, LEE

USA

Born: 14.7.34

Appearances: 1979

Record: P4 W1 L3 H0

In 1974, at the Monsanto Open, Lee Elder holed a birdie putt at the fourth extra hole of his play-off against Peter Oosterhuis and won his first PGA tournament. By so doing, he qualified to play in the Masters at Augusta, and became the first black to do so. No doubt the pioneering black American golfers who had gone before him, such as Bill Spiller, Ted Rhodes and Charlie Sifford, could scarce forbear to cheer.

Before his first victory, Elder had made colourful progress through the lower echelons of golf. He had been a caddie at Tenison Park, Dallas – where Lee Trevino later learned to play – and originally swung the club cross-handed, left hand below right. Tuition from Lloyd Mangrum sorted out his swing and in the late Fifties Elder caddied for the legendary hustler, Titanic Thompson. He did his own share of hustling, too; for example, he won money when hitting his shots standing on one leg and, on another occasion, when he had to play encased in a rubber suit.

In 1964, Lee Elder joined the United Golf Association tour, which mainly comprised black players and was contemptuously called the 'peanut circuit' because of its limited prize money. In one year, he won 21 out of 23 events and qualified in 1968 for the PGA tour. In his first year, he tied with Frank Beard and Jack Nicklaus in the American Golf Classic but lost the play-off. In 1972 he lost another play-off, to Lee Trevino, in the Greater Hartford Open but at last, two years later, he had his first triumph on the tour.

Elder's strength as a golfer was his accuracy and his two victories in 1978, in the Greater Milwaukee Open and the Westchester Classic, ensured that he was chosen for the Ryder Cup team at The Greenbrier in the following year. In his mid-forties, it was late to make a debut, but he began with a win, in partnership with Andy Bean, over Nick Faldo and Peter Oosterhuis. The Americans played splendid golf and their better ball was eight under par when they won. But that was to be Elder's only success in the match.

Lee Elder has played on the American Seniors tour since 1984 and has won eight tournaments.

ESPINOSA, AL

USA

Born: 24.3.94

Appearances: 1927, 1929, 1931

Record: P4 W2 L1 H1

Al Espinosa was a member of the first American Ryder Cup team in 1927 but did not play a match. He made up for the omission in the next two fixtures. At Moortown, in 1929, he and Leo Diegel easily defeated Aubrey Boomer and George Duncan in the foursomes and he halved his singles with Ernie Whitcombe; two years later, at Scioto, he and Diegel lost their foursomes but Espinosa defeated Whitcombe in the singles.

He won nine tournaments in America, including the Missouri, Houston, Indianapolis and Ohio Opens and came close in two majors. In the USPGA Championship he was runner-up to Leo Diegel in 1928, and in the following year, at Winged Foot, he tied the US Open with Bobby Jones, only to lose the 36 hole play-off by 23 strokes.

F

FALDO, NICK

GB & Europe

Born: 18.7.57

Appearances: 1977, 1979, 1981, 1983, 1985 1987, 1989, 1991

Record: P31 W17 L12 H2

It was the sight of Jack Nicklaus, on television, as he played in the 1971 Masters at Augusta that set Nick Faldo off on his quest for golfing glory. He was a gifted sportsman but, from the age of 14, he devoted himself to golf with the single-mindedness which has always characterised him. Four years later, Faldo became the youngest winner of the English Amateur

Championship, one of the nine amateur titles he won in 1975.

A year later he became a professional golfer, after terminating his visit to an American college on a golf scholarship. Faldo already had an elegant and powerful swing but Henry Cotton commented on a noticeable looseness in his action: there was a loop at the top of the swing and the maestro thought that Faldo's leg action was weak. Nevertheless, Faldo won enough money in 1976 to reach 58th position in the Order of Merit. A year later he won his first tournament and was eighth on the money list.

At Lytham, in 1977, Faldo made a wonderful start to his Ryder Cup career, despite being diagnosed as having glandular fever. The captain Brian Huggett, paired him with another very tall man, the experienced Peter Oosterhuis and, despite losing the first three holes of their foursomes against Raymond Floyd and Lou Graham, they rallied in fine style to win by two and one. In the fourballs Floyd was partnered by the best player in the world, Jack Nicklaus, but the young Faldo was hitting his drives way past those of the great American. It was almost a case of *lese-majeste*, especially when the British pair won on the 17th green. Faldo finished in triumph by defeating the current Open champion, Tom Watson, in the singles.

A new golfing star seemed to be in the making but over the next few years Faldo's progress was steady, rather than spectacular. He won the PGA Championship three times from 1978 to 1981 and the Tournament Players Championship in the following year. In the 1979 Ryder Cup at The Greenbrier, he and Oosterhuis continued their winning ways with two victories in three matches and Faldo beat Lee Elder in the singles. In his two appearances he had won six points out of a possible seven, a dazzling start for such a young man. But at Walton Heath in 1981 Faldo's record was dented when he and Oosterhuis were easily beaten in the foursomes by Jack Nicklaus and Tom Watson; and in the fourballs he and Sam Torrance were annihilted seven and five by Lee Trevino and Jerry Pate. But Faldo bounced back to defeat another Open champion, Johnny Miller, in the singles.

In 1983, Faldo had his first concerted sequence of successes as a professional. He won five

tournaments, including the French and the Swiss Opens and finished as leader of the Order of Merit. In the Ryder Cup at the PGA National he asserted himself in formidable style to win four points from five outings, three of them in partnership with Bernhard Langer.

Faldo's advance towards golfing glory continued in the following year, as he achieved his first American victory in the Heritage Classic. In three of the year's major championships, he played himself into a position to win; but in the Open, the Masters and the USPGA Championship one poor round took him out of the reckoning.

It was at this stage of his career that Faldo's single-minded desire to be a champion golfer asserted itself. He decided that his technique was not good enough to win the only championships that matter, the majors. It took great courage to make that decision, especially in the face of critics who never tired of telling him that a swing which had already won him over a dozen professional tournaments and a great deal of prize money should be left alone.

In 1985 Faldo met a man who agreed with his diagnosis and was prepared to work with him to achieve a solid, repetitive swing which would bring him the major championships he craved. Under David Leadbetter's tutelage the changes were made slowly and painfully. In 1985 and 1986 Faldo did not win any tournaments and his participation in the exhilarating European victory in the Ryder Cup at the Belfry was muted: he lost both his matches. But Faldo saw the edges of his new dawn when he won the Spanish Open early in 1987; and the new day burst into glorious sunlight a few months later when he won the Open Championship at Muirfield. He was a stroke behind Paul Azinger as the final round began and three behind him with nine holes to play. Nothing attested more to the consistency of Faldo's newly wrought method than his play over those last 18 holes. He parred every one of them, won the championship by one shot and had vindicated himself.

In the following year, he won the French Open for the second time and the British Masters title and played splendid golf from tee to green in the US Open at Brookline. He hardly missed a fairway, but he could not hole a putt of any distance and lost a play-off to Curtis Strange. He was third in the Open Championship, equal fourth in the USPGA Championship and finished in second place in eight tournaments during the year. A year later he became the first Englishman to win the Masters at Augusta. A poor third round of 77 had left him five shots behind Ben Crenshaw but, on the final day, he went to the turn in 32 strokes and had four birdies during the second nine, to score a 65 and force a play-off with Scott Hoch, whom he defeated at the second extra hole. In Europe he won the PGA Championship for the fourth time, the British Masters for the second time, the French Open for the third time and the World Matchplay Championship at Wentworth.

In the Ryder Cup at Muirfield Village Faldo first teamed up with Ian Woosnam to form a devastating partnership. They were unbeaten, with three and a half points out of four, and their results included a demolition of Tom Kite and Curtis Strange by five and four. At the Belfry two years later they carried on in similar vein with two and a half points out of four, and their final fourball match against Azinger and Beck produced golf of such an exalted level that 18 birdies were scored by the time the Americans won on the 17th green.

In 1990 Nick Faldo had a flying start to the season as he retained his Masters title. Once again he needed extra holes, this time against that most competitive of golfers, Raymond Floyd. It was the American who succumbed to the intense pressure as he hit his second shot at the 11th hole into the water and Faldo donned the famous green jacket for the second time.

Such was Faldo's consistency that there was speculation that he could achieve the grand slam of the four major championships in one year. Only two other golfers since the war had merited such conjecture: Ben Hogan and Jack Nicklaus. That was a measure of Faldo's stature in the game. In the second major of 1990, the US Open, Faldo's putt on the 72nd green hung on the edge of the hole and failed to drop; if it had, he would have been in the play-off with Hale Irwin and Mike Donald. But he made no mistakes in the Open at St Andrews. From the first drive he looked impregnable; he won by five shots and broke the record score for an Open Championship at St Andrews by six shots. In the third round he played with Greg

 Faldo and Woosnam, usually a dependable Ryder Cup partnership

Norman and destroyed him, and the rest of the field, with a superb round of 66.

Faldo is undoubtedly a great champion. His whole being is devoted to golf; the same demons that drove Ben Hogan in the pursuit of golfing perfection also drive Faldo. He is aloof on the golf-course because of his intense concentration, so he has never had the popular appeal of Ballesteros, Trevino or Lyle. Perhaps he should remind himself, before every round, of the old music hall saying: 'Always smile when you walk on'.

Faldo only won one event, the Irish Open, in 1991, although he was hampered early in the season by injury. As the season went on the success eluded him, he seemed to get more and more absorbed in the mechanics of his golf swing. Consequently, his form in the Ryder Cup at Kiawah Island was uninspiring. His dependable partnership with Woosnam foundered as they narrowly lost their foursomes to Payne Stewart and Mark Calcavecchia and then were outplayed by Fred Couples and Ray Floyd. In his second foursomes, Faldo retired into his shell and seemed unable to give the support that his partner, the inexperienced David Gilford, had every right to expect. Nevertheless, Faldo fought hard on the final day to wrest a valuable point from Floyd.

It would be no surprise if Faldo added several more major championships to his tally, such is his great skill and immense dedication.

FALLON, JOHN

GB

Born: 29.4.13

Appearances: 1955
Captain 1963

Record: P1 W1 L0 H0

With John Jacobs as his doughty partner, John Fallon played in one of the most thrilling matches in Ryder Cup history at Thunderbird Ranch, California, in 1955. In the top foursomes match, the British pair were drawn against Chandler Harper and Jerry Barber. The match see-sawed from one pair to the other: Fallon and Jacobs were two down at lunch, one up after 27 holes and still one ahead on the final tee. When the British ball lay about four feet from the final hole in three strokes and the American ball was still off the green in the same number, it seemed a British win was assured. But that great short-game exponent, Jerry Barber, chipped the ball in, not for the first time in the match, for a par. Suddenly Johnny Fallon was faced with a very intimidating putt to win the match. Henry Longhurst described it as 'a horrible four footer across a sharp slope. He looked ashen grey ... He went slowly up, like the condemned man, and in the dead silence holed it to win.'

Fallon had had some successes before the war but he owed his place in the 1955 team to being the runner-up in the *News of the World* Championship in the previous year and to his second place, behind Peter Thomson, in the 1955 Open at St Andrews.

In 1963 Fallon succeeded Dai Rees as captain and made the inspired decision to send two of his 'new boys', Brian Huggett and George Will, out together in the first foursomes match and they duly beat Arnold Palmer and Johnny Pott. But that was the limit of his inspiration and he undid his successful beginning by parting Neil Coles and Bernard Hunt after they had fought back superbly to wrestle a half from Tony Lema and Julius Boros. Neil Coles still recalls his astonishment when Fallon put them out with different partners in the afternoon foursomes. Their momentum and confidence were lost – as were all four of the matches.

FARRELL, JOHNNY

USA

Born: 1.1.01

Appearances: 1927, 1929, 1931

Record: P6 W3 L2 H1

One of the most successful professional golfers of his time, Johnny Farrell was a consistent winner during the 1920s and the early 1930s. In 1926, he won four events and a further seven in 1927.

It was no wonder that Walter Hagen selected him for the inaugural Ryder Cup match and he won both his matches by a wide margin. He and Joe Turnesa had no trouble with George Duncan and Archie Compston, and he took care of Aubrey Boomer in the singles. He was not so successful in the next match when he only gathered half a point out of a possible two, but in the process he played the shot of the year. He and Joe Turnesa were one down at the 36th hole to Charles Whitcombe and Archie Compston; Turnesa put their ball behind a marquee with their second shot but Farrell played a miraculous shot over the obstruction to within a few feet of the flag and the American pair snatched an unlikely half. In his last appearance, in 1931, Farrell won a point in the foursomes with Gene Sarazen.

The pinnacle of Farrell's career was his win in the US Open of 1928, when he had the distinction of beating Bobby Jones, by one shot, in a play-off. In the following year, he was beaten in the final of the USPGA Championship by Leo Diegel.

Farrell was a rather short hitter, although he hooked the ball to gain the maximum length he could; but his accurate short game and brilliant putting more than made up the difference. An elegant figure, who really looked the part in his white plus-fours, Johnny Farrell eventually became the professional at Baltusrol.

FAULKNER, MAX

GB

Born: 29.7.16

Appearances: 1947, 1949, 1951, 1953, 1957

Record: P8 W1 L7 H0

It was a safe bet that Max Faulkner would follow his father into golf. Gustavus Faulkner was the professional at Pennard, in South Wales, and was good enough to win the *Western Mail* tournament and to come second in the Welsh Open; he was on the fringes of the Ryder Cup team in 1931. He gave the young Max Faulkner every encouragement. The Second World War interrupted Faulkner's career before he had won anything of consequence but he played well enough afterwards to earn his selection for the Ryder Cup of 1947 in Portland, Oregon. The team travelled in style on the *Queen Mary* and Faulkner enlivened the train journey of several days' duration by giving a commentary on the various landmarks along the route.

He could not have had a tougher introduction to Ryder Cup golf, since he went out with Jimmy Adams against Ben Hogan and Jimmy Demaret, who were judged to be the American 'bankers'. The British pair were not the slightest overawed: they were four up at the turn and two up at lunch. The turning-point came at the 34th hole, when the match was level. Although the Americans were bunkered off the tee, they made a birdie and increased their lead to win by two holes. In his singles match Faulkner was drawn against another tough customer, Lloyd Mangrum, and was defeated.

The British suffered their heaviest defeat, by eleven matches to one, despite the pre-match plea for divine intervention by the captain, Henry Cotton. Faulkner has a vivid memory of the whole team being summoned to Cotton's hotel room and being asked to kneel down as the captain read a prayer.

It was, however, a different story at Ganton two years later. Faulkner and Adams were out first against 'Dutch' Harrison and Johnny Palmer and they played glorious golf all day, to win on the 35th hole. But Harrison had his revenge on Faulkner in the singles. He had five 3s in his first six holes, to go four up, and was seven up at lunch after a morning round of 67. The Englishman could not make any impression against such brilliance and lost; as did the British team, by seven points to five.

In the meantime, Max Faulkner had been winning tournaments. He was a powerful man, a shade under six feet in height, and was extremely fit throughout his playing career. With a very wide arc to his swing and a superb rhythm, he struck the ball as well as anyone in the game. In his prime he won several long-driving contests against the likes of Harry Weetman. He was also blessed with a very sure and delicate touch with his putter, of which he used some bizarre examples, several of them home-made.

His presence on the post-war golf-courses was also a great tonic for the fans. He was a

cheerful and engaging person, who had a word for everyone within chatting distance. If he hit a bad shot or had a bad round there were no scowls or dramas: it was just an occasion for a joke and anticipation of something better on the morrow.

Faulkner was the first British professional to dress in colourful clothes. Amid the drab austerity of post-war Britain, with its clothing coupons and 'utility' products, he stood out like a beacon with his outrageously bright co-ordinated outfits. In the final round of the Open in 1951 he wore canary yellow plus-twos, shoes and socks to match and a blue-and-white striped shirt.

Max Faulkner won the Open at Portrush in 1951, the last Briton to do so for 18 years. He had shown his liking for the great occasion in the previous two years; in 1949, at Sandwich, he led after three rounds and a year later, at Troon, he was one stroke behind the leader at the same stage.

Bobby Locke won on both occasions. But at Portrush Faulkner never wavered and his putting, on the magnificent and very fast greens, was especially sure. He was six ahead of his nearest rival, Antonio Cerda, after three rounds and eventually won by two shots.

There are many stories about Faulkner's Open, most of them, like all good stories, exaggerated. Henry Longhurst claimed that he saw him signing autographs after the second round as 'Open Champion, 1951'. Longhurst said that he moved silently away, 'lest fate mistake me for an accomplice and in some way give me the hammer, too.' The true story is that Faulkner, on the way to the first tee for the final round, was asked to autograph a golf ball. The supporter asked him to put 'Open Champion' below his name and Faulkner, despite his qualms, did so. He says that he still has nightmares about it.

Faulkner played again in the Ryder Cup at Pinehurst in 1951 and lost both his matches, including a singles with Sam Snead who was four up at lunchtime after scoring 67. In the very close match at Wentworth two years later, he and Dai Rees, who had contested the final of the PGA Matchplay Championship (won by Faulkner), were amazed when they were not asked by the captain, Henry Cotton, to play in the foursomes.

By this time, Max Faulkner had won the Open, the PGA Matchplay and the Dunlop Masters, a trio of tournaments which no other British golfer has ever won.

He made his last appearance in the Ryder Cup at Lindrick in 1957, when Britain at last won it back. He and Harry Weetman played very badly against Ted Kroll and Jackie Burke and Faulkner asked to be omitted from the singles. He was insistent that Peter Mills took his place, a shrewd proviso, since Mills beat Burke easily. On the final day Faulkner was charging all over the course in his enthusiastic, self-appointed role of chief motivator.

Faulkner's last major win was in the Portuguese Open of 1968, when he was 54 years of age. He won the Seniors title in 1968 and 1970 and then retired from tournament play. He put his clubs in the attic and did not hit a golf ball for nearly 20 years. Instead he indulged his great love of fishing; but now he plays again, often at West Chiltington Golf Club, half of which he owns. It is just over the hill from his farmhouse in Sussex.

With his natural and uninhibited swing Max Faulkner was a worthy winner of the Open Championship; above all he was a breath of fresh air on the post-war British golf circuit. Apart from his overseas exhibition tours he travelled the length and breadth of Britain to give exhibition matches in the cause of the Cancer Relief Fund. His engaging presence was always welcomed.

FEHERTY, DAVID

Europe

Born: 13.8.58

Appearances: 1991

Record: P3 W1 L1 H1

Three visits to the qualifying school were needed by David Feherty before he joined the European tour in 1979 and he first finished in the top 50 in the Order of Merit in 1982. His initial success came in South Africa, but he won two events in 1986, the Italian Open and the Scottish Open, and ended the season in the top 20 on the money list.

Feherty has a clear-eyed view of tournament golf: to him

it is a successful way to earn a good living. Perhaps that is why he has such an intense look on the golf course, as he goes about his business; he regards the idea of playing golf for pleasure as a contradiction in terms. Off the course he is relaxed and approachable, with a good ear for a witty phrase and a keen eye for the essential absurdity of the game. 'As soon as you think you've got the answers to this game, somebody changes the questions', he once said.

Feherty consults a sports psychologist to help him unearth the right questions and from 1989 onwards seems also to have provided the right answers. He won the BMW International Open and the Cannes Open, and led Ireland to victory in the Dunhill Cup.

His first appearance in the Ryder Cup, at Kiawah Island in 1991 was marked by mixed success. He and Sam Torrance earned a half in their fourball against Mark O'Meara and Lanny Wadkins, but were easily beaten by Wadkins and Hale Irwin in their foursomes. However, Feherty showed his quality as a golfer by defeating Payne Stewart, the US Open Champion, in his singles. He was three up after four holes and, despite a slight wobble towards the end of the match, went on to claim a crucial point on the 17th green.

Feherty has the ability and the intelligence to win many tournaments, in America, where he finished joint seventh in the 1991 USPGA championship, as well as in Europe. He also has a refreshing appreciation of the wider horizons that lie beyond tournament golf. For example, he has ambitions to develop his golf course design business. He has decided views on the subject and pours scorn on the outlandish creations of the Trent Jones family and of Jack Nicklaus. He wants to build courses that will not only appeal to ordinary golfers but will at the same time offer a fair challenge to professionals.

FINSTERWALD DOW

USA

Born: 6.9.29

Appearances: 1957, 1959, 1961, 1963
Captain 1977

Record: P13 W9 L3 H1

Such was his remarkable consistency that the golfing cognoscenti were at one stage talking of Dow Finsterwald as the natural heir to Ben Hogan. He did not possess the genius of the iron man from Texas, but during the years from the end of the Fifties to the early Sixties, he was one of the foremost players on the American tour. In total he had eleven victories but seven of those came in the three years from 1958 to 1960.

Finsterwald had given notice of his talent as early as 1950. Though still an amateur he scored a 61 in the St Louis Open; a year later he became a professional. His first win came in 1955 and he was the runner-up to Lionel Hebert in the USPGA Championship of 1957. This was its last year as a matchplay event and in the following year Finsterwald was the winner. He followed this with victories in the Greater Greensboro, Carling and the Los Angeles Opens.

Finsterwald's first outing in

Dow Finsterwald receives the Ryder Cup from Princess Alexandra in 1977

Dow Finsterwald celebrates the American win with his team

the Ryder Cup was at Lindrick in 1957. Although he and Doug Ford won their foursomes, he was heavily defeated by Christy O'Connor in the singles. After a misunderstanding at the third hole over whether a putt by Finsterwald had been conceded or not (it had not), the match was played in virtual silence. This did not worry O'Connor, who won six of the first eight holes after lunch and breezed home to victory.

Finsterwald was undefeated in 1959 at Eldorado, and got his revenge on O'Connor in 1961 at Lytham. He beat the Irishman in the first singles but lost to Neil Coles in the second series. His final appearance was at East Lake, Atlanta, two years later and he played magnificently to score four wins and a half out of six games.

In the 1962 Masters at Augusta Finsterwald had a great chance to win but gave best to the brilliance of Arnold Palmer in the play-off. He played on the tour until the mid-Seventies and his consistency never wavered. At one stage of his career he finished in the money in 72 tournaments in succession.

In 1977 Dow Finsterwald captained the American Ryder Cup team to victory at Royal Lytham.

FLOYD, RAYMOND

USA

Born: 4.9.42

Appearances: 1969, 1975, 1977, 1981, 1983, 1985, 1991
Captain 1989

Record: P27 W9 L15 H3

The most notable aspect of Ray Floyd's Ryder Cup record is its longevity: he has played in the matches over a span of four decades, an achievement only equalled by Dai Rees. With his victory in the 1992 Doral Open, Floyd has equalled Sam Snead's feat of winning tournaments in four decades. Floyd is the only golfer who, after being appointed as a non-playing captain, has later been selected again as a player.

In the early days of Floyd's career, not many people in golf would have backed him to put his mark on the Ryder Cup in such a distinctive way. As a young man he had a deserved reputation as a playboy and his preferred company was other hell-raisers, such as Doug Sanders and Al Besselink. He was more interested in hustling bets in big-money matches than in concentrating on tournament golf; his investment in a topless female rock group was also a distraction for 'Pretty Boy' Floyd, as he was called in those days.

Floyd had a bizarre start to his career on the American tour. In 1963 he missed the cut in his first ten events but won the eleventh, the St Petersburg Open. He was one of the youngest winners in the history of the American tour. Until 1969 he won only one other tournament but his achievements in that year emphasised his great ability. He won the Jacksonville Open, the American Golf Classic at Firestone with a record score of 268, and then secured his first major victory in the USPGA Championship. He finished eighth in the money list and made his debut in the tied Ryder Cup match at Birkdale. His play was undistinguished, since he only managed two halves out of four matches.

During the early years of the Seventies Floyd drifted back into mediocrity but the responsibilities of marriage and fatherhood spurred him back into more forceful action. In 1974 he finished in 18th position on the money list and a year later he won the Kemper Open. But it was in 1976 that he was to have his greatest triumph. He went into the Masters at Augusta with a specific plan; he had decided that the higher flight provided by a 5-wood would enable him to attack the par-5 holes to better effect. Floyd was absolutely right; by the end of the tournament he was 13 under par for those holes (four par-5s played four times). After two rounds Floyd, with a record score of 131, had killed off the opposition; he eventually won by eight shots. Club golfers all over America rushed to buy 5-woods, as well as the Zebra putter which the new Masters champion had used to such remarkable effect. Later in the year he was the runner up to Dave Stockton in the USPGA Championship.

The golfing prodigal son had returned and was never to wander off again. Over the next decade Floyd was to take his total number of victories to 21 on the American tour, including the World Open, the Byron Nelson Classic, the Tournament Players Championship, the Doral Open and the Houston Open. He added to his tally of major championships, too. In 1982 he won the USPGA Championship for the second time, at Southern Hills. He opened with a record score of 63 and led all the way, to win by three shots.

By this time Floyd had made three more appearances in the Ryder Cup. By any standards his record was poor; in 1975, at Laurel Valley, he had one victory, over Tony Jacklin in the singles, and it was the same story two years later at Lytham, when his only point was a defeat of Mark James; in 1981, at Walton Heath, he improved matters by winning three points out of five matches. But his 1983 record at the PGA National was disastrous, with four defeats in four games. Nevertheless, he forced his way back into the team for the Belfry in 1985 by dint of his fifth position in the money list. He and Lanny Wadkins won their first two matches together but lost the third; in the singles Floyd was four down at the turn to Paul Way, recovered to one down with one to play and then found the water on the final hole, to lose the game.

It seemed that Floyd's participation in the Ryder Cup

had drawn to its close, but his will to win major championships burned as brightly as ever. In 1986 he became the oldest man to win the US Open. At Shinnecock Hills he scored a final round of 66 for a victory by two shots.

In 1989 Floyd was the non-playing captain of the American team which tied the Ryder Cup match at the Belfry. It might have been supposed that his sights were set on a rewarding foray on the Seniors tour in 1992 rather than any further test in the fires of the Ryder Cup. But in 1991 Floyd tied for the Masters at Augusta, even though he lost the play-off to Nick Faldo; he was eighth in the US Open and sixth in the USPGA Championship. The new captain, Dave Stockton, recognised a battler and picked him as one of his wild cards. Floyd was thrilled and commented that he 'would pay to be on the Ryder Cup team'.

It was a choice which was initially criticised, since Floyd had lost more Ryder Cup matches than any other American golfer. But Stockton already had a role in mind for Floyd: he saw him as the seasoned campaigner who would assume the role of a father-figure to someone like Fred Couples, a player of great brilliance but with an insecure temperament. It was a shrewd tactic; the American pair saw off Bernhard Langer and Mark James in the first foursomes and routed Nick Faldo and Ian Woosnam in the fourballs.

They were, however, unseated by the brilliance of the Spaniards, Ballesteros and Olazabal, in the second series of foursomes and Floyd lost a tough battle against Nick Faldo in the singles.

Raymond Floyd has never been an elegant golfer: there is a lot of movement and a noticeable loop in his swing. But over the space of four decades he has been one of the most successful of American players and, with victories in three major championships, he has a secure place in the history of the game.

FORD, DOUG

USA

Born: 6.8.22

Appearances: 1955, 1957, 1959, 1961

Record: P9 W4 L4 H1

One of the most consistent and industrious professionals on the US tour, Doug Ford had 19 victories and, during the years from 1950 to 1963, usually finished in the top ten in any event. In 1957, for example, he was among the top 25 players in every event in which he played (32), in the top ten on 24 occasions and won three times. In 1961 he was working as hard as ever and played 29 events in the first nine months of the year. His career covered a considerable span, since he became a professional in 1941 and made his last appearances in major tournaments in 1975. He now plays on the Senior tour.

Ford's first victory was in the Jacksonville Open of 1952 and his last in the Canadian Open of 1963, and along the way he won the Miami Open, the Greater Greensboro Open, the Los Angeles Open and the Western Open. He also won two majors: the USPGA championship in 1955, when he beat Cary Middlecoff in the final, and the Masters two years later: after three rounds he was three shots behind Sam Snead but scored a 66, up to then the lowest final round ever recorded, to win by three strokes.

Ford played in the American Ryder Cup team on four successive occasions and ended up on the right side of the ledger, with four wins and a half from his nine matches. He began with two wins at Thunderbird Ranch in 1955 and won his foursomes two years later at Lindrick. But he was walloped by Bernard Hunt in the singles as Britain won a famous victory. At Eldorado in 1959 he and Art Wall lost to Christy O'Connor and Peter Alliss and Ford, four holes in the lead at lunchtime, let Norman Drew off the hook in the singles and the game was halved.

In his final appearance in the fixture, at Lytham in 1961, Ford, in company with Gene Littler, was defeated again by O'Connor and Alliss; but he was handed an unexpected victory in his singles by Harry Weetman, who missed a very short putt on the final green. In the second singles, however, Dai Rees beat Ford easily.

Doug Ford had a long a highly successful career in golf, a career which was marked by his intelligent application to the game. In the Sixties, he published a book called *The Brainy Way to Better golf* - a neat summary of his philosophy.

FURGOL, ED

USA

Born: 22.3.17

It was a wonder that Ed Furgol could swing a golf club with any facility at all, since he broke his left arm in a childhood accident; it was badly set and was bent rigid. The arm was not much use in the swing except to help him to guide the club. He had to compensate in various ways: he built up the left hand grip on his clubs to tennis-racket thickness, and made up for his short swing by lunging hard through the ball. Despite his handicap, he was able to hit the ball very powerfully and became one of the leading American amateurs when he won the North and South Amateur event in 1945.

Furgol turned professional soon afterwards. His most successful year was in 1954 when he won two tournaments, one of which was the US Open at Baltusrol, where he just stayed ahead of Gene Littler. In 1956 he won two more events, was fourth in the US Open and reached the semi-finals of the USPGA Championship.

He was selected for the Ryder Cup in 1957, when the American team were beaten at Lindrick. He had the misfortune to draw Dai Rees in the singles. The British captain would have beaten anyone in the world on that particular day and he was far too hot for Furgol to handle.

Furgol won another event in 1957, the Agua Caliente Open, and gradually withdrew from the tournament scene to become a club professional. In his rare appearances he was still a formidably determined player and at the 1963 Masters, for example, he was only one behind the eventual winner, Jack Nicklaus, at the start of the final round.

FURGOL, MARTY

USA

Born: 5.1.18

Appearances: 1955

Record: P1 W0 L1 H0

Marty Furgol became a professional golfer in 1941 but spent five years as a sergeant in the US Army before he could resume his chosen career, which lasted until the middle of the 1960's. His major victories all came in the previous decade: the Western and Houston Opens in 1951 and the El Paso and San Diego Opens in 1959. He was also the runner-up in the 1956 Canadian Open.

In his one outing in the Ryder Cup, at the Thunderbird Golf Club, California, in 1955, he lost his singles match to Arthur Lees, but the Americans won the tie with ease.

Marty Furgol was born in the same New York town as Ed, and caddied for a time at the same club, but they are not related.

G

GADD, GEORGE

GB

Born: 1890

Appearances: 1927

George Gadd was one of seven British players who were unfortunate enough to be picked for the Ryder Cup and then did not play a single match. It is ironic that he played against an American team at Wentworth in 1926 in the match which is regarded as the forerunner of the Ryder Cup. He won both his matches, too.

In 1927 the six-day crossing to New York was extremely rough and Gadd suffered more than anyone. He could not rediscover his form in the practice rounds at Worcester, Massachusetts, and asked to stand down. A critical observer of the American triumph, he said that the opposition had 'mechanicalised the game'. He also noted that the Americans 'hardly missed a putt'. This was to be a familiar cry down the exciting years of the Ryder Cup.

He cut a chubby, cheerful figure and had some considerable tournament successes, including wins in the *News of the World* Matchplay Championship in 1922 and the Northern Professional Championship in 1924 and 1926.

GALLACHER, BERNARD

GB & Europe

Born: 9.2.49

Appearances: 1969, 1971, 1973, 1975, 1977, 1979, 1981, 1983
Captain 1991

Record: P31 W13 L13 H5

Bernard Gallacher grew up in a traditional Scottish sporting environment: he played football in winter and golf in summer. The course in his native Bathgate was a few minutes walk from his home and had the advantage of a thriving and competitive junior section. In 1967 Gallacher won the Scottish Amateur Strokeplay Championship and turned professional a year later. In only his second season he was top of the Order of Merit after winning the PGA Championship and the Wills Open.

It was a dazzling start to his career and he became the youngest golfer to play in the Ryder cup team when he was selected for the 1969 match at Birkdale. In tandem with Maurice Bembridge he won his first game, a foursomes against Lee Trevino and Ken Still, but the British pair lost their second foursomes to Trevino and Gene Littler. His fourball match, in partnership with Brian Huggett, against Ken Still and Dave Hill was marred by a series of disputes. On the seventh hole, Still putted out of turn; the British pair queried this and were awarded the hole. There was another argument on the next green and the two captains, aided by the President of the PGA, arrived to calm matters down. Gallacher remembers that the source of the trouble was the indecisiveness of the referee and the two Americans' lack of knowledge of the rules of matchplay. In addition, Hill and Still were unwise enough to try to intimidate the two resolute Celts, who were not going to step aside for anyone.

Dave Hill played brilliantly and won the match for the Americans. On the final day, Gallacher was pitted against Lee Trevino. He showed his steadfast qualities by beating the great American player by four and three and in a nerve-wracking finish, the match was tied for the first time.

In 1971 Gallacher won another tournament, the Martini International, and was once again called to the Ryder Cup colours. Controversy, though not of his own making, followed him. After winning his first match, he and Peter Oosterhuis were drawn to play Arnold Palmer and Gardner Dickinson in a fourball. On the seventh tee, the Americans were one up and, after Palmer had hit a beautiful shot on to the green, Gallacher's caddie innocently asked the great man what iron he had used. It is Gallacher's recollection that Dickinson reported the breach of the rules to the referee and the Americans were awarded the hole. The decision was technically correct but hardly within the spirit of the Ryder Cup. It knocked the stuffing out of the British pair, who were heavily defeated. Nevertheless, Gallacher went on to win his second foursomes against Trevino and Casper, to halve his first singles with Dave Stockton and to beat Charles Coody in his second singles.

Gallacher's reputation as an implacable matchplayer was already being formed and his record against Lee Trevino illustrates how difficult an opponent he was. He played the American on seven occasions, won five times and only lost once. Trevino acknowledges just how determined Gallacher was: 'He was very difficult, very tough and very fierce; he always kept on trying; he was the only one who got the better of me.' For his part Gallacher recalls that he enjoyed his battles with Trevino: 'I enjoyed his company; he inspired me.'

Another player who inspired him was Brian Barnes, or rather they inspired each other and formed one of the most effective British partnerships in the Seventies. Their strengths were complementary, since Brian Barnes hit the ball long and straight, while Gallacher was wonderfully accurate with his medium and short irons and was a supremely confident putter. Leonard Crawley described him as 'a versatile genius on the greens . . . he has a cool head and an astute golfing brain'. Above all, the two men were friends and had a great respect for each other's abilities.

In 1973 at Muirfield, Barnes and Gallacher gave a surging impetus to the British team; they won both their games on the first day and by evening Britain were three points in the lead. With

another similar effort on the morrow, it seemed that Britain might take an unassailable lead into the final day. But during the night Gallacher was struck down by food poisoning and all the fizz left the team. By the end of the second day, the Americans had drawn level and they went on to win by a margin of six points.

During the Seventies, Gallacher played some of his finest golf. He was usually in the top 20 of the Order of Merit and he won several prestigious events, including the Dunlop Masters two years in succession (1974 and 1975), the Spanish and French Opens and the Tournament Players Championship. He also managed to combine his tournament career with his duties as the club professional at Wentworth, where he remains to this day. His record in the 1975 Ryder Cup encounter at Laurel Valley was moderate by his standards, although he halved his singles matches with Trevino and Al Geiberger. Two years later, at Lytham, he drew Jack Nicklaus in the singles. Between the putting green and the first tee Gallacher's putter was stolen and he had to dash into the professional's shop and buy another. It might have unsettled lesser men but Gallacher was intent on his tactic of ignoring the intimidating presence of Nicklaus and of getting on with his own game. It worked outstandingly well since the Scot won the first four holes. Although Nicklaus levelled the match after 16 holes, Gallacher sank a huge putt on the 17th green to go ahead again and then settled matters with another good putt on the final green.

At The Greenbrier in 1979 Gallacher was at the top of his form and won four points out of five. His only defeat was in a foursomes against Lanny Wadkins and Larry Nelson; he and Brian Barnes won their other three outings comfortably. Gallacher was sent out first in the singles and relished the battle to come with Lanny Wadkins, the abrasive Virginian who had won all his Ryder Cup matches until then. Gallacher saw him off by the margin of three and two. Gallacher's final two appearances, at Walton Heath in 1981 and at the PGA National in 1983, were to blight his record somewhat, since he won only one and a half points from six matches. In the latter encounter he was in the thick of the battle. At one stage it seemed that the European side might at last win the Cup on American soil for the first time, and, with the match tied, everything rested on the last game out on the course, between Tom Watson and Gallacher. Watson was one up on the 17th tee and both men missed the green. Gallacher thought that he had hit a perfect shot, but his ball went through the green into a horrible lie in the Bermuda grass. His first chip left the ball on the bank at the back of the green and his next one left him four feet from the hole. Watson had got down in four strokes but Gallacher missed his putt to lose the game and the USA retained the Ryder Cup by the narrowest of margins.

Bernard Gallacher soldiered on to good effect on the expanding European tour and was always in the top hundred in the Order of Merit up to 1989. He also became Tony Jacklin's trusted lieutenant in each of the Ryder Cups from 1985 to 1989. He assumed full command in 1991 at Kiawah Island and began his term of captaincy with the same result that Tony Jacklin attained in his first fixture in charge of the European team: a defeat by a single point. Gallacher is confident that the European side will win back the Ryder Cup at the Belfry in 1993, and the destiny of the European team could not be guided by a more confident and resolute captain.

GARNER, JOHN

GB

Born: 9.1.47

Appearances: 1971, 1973

Record: P1 W0 L1 H0

Although he was known as a very consistent player (he had been second in four British events in 1969, for example), John Garner was a controversial selection for the 1971 Ryder Cup team to play in St Louis. Opinion had it that he lacked the weight of shot for the hurly-burly of such a match; and especially in America, where golfers who could flight the ball high into the yielding greens were the best bet.

So it proved and John Garner only had one match in the four-ball series. He and Neil Coles lost to Frank Beard and J C Snead.

Garner was picked again in 1973 after finishing ninth in the Order of Merit; he had also won the PGA Matchplay Championship in the previous year, but the captain, Bernard Hunt, did not give him a game.

John Garner is now a prominent and well-respected teacher of the game.

GARRIDO, ANTONIO

Europe

Born: 2.2.44

Appearances: 1979

Record: P5 W1 L4 H0

Golfers from mainland Europe were included in the Ryder Cup team for the first time in 1979 and Antonio Garrido, together with Severiano Ballesteros, were the welcome newcomers.

The stocky, bearded Garrido's best year on the European circuit was 1977 when he won the Madrid Open (he was born in Spain's capital city) and the Benson & Hedges International; he also won the World Cup with Ballesteros and finished third in the Order of Merit.

Neither of the Spaniards was seen at his best at The Greenbrier in 1979 but, sent out in partnership for both foursomes and both fourballs, they were unlucky enough, in three of the games, to encounter Larry Nelson, who was in magnificent form. The Spaniards only managed one victory, in a foursomes against Fuzzy Zoeller and Hubert Green, and Garrido lost his singles to Mark Hayes on the final green.

In the Eighties, Garrido's best year was 1982 when he won the Tunisian Open and finished 17th in the Order of Merit.

GEIBERGER, AL

USA

Born: 1.9.37

Appearances: 1967, 1975

Record: P9 W5 L1 H3

Al Geiberger had unparalleled success as a junior and as an amateur golfer. As a member of the University of Southern California golf team he lost only twice in nearly 40 matches and was clearly destined to become a successful professional.

Tall and slim, with a relaxed rhythmic swing, Geiberger's golfing watchword was accuracy. It stood him in good stead because even when he did not win events, his consistency enabled him to finish well up in the money. For example, in 1967, he entered 24 tournaments, completed every one and finished in the top ten on nine occasions, without winning an event.

He won his way into the Ryder Cup in 1967, at the Champions Club at Houston, and met his only defeat in his first match. He and Gene Littler were easily defeated by the big-hitting Dave Thomas and an effervescent Tony Jacklin. The Americans got their revenge on the same pair in the first series of fourballs and the honours were shared as the respective pairs halved their second fourball encounter. Geiberger was much too accomplished for Malcolm Gregson and beat him twice in the singles.

By this time Geiberger had already won a major event, the USPGA Championship at Firestone in 1966. Thereafter, despite his consistency, he failed to win a US tour event until 1974 but he won six tournaments over the succeeding three years, including the Tournament Players Championship and the Tournament of Champions. He seemed to relish long and demanding courses, such as Firestone and the Colonial Country Club at Forth Worth, where he won the TPC. Just to emphasise his liking for the latter course of over 7,000 yards, he scored an astonishing 59 in the third round of the Danny Thomas Memphis Classic in 1977. This equalled Sam Snead's record and still stands.

Geiberger made his second appearance in the Ryder Cup at Laurel Valley in 1975 and was unbeaten in his four matches, with two wins and two halves.

He played on the American tour until the late Eighties and then joined the expanding and very lucrative Seniors tour. In 1991 he finished tenth in the money list with over $500,000.

GILDER, BOB

USA

Born: 31.12.50

Appearances: 1983

Record: P4 W2 L2 H0

Bob Gilder has been on the American tour since 1976; his career began well, since he won his second professional tournament, the Phoenix Open. He did not win again until the 1980 Canadian Open and his best year was in 1982 when he won three events and finished sixth in the money list.

His one Ryder Cup appearance was at the PGA National in Florida in 1983. He lost both his foursomes games but won his fourball, in partnership with Tom Watson, against Ian Woosnam and Sam Torrance. He drew Gordon J Brand in the singles and beat him by two holes.

Gilder suffered a decline in his golf which lasted through the middle of the Eighties but he has revived his career in the last few years. In 1991 he won $250,000 and finished in the top ten on four occasions, including a fifth place in the USPGA Championship at Crooked Stick.

GILFORD, DAVID

Europe

Born: 14.9.65

Appearances: 1991

Record: P2 W0 L2 H0

David Gilford accumulated a most impressive amateur record before becoming a professional in 1986. He won the English Amateur Championship in 1984 and played in the Walker Cup a year later; he represented England and Great Britain in international matches and won the British Youths' Championship in 1986.

Diffident in manner and unspectacular in play, Gilford won his way into the Ryder Cup side by some consistent play which culminated in a victory in the English Open. But he experienced a miserable start to the match since he and another newcomer, Colin Montgomerie, drew Lanny Wadkins and Hale Irwin in the first series of foursomes. The battle-hardened Americans birdied the first three holes and were never in danger of being caught by the young British pair. On the second morning Gilford was teamed with Nick Faldo in a foursomes against Mark Calcavecchia and Payne Stewart. Gilford was certainly at odds with his game, but Faldo, rather than assume the role of mentor that his experience would have merited, appeared uninterested. The Americans won by a dog licence, seven and six.

The cruellest piece of misfortune was yet to come. On the morning of the final day, Steve Pate, injured earlier in the week in a car crash, declared himself unfit to play and Gilford was the unfortunate European nominated by the captain, Bernard Gallacher, to stand down. One hopes that Gilford has another chance to test his mettle in the Ryder Cup.

GOALBY, BOB

USA

Born: 14.3.29

Appearances: 1963

Record: P5 W3 L1 H1

Bob Goalby played splendid golf in his one Ryder Cup appearance, at Atlanta in 1963. His only loss was in a fourball match, partnered by Dave Ragan, against Neil Coles and Christy O'Connor, who closed the door on the American pair with a birdie two at the 18th hole. In the afternoon he and Ragan halved their game with Brian Huggett and David Thomas, but Goalby finished the tie in fine style by winning both his singles, against David Thomas and Bernard Hunt.

At the University of Illinois Goalby was a notable sportsman. Although several major league baseball clubs wanted him to sign on, he preferred to play football. After graduation he sold cars for a while and then became a professional golfer. His first win was in the Greater Greensboro Open in 1958 and he had 11 victories, the last in 1971.

Although he was second in the US Open of 1961 and in the USPGA Championship in the following year, his most important victory was in the Masters in 1968. His triumph was clouded by the unfortunate error made by the Argentinian golfer, Roberto de Vicenzo, who signed for a four at the 17th hole in the final round when he had actually scored a birdie three. The rules of golf, implacable as always, stated that the score for which he had signed must stand. Vincenzo was therefore deprived of a play-off with Goalby. But Bob Goalby had scored a magnificent final round of 66 and was a worthy winner.

Goalby has played on the Seniors tour since 1980.

GOLDEN, JOHN

USA

Born: 2.4.96

Appearances: 1927, 1929

Record: P3 W3 L0 H0

The possessor of a perfect Ryder Cup record, John Golden won two of his victories in partnership with his captain, Walter Hagen. In their match in 1927 against Ted Ray and Fred Robson, the American pair won four holes in a row in the morning to take them from a perilous position of three down to one up. Golden easily defeated Herbert Jolly in the singles. In 1929 he had only one match, which he again won with Hagen.

Golden was born in New York, became a professional golfer in 1924 and won nine tournaments between 1927 and 1935. He was known as a very dependable golfer, very strong with his irons and reliable with his putter.

He tried his luck in the cold and windy Open of 1929 at Muirfield and finished in a tie for 13th place.

GRAHAM, LOU

USA

Born: 7.1.38

Appearances: 1973, 1975, 1977

Record: P9 W5 L3 H1

Although he joined the American tour in 1964, Lou Graham's most

Lou Graham

productive years were in the Seventies when he won five of his six victories. They included the US Open at Medinah in 1975 when he beat John Mahaffey in a play-off; in that year he and Johnny Miller won the World Cup team title in Bangkok. Two years later he was the runner-up in the Open at Southern Hills to Hubert Green. In 1979 he had another purple patch and won three events, including the Philadelphia Classic and the Texas Open.

Graham played in three Ryder Cup teams and had a very respectable record of five wins from nine matches. At Muirfield in 1973 he made an undistinguished debut, with only half a point from two outings; but two years later, at Laurel Valley, he took three points with three different partners in the fourball and foursomes games. At Lytham in 1977 Graham lost his opening foursomes match to Nick Faldo and Peter Oosterhuis but ended in style by winning his fourball in partnership with Hale Irwin and by demolishing the formidable Neil Coles in his singles.

Graham joined the American Seniors tour in 1988 and played with great success for three years. A wrist injury curtailed his golf in 1991.

GREEN, ERIC

GB

Appearances: 1947

Eric Green has proved to be a mystery man, since his name does not appear in any of the usual reference books. Even the resources of the R&A and the USPGA have unearthed very little about the man. His club affiliation was listed as Hurst Park but the course no longer exists.

It seems probable that he was selected for the 1947 Ryder Cup team on the basis of his victory in the Northern Professional Championship; he thereby qualified for the *New of the World* Matchplay Championship in which he was beaten in the quarter-finals by the eventual winner, Fred Daly.

The captain, Henry Cotton, wrote that he intended to give Green and Reg Horne a match in the singles if any of the other eight players fared badly in the foursomes. But only Fred Daly and Cotton himself played poorly and the captain felt that he could not omit either himself or Daly, who was the current Open champion.

Green went all the way to Portland, Oregon, and did not play a game. Max Faulkner remembers him as a powerful player who was unlucky not to participate in the match.

GREEN, HUBERT

USA

Born: 28.12.46

Appearances: 1977, 1979, 1985

Record: P7 W4 L3 H0

If ever a golfer proves the adage 'it's not how, its how many', it is Hubert Green. At first sight his swing seems suited to a Sunday morning fourball rather than to a major professional tournament. He crouches over the ball, his hands well ahead of the clubhead and then attacks the ball with a short and very fast swing. Green once said: 'I don't try to analyse my swing. I looked at it once on film and almost got sick.' His putting style breaks all the rules, too, since his hands are well separated on the top of the club.

Despite these apparent stylistic handicaps Green has won 19 tournaments in America, including the US Open and the USPGA Championship.

He became a professional in 1970 and won his first event in the following year; from 1973 to 1979 he was usually in the top ten of the money list and his worst position was 13th. He won four tournaments in 1974 and two years later accomplished the remarkable feat of winning three events in succession: the Doral Open, Greater Jacksonville Open and the Sea Pines Heritage Classic. In 1977 he won the US Open at Southern Hills, Tulsa, by one shot from Lou Graham and ignored a threat that he would be killed on the 15th green during the final round: with due consideration, he told his caddie not to stand too close to him.

Green made his Ryder Cup debut in 1977 at Lytham, and won both his matches. He and Tom Watson were too strong for Brian Barnes and Tommy Horton in their fourball match and in the singles he defeated Eamonn Darcy on the final green. Two years later Green lost his foursomes game but became the first American to conquer Peter Oosterhuis in a singles.

Green had an excellent chance to win the Masters at Augusta in 1978. After a fine score of 65 in the third round, he was three shots ahead of the field. Even when Gary Player shot into the lead with a final round of 64, Green had a putt of about three feet to force a play-off. To everyone's surprise he missed it.

In the early Eighties Green's golf deteriorated, partly due to a shoulder injury which necessitated an operation in 1983. His recovery was completed in 1985 when he won the USPGA Championship at

Cherry Hills, Denver, even though he was chased all the way home by the defending champion, Lee Trevino. Green was an automatic selection for the Ryder Cup match at the Belfry in that year, under the captaincy of Trevino. He lost both his fourballs, in partnership with his close friend, Fuzzy Zoeller, but beat Nick Faldo in the singles.

Green has won tournaments in various parts of the world, including the Dunlop Phoenix in Japan and the Irish Open. He has also been a regular visitor to Britain for the Open Championship and has often finished in the top ten; his best position was third place, at Turnberry in 1977. He has not won a tournament since 1985 but is an exempted player on the American tour until 1995 when the rich pickings of the Seniors tour await him.

GREEN, KEN

USA

Born: 23.7.58

Appearances: 1989

Record: P4 W2 L2 H0

Ken Green had his first victory on the American circuit at the Buick Open in 1985 and his most successful year was in 1988 when he won the Canadian Open and the Greater Milwaukee Open. He finished fourth on the money list with nearly $800,000.

His first appearance in the Ryder Cup, at the Belfry in 1989, began with two comfortable wins, in company with Mark Calcavecchia, in the foursomes. But the Americans then met their match in the form of the ebullient Spaniards, Ballesteros and Olazabal, in the second series of fourballs.

In the singles Green had a close game, marked by excellent scoring, with Jose Maria Canizares. They were level and both on the final green in two shots. From the back of the green, Canizares laid his long putt dead but Green had the misfortune to take three putts and lost the game. This was a vital point for the European team since it ensured that, at worst, the whole match would be tied and the Ryder Cup retained. The Americans won all of the final four matches to ensure a tie, the second in the series.

Ken Green, advised by Mark Calcavecchia, lines up a putt

GREGSON, MALCOLM

GB

Born: 15.8.43

Appearances: 1967

Record: P4 W0 L4 H0

After leaving Millfield School, Malcolm Gregson became a professional golfer and he won the Assistants' Championship in 1964. His great year was in 1967 when he won the Schweppes, the Daks and Martini tournaments. He was awarded the Harry Vardon Trophy and represented England in the World Cup. Although Gregson won the Daks again in 1968 and the Sumrie Tournament in 1972, and had some successes on the Safari Circuit, he never again attained such standards.

Gregson won his way into the Ryder Cup team which was soundly beaten at Houston in 1967. He was never in the hunt in any of his matches and was often the victim of some sparkling golf by the Americans.

A good example was the brilliant start made by Arnold Palmer and Gardner Dickinson, who scored 32 shots to the turn in their foursomes against him and Hugh Boyle. Gregson lost both his singles against Al Geiberger.

GULDAHL, RALPH

USA

Born: 22.11.11

Appearances: 1937

Record: P2 W2 L0 H0

It was a puzzle that a man like Ralph Guldahl, who lit up the golfing heavens with such intensity, should subside so suddenly. He won his first tournament, the Santa Monica Open, in 1931, a year after becoming a professional and was second in the 1933 US Open behind the amateur, Johnny Goodman.

Guldahl abandoned golf for a time in 1934 and 1935. He tried his hand at selling cars and then became a stagehand at the MGM studios in Hollywood. But it was on his return in 1936, the following year, that his game flourished. For the space of five years, he was the pre-eminent American golfer and won 16 tournaments. In 1937 he won two events, came second on six occasions and was rarely out of the top ten. Among his victories during that period were three Western Opens in succession, the US Open in 1937 and 1938 and the Masters in 1939.

A measure of Guldahl's skill was that all his rounds at the 1937 Open at Oakland Hills were under par. Everyone expected Sam Snead to prevail, especially when he finished with a total of 283 but Guldahl's final round of 69 won the day. He retained his Open title easily in 1938 and at the 1939 Masters confounded Sam Snead yet again. He played the last nine holes in 33 strokes, to set a new record of 279 for the event, a record which stood until Ben Hogan's epic performance of 1953.

Guldahl played in only one Ryder Cup fixture, at Southport in 1937, when the American team were the victors. With Tony Manero he won a close foursomes match over Arthur Lacey and Bill Cox and easily defeated Alf Padgham, who was out of sorts with his game, in the singles.

Ralph Guldahl won a couple of tournaments in 1940 but then lost his game and never recovered it. All sorts of theories were advanced to explain his spectacular decline. Gene Sarazen thought that his club head had always come into the ball slightly closed and a minor decline in his natural timing made it too difficult for him to correct the fault; Sam Snead felt that Guldahl's grip had changed since his early days and he tried, without success, to persuade Guldahl to correct it.

Certainly, something had gone sadly wrong with his rather peculiar technique. His height, well over six feet, posed its own problems for Guldahl. In addition he took the club a long way back at great speed and then lunged savagely through the ball. It was not a pretty swing and he had some irritating mannerisms; for example he was a slow player and shuffled around as he addressed the ball 'like a man squirming into a telephone box with an armful of parcels', as a contemporary put it.

Sarazen was probably nearest the truth in that Guldahl, as he grew older, became unable to compensate for his suspect technique. Guldahl maintained that he had achieved all his ambitions in golf and that may also have been a factor in his spectacular decline. Nevertheless, for a few glorious years, Guldahl's abundant power and accuracy made him one of the best golfers in the world.

He became the professional at Braemar in California and remained there until his death in 1987.

H

HAAS, FRED

USA

Born: 3.1.16

Appearances: 1953

Record: P1 W0 L1 H0

There is a small niche in golfing history for Fred Haas because he was the first player to compete in both the Walker Cup and the Ryder Cup. In 1938 he played for America and lost both his Walker Cup matches at St Andrews; and in 1953 he was beaten by Harry Bradshaw in the Ryder Cup singles.

As an amateur in 1945 Haas had the distinction of ending Byron Nelson's extraordinary run of 11 wins out of 11 tournaments. Haas won the Memphis Invitational and Nelson finished fifth. He went on to win four tournaments as a professional during the years from 1949 to 1954 and he served on the PGA Tournament Committee in the mid-Fifties.

HAAS, JAY,

USA

Born: 2.12.53

Appearances: 1983

Record: P4 W2 L1 H1

After playing in the 1975 Walker Cup team, Jay Haas first played on the American tour in 1977. His inaugural victory was in the San Diego Open a year later and since then he has been one of the most consistent players on the circuit. He won four tournaments in 1981 and 1982, including the Texas Open.

The latter year was his highest finish (13th) in the money list and he was selected for the Ryder Cup at the PGA National Club, Florida. With three different partners he won two and a half points out of three in the fourball and foursomes matches, but lost to Nick Faldo in his singles.

HAGEN, WALTER

USA

Born: 21.12.92

Appearances: 1927, 1929, 1931, 1933, 1935
Captain 1937

Record: P9 W7 L1 H1

It was entirely appropriate that Walter Hagen should play as captain of the American team in the first-ever Ryder Cup match. He was the pre-eminent professional golfer in the world, and only the legendary amateur, Bobby Jones, equalled him in reputation.

In the early years Hagen also picked the American team; a proper selection process was later devised, but Hagen's was still a dominant influence.

His record shows a total of around 40 tournament wins in the USA, including the Open in 1914 and 1919. He won the USPGA Championship in 1921 and was the champion four times in succession from 1924. He also won the Open Championship on four occasions, and the French, Belgian and Canadian Opens.

His victories in the major championships, and his brilliant record in the Ryder Cup, put Walter Hagen at the very pinnacle of professional golf. But the manner of his victories and his radical view of how a professional golfer should behave and how he should be treated made him the most profoundly influential figure in the game. He was the first great showman, a flamboyant personality who dressed in monogrammed silk shirts, flannel trousers and two-tone shoes when most golfers still played in tweeds. Off the course he wore Savile Row suits and had a love of expensive cars: he drove Cadillacs and Stutz Bearcats when these were the playthings of the very rich.

Hagen had a fine sense of humour, a glib and witty tongue and supreme self-confidence. His loud enquiry on the first tee of 'who's gonna be second' was only partly tongue-in-cheek because he had the golf game to beat anyone. And the golf fans loved him.

As a young unknown golfer, who had recently become a professional, he entered the US

Open in 1913. In those day, as long as you had your clubs and the entry fee, you could play. Hagen finished equal fourth and in the following year he led the championship all the way, after an opening round of 68, and won it with a record score at Midlothian, Illinois. He won again in 1919 after a play-off with Mike Brady. It is said that Hagen had been at a party with Al Jolson for most of the night but nevertheless he won by a shot. He then made the revolutionary decision to become a full-time tournament professional and abandoned his job at Oakland Hills at a time when such employment provided the main income for golf professionals.

Walter Hagen had the vision and the courage to seek a different role in the game. He also decided that he must visit Britain and win the Open. In 1920 he arrived at Deal and found that professionals were not even allowed inside the clubhouse. He parked his chauffeur-driven Austro-Daimler right in front of the club and had his meals served from its boot each day by his footman. This was 'Sir Walter's' style. In the high winds at Deal he finished tied for 53rd place (no doubt to the amusement of the championship committee) but, undaunted, went over to La Boulie, near Paris, and won the French Open.

The following year saw the start of a remarkable sequence of victories that has never been equalled. He even had the foresight to acquire a business manager-cum-press agent to help him capitalise on his successes. He won the Open in Britain in 1922, 1924, 1928 and 1929, and the American PGA Championship in 1921 and four times in succession from 1924 to 1927. He registered 22 straight wins over the best American golfers of those years, including the likes of Gene Sarazen, Leo Diegel, Bill Mehlhorn and Tommy Armour.

Someone said that he had a swing that started with a sway and ended with a lunge, but Hagen had a nerveless approach to matchplay and a magical facility to follow a poor stroke (and he perpetrated more than any other great player, especially off the tee) with a remarkable recovery. Bobby Jones called him 'a veritable wizard with the pitch' and Ben Hogan said that he had 'the greatest mental approach to golf of any player I ever knew'. Two remarkable testimonies to a man who was virtually impregnable in matchplay in the 1920s. He had also mastered the handbook of gamesmanship. One of his tricks was to keep his opponent waiting on the first tee; and another was to study the alternative routes for a difficult shot until his opponent's nerves were screaming. He usually knew exactly what he would do and his secondary motive was to entertain the gallery. As Gene Sarazen, the constant rival to Hagen, wrote: 'There has never been a golfer who could out-think and out-manoeuvre a matchplay opponent as Walter Hagen could. You couldn't rattle Hagen, whatever you did.'

In 1922 Hagen achieved another of his ambitions by winning the Open at Royal St George's – the first American-born golfer to win it. With his champagne and caviare style of living, from his usual base at a suite at the Savoy Hotel, he

Walter Hagen with the Ryder Cup in 1937, the first time the American team was victorious

reckoned that a visit to the Open usually cost him $10,000. He gave his prize of £75 to his caddie, whose celebrations of his good luck sent him to a premature grave.

He was the runner-up to Arthur Havers in the following year at Troon, where the professionals were not just barred from the clubhouse, they were not even allowed at the back door to collect their mail. This so incensed 'the Haig' that he sabotaged the prize-giving ceremony by inviting the gallery back to the local pub for a drink. The committee were left in solitary state to conduct affairs.

By the latter part of the 1920s, Hagen was said to be earning nearly $200,000 a year from golf and this included his income from his own golf-club manufacturing company which he had set up in 1922. He eventually sold it to the Wilson Company and his royalties assured him of a reasonably comfortable old age.

His victories in the Opens of 1928 and 1929 illustrated Hagen's skill and resolution. In 1928 he suffered an astonishing reverse in a challenge match over 72 holes at the hands of Archie Compston. Hagen had admittedly just stepped off the boat from New York on the day before the match, but the margin was an

extraordinary one of 18 and 17. His comment was typical, 'when you are laid out good and flat, you must not squawk.' A week later Hagen won the Open at Sandwich. In the following year he won again at Muirfield, in gale-force winds and freezing temperatures; Hagen called it 'the Arctic Circle part of Scotland'. He deployed a special mallet-headed driver to hit the ball low through the wind and he described his second round of 67 as one of the best of his career. On the final day, his consummate skill and determination gave him two rounds of 75. He had started two shots behind Leo Diegel and finished six ahead. American players filled eight of the first ten places.

In the Ryder Cup, his prowess as a matchplayer made Hagen a fearsome opponent and he lost only one match, in 1929, when the American side was defeated at Moortown. He deliberately arranged to play his opposing captain, George Duncan, and, with his usual self-confidence, told his team that they had 'one point in the bag' on the morrow. The British captain played superbly and Hagen was given what he described as 'a terrific shellacking' by 10 and 8.

But Walter Hagen did not lose another match in the series and was the non-playing captain in 1937 when the Americans won for the first time in Britain. He was rated as an excellent leader and his brand of self-confidence rubbed off on the rest of the team. But he also picked his pairings wisely, by matching players of similar temperaments who would get on well together. It was also typical of Hagen that he was conscious of the American team's image and had their clothes specially made for them; their blazers incorporated the American eagle on the breast pocket. He paid the bill out of his own pocket, too.

Walter Hagen's triumphs were limited in the 1930s to half a dozen tournament wins, even though he was third in the US Open in 1935, 22 years after his first appearance.

He travelled America and the rest of the world to play exhibition matches for large sums of money, even if the money never quite kept pace with his ability to spend it. His much-quoted remark that he never wanted to be a millionaire, only to live like one, was apt. But he was a great ambassador for golf and wherever he went, 'Sir Walter' pulled in the crowds and never failed to entertain them.

Walter Hagen was one of the greatest of all golfers and took professional golf to a new and unimagined level of public acceptance and awareness. His great rival and friend, Gene Sarazen, praised him as the finest short-iron player the game has ever known, as a magnificent putter, above all as a golfer with unique faith in himself. He wrote that 'golf has never had a showman like him. All the professionals who have a chance to go after the big money today should say a silent thanks to Walter . . . it was he who made professional golf what it is.'

Hagen's epitaph should properly be his own: 'I never hurried, there was no use worrying – and I always took time to smell the flowers along the way.'

HALIBURTON, TOM

GB

Born: 5.6.15

Appearances: 1961, 1963

Record: P6 W0 L6 H0

Tom Haliburton's record in the Ryder Cup did no justice to his talents as a golfer. It must be said in his defence that five of his six losses were by very narrow margins: three times by one hole and twice by two and one. Only Gene 'the Machine' Littler inflicted a heavy defeat on him, in the singles of 1963 at East Lake, Atlanta.

With his easy style, Tom Haliburton played excellent golf until well past his forties and was capable of inspired bursts of scoring. His score of 61 in an event at Worthing in 1952, and his two round total of 126 in the same tournament, was a British professional record for nearly two decades.

But he seemed to be a perennial runner-up, rather than a winner. He was second in the Daks three times and also in the Spanish Open and the PGA Championship. His victory in the *Yorkshire Evening News* Tournament of 1963, by one shot over Peter Thomson, assured him of his second Ryder Cup appearance.

In 1969 he was elected Captain of the PGA.

HAMILTON, BOB

USA

Born: 10.1.16

Appearances: 1949

Record: P2 W0 L2 H0

Bob Hamilton won the Amateur Championship of his native Indiana in 1936 and went on to win the Indiana Open twice. But his first major win was the North and South Open in 1944 and in the same year he won the USPGA championship. To do so he beat the two most formidable American golfers of the day, Jug McSpaden and Byron Nelson; the latter in the final by one hole.

Hamilton was a personable man with a penchant for large cigars and even larger bets. He was a regular on the American tour until the 1950s and won five events. Apart from the USPGA Championship, his best finish in a major was third place in the Masters of 1946.

He lost both his matches in the 1949 Ryder Cup at Ganton. In the foursomes Fred Daly and Ken Bousfield played superb golf to beat him and Skip Alexander; in the singles he ran into Dai Rees, who was in irresistible form. The Welshman was four holes up at lunch after a round of 65 and easily beat Hamilton by six and four.

HARBERT, MELVIN

USA

Born: 20.2.15

Appearances: 1949, 1955
Captain 1955

Record: P2 W2 L0 H0

Chick Harbert was one of the longest drivers of a golf ball ever seen in the game and he allied this strength to a fine skill with his putter. It was not surprising that he was a formidable matchplayer, as was shown by his record in the USPGA Championship. He lost in the final to Jim Ferrier in 1947 and to Jim Turnesa in 1952 but at last got his due reward with a victory in 1954 over Walter Burkemo.

Harbert had shown early promise when he won the Michigan Open as an amateur in 1937 and he won it twice more after he became a professional. He won seven major events on the American tour, including the Texas Open. In 1955 he teamed up with Ed Furgol to win the Canada (World) Cup for America.

He played in two winning Ryder Cup teams and won both his singles matches. At Ganton in 1949 he defeated Sam King, and Syd Scott was his victim at Thunderbird Ranch in 1955, when Harbert was also captain of the American side. Harbert made his own incisive comment on the tensions involved in playing Ryder Cup golf. Of his first appearance at Ganton he said: 'When I stood on the first tee and they played the "Star Spangled Banner" you couldn't have driven a nail into my ass with a sledgehammer.'

An intelligent and articulate man, Chick Harbert served on the USPGA Tournament committee from 1946 to 1950 and was its chairman for two of those years.

HARGREAVES, JACK

GB

Born: 12.2.14

Appearances: 1951

Jack Hargreaves, a cheerful and chubby-faced man, had the ill luck to travel to Pinehurst with the British team in 1951 and not to be given a game by the captain, Arthur Lacey.

Hargreaves had his successes as a professional: he won the Spalding Tournament in 1951 and was the runner-up in the Daks in the following year. His best finish in the Open was a tie for third place in 1948 behind Fred Daly and the winner, Henry Cotton.

HARPER, CHANDLER

USA

Born: 10.3.14

Appearances: 1955

Record: P1 W0 L1 H0

In his only game in the Ryder Cup, the opening foursomes match of 1955 in Palm Springs, Chandler Harper lost a cliff-hanger to John Jacobs and Johnny Fallon, who had to hole a putt of around four feet on the final green.

Harper had turned professional in 1934, although he also fancied his chances as a baseball player. He won eight US tour events, and his major success was his victory in the 1950 USPGA Championship. In 1954 he won the Texas Open with a record score of 259, which included the best-ever total over 54 holes of 189.

He had various club jobs during his career and even ran a finance business, and he built his own golf course in the Fifties. Chandler Harper claimed that he rarely practised but his game was good enough to win the American and the World Seniors tournaments in 1968.

HARRISON, ERNEST JOE

USA

Born: 29.3.10

Appearances: 1947, 1949, 1951

Record: P3 W2 L1 H0

Universally known as 'Dutch', Harrison came to notice as a golfer by winning the Arkansas Amateur Championship. He became a professional in 1934 but it was some time before he won an event of consequence: in 1939 he won the Bing Crosby Open and the Texas Open. In those years, he earned far more from hustling bets in unofficial matches than he ever did from tournaments.

Harrison had a remarkably long career which stretched from the Thirties to the Sixties. In between, he won 18 tournaments but was unable to put his name on a major trophy. His best effort was in 1950, when he finished one stroke behind Ben Hogan, George Fazio and Lloyd Mangrum at the US Open at Merion.

Nevertheless, he was acknowledged as one of the finest American golfers of his time, a superbly accurate player and a brilliant putter. He was a very tall man, several inches over six feet, and he played his shots from a rather narrow stance. In his youth he played golf left-handed for a couple of years and then changed back.

Dutch Harrison's Ryder Cup career began at Portland, Oregon, in 1947 when he had an easy singles victory over Fred Daly. In 1949, at Ganton, he and Johnny Palmer lost to Max Faulkner and Jimmy Adams but he revenged himself on Faulkner in no uncertain manner in the singles. Harrison began the match with five 3s in the first six holes and went in to lunch, a contented man no doubt, with a lead of seven holes. He finished his opponent off without any trouble.

Although Harrison was chosen for the 1951 tie at Pinehurst, he was not called upon by his captain, Sam Snead. He had won the Texas Open that year and some of his best golf still lay ahead of him. He won the Western Open, the All-American Open and the Tijuana Open in the 1950s; and he was good enough to finish in a tie for third place, behind Arnold Palmer and Jack Nicklaus, in the US Open in 1960 at Cherrry Hills.

Dutch Harrison had a highly successful career in golf and a remarkable one, in that he competed with distinction with golfers as diverse as Hagen and Sarazen, Hogan and Snead, and Palmer and Nicklaus.

HAVERS, ARTHUR

GB

Born: 10.6.98

Appearances: 1927, 1931, 1933

Record: P6 W3 L3 H0

Arthur Havers was a remarkably precocious golfer in that he qualified for the Open in 1914 at the age of 16. The very tall and thin youth grew into a big-framed, formidably strong man, who retained his high level of fitness throughout his golfing career.

He won the Open at Troon in 1923 with Walter Hagen breathing down his neck. The American needed a birdie three at the 72nd hole to force a play-off but left his bunker shot a few inches short. Havers was the only British winner between George Duncan in 1920 and Henry Cotton in 1934. It was a period of American domination by Walter Hagen (three wins), Bobby Jones (three wins), Gene Sarazen, Tommy Armour and Densmore Shute.

Havers played in the first Ryder Cup match in the USA, in 1927, and remarked how the British team were 'submerged by hospitality and kindness . . . in a world of luxury and plenty'. This did not extend to the golf course, where the Americans, led by Walter Hagen, won easily. Havers lost to Hagen narrowly in the singles. They were to meet again, in the foursomes, four years later at Scioto, Ohio, when Hagen and Densmore Shute hammered him and his partner, George Duncan, by ten and nine.

Havers had the consolation of winning his singles, and ended his Ryder Cup career in 1933 in triumph when Britain won a close match. He won both his foursomes and his singles matches; in the latter he defeated Leo Diegel by four and three. His association with the Ryder Cup continued when he became a selector in 1949.

In the days between the wars British professional golfers did not travel very far, but Havers was an exception, with trips to America, Europe and Argentina. In 1924, for example, he travelled to America and beat Bobby Jones over 36 holes and Gene Sarazen over 72 holes.

Despite his likeable, almost gentle demeanour, he was a formidable matchplayer and he emphasised this again in 1938 when he reached the semi-final of the *News of the World* Matchplay Championship.

He had an orthodox swing, characterised by an open stance which produced a slight fade. He was a long hitter, nevertheless, and particularly accurate with his wooden clubs.

HAWKINS, FRED

USA

Born: 3.9.23

Appearances: 1957

Record: P2 W1 L1 H0

Fred Hawkins had the distinction of being the only American player to win his singles at Lindrick in 1957, when the British team stormed through to win a famous victory. Having lost his foursomes, in partnership with Art Wall, he beat Peter Alliss to level the match at four matches to both teams, with four to play.

Hawkins was a particularly consistent player on the American tour and during the years from 1949 to 1963 he usually finished in the top 25 and often in the top 10. But he only won one PGA event, the Oklahoma City Open in 1956. He reached the quarter-finals of the USPGA Championship twice and tied for second place behind Arnold Palmer in the 1958 Masters.

HAYES, MARK

USA

Born: 7.12.49

Appearances: 1979

Record: P3 W1 L2 H0

Mark Hayes was called to the American colours on the eve of the 1979 Ryder Cup match at The Greenbrier when Tom Watson withdrew because of the imminent birth of his first child. Hayes's best years were in the late Seventies when he won his three victories: in the Byron Nelson Classic and the Pensacola Open (1976) and the Tournament Players Championship (1977). He also made an impact on the Open Championship at Turnberry in 1977 when he scored a 63 in the second round; it was the lowest round ever recorded in the Open and Hayes finished in a tie for ninth place.

On the second day at The Greenbrier he and Fuzzy Zoeller were victims of the assured foursomes partnership of Barnes and Gallacher; and in the afternoon Hayes and Lee Elder lost on the last green to Nick Faldo and Peter Oosterhuis. But Hayes won his one and only point by defeating Antonio Garrido in the singles; and he did it in style, with a birdie on the 18th hole.

HEAFNER, CLAYTON

USA

Born: 20.7.14

Appearances: 1949, 1951

Record: P4 W3 L0 H1

A man who weighs in at well over 200 pounds and is renowned for his bad temper, is a man of whom to be wary. Such a man was Clayton Heafner, a former Army sergeant from North Carolina, whom Sam Snead described as 'the most even-tempered golfer I ever saw. He was mad all the time.' No doubt Heafner played up to his image but it is well documented that, when an announcer mispronounced his name on the first tee, he replaced his driver in his bag and departed the tournament.

With his brawny arms covered in reddish blond hairs and a moustache of the same hue adorning a lip shadowed by a bulbous nose and a craggy brow, this lumbering bulk of a man was a forbidding sight. His looks did not belie his character because he was also a fierce competitor.

He had an awkward, rather unprepossessing swing, but it was a very sound one and he was a superb putter. His first important victory was in the 1947 Jacksonville Open and he was the runner-up in the US Opens of 1949 and 1951.

He was undefeated in his four Ryder Cup matches. At Ganton, in 1949, he and Jimmy Demaret beat Charlie Ward and Sam King, and in the singles he edged away from Dick Burton mainly by dint of an eagle three at the 31st hole. At Pinehurst two years later he and Jack Burke had an easy foursomes win; but in the singles Fred Daly surprised him by fighting back from an almost hopeless position of three holes down with three to play to force a half.

HEBERT, JAY JUNIUS

USA

Born: 14.2.23

Appearances: 1959, 1961
Captain 1971

Record: P4 W2 L1 H1

Jay Hebert turned his full attention to the US golf tour only in 1956, when he was well into his thirties but he made up for lost time by winning seven tournaments between 1957 and 1961, including the USPGA Championship.

After serving in the US Marines during the war (he was wounded at Iwo Jima), Hebert went to Louisiana State University and finally graduated in 1948.

Hebert was well liked on the tour and possessed a very sound and consistent swing, although he convinced himself that his short game was not up to standard. The evidence does not really support that view since, apart from his seven tournament victories, he finished in second place on 16 occasions between 1955 and 1960.

In 1959 he played one Ryder Cup match at Eldorado and halved with Peter Alliss. Two years later, at Lytham, when the format was altered to 18-hole matches, he won both his foursomes games in partnership with Art Wall. The second game could not have been more tense and Hebert sank a putt for a birdie three on the 18th hole to steal a point from Christy O'Connor and Peter Alliss. However, he was beaten in the singles by Dai Rees.

In 1971, Jay Hebert was the non-playing captain of the American team which won a close match at the Old Warson course in St Louis.

HEBERT, LIONEL

USA

Born: 20.1.20

Appearances: 1957

Record: P1 W0 L1 H0

The elder brother of Jay, Lionel Hebert also went to Louisiana State University, where he took a degree in music. He became a professional golfer in 1950 and his first major success was to win the 1957 USPGA Championship. This was its last year as a matchplay event and he beat Dow Finsterwald in the final. He also won the Tucson Open in 1958 and the Memphis Open in 1962.

Hebert played in the 1957 Ryder Cup match at Lindrick. His defeat in his only match, a singles against Ken Bousfield, gave Britain the crucial point which won the match.

HILL, DAVE

USA

Born: 20.5.37

Appearances: 1969, 1973, 1977

Record: P9 W6 L3 H0

Dave Hill has spent much of his career in a relentless search for the impossible, the perfect golf swing. Lean of figure and jumpy of disposition, one pictures him hauling voraciously on a succession of cigarettes during the course of a round. An irascible and outspoken man, he also expended a lot of his energies in criticising the golf administrators, especially the USGA, which runs the US Open Championship. At Hazeltine in 1970, when he finished second to Tony Jacklin, Hill called the course a 'cow pasture' and was fined. Two years later he was at it again when he found that the USGA had tinkered over much with Pebble Beach. His view was that they had 'turned a show dog into a bitch'. In 1973 he played the first four holes of his practice round at Oakmont and disliked the course so much that he withdrew from the tournament.

Hill became a professional golfer in 1958, won a couple of tournaments and then suffered a prolonged slump throughout most of the 1960s. But he was to have his most successful year in 1969 when he won three tournaments and was awarded the Vardon Trophy for the lowest stroke average: 70.3 over 90 rounds.

Hill called himself 'a skinny little cat who has to win with style, not strength' and his skill and his rough-edged determination were much in evidence at his Ryder Cup debut in 1969 at Royal Birkdale. The match was drawn and the United States team was in Hill's debt since he gathered four points out of a possible six. But trouble was inevitable when Hill and his even more aggressive partner, Ken Still, were drawn to play a fourball against the highly combative pair of Celts, Brian Huggett and Bernard Gallacher. As early as the first green Hill had to be asked to stand still while Huggett putted. It was downhill all the way from there, with disagreements so heated that the two captains and the PGA President, Lord Derby, had to be summoned to calm not only the players but also the crowd. Hill reacted in the best way possible for his team and played brilliantly to win the game for America. On the final day he won both his singles, against Peter Townsend and Brian Barnes.

Dave Hill played twice more in the Ryder Cup. At Muirfield in 1973 he seemed to be an unwilling participant and only played one game, in which he and Arnold Palmer were beaten by Peter Oosterhuis and Tony Jacklin. At Lytham in 1977, however, Hill won both his matches and his defeat of Tommy Horton was the decisive point by which America retained the trophy. It was ironic that Hill made all his Ryder Cup appearances in Britain since he was certainly no fan: he did not like the courses, the weather or the hotels.

Hill played the American golf tour for well over 20 years and won 13 tournaments. His remarkable skill should have brought him more victories but perhaps he spent too much energy in tilting at windmills. His temperament was fragile, as the colourful Hill himself admitted: 'I buried a few (clubs) in the ground, you know. It took two men to get one of them out!' He now enlivens the Senior tour on which he has won nearly $2 million.

Dave Hill (left and above) gives his all

HITCHCOCK, JIMMY

GB

Born: 38.7.30

Appearances: 1965

Record: P3 W0 L3 H0

As an assistant to Dick Burton at Coombe Hill, where his father was a greenkeeper, Jimmy Hitchcock had an excellent start in golf. His development was slow, partly because he was relatively small but he built his strength up by a tough regime of exercise and his determination was expressed in the diligence of his practice.

In 1959 Hitchcock began to show his form as a professional. He was well up in several events, finished eleventh in the Open at Muirfield and was close to selection for the Ryder Cup. In the following year he broke through to win his first important tournament, the Dunlop Masters at Sunningdale. After a 66 in the first round to lead the field, he won it in fine style with a birdie at the 72nd hole.

He qualified for the Ryder Cup at Birkdale in 1965 mainly because of his victory in the Agfa-Gevaert and lost all his matches. He and Jimmy Martin were demolished by the formidable pair of Tony Lema and Julius Boros in the foursomes and worse was to follow for Hitchcock. In the singles he was first out against Arnold Palmer, who was much too powerful for him; and in the afternoon he was never in the hunt against Julius Boros.

HODSON, BERT

GB

Born: 22.7.05

Appearances: 1931

Record: P1 W0 L1 H0

Bert Hodson had a very little in the way of serious golfing credentials to his name when picked for the match at Scioto Country Club, in Ohio, as a late substitute for Henry Cotton, who was embroiled in a disagreement with the PGA and withdrew from the team.

He had won the Welsh Professional Championship and the Essex Open and had been equal seventh in the St Andrews Open of 1927, which was won by Bobby Jones. From his base at Chigwell Golf club, Hodson played in the Open throughout the Thirties and occasionally finished in the top 20 (he was equal seventh again in 1934).

It was not surprising that in his one Ryder Cup game he was easily defeated by Densmore Shute.

HOGAN, BEN

USA

Born: 13.8.12

Appearances: 1947, 1951
Captain 1947, 1949, 1967

Record: P3 W3 L0 H0

On 2 February 1949, a head-on collision with a bus in heavy fog nearly killed Ben Hogan just as his career had touched full bloom. As the bus hit his car, Hogan threw himself across his wife, Valerie, to protect her; his action saved him from being impaled on the steering column. His injuries were such that no one, much less his doctors, thought Hogan would ever play golf again. When he left the hospital he weighed less than 100 pounds.

Hogan's arrival as a great golfer had been much delayed and the journey had been full of hardship. He had turned professional in 1931 and in the next nine years won only one tournament. There were several occasions when, penniless, he was near to giving the game up. In 1937, Henry Picard's promise of a loan whenever he needed it stopped Hogan from abandoning the tour. This small lifeline helped him although he never called upon Picard for money. Hogan dedicated his first instructional book to his mentor.

Hogan's breakthrough came in 1940 when he won four events, including the prestigious North and South Open at Pinehurst with a record score of 277 and the Greater Greenboro Open. In the next two years he was first in 11 tournaments and then did his stint in the American Army, to return in 1945 with another five tournament victories.

Hogan was now ready to dominate professional golf. For one thing he had the game to do it. In his early days he had a very long swing and hit the ball low and with a hook which often took him into trouble. So he taught himself to fade the ball, to hit the safe and accurate shot, to 'play the percentage game'. By dint of a practice regime that had never been imagined until then, Hogan created his new swing. He was merciless on himself in his pursuit of a perfection which can never be attained in a game such as golf but Hogan got as near to it as anyone, before or since. It was

no wonder that Henry Longhurst called him 'the hard case from Texas'.

Between 1946 and 1958 Hogan won 30 tournaments, including the USPGA Championship on two occasions and the US Open at Riviera, Los Angeles. He was also the runner-up in the Masters in 1942 and 1946.

Then came the almost fatal crash and it seemed unlikely that Hogan would ever walk properly again, let alone play golf. But, with what may have seemed a sentimental gesture, the PGA asked him to captain the Ryder Cup team at Ganton, in September 1949. Although Hogan could only hobble as far as the first tee it was apparently extremely unwise to refer to him, in his presence, as the 'non-playing' captain. The practice schedules he set for the American team were rigourous and his planning had its reward when the USA won a close match. Jimmy Demaret, Hogan's closest golfing friend and usual golfing partner, complained that he had to practise twice as hard as he wanted, but that was only half as hard as Hogan wanted. Hogan was not averse to asking for an inspection of the British golfers' clubs either. He suspected that the grooves were too deep and therefore imparted extra back-spin. Bernard Darwin, who was Chairman of the Royal and Ancient Club's rules committee, agreed with him and the British players had to get to work with their files.

In January 1949, Hogan entered for the Los Angeles Open at the Riviera Club: 'just to see whether he could still play the game'. With his legs heavily bandaged he scored a 73 followed by three rounds of 69, to tie for first place with Sam Snead. 'Slammin' Sam' won the play-off, after which Grantland Rice made his famous remark of Ben Hogan: 'His legs weren't strong enough to carry his heart around'.

After finishing fourth in the Masters, Hogan decimated The Greenbrier course to win the White Sulphur Springs Open with a score of 259, the lowest ever recorded in an official tournament. The scene was set for the US Open at the difficult Merion course. The final day, when 36 holes were played, would test Hogan's physical reserves to their limits. He finished in a tie with Lloyd Mangrum and George Fazio and won the play-off. His come-back

was complete.

In 1951 Ben Hogan won the US Open again at Oakland Hills, a course which had been tightened up in the most spiteful fashion by Robert Trent Jones to prevent low scoring. With a remarkable final round of 67 Hogan was justifiably able to say that he had 'brought this monster to its knees'. He also won the Masters in the same year but he had a rather fallow year in 1952.

However, 1953 was to be his greatest year in golf. First, he won the Masters with a score of 274, which cut five shots off the record; and then he won the US Open at Oakmont by six shots and led the field all the way. Hogan was not particularly keen to travel to Britain for the Open, which had lost some of its international lustre since the war but, once decided, he gave his all to the campaign. He arrived two weeks early to get used to the conditions, and especially to the small British ball, and he picked the course apart in his usual meticulous way. 'Management is eighty per cent of winning,' he said and went on to prove it at Carnoustie.

Every player had to qualify for the Open at that time and Hogan, watched by huge crowds, did so with ease. In the tournament proper, each of his four rounds was lower than the preceding one (73, 71, 70, 68) and he won the Open by four shots, without ever holing a putt of any length. Pat Ward-Thomas described one of Hogan's strokes as 'a two-iron rifled into the teeth of the wind, with that compelling, searing flight we came to know so well'.

Hogan had won three of the four major tournaments in the same year, a feat unequalled by any other professional golfer. He would not enter the USPGA Championship, which called for two matches a day, because of his physical condition; and it was scheduled for the week after the Open. No doubt he would have won it if he had wished; that is not a fanciful idea: Hogan had the single-mindedness and heightened resolution that would override all difficulties. Among modern sportsmen, only Don Bradman can be compared to him.

Ben Hogan did not win another major tournament, although he was second in the Masters in 1954 and 1955 and should have won the US Open again in 1955; but to everyone's amazement, he was beaten in the play-off by an 'unknown', Jack Fleck. He was equal second in 1956 but an inability to hole short putts troubled him more and more. His game from tee to green was still better than anyone's and he had a chance, in 1960, to deny Arnold Palmer his US Open victory at Cherry Hills. In 1967, at the age of 54 and despite his miseries on the greens, he finished tenth in the Masters and recorded the lowest round of the tournament. His 66 included a score of 30 shots for the last nine holes. Hogan had six birdies and three pars and not a single error in judgement or technique could be discerned; he even holed a putt of over 12 feet on the final green for a birdie. The applause rolled on and on. There wasn't a dry eye to be seen.

A measure of his consistency was that in fourteen consecutive US Opens up to 1960 and in fourteen consecutive Masters tournaments up to 1956, Ben Hogan was always in the top ten, and was in the top four on eighteen occasions.

He had a perfect record in the Ryder Cup, as would be expected. In the 1947 massacre at Portland, when Britain only won one point, he played only in the foursomes and did not feel it necessary to go out in the singles. In 1951 he and Demaret were back in harness and beat Fred Daly and Ben Bousfield easily; in the singles, despite a round of 67 in the morning, he found it difficult to pull away from Charlie Ward but eventually did so with some superlative shots.

Hogan was captain of the team again in 1967 at Houston, Texas, and demonstrated just how much he was in charge when the superstar of golf, Arnold Palmer, questioned his decision to use the smaller British ball in the match. Hogan's reply was: 'Who said you're playing, Palmer?'

No one could call Ben Hogan lovable. Pat Ward-Thomas wrote a revealing cameo of him: 'Standing motionless on a fairway . . . wide mouth drawn into a thin line, with a cigarette between his lips, and the eyes, bleak as an Arctic dawn, piercing the distance as if to shrivel the hole into submission.' The crowds respected Ben Hogan but, in contrast, they warmed to his great rival, Sam Snead, who noticed that while the fans actually watched his swing, they just looked down the fairway to see where Hogan's ball would land. Hogan was irritated by this but he had very little communication with his public. He sheltered himself behind the walls of his own impenetrable concentration. He rarely signed an autograph and, as Snead said, he didn't talk at all on the course, 'and didn't have much to say off it either. He's been consistent there'. His contemporaries said that his only utterance during a round of golf was 'you're away'.

During the Canada Cup at Wentworth in 1956, which the two of them won, Hogan is reputed to have told Snead that he had spotted a tiny flaw in his swing. On the flight home, Snead pressed Hogan to tell him what the problem was. After a little thought, Hogan said 'Hell, no!' and went back to sleep.

Hogan was certainly a hard case. But he had come through early adversity and a near-fatal accident to become the most successful golfer in the world. He was a supremely analytical player, who examined every iota of his own swing and plotted his way round the golf course with inch-by-inch precision. He was a perfectionist, who got as near to taking the risk and the emotion out of golf as anyone. With his frightening intensity and high intelligence, he would have reached the top of any profession; Ben Hogan happened to choose golf.

HORNE, REGINALD

GB

Born: 19.7.08

Appearances: 1947

A quiet and unobtrusive golfer and little known outside Hampshire, Reg Horne suddenly found himself in the limelight when he won the first post-war PGA championship at Walton Heath against the formidable Percy Alliss.

He was in the spotlight again in the 1947 Open Championship when he was in the lead on the final day but Fred Daly beat him by one shot and Horne finished equal second with Frank Stranahan.

Horne was picked for the 1947 Ryder Cup match at Portland, Oregon, but was not asked to play a game by his captain, Henry Cotton. Reg Horne was no doubt disappointed but perhaps reflected later that it was just as well – the British team lost 11 of the 12 matches.

HORTON, TOMMY

GB

Born: 16.6.41

Appearances: 1975, 1977

Record: P8 W1 L6 H1

Tommy Horton probably despaired of ever making the Ryder Cup team. In 1969 he was passed over despite being in the top ten of the Order of Merit for two years running; in 1970 he won the South African Open and the PGA Matchplay Championship and was the runner-up in the Piccadilly Matchplay tournament in the following year. Once more he was ignored, and it was no coincidence that a degree of antipathy existed between Horton and the captain in those years, Eric Brown.

From the mid-Sixties to the end of the Seventies Tommy Horton was usually high up in the Order of Merit. A slight figure, his head usually crowned with a floppy white hat, he won other important tournaments, including the Piccadilly Medal, the Penfold tournament and the Dunlop Masters. Horton was never a long hitter but an adept short game compensated for his lack of power.

Horton made his long-awaited appearance in the Ryder Cup matches of 1975 and 1977 and was one of the players who suffered in comparison to the Americans' strength in depth. Nevertheless, he showed his skill and determination to their full extent at Laurel Valley where he halved his singles match with Hale Irwin, the US Open champion of the previous year and beat Lou Graham, the current US Open champion. Two years later, at Lytham, he lost all his three matches by wide margins.

A popular figure in the game, Horton has established his reputation as a teacher. He was captain of the PGA in 1978 and is now a director of the PGA European tour, as well as commentating on the game on radio and television. He keeps his golfing hand in by playing some of the Seniors tournaments.

HUGGETT, BRIAN

GB

Born: 18.11.36

Appearances: 1963, 1967, 1969, 1971, 1973, 1975
Captain 1977

Record: P25 W9 L10 H6

With his strong, square frame and resolute bearing, Brian Huggett looked every inch a matchplay battler. So his Ryder Cup record proved: with nine wins and six halved matches in his 25 games, his ledger was well in credit. Most British supporters would have picked him to hole a vital putt, perhaps the one to win the Cup for Britain. In 1969, at Birkdale, Brian Huggett thought that he had done exactly that.

In the final series of the singles he was playing the penultimate match against Billy Casper. They came to the final hole with the match level and the Welshman had holed a five-foot putt on the 17th green to keep it that way. Both players hit the green of the par-five 18th hole in two shots and, after Casper had registered his four, Huggett putted to win his match. The putt was strong and left him four or five feet past the hole. At this point there was a huge roar from the 17th green, where Tony Jacklin and Jack Nicklaus were contesting the final match. It sounded to Huggett like 'a winning roar' and he thought that his putt for a half with Casper would win the Ryder Cup. Huggett was an excellent putter, knew the line (just inside the left edge) and told himself to trust his stroke. In it went, he shook hands with Casper and collapsed in tears. But the roar which had gone up had not been for a win but for an eagle by Jacklin, to bring him level with Nicklaus. That match was also halved to ensure the first tied match in the history of the Ryder Cup.

Huggett recalls with feeling that 'you wouldn't want too many of those sort of putts'. It proved to be one of the abiding memories of his career, and golf fans still recall it vividly as one of the high spots of the Ryder Cup.

Brian Huggett followed his father, who was the professional at Porthcawl and Neath, into golf. After doing his national service, he soon began to win tournaments, including the Dutch and German Opens and the Cox-Moore tournament. In the Open he was equal third in 1962 at Troon behind Palmer and Nagle and equal second in 1965 at Royal Birkdale when Peter Thomson won.

He was selected for the Ryder Cup match at East Lake, Atlanta, in 1963 and went out first in the foursomes with another newcomer, George Will, against Arnold Palmer and Johnny Pott. It was a brilliant start to his Ryder Cup career, as the British pair won fairly comfortably, partly because Pott seemed 'scared to death' of Palmer. Although Huggett only won half a point from his next three matches, he beat Pott in his singles to conclude an excellent debut. His next appearance was at Houston in 1967 when the British were heavily defeated. His one and a half points out of a possible five, which included a win over the redoubtable Julius Boros, represented a better return than average.

The tied match at Birkdale in 1969 was a blessed relief for British golf, so long overawed by the powerful Americans, and the close encounter two years later in St Louis, won by the American team by a margin of only five points, seemed to pressage more promising times for the British. Huggett believed that they could win at Muirfield and no player could have done more, since he was unbeaten in his four games. He and Maurice Bembridge even took on the might of Arnold Palmer and Jack Nicklaus in the second series of fourballs and won by three and one. In his singles against Homero Blancas, Huggett was two down but then had six 3s in succession to win by four and two.

But the American side proved to be too powerful and won by six points. The margin was even greater at Laurel Valley in 1975 when Huggett played his last matches. He and Tony Jacklin won their foursomes but Huggett lost his one singles game to Gene Littler.

During these years Huggett had won a string of events in Britain, including the Sumrie, PGA Close, Martini, Daks, Bowmaker and Carrolls events, the Dunlop Masters and the PGA Matchplay Championship. He won the Vardon Trophy in 1968 and represented Wales in the World Cup on nine occasions.

It was wholly appropriate that Huggett should have been appointed the non-playing captain for the 1977 match at Lytham. The new format of five foursomes, five fourballs and ten singles over three days was thought to favour Britain, but nobody liked it – least of all the spectators who had much less to watch each day.

The British team got off to a bad start in the foursomes and were even worse in the fourballs. With the Americans five points in the lead and only ten singles to come, Huggett was in an impossible position. The one questionable decision he made was to exclude Tony Jacklin, still a popular hero with the British supporters, from the singles. According to the captain, he had not only played badly in the fourball defeat at the hands of Dave Hill and Dave Stockton but was in a bad frame of mind and seemed to have left his partner, Eamonn Darcy, to struggle along on his own. Huggett was not the sort of man to shirk an unpopular decision and the subsequent controversy revived memories of the similar squabble between another Welsh captain, Dai Rees, and another Englishman, Harry Weetman, in 1957.

Brian Huggett had a remarkably successful career in professional golf with a fine tally of victories during his two decades as one of the best British players. His splendid Ryder Cup record pointed up his extraordinary resolution and he will rightly be remembered as the man who holed the putt that almost won the Ryder Cup.

Brian Huggett lives in Wales, and among his various business interests designs golf courses.

HUNT, BERNARD

GB

Born: 2.2.30

Appearances: 1953, 1957, 1959, 1961, 1963, 1965, 1967, 1969
Captain 1973, 1975

Record: P28 W6 L16 H6

There was an inevitability to Bernard Hunt's choice of career since his father was a professional golfer. Hunt was a leading figure in British golf for over two decades; he won his first important professional event, the Sumrie, in 1953 and won it again exactly 20 years later. A measure of his consistency was his winning of the Vardon Trophy (for the best stroke average throughout the season) on three occasions, in 1958, 1960 and 1965.

He won many of the prestigious tournaments in Britain – the Bowmaker, Daks, Martini, the Dunlop Masters (twice), the Penfold and the Wills – without threatening to win one of the majors, although he was third in the 1960 Open Championship at St Andrews and fourth in 1964. He also won the Belgian, German and French Opens.

Hunt had a short swing which repeated itself with great ease. Henry Cotton wrote of him as having 'one of the most precise and economical and brief actions of modern times'. Hunt also possessed a very calm temperament and was an excellent putter. Cotton was the non-playing captain of the Ryder Cup team in which Hunt made his debut, in 1953 at Wentworth. Despite his admiration for his swing, Cotton advised him to alter it: to make it longer and more upright. Hunt tried to follow the maestro's advice and played very badly for a couple of years until he reverted to his old swing.

Bernard Hunt had a tremendously long career in the Ryder Cup, with eight appearances as a player and two as a non-playing captain. But his first appearance in 1953 was an ordeal best forgotten. He and Jimmy Adams were no match in the foursomes for Ted Kroll and Jack Burke who were seven holes ahead by lunchtime. On the second day, with one of those unfair rolls of the dice in which the golfing fates specialise, the result of the whole match rested on the young and inexperienced shoulders of Peter Alliss and Hunt. Alliss made a mess of the 36th hole to lose his match, but Hunt, one up on the 36th tee, was fairly sure that, with a par five, he would win his match against Dave Douglas and secure the first tie in Ryder Cup history. Hunt was short of the green in two shots, rather overdid his run-up shot to the green and took three putts to let the Americans in for a narrow win.

Both Alliss and Hunt were omitted from the 1955 team but they had the consolation of being in the side which won the Ryder Cup back in 1957, at Lindrick. The two paired up in the foursomes and lost to Doug Ford and Dow Finsterwald but Hunt

hammered Ford in the singles by six and five.

Hunt was not to play in another successful Ryder Cup team until 1969 when the fixture was tied. In 1961 the format changed from 36-hole to 18-hole matches and in 1963 and 1965 Hunt was sent out in every series, 12 matches in all. These were the days when the Americans dominated the Ryder Cup and Hunt's record of four wins and two halved matches out of twelve was praiseworthy. His partnership with Neil Coles began in 1963 and they played eight matches in harness.

In his final appearance, at Birkdale in 1969, Hunt finished on a positive note. Although he and Peter Butler lost by one hole in the foursomes to Jack Nicklaus and Dan Sikes, he and Maurice Bembridge prised a half from Tommy Aaron and Ray Floyd.

Hunt's association with the Ryder Cup continued when he captained the team at Muirfield in 1973 and at Laurel Valley in 1975. According to Hunt, the result at Muirfield would probably have been much closer if Bernard Gallacher had not been taken ill after the first day. He also tells how Christy O'Connor did not want to play a second singles on the final day but, after a few cheering glasses of red wine at lunchtime, he agreed to go out and drew the great Tom Weiskopf, who had won the Open Championship at Troon earlier that year. Hunt told a sceptical Weiskopf that after a couple of glasses of 'the red infuriator' O'Connor was unbeatable. So it proved; the match was halved.

Hunt has always been a keen student of the game and travelled far and wide in his playing days to improve both his game and his bank balance. In the early Sixties he was a regular visitor to the American circuit during the early part of the year; he would then play the British tournaments and finish up in South America at the end of the year. Although he did not win an event in the USA, he won the Egyptian Open in 1956 and the Brazilian Open in 1962.

Bernard Hunt is now the professional at Foxhills, in Surrey, and thoroughly enjoys the life, especially teaching the game. His swing, as compact and solid as ever, still makes him a force in pro-am and Senior tournaments.

HUNT, GEOFFREY

GB

Born: 28.12.35

Appearances: 1963

Record: P3 W0 L3 H0

When Geoff Hunt joined his well-established older brother, Bernard, in the Ryder Cup team of 1963, they became only the second pair of brothers to appear in the fixture since the famous Whitcombes in the Thirties. Hunt won the last place in the team, selected on a points basis through the season, although he had not been near to winning a tournament.

At the East Lake course in Atlanta, Hunt narrowly lost both his foursomes, with Neil Coles, and his fourball match, with Tom Haliburton. He went out first in the morning singles when the match was virtually in the Americans' pocket, and was out of his class against Tony Lema.

HUNT, GUY

GB

Born: 17.1.47

Appearances: 1975

Record: P3 W0 L2 H1

A small, chunky man, Guy Hunt had climbed to second in the Order of Merit in 1972 and represented England in the World Cup in that year and in 1975. His best win was to be in the Dunlop Masters of 1977.

At Laurel Valley, in Pennsylvania, the match was over by lunchtime on the third day as the USA coasted to victory. It was a familiar story in the Seventies, but at least Guy Hunt had a halved match to remember. In the second series of fourball matches he and Eamonn Darcy held Al Geiberger and Raymond Floyd, but in the afternoon he lost his foursomes with the same partner.

Hunt was out second to last in the singles on the next day and met Tom Weiskopf, whose fire-power was far too heavy for him. With that win, by five and four, the American team had triumphed once again.

Guy Hunt (below)

I

IRWIN, HALE

USA

Born: 3.6.45

Appearances: 1975, 1977, 1979, 1981, 1991

Record: P20 W13 L5 H2

In 1991 at Kiawah Island, Florida, the result of the Ryder Cup fixture depended on the final putts on the final green in the final match. Hale Irwin, grey-faced and exhausted by the tension, watched as his opponent, Bernhard Langer, tried to hole out from a few feet to win their match and secure a tie for only the third time in the history of the famous encounter. He missed and the Cup went back to the USA. Hale Irwin was one of the oldest players in the match but Langer could not have met a tougher opponent.

Irwin has had a remarkable career in golf which encompasses 19 American tour victories, including three US Open triumphs. After attending the University of Colorado, where he revealed his talents for American football as well as golf, he became a professional in 1968. His first win arrived in 1971 at the Heritage Classic, which he won again two years later. It was no coincidence that both these victories were won at the Harbour Town course, a particularly stern test designed by Pete Dye. Irwin's neat and controlled swing, his remarkable consistency with his long irons and his inventive skills with his short irons, especially from a range of a hundred yards and less, are especially suited to such tough courses. In 1974 the US Open was played at Winged Foot, difficult enough anyway but made even more challenging by the US Golf Association. It was tailor-made for Irwin's game and he won the title with a score of 287, seven over par.

Sober of dress and diffident of manner, Hale Irwin looked as anonymous as a computer salesman, especially before he abandoned his large-lensed spectacles in favour of contact lenses. He even described himself, self-deprecatingly, as a plodder on the golf course. Perhaps his golf was unspectacular but he was remarkably consistent between 1971 and 1983: only once did he fail to make the top 20 in the money list and between 1975 and 1978 he played in 86 events without missing the cut. He won a string of tournaments, including the Atlanta Classic, and the Western, Los Angeles, Texas and Buick Opens. In 1974 he won the World Matchplay Championship at Wentworth and retained the title in the following year. In 1976 he only relinquished his grip on the tournament at the 38th hole of the final against David Graham.

In 1979 Irwin won his second US Open Championship at another unrelenting course, Inverness. He was three shots ahead of the field after three rounds and six ahead after ten holes of the final 18 holes. He won at a canter, able to afford the luxury of dropped shots at the final holes.

Irwin's steely disposition, allied to his unbending consistency, was ideally suited to Ryder Cup play and he began with an undefeated sequence at Laurel Valley in 1975. He carried on in a similar vein two years later at Lytham, with wins in both the foursomes and the fourball matches but he suffered his first defeat at the hands of Brian Barnes in the singles. At The Greenbrier in 1979 he dropped just one point out of four and, when he defeated Des Smyth on the last day, secured the point required for an American victory.

Irwin's appearance at Walton Heath in 1981 seemed as if it might be his last in the Ryder Cup. He was as successful as before, with three points won out of four. He admits that his game declined during the latter part of the Eighties, as his interest in his golf course design business grew. He slipped down the money list and was in 93rd place in 1989.

Irwin's exemption into the US Open had lapsed and he was specially invited by the USGA to play in the 1990 Championship at Medinah. At the 72nd hole he scored a birdie with a slippery putt of about 15 yards and forced a play-off with Mike Donald. He raced around the green and punched the air in his exhilaration; at that moment he looked anything but a 45-year-old veteran. After 18 holes the two players were still level but Irwin won at the first sudden-death hole. He became the oldest man to win the US Open and it was his third major championship. In the following week he won the Buick Classic and eventually finished sixth in the money list with over $800,000.

So, at the age of 46, Irwin took his place in the Ryder Cup team again and started with two wins, in company with Lanny Wadkins, in the foursomes. He lost his one fourball match, with Paul Azinger, to Ian Woosnam and Paul Broadhurst, but, such

was his captain's confidence in his quality as a matchplayer, that he was nominated to go out last in the singles as the anchorman. He justified his captain's faith and put the seal on a superb record in the Ryder Cup.

J

JACKLIN, TONY

GB & Europe

Born: 7.7.44

Appearances: 1967, 1969, 1971, 1973, 1975, 1977, 1979
Captain 1983, 1985, 1987, 1989

Record: P35 W13 L14 H8

Tony Jacklin has already had two distinct careers in golf and his successes inspired first British and then European golf to new plateaux of self-confidence and success.

As a player his first major triumph was in the 1967 Dunlop Masters tournament and perhaps it was an omen that in his final round of 64, he had a hole in one, the first to be seen on national television. Jacklin was in his early twenties; he was cocky and self confident and his personality mirrored the brash, egalitarian and assured atmosphere of Britain in the Sixties. Even his bright clothes stood out among the dowdier attire of the rest of the British golfers.

Jacklin had no hang-ups about the supposed superiority of golfers such as Nicklaus and Palmer; with the arrogance of youth, he could not wait to prove himself against them. Like another great champion before him, Henry Cotton, he realised that he had to hone his game in America, and above all that he had to learn how to win in the toughest company before he could hope to claim the greatest prize in golf, the Open Championship. He had played in the Masters at Augusta in 1967, when he had led the field for a short time before finishing in 15th place, and it did not take

Jacklin long to make an impact on his first serious foray on the American tour.

He won the Jacksonville Open in 1968, which was the turning-point of his career, as he proved to himself that he was capable of beating anyone in the world. For four years or so Jacklin certainly retained that self-belief. He struck a golf ball as well as anyone in the world and his self-confidence never wavered. In 1969 he arrived at Lytham for the Open Championship with the hopes of Britain's golf fans resting on him. A British golfer had not held the old claret jug aloft in triumph since Max Faulkner in 1951. Strengthened in the fierce arena of American golf, Jacklin's knees did not buckle under the weight of his supporters' expectations. After three rounds he was two strokes ahead of the 1963 champion, Bob Charles. Memories of him on that final day remain: of his purple outfit; of his powerful swing, unfaltering in its rhythm; of several adept bunker shots by which he preserved his lead; finally of his towering drive down the final hole and a smooth 7-iron to within a few yards of the flag.

The champion, for whom the British public had longed, was at last in their midst. In the following year, he confirmed his stature by leading the US Open from start to finish to win the title by seven shots, the widest margin since Jim Barnes's victory in 1921. The conditions at Hazeltine were extremely testing, especially on the first day. Arnold Palmer scored 79, Gary Player 80 and Jack Nicklaus 81. Dave Hill, who eventually finished in second place, called the course 'a cow pasture' and was fined by the USGA. But Jacklin just got on with it – to telling effect. Not since Ted Ray in 1920 had a British player won the US Open and for a few weeks Jacklin was in possession of both Open titles.

At St Andrews in 1970 he began his defence of the Open with unparalleled brilliance. He covered the first nine holes in 29 shots and birdied the tenth hole. It seemed that an astonishingly low score was in his grasp. But the golfing Fates, perhaps offended by Jacklin's presumption, decreed otherwise. A thunderstorm forced the abandonment of play just as he hit his second shot at the 14th hole into a gorse bush. In the morning, the inspiration had whistled away on the wind and he finished in 67 and eventually came fifth.

Jacklin began his long Ryder Cup career in 1967, at Houston. The British team were heavily defeated but the ebullient young golfer, teamed with the powerful and experienced Dave Thomas, won his first two foursomes games easily. The pair gained one half in their fourballs but Jacklin lost his singles games to Arnold Palmer and Gardner Dickinson.

Two years later, at Birkdale, he was to have a singular effect on the fixture. Jacklin was the Open champion and had signalled a renaissance in the British game. This confidence spilled over into the Ryder Cup team, where it was reinforced by the unbending and truculent spirit of the captain, Eric Brown, who had won all his singles matches in the biennial fixture. There were other young men in the team, too, who sought to emulate Tony Jacklin and who were certainly not in awe of the Americans: Bernard Gallacher, Peter Townsend, Brian Barnes and Maurice Bembridge.

Jacklin and Townsend at once fired the British team's enthusiasm by winning both their foursomes games. They began with three birdies against Dave Hill and Tommy Aaron and never looked back. Nobody will ever forget Townsend's soaring 3-wood to the 17th green. It finished about six feet from the hole and was knocked in for an eagle by Jacklin, to sink the American pair. In the fourballs Jacklin teamed up with Neil Coles and only dropped half a point and, on the nerve-wracked final day, defeated Jack Nicklaus in the first series of singles.

In the end the result of the 1969 Ryder Cup depended on those two golfers who were drawn together in the final singles match. Jacklin had holed a very long putt on the 17th green for an eagle to draw level with Nicklaus, and the match was also level at fifteen and a half points to each side. Both men hit their drives down the 18th fairway and, as they moved off in pursuit, Nicklaus broke the tension by asking his opponent how he felt. 'Petrified' was Jacklin's reply and the great American confessed that he felt exactly the same. Jacklin putted first and left his ball about two feet short of the cup. Nicklaus went boldly for the winning putt but went three or four feet past. He holed his tricky putt back and then, in a

Seve Ballesteros and Tony Jacklin, the architects of Europe's success in the 1980s

gesture which encapsulated the honourable spirit in which Ryder Cup golf should be played, conceded Jacklin's putt for a half. Nicklaus told Jacklin: 'I was sure that you would hole the putt, but I was not prepared to see you miss.' It was a supreme moment in golf and ensured the first tied match in Ryder Cup history.

Two years later the British team were again captained by Eric Brown and were just as buoyant. They lost the fixture by a margin of five points in St Louis but performed admirably, even if Jacklin only won one and a half points; both his singles were lost by one hole to Jesse Snead and Lee Trevino.

Tony Jacklin had become a sporting superstar. He endorsed a wide variety of products; he commanded appearance money in tournaments around the world; he was in demand for personal appearances and he even made a pop record. He was winning tournaments, too: the Wills, the Lancome Trophy, the Benson & Hedges and the PGA Close tournaments and the Jacksonville Open (for the second time) were won by him in 1971 and 1972. Above all, Jacklin's talents had revived British golf and John Jacobs, who was now the PGA Tournament Director, was shrewd enough to realise that such a player could provide the impetus for a huge expansion of European golf. sponsors will always pay a lot more for a star; and so it proved.

He should have won the Open again in 1972, at Muirfield, but the portly figure of Lee Trevino intervened. The wisecracking Mexican could hardly be termed a dark avenger but he certainly became Jacklin's nemesis. Jacklin might have been a few shots clear of him by the end of the third round, but he finished with five birdies, which included a holed bunker shot and a holed chip shot. At the 71st hole Trevino was in trouble all the way and finally hacked his ball to the back of the green in four, whereas Jacklin was on the green in three. He watched in amazement as Trevino strode up to his ball, hardly bothered to line up the shot and then chipped it into the hole. Jacklin, sitting on the edge of the green, covered his face in anguish. It seemed inevitable that he would take three putts and that Trevino would win his second Open Championship.

A few months later Trevino struck again in the semi-final of the World Matchplay Championship at Wentworth. In one of the great matches he beat Jacklin on the 36th green.

It seemed that his ill luck at Muirfield knocked the stuffing out of Tony Jacklin. Certainly he never threatened again to win a major championship. His brilliance became tarnished by self-doubt, sometimes expressed in querulous terms. He became more and more at odds with his putter and tried all sorts of remedies to revive his game: even the scientologists were consulted at one stage. Nevertheless, he was capable of competing effectively at the highest level. In 1977 he finished well in the Tucson Open and was the runner-up to Tom Watson in

the Bing Crosby tournament at Pebble Beach. He won the German Open in 1979 and the PGA Championship in 1982, chased all the way on both occasions by Bernhard Langer.

He was more than good enough to keep his place in the Ryder Cup, too, even if he seemed at times fatalistic about Britain's chances. At Muirfield in 1973 he teamed up with Peter Oosterhuis and won three and a half points out of six; and two years later won two and a half points. The match at Lytham in 1977 saw him at a low ebb under Brian Huggett's captaincy. He was dropped for the singles matches and in Jacklin's opinion it was an argument between the two men on the second afternoon of the fixture that ensured his exclusion from the final day's play. Other experienced players, such as Brian Barnes and Peter Oosterhuis, have opined that Huggett's decision was ill-judged, since Jacklin's great pride would have guaranteed a good performance in the singles, especially at Lytham, where he had won the Open.

Tony Jacklin made one more appearance in the Ryder Cup two years later at The Greenbrier and was bitterly upset when he was passed over in 1981 in favour of Mark James. At this point he had undoubtedly lost all interest in the Ryder Cup, just as had Severiano Ballesteros, who had also been excluded from the team following his disputes over appearance money earlier that season.

But, fortunately for Jacklin and for European golf, his career was to be linked yet again with the Ryder Cup. It was an imaginative decision to approach him to captain the 1983 team and it fell to Ken Schofield, the executive director of the PGA tour, to do so. Jacklin eventually agreed to take on the task, but only if certain conditions were met. In essence, the team had to 'go first class' in every meaning of the word: travel, clothes, accommodation, equipment. Never again must the players go to the first tee feeling inferior. Jacklin got everything for which he asked.

Above all, he had to get Ballesteros, one of the best golfers in the world but an extremely stubborn man who felt he had been treated badly by the PGA tour. The Spaniard had no interest in the Ryder Cup. Jacklin talked and talked to him, especially during the Open at Birkdale. The eggs and bacon in the breakfast room of the Prince of Wales Hotel grew cold as the two men argued. Ballesteros finally agreed to support the Ryder Cup team, and his genius and fire became a crucial factor in Europe's success.

In 1983 Jacklin's heroes came within a couple of putts of beating the Americans on their own turf for the first time. In 1987 they did so, after regaining the cup at the Belfry in 1985. Two years later one of the great Ryder Cup encounters ended in a tie. Jacklin had once again experienced wonderful success and in the process he had rejuvenated his own career in golf.

Tony Jacklin has been fortunate enough to be in the forefront of two notable expansions of golf. His great talents as a golfer set off the boom in British golf in the Seventies; in the Eighties he was able to weld together the diverse personalities of stars such as Ballesteros, Lyle, Faldo, Woosnam and Olazabal to demonstrate that the best European golfers were at the very least the equal of their American counterparts.

JACOBS, JOHN

GB

Born: 14.3.25

Appearances: 1955
Captain 1979, 1981

Record: P2 W2 L0 H0

It was singularly appropriate that John Jacobs was captain of the Ryder Cup team in 1979, when European golfers were first made eligible for selection. He was ever an intelligent and progressive administrator who was poised to direct a new course for the Ryder Cup matches, a course that was to resurrect the fixture after years of American domination.

By then, Jacobs was popularly known as 'Dr Golf', an eminent teacher of the game. He had also been the Tournament Director of the PGA from 1971 to 1975 and had had a profound influence on the future of professional golf in Europe.

In the Fifties and early Sixties, Jacobs had been an accomplished player and Tony Jacklin recalls how he, as a very young tournament professional, had admired his swing and in particular his rhythm. Although Jacobs had never won a significant tournament in Britain, in 1957 he won the Dutch Open and beat Gary Player in the final of the South African Matchplay Championship.

In the Ryder Cup he had a perfect record: played two, won two. The tie was at Thunderbird Ranch, Palm Springs, and on the first day Jacobs went out with Johnny Fallon in a foursomes against Chandler Harper and Jerry Barber. It was one of the most thrilling matches in the history of the Ryder Cup. Barber chipped in several times but the British pair won on the last green. In the singles, Jacobs drew Cary Middlecoff, the US Masters champion. It was another thriller, with Jacobs two down after 18 holes, and level after 27. It all came down to a very nasty putt on the final green, which Jacobs holed to win. In his morning round he had broken 70, and in the afternoon he had scored a 65.

In the Sixties John Jacobs became a willing victim of his great skills as a teacher and eventually devoted himself to this aspect of golf. He set up a chain of golf centres and coached many individuals and teams, including the victorious Walker Cup side of 1971. His was a familiar figure on the practice ground at major tournaments, just like David Leadbetter and Bob Torrance today. He was a regular television commentator; he made several excellent instructional videos; and his *Practical Golf*, published in 1972, is one of the best instructional books ever written. It is still in print.

John Jacobs has been a very influential figure in British professional golf and was a popular choice as captain of the Ryder Cup teams of 1979 and 1981.

JACOBS, TOMMY

USA

Born: 13.2.35

Appearances: 1965

Record: P4 W3 L1 H0

Tommy Jacobs was one of those consistent golfers who was able to grind out a comfortable living on the American tour. His best years were certainly in the mid-Sixties. He was the runner-up to Ken Venturi in the 1964 US Open and in the process set a record score of 64 in the second round. In the Masters of 1966 he came second again after a play-off with Gay Brewer and Jack Nicklaus.

Jacobs had a splendid Ryder Cup at Birkdale in 1965, with three wins out of four. He and Don January teamed up to beat Dave Thomas and George Will twice in one day in the fourball matches. Jacobs then defeated Dave Thomas, who must have been sick of the sight of him, in the first series of singles. He lost his final match to Lionel Platts, although the American team had by then already retained the Cup.

JACOBSEN, PETER

USA

Born: 4.3.54

Appearances: 1985

Record: P3 W1 L2 H0

A tall man with a powerful swing, Peter Jacobsen's best year on the American tour was in 1984 when he won two tournaments and finished in tenth position on the money list. This won him a place in the Ryder Cup team which lost to Europe at the Belfry in the following year. He lost his fourball match to Ballesteros and Pinero and his singles to Sandy Lyle but he won one point, with Curtis Strange, by defeating Paul Way and Ian Woosnam in a foursomes.

A ruptured disc in his back interrupted Jacobsen's progress in 1985 but he returned to form in 1988 when he was second in the Western Open and in two other events. In 1990 he won the Bob Hope Classic. He is capable of inspired sequences of scoring, as when he achieved seven 3s in succession during a final round of 64 in the US Open at Brookline in 1988.

Known for his mickey-taking impersonations of the superstars' golf swings, Jacobsen is a regular visitor to the Open in Britain, and finished in 64th position on the American money list in 1991 with just over $250,000.

JAMES, MARK

GB & Europe

Born: 28.10.53

Appearances: 1977, 1979, 1981, 1989, 1991

Record: P19 W7 L11 H1

After an impressive amateur career during which he won the English Amateur Championship and played in the Walker Cup in 1975, Mark James made the change to the professional ranks with great assurance. In his first season, in 1976, he finished fifth in the Open championship, mainly due to a courageous final round of 66; he was second in the Benson & Hedges Festival and ended the year in 15th place in the Order of Merit.

In his decade and a half on the European tour James has won 14 tournaments, including the PGA Matchplay Championship, the Irish Open (twice), the Italian, Spanish and English Opens and the British Masters. It is an impressive list and explains why James has rarely been outside the top 20 on the tour. In addition to his high finish in 1976, he has performed well in the Open on two other occasions: he was fourth in 1979 and equal third in 1981.

As he walks along the fairways, his shoulders slumped as if in terminal despair, or as he grimaces painfully after hitting a shot, nobody would guess that James actually enjoys his golf (apart from his putting, which he claims is below average for a professional); nor would a spectator imagine that he is well liked by the other players and has a reputation as a humorist, even if the flavour of the humour is dry. James has had several brushes with the golf authorities but it now quite a pillar of the establishment in his role as a director of the European tour.

He made his debut in the Ryder Cup only a year after turning professional and had a very tough baptism. At Lytham in 1977 he lost all his matches and two years later, at The Greenbrier, lost his only match, a fourball to Fuzzy Zoeller and Lee Trevino. He then withdrew from the match through injury but not before his and Ken Brown's immature behaviour had alienated the rest of the team. On his return to Britain James was fined £1,500 by the PGA.

In view of this, it was surprising that he was a special selection for the 1981 team at Walton Heath; even more so when it was a direct choice between him and Tony Jacklin. But at last James registered a victory; he and Sandy Lyle won both their matches on the opening day, and they played exciting golf in the process. When they beat Ben Crenshaw and Jerry Pate on the 16th green in their fourball the European pair were eight under par. It was a false dawn, since Europe were comprehensively beaten by the USA and James lost his next three games.

James had hardly justified his reputation as an accomplished matchplayer in his first three appearances in the Ryder Cup; he won a mere two points out of nine. But when he returned to the fray at the Belfry in 1989, a more mature golfer, he at last showed his mettle and his three wins were vital to the European cause. He and Howard Clark lost their opening foursomes to Lanny Wadkins and Payne Stewart but they won their next two games. In the heat of the battle on the final day James beat Mark

O'Meara convincingly.

Two years later, at Kiawah Island, James was once again a wild card selection and he formed a very effective partnership with Steven Richardson. They won both their fourball games and it was only Richardson's missed putt of a few feet on the final green that deprived the British pair of a half in their foursomes. In the singles James never got to grips with Wadkins and lost on the 16th green.

James's unorthodox and highly effective swing will be seen on the fairways of Europe for many years to come and he is recognised as a particularly tough opponent in a tight finish to a tournament.

JANUARY, DON

USA

Born: 20.11.29

Appearances: 1965, 1977

Record: P7 W2 L3 H2

His appearances in Ryder Cup ties 12 years apart paid testimony to Don January's stamina and discipline as a top tournament golfer. As early as 1956 he won the Dallas Open and 20 years later he won his last US tour event, the Tournament of Champions. His success continued on the American Seniors tour as he notched up over 20 victories during the 1980s; he finished 28th on the Senior money list in 1991.

He began his roll of victories in great style at the 1956 Dallas Open when he holed a bunker shot for an eagle on the 72nd hole; and in 1961 he won $50,000 for a hole in one, an astonishing sum of money for the time.

Don January won a major title in 1967, the USPGA Championship, and was a runner-up on two other occasions. Some idea of his consistency may be gained by his record in 1971 when he played in 22 American tournaments; five times he finished in the top five and eight times in the top ten.

In his first Ryder Cup appearance, at Birkdale in 1965, his balance was just in credit, with two and a half points won against two lost. Twelve years later and at the age of 47, he halved his foursomes match (with Ed Sneed) against Tony Jacklin and Eammon Darcy but was easily beaten in the singles by Peter Dawson.

JARMAN, EDWARD

GB

Born: 2.7.07

Appearances: 1935

Record: P1 W0 L1 H0

Edward William George Jarman had two highly successful golfing years in 1934 and 1935. He had several high finishes, including eighth place in both the Open and the Irish Open.

He was selected for the match at Ridgewood, New Jersey when a strong American team easily defeated Britain. In his one foursomes match, Jarman, partnered by Bill Cox, was heavily defeated nine and eight by Horton Smith and Paul Runyan.

JOLLY, HERBERT

GB

Born: 8.1.95

Appearances: 1927

Record: P2 W0 L2 H0

Herbert Jolly was one of several fine golfers who were born in the Channel Isles. He survived his stint as an infantryman in the trenches of the First World War and then resumed his career in golf. Although he reached the semi finals of the PGA Matchplay Championship in 1928, his most notable feat was to beat the mighty Walter Hagen in the *Yorkshire Evening News* Matchplay Tournament of 1923. He won the event again in 1930.

Although Jolly played in the 1926 match which is regarded as the forerunner of the Ryder Cup and won both his games, he was a late substitute for the inaugural match of 1927. He replaced the captain, Abe Mitchell, who was ill, and sailed to New York on the *Majestic* four days after the rest of the British team.

Paired with Arthur Havers in the foursomes, he lost to Gene Sarazen and Al Watrous, who were hardly pressed since they were well over par when they won; and he was heavily defeated by Johnny Golden in the singles. After the match Jolly said good-humouredly: 'He holed out from all over the place; I putted beautifully to where the hole wasn't.'

K

KEISER, HERMAN

USA

Born: 7.10.14

Appearances: 1947

Record: P1 W0 L1 H0

The Masters Tournament was resumed, after the war, at Augusta in 1946. At the final hole the great Ben Hogan had a putt of around 12 feet to win the event. With an uncharacteristic lapse, which was perhaps a portent of his future putting problems, he took three putts and Herman Keiser was the unheralded Master golfer.

Keiser had played professional golf before the war. He had won the Iowa Open in 1939 and was to win several events in the late Forties and early Fifties. After doing his time with the American Navy he resumed his career with his notable victory in the Masters, to which he owed his selection for the Ryder Cup fixture at Portland, Oregon, in 1947.

It was almost a whitewash of the British, but Sam King rescued one point for Britain in the final singles match – and his victim was Herman Keiser.

KING, MICHAEL

Europe

Born: 15.2.50

Appearances: 1979

Record: P1 W0 L1 H0

After attending Millfield School, Michael King had a successful career in amateur golf and played for England on several occasions. He tied for first place in the Lytham Trophy in 1973 and played in the Walker Cup in 1969 and 1973.

King became a professional in 1974 and his only important victory was in the Tournament Players Championship in 1979. In that year, he won a place in the Ryder Cup team to play at The Greenbrier in West Virginia. He lost his one match to Andy Bean by four and three. He represented England in the World Cup in the same year.

KING, SAM

GB

Born: 27.3.11

Appearances: 1937, 1947, 1949

Record: P5 W1 L3 H1

Sam King counts himself a lucky man to have lived all his long life in Knole Park, Kent. He talks with as much enthusiasm of his rural surroundings as he does of golf, and remembers with real sadness the hundreds of trees that were lost in the great storms of 1987.

King's father and grandfather were charcoal burners on the Knole Park estate when it was owned by Lord Sackville but his family had golfing connections. Their pony used to pull the mowers along the fairways of the Wildernesse Club and the young Sam used to ride it back on the way home from school; and during the First World War his sister was a greenkeeper at the club. He picked the game up 'on the village green' and by caddying at the Wildernesse.

King first announced his golfing presence by winning the Kent Professional Championship in 1932 and played in the Open at Prince's, Sandwich, in the same year. In 1936 he was the runner-up to Alf Padgham in the *Daily Mail* tournament and won it in the following year at Little Aston. This was not only an important victory financially, since the first prize was £500, but it secured King's place in the Ryder Cup at Southport.

He was not selected for the foursomes but drew Densmore Shute, a former Open champion, in the singles. He still remembers vividly that he was so nervous that he had to be urged towards the first tee by Commander Roe. He was not normally nervous in tournaments, not even in the Open, but the Ryder Cup was quite a different matter. At lunchtime he was level with the American champion, lost four holes soon after but reduced the arrears to be one down on the 36th tee. He managed to hole a downhill putt of about ten feet for a birdie to halve the match. Sam King recalls that he 'never thought about missing it'. He was brimful of youthful confidence.

The next golfing encounter between the nations was in 1947 at Portland, Oregon, when the British team suffered their worst-ever defeat, by 11 matches to one. Sam King was the anchorman in the singles and saved the British team's blushes by beating Herman Keiser. With typical modesty King recalled that the course was inundated with rain and that Keiser did not like the conditions. Two years later, at Ganton, the Americans won again. In the foursomes King and Charlie Ward lost to Jimmy Demaret and Clayton Heafner, who finished the British pair off with five birdies in the course of seven holes in the afternoon. In the singles King met Chick Harbert, who was known as a very powerful but erratic player. But there was very little wildness apparent, as he scored 68 in the morning and eventually won by four and three.

Sam King was one of the most consistent British professionals and had a splendid record in the Open Championship. In 1939 he was equal third at St Andrews and, when the tournament resumed in 1946, he finished in the top ten on seven occasions up to 1954. He also reached the semi-final of the prestigious PGA Matchplay Championship three times. His last important victories were in the British Seniors event in 1961 and 1962; but he lost both his matches with his American Seniors counterpart, Paul Runyan.

King remained as the professional at his beloved Knole Park until 1976 and still visits the club each day.

KITE, TOM

USA

Born: 9.12.49

Appearances: 1979, 1981, 1983, 1985, 1987, 1989

Record: P24 W13 L7 H4

Tom Kite is one of the money machines of American golf: he has won over $7 million in official earnings. For much of his career the question has been posed, more and more pointedly, of whether he would win a major championship. At Pebble Beach, in June, 1992, Kite at last answered that question by winning the US Open in fine style. He had had several previous chances in the big events: in 1978 he was second to Jack Nicklaus in the Open championship at St Andrews; and he has been the runner-up in the Masters twice, to Ballesteros in 1983 and to Nicklaus in 1986, when Kite's putt on the final green to force a play-off was as close as a whisper. Above all, Kite should have won the US Open at Oak Hill in 1989. He was in the lead after three rounds but was then unseated by the shadowy shapes of glory that beckoned to him. His repeated errors handed the championship to Curtis Strange.

Kite became a professional golfer in 1972 after representing his country in the Walker Cup in the previous year. He got into his stride quickly and from 1975 to 1990 his consistency ensured that he was always in the top 35 on the money list; in 1981 and 1989 he was the leader and has won more money than anyone on the American tour. He has 16 tournament victories to his name, including the Bay Hill Classic, the Doral Open, Tournament of Champions, Western Open, Kemper Open and the Tournament Players Championship. In 1981 he played in 26 events and finished in the top ten on 21 occasions; by the end of 1990 he had finished in the top ten of the four major championships on 19 occasions. In 1992 he found the last piece of the mysterious jigsaw that makes a champion golfer.

Kite has an excellent record in the Ryder Cup and has never lost a singles. He began at The Greenbrier in 1979 when he won three points out of four. His first two results must have rocked his ordered golfing world; in his first foursomes, he and Hale Irwin routed Des Smyth and a disaffected Ken Brown by seven and six, but he and Andy Bean were clinically dispatched in the second foursomes by Nick Faldo and Peter Oosterhuis. The British pair were six holes up at the turn and maintained their lead to win on the 13th green.

Kite is capable of inspired sequences of scoring, as he

showed at Walton Health in 1981. He won four and a half points out of five and his singles match against Sandy Lyle is still recalled with awe. Both players were six under par and level after 11 holes. But Kite found another reserve of brilliance and won the game on the 16th green; he was ten under par by then.

During the years of Europe's successes in the Ryder Cup, Kite in his turn suffered unexpected reverses. In 1983, at the PGA National, he came to the final hole one up on Sam Torrance but the Scot's birdie levelled the match; two years later, at the Belfry, Kite was three holes up on Ballesteros with five to play but the dashing Spaniard managed to halve the match. In the 1987 and 1989 matches Kite's potentially potent partnership with Curtis Strange failed to take wing. They won two foursomes matches at Muirfield Village but lost a fourball match to the Spaniards, Ballesteros and Olazabal, and were hounded to defeat by Ian Woosnam and Nick Faldo in their second fourball. The British pair were five holes up at the turn with a better ball score of 29 and never relaxed their grip. At the Belfry in 1989 Kite and Strange halved their foursomes with Faldo and Woosnam, but again lost to the Spaniards. Nevertheless, Kite won his singles against Sandy Lyle in 1987 and humiliated Howard Clark at the Belfry by the record margin of eight and seven.

Although Tom Kite had a modest year in 1991 and finished in 39th position on the money list, it would be no surprise to see him in the American Ryder Cup team at the Belfry in 1993.

KROLL, TED

USA

Born: 4.8.19

Appearances: 1953, 1955, 1957

Record: P4 W3 L1 H0

Ted Kroll probably thanked his stars that he was able to play golf at all. He was wounded on four occasions during the Second World War, during which he served as a sergeant in the US Army.

In the Ryder Cup he was a highly successful foursomes player; in the company of Jack Burke (twice) and Doug Ford he won all his matches. But he was overwhelmed by Fred Daly in their 1953 singles match at Wentworth. His captain in the match two years later, Chick Harbert, obviously remembered this because he did not invite Kroll to participate in the singles. He was forgiven by 1957 and was down to play Peter Mills, but withdrew because of illness.

Kroll's best finishes in major tournaments were as a runner-up in the USPGA championship in 1956 and equal second in the US Open of 1960. He won seven tournaments on the American circuit during the Fifties, including the San Diego, Tucson and Houston Opens, and the lucrative World Championship of Golf. His final victory was in the 1962 Canadian Open. For several years his score of 60 in the 1954 Texas Open was a record for 18 holes.

In his later years, Ted Kroll gained a high reputation as a 'golf doctor', a man to whom the other professionals turned to diagnose their swing faults.

L

LACEY, ARTHUR

GB

Born: 20.5.04

Appearances: 1933, 1937
Captain 1951

Record: P3 W0 L3 H0

A cheerful man with a strong physique, Arthur Lacey was described by Dai Rees as 'a large chap, with the bluff geniality and strength of a yeoman farmer'.

He learned his golf at Burnham Beeches and had some considerable successes in the 1930s. He won the Belgian Open twice, the French Open, was a semi-finalist in the *News of the World* Matchplay Championship twice, and finished sixth in the Open in 1937.

Arthur Lacey adopted a very wide stance and lashed into the ball very hard and very late. It was not a pretty style, but he propelled the ball great distances and was capable of some inspired, if sometimes erratic, golf. He lost all three of his Ryder Cup matches, albeit by narrow margins; and his two singles defeats were at the hands of two of the great American players of their time, Walter Hagen and Henry Picard.

Lacey was appointed captain in 1951 when Britain was defeated at Pinehurst. It was here that he met his future wife and he eventually went to live in the USA.

LAFFOON, KY

USA

Born: 23.12.08

Appearances: 1935

Record: P1 W0 L1 H0

A man who ties his putter to the rear bumper of his car and drags it all the way to the next tournament 'to teach it a lesson' might be termed eccentric; and a man who angrily breaks his putter by smashing it against his foot but in the process breaks his own toe might be described as colourful (and unlucky). Such a man was Ky Laffoon, a brilliant and erratic golfer who had a career which stretched from 1931 to 1951 but who was at his best in the 1930s. He started his career in golf by caddying for the legendary hustler, Titanic Thompson, whose favourite line to a victim was: 'Hell, my caddie could beat you.' And Ky Laffoon could.

Laffoon won four tournaments in 1934 and reached the semi-finals of the USPGA championship in 1937. In the US Open of 1936 he was tied for the lead with Tony Manero after three rounds but declined into fifth place. In the late Forties, Laffoon was still good enough to finish fourth in the Masters and runner up in the Canadian Open. He won his last official PGA event, the Montgomery Invitational, in 1946.

He had a magnificent short game and was deadly with his shots from just off the green. Despite his propensity for fits of bad temper, Laffoon could concentrate very well and was capable of brilliant bursts of low-scoring golf. In the Thirties he was the first professional golfer to go through the season with a stroke average per round of below 70.

Laffoon had a loop in his swing, chewed tobacco and throughout his career went along with story that he was partly of Red Indian descent. It was untrue, despite his high cheek-bones and sun-tanned complexion, but he thought it was good for publicity. He was certainly one of the characters of the American golf scene and he was highly conscious of his status as a top professional golfer. He scratched from the Western Open once because the car park was too far from the clubhouse.

He only played one Ryder Cup match and with his partner, Olin Dutra, lost his foursomes in 1935 to the Whitcombe brothers, Charlie and Ernie.

LANGER, BERNHARD

Europe

Born: 27.8.57

Appearances: 1981, 1983, 1985, 1987, 1989, 1991

Record: P25 W11 L9 H5

The result of the 1991 Ryder Cup hinged on the final putt in the final match on the final green. It was ironic that the European attempting the fateful putt was Bernhard Langer, who had already suffered the yips, that chronic inability to hole even the simplest of short putts, several times in his career. Yet, paradoxically, he was the player whom most of the European team would have nominated to hole that critical putt. Such is Langer's strength of mind that he has overcome his problem and has made himself into one of the best putters in the world. Henry Longhurst once wrote an article about the yips in which he maintained that 'once you've had 'em, you've got 'em' but Langer has proved him wrong. Langer missed his putt at Kiawah Island and the halved match with Hale Irwin ensured that the Ryder Cup went back to the American team; but he had already holed difficult putts on the three previous greens to keep his match and the European team's hopes alight.

Langer, the son of a Czechoslavakian refugee who settled in Bavaria, learned his golf by caddying at the course at Augsburg. His dedicated regime

of practice made him into the best golfer in Germany by the time he was 17, and two years later he joined the European circuit when his troubles on the greens were already afflicting him. His tortured putting stroke was so unnerving that his partners used to avert their eyes in case they too caught the disease. He putted left handed for a while but eventually developed an efficient and conventional stroke.

Langer's first important victory came in the World Under-25 Championship in 1979; he won the event by the extraordinary margin of 17 shots. A year later he became the first German to win a European tour event when he came first in the Dunlop Masters. Langer finished ninth in the Order of Merit and first in 1981 when he won two tournaments, including the German Open.

In the 1981 Ryder Cup at Walton Heath, Langer made a muted debut with only one and a half points from four games but, in the very close encounter two years later at the PGA National, he and Nick Faldo formed a tenacious partnership and won three matches out of four. Langer also defeated Gil Morgan in his singles.

By this time Langer had managed to conquer the yips for the second time. On the shorter putts he switched to a cross-handed grip with the left hand below the right. His method worked; in the three years from 1982 to 1985 he won the German Open twice more and the Italian, French, Dutch, Colombian, Irish, Spanish and European Opens, and the Australian Masters. Above all he won his first major championship, the Masters, and showed just how well he could putt by taking no more than two putts throughout a tournament which is played on the fastest greens in professional golf. It was an astonishing display which confirmed him as one of the most prominent golfers in the world. In the week after the Masters he won the Heritage Classic.

Langer played a crucial part in Europe's two triumphs in the Ryder Cup in 1985 and 1987. At the Belfry he won three points from five games and, with Sandy Lyle, managed to inflict some severe psychological damage on the American team. In their fourball against Strange and Stadler on the Saturday morning the Europeans were two down with two to play. Lyle eagled the 17th hole to reduce the deficit and Stadler missed a tiny putt on the final green to allow Langer and Lyle to escape with half a point. The damage was partly self-inflicted, which may explain why the balance of the Ryder Cup match swung markedly in Europe's favour. Langer outclassed Hal Sutton in the singles as Europe won a great victory.

Two years later, at Muirfield Village, Langer and Lyle won three matches in a row, two of them against the staunch American pair of Wadkins and Nelson, with whom Langer later halved his singles. In 1989, at the Belfry, Langer's game was not at its best and he suffered three defeats in the tied match.

Throughout the Eighties, Langer added to his victories on the European tour and was rarely out of the top ten of the Order of Merit. When he won the PGA Championship at Wentworth in 1987 Severiano Ballesteros said that during that week Langer had probably played the game as well as it could be played. At the same time he was playing regularly in the USA and was 13th on their money list in 1985, tenth in 1986 and 23rd in 1987. He has won over $1.5 million on the American tour.

Langer had to overcome a third attack of the yips, which struck him down as he defended his PGA title in 1988. He now adopts a curious style, his right hand clamping the shaft of the putter to his left forearm. Once again he found a solution to his problems and proved it by finishing fourth in the European Order of Merit in 1990 and third in 1991. He won the Madrid and the Austrian Opens, the Benson & Hedges International and the German Masters. In 1990 he and Torsten Giedeon won the World Cup for Germany for the first time.

Langer has many virtues: he practises as intensely as anyone in professional golf and is one of the best iron players in the game; his methodical and unhurried approach is another of his strengths. But perhaps he should hurry a bit more: he is known as one of the slowest players on the circuit. A dedicated Christian, Langer leads Christians on Tour, a group of players and their wives who meet regularly for prayers and discussions.

No doubt all these factors helped Langer as he assessed his putt on the final green at Kiawah Island in 1991; even more, they would have helped him after he missed it. A lesser person might have been irrevocably harmed by the glaring publicity which attended the aftermath of his fateful putt. Bernhard Langer focused his attention on the following week's tournament, the German Masters. He won it.

LEES, ARTHUR

GB

Born: 21.2.08

Appearances: 1947, 1949, 1951, 1955

Record: P8 W4 L4 H0

Arthur Lees was one of the foremost professionals in Britain for a decade or so after the Second World War. He won the Dunlop Masters in 1947, the Penfold tournament in 1951 and 1953 and several other events, including the British Seniors in 1959.

From a wide and solid stance his swing was short and very dependable, and his short game was superb. For many years he was the professional at Sunningdale and the tales of his prowess around that delightful course, especially when high stakes had been wagered, are legendary. Lees was a brilliant putter and once, when he missed a putt of about 30 feet, he inspected his ball closely. 'I thought so, the bugger isn't round,' he said and hurled it into the nearest bush.

His qualities as a matchplayer were never in doubt, as his record in the Ryder Cup demonstrated. Although he lost both his games in 1947, at Portland, so did everyone else except Sam King, who alone saved Britain from a whitewash. Lees and Henry Cotton were put to the sword in the opening foursomes, ten and nine, by Porky Oliver and Lew Worsham. Two years later Lees won his first point in the series at Ganton when he and Dick Burton defeated the toughest of the American pairs, Sam Snead and Lloyd Mangrum.

Arthur Lees was at his doughtiest at Pinehurst in 1951 when he won both his matches. He and Charlie Ward defeated Oliver and Ransom in the foursomes and then Lees triumphed again over Oliver in their singles game.

His final appearance was in

Arthur Lees (above)

1955, at Thunderbird Ranch, California. Paired with Harry Weetman, he fought a stern battle with Jack Burke and Tommy Bolt. The golf was exceptional. The British pair went round in 68 in the morning but were only one hole up; out in 34 in the afternoon they had not improved their position and the Americans struck back to be one up in their turn on the 36th tee. Harry Weetman holed a marvellous putt for a birdie, but Burke followed him in to win the match. But the determined battler, Lees, finished in fine style by beating Marty Furgol in the singles.

LEMA, TONY

USA

Born: 25.2.34

Appearances: 1963, 1965

Record: P11 W8 L1 H2

By virtue of his victory in the Open championship at St Andrews in 1964, Tony Lema has a special place in golfing history. It was not just the brilliance of his victory, five shots ahead of the menacing Jack Nicklaus, but also the fact that he had never played golf in Europe before, let alone on a links course, and had left himself only enough time for one complete practice round. Lema borrowed Arnold Palmer's caddie, Tip Anderson, for the championship and claimed, with typical modesty, that he just hit the ball where his caddie indicated. He started with an excellent 73 in very windy conditions and played superbly on the second day for a score of 68. Lema was driving beautifully and putting just as well.

On the final day, when two rounds were played, Lema began poorly and, when he and Nicklaus coincided on the huge double green that accommodates both the 6th and 12th hole, he learned that the 'Golden Bear', who had been nine shots behind, was now only one behind. Many a player would have collapsed at that point but Lema played the next five holes in 15 shots and recorded a total of 68 for the third round. His score of 70 in the afternoon saw him home at a canter.

Tony Lema's father, a labourer of Portuguese descent, had died when the boy was 3 years old and he had undergone a tough upbringing in Oakland, California. As a boy he caddied on the local course and later enlisted as a Marine and fought in the Korean War.

He became a professional golfer in 1958 and endured several disappointing seasons before he won his first tournament, in Orange County in 1962. He treated the assembled golfing journalists to champagne and the label, 'Champagne' Tony, stuck with him throughout his career. It was certainly appropriate because Lema was an ebullient and relaxed man, tall and handsome, who, whatever the state of his finances, lived in style. As he said to the assembled journalists at St Andrews in 1964: 'I think right now I'm third in money winning and first in money spending.' He was a latter-day Walter Hagen in more ways than one.

Lema won another tournament in 1962 and was second to Jack Nicklaus in the Masters in the following year, in which he finished fourth on the US tour's money list. The next two years saw his great talent ripen and blossom as he won the Open Championship, the World Series and the Carling Tournament. He made a marvellous defence of his Open title at Birkdale in 1965, but faded in the final round and was

overtaken by Peter Thomson. In that year Lema was involved in a remarkable match in the World Matchplay Championship at Wentworth. He was 7 holes up on Gary Player on the 20th tee but eventually lost on the 37th green. Lema took the setback with the dignity and good humour which endeared him to golf fans wherever he played.

He played in two Ryder Cup matches and has one of the best records, with eight wins and only one defeat in eleven games. It is curious to note that six of the results were by a margin of one hole. In 1963, at Atlanta, he was undefeated and Bernard Hunt, who was drawn against him three times with different partners, had probably had enough of him by the end of the second day. Just as a variation, Lema drew Guy Hunt (no relation to Bernard) in the singles and beat him too.

Bernard Hunt drew him again in both the fourball series at Birkdale in 1965, but honours were even, with a point for each team. Lema ended in style by winning both his singles matches against Peter Butler and Christy O'Connor. He was six under par when he beat O'Connor.

With Tony Lema's death in a plane crash in 1966, golf lost one of its finest players and most appealing personalities. With such an elegant and rhythmic swing and such a masterly short game he would surely have won many more major championships. But, above all, Lema was an entertainer, a very likeable man who brought his own brand of enjoyment and sense of style to the game.

LEVI, WAYNE

USA

Born: 22.2.52

Appearances: 1991

Record: P2 W0 L2 H0

Wayne Levi owed his selection for the American team at Kiawah Island to his performances in the 1990 season when he won four events, including the Western Open and the Canadian Open; he secured prize money of over $1 million to finish second in the money list behind Greg Norman. Such form deserted him in 1991 and, when the Ryder Cup began, he was not even in the top 70 on the American money list.

Levi joined the American tour in 1978 after three attempts to qualify and by 1985 had won eight tournaments; but he did not win another event until his brilliant year of 1990.

Because of his poor form he was apparently a reluctant participant in the Ryder Cup and the captain, Dave Stockton, did not send him into battle until the afternoon of the second day. He and Lanny Wadkins were always down to Mark James and Steven Richardson and lost by three and one. Levi's enthusiasm would hardly have been rekindled when he came out of the hat opposite Severiano Ballesteros and the Spaniard disposed of him on the 16th green.

LIETZKE, BRUCE

USA

Born: 18.7.51

Appearances: 1981

Record: P3 W0 L2 H1

It is surprising that the talented Bruce Lietzke has only played in one Ryder cup match, at Walton Heath in 1981, when he lost both his fourball and his foursomes matches in partnership with Bill Rogers; but he salvaged some pride by halving his singles with Bernhard Langer.

Lietzke turned professional in 1974 and had his first victory in the Tucson Open in 1977. In all, he has won 11 events on the American tour, including the Canadian Open (twice), the Bob Hope Desert Classic and the Byron Nelson Golf Classic (twice). In 1991 he played very consistently to finish 19th on the money list with over half a million dollars.

LITTLER, GENE

USA

Born: 21.7.30

Appearances: 1961, 1963, 1965, 1967, 1969, 1971, 1975

Record: P27 W14 L5 H8

Gene Littler's golf swing was admired the world over. Henry Cotton called him 'one of the game's supreme stylists' and conjectured that few players could ever have hit as many pure shots. Littler's style was beautifully orthodox and he had a grace and a rhythm that was only matched by Sam Snead. It was no wonder that he was called 'Gene the machine'; and it was of him that Tommy Aaron, as he watched him on the practice ground, remarked: 'It doesn't take a Rolls-Royce long to warm up, does it?'

Littler's first notable win was in the US Amateur Championship of 1953 and he played in the Walker Cup in the same year. In 1954, he was still an amateur when he won the San Diego Open. It did not escape his notice that while he had the congratulations, Dutch Harrison had a substantial cheque to enjoy. Littler became a professional a week later and won four tournaments, including the prestigious Tournament of Champions, in the following year. During the years from 1954 to 1962 he won 19 victories, including a hat-trick of wins in the Tournament of Champions.

Littler came second in the US Open at Baltusrol in 1954 and won the championship at Oakland Hills in 1961. It was his first major victory and it was assumed that many more would follow. But they did not, and the reason that his remarkable talents did not bring him any more major championships lay with his diffident personality. The fierce desire to win tournaments that drove golfers such as Hogan, Nicklaus and Player was not a part of Littler's modest and retiring temperament. He seemed somewhat surprised by his own immense ability and often said deprecatingly of himself that he had not played really well since his mid-twenties. In any case he really preferred to be at home with his family rather than slogging it out on the golf course; and his hobby of collecting classic cars, especially Rolls-Royces, took up a lot of his time.

Nevertheless, over the span of a quarter of a century from 1954 Littler played well enough to win 29 tournaments on the US tour; and in those years he was only once out of the top 60 on the money list. That was in 1972 when he had successful treatment for cancer of the lymph glands. He bounced back to win an event in the following year and in 1975 won three events and finished in fifth place on the money list.

Littler's record in the Ryder Cup reflected his outstanding ability. He played in seven of the matches between 1961 and 1975 and only lost five games out of 27. His metronomic swing and mesmerically straight hitting, allied to a wonderful short game, must have been heart-breaking to oppose in matchplay. His first call to the American colours was at Lytham in 1961 and he lost his opening game, a foursomes against Christy O'Connor and Peter Alliss. In the singles he halved both his matches; a birdie at the final hole saved him against Neil Coles and honours were also even with O'Connor. Two years later, at East Lake, Atlanta, he was unbeaten and in the process he crushed Tom Haliburton in the second series of singles by the margin of six and five.

At Birkdale in 1965 he and Billy Casper teamed up and were involved in a wonderful foursomes match against their old adversaries, Christy O'Connor and Peter Alliss. Each side bombarded the other with birdies and, although the British pair went to the turn in a remarkable 31 shots, they were only one hole ahead. But they clung on to win on the 17th green. Littler eventually gained three points out of a possible six, and two years later, at Houston, he won two points from four games, as the American team crushed the British.

Littler played on three more occasions in the Ryder Cup and won eight matches out of nine. The only man to overcome him was Peter Oosterhuis, in a singles

game at Old Warson in 1971. His parting shot was to win three points out of three at Laurel Valley in 1975 when he was 45 years of age. He won all his games in that year by the considerable margin of at least four holes.

Littler's method was so good and his swing so devoid of any strain that he was able to play on until the early Eighties when he headed off to win more titles on the Seniors tour. He should have won more major championships and had his chances. In 1970 he lost a play-off in the Masters at Augusta to Billy Casper. In 1977 at Pebble Beach he seemed to have the USPGA championship in his grasp. He led the event from the first round onwards and was five shots ahead of the field with nine holes to play. He dissipated his lead over the next six holes and then lost the play-off to Lanny Wadkins.

But the memory of Gene the Machine's peerless classical style will remain long after the achievements of other golfers have been forgotten.

LYLE, ALEXANDER

Europe

Born: 9.2.58

Appearances: 1979, 1981, 1983, 1985, 1987

Record: P18 W7 L9 H2

The son of the professional at Hawkstone Park, Shropshire, Sandy Lyle is reputed to have hit his first golf shot at the age of 3. He was born to the game and his progress through the golfing ranks was swift and sure. As early as 1974, when he was only 16, Lyle qualified for the Open Championship at Lytham and one remembers his gangling figure, his trousers at half-mast, as he strolled down the fairways of a major event for the first time. Within a year he had won the English Amateur Strokeplay Championship and he won it again in 1977 and represented Britain in the Walker Cup.

Under the tutelage of his father, his transition to the professional ranks was made with great facility. He won the Nigerian Open in 1978, his first season, and finished 49th in the Order of Merit. He was first in the next two years and up to 1985, when he led the table again, his worst position was 5th. By then he had won several notable events, including the European, French, Madrid and Italian Opens, the Lancome Trophy, the individual title in the World Cup and the World Open. His first major triumph was in the 1985 Open Championship at Royal St George's when he became the first Briton since Tony Jacklin to win the title.

Not only did Sandy Lyle show that he was a winner but, blessed with a remarkable natural talent, he made golf look so easy. There was no need for any displays of grim-faced intensity: the gentle giant ambled up to the ball and sent it on its way with the minimum of fuss. At times he looked too casual, especially on the greens when it seemed that, with a little more care, he might hole more putts. Lyle's amiable and approachable mien has made him one of the most popular figures in the game; in particular, the fans were enchanted by the enormous power generated by his highly individual swing. Surely no golfer has ever hit a 1-iron further?

Lyle was introduced to the Ryder Cup encounters in 1979, at The Greenbrier, when he was only 21 years of age. In tandem with Tony Jacklin, he halved his first foursomes game against Lee Trevino and Gil Morgan and they beat Lee Elder and John Mahaffey easily, after a flying start during which they won four of the first five holes. The British pair lost their fourball to Irwin and Kite and Lyle was defeated in the singles by the wily and experienced Lee Trevino. Two years later, at Walton Heath, he teamed up with Mark James and they came out even with two wins and two defeats. In the singles Lyle and Tom Kite fought out one of the most brilliant matches ever seen in the Ryder Cup. After 11 holes both players were six under par and when Kite won on the 16th green, he was ten under. In 1983, at the PGA National, Lyle was out of form and lost both his games.

As the Open Champion of 1985, Lyle was expected to assume a prominent role in the match at the Belfry. But, as in previous Ryder Cups, his brilliance flickered only fitfully. On the second morning he and Bernhard Langer halved a fourball against Strange and Stadler which they should have lost, partly due to Lyle's eagle at the 17th hole and partly due to Stadler's inexplicable lapse with his short putt at the final hole. But Lyle played well to defeat Peter Jacobsen in the singles.

Lyle made the correct decision in 1986 to spend part of his season on the American tour, where he had played occasionally in the two previous years. Once again his entrance to a new and different stage was smooth and accomplished; he won the Greater Greensboro Open and finished in 64th position on the money list. In the following year he came first in the important Tournament Players Championship and was 34th on the money list.

The scene was set for the most successful year in Lyle's career. He began the season in America in grand style by winning the Phoenix Open and the Greater Greensboro Open for the second time. For the first time ever a British golfer went to Augusta as one of the favourites to win the Masters. After three rounds Lyle led the field; in the final round his first mistakes came at the 11th hole, where he took three putts, and at the 12th, where he put his ball into Rae's Creek and dropped two shots. After a courageous birdie at the short 16th hole, he was aware that he needed two pars to force a play-off with Mark Calcavecchia. The first came at the 17th and one can only imagine Lyle's despair when he hit his drive into the bunker which guards the left-hand edge of the 18th fairway. With just over 140 yards to the flag Lyle risked all with his 7-iron. No one will ever forget the perfection of the shot as he picked his ball cleanly off the sand and flew it all the way to the green and beyond the pin. The ball gripped and spun down a ridge to within a few feet of the hole. If Gene Sarazen's double-eagle at Augusta in 1934 was a golf shot that 'rang around the world', Lyle's shot was seen, over and over again, on the television screens of the world. It was an audacious shot and a precise one and deserved to win a great championship; as it did, when Lyle casually knocked his putt of ten feet into the hole.

After his victory in the Masters, Lyle led the money list in the USA and he then returned to Europe and won the British Masters. Later in the year, he at last won the World Matchplay Championship at Wentworth, after being the runner-up on four previous occasions. In the final he beat his great rival, Nick Faldo.

At this stage in his career Sandy Lyle was one of the pre-eminent golfers in the world, along with Ballesteros and Faldo. He had even improved his moderate Ryder Cup record. In the 1987 fixture, at Muirfield Village, his three victories in partnership with Bernhard Langer had been vital contributions to Europe's first triumph on American soil.

Lyle began the 1989 season in America in his usual relaxed and successful style: equal tenth in the Tournament of Champions, third in the Pebble Beach Pro-Am, second in the Los Angeles Open, and runner-up after a play-off in the Bob Hope Classic. But Lyle's game suddenly left him, a highly malevolent ghost had infiltrated the machine, and he missed nine cuts out of the next ten tournaments, including the Masters at Augusta. He struggled on through 1989 when he finished 53rd in the European Order of Merit and he fared even worse in 1990 when he finished in 59th position. He recalls that his blackest moment was when he contacted Tony Jacklin prior

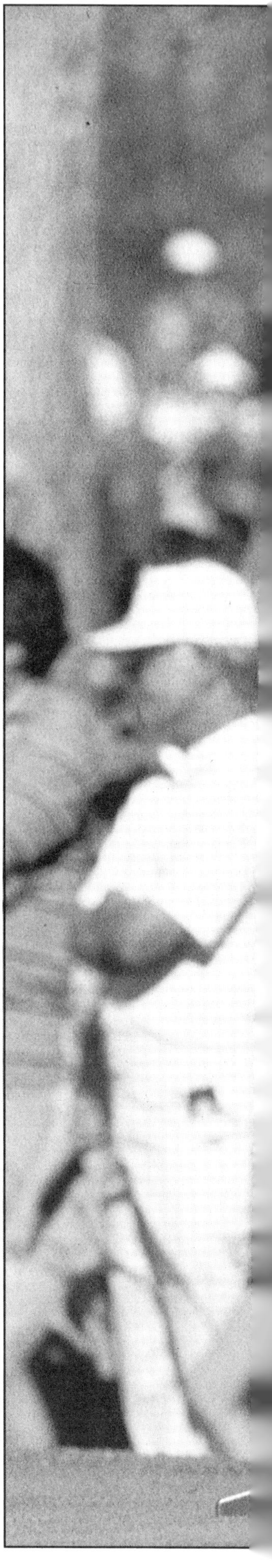

Sandy Lyle sizes up a putt with Bernhard Langer. Their partnership is undefeated in the Ryder Cup

to the final selection of the 1989 Ryder Cup team and asked the captain not to consider him; he could not bear the thought of letting the European team down.

Lyle battled on and his despair must have been heightened because until then he had never had to face adversity; his career had been a prolonged and uninterrupted success. He sought advice from all and sundry before settling on Nick Faldo's coach, David Leadbetter. There were glimmers of hope in the darkness. At the 1990 Open Championship, at St Andrews, Lyle finished in a tie for 16th place and it was noticeable how warm was his reception from the fans.

But it was not until 1991 that his uncomplaining hard work began to bear fruit. He had some finishes in the top ten, including second place in the European Open. Finally, he won a tournament, the BMW International Open, almost three years to the day since his previous success and continued his progress in 1992 by winning the Italian Open. Lyle has been a long time in the depths and everyone hopes that he has arrived again at the broad, sunlit uplands of his career in golf. He is young enough to win many more major championships and to carry the European flag into the Ryder Cup battles to come.

M

McCUMBER, MARK

USA

Born: 7.9.51

Appearances: 1989

Record: P3 W2 L1 H0

Although he won the Doral-Eastern Open in 1979, his second year on the tour, Mark McCumber found it difficult to make a real impact for some years. His best year was to be 1983 when he won two events, the Western Open and the Pensacola Open and finished in eighth place on the money list. His most prestigious victory was in the Tournament Players Championship in 1988 and he won the Western Open for the second time a year later. In partnership with Ben Crenshaw he won the World Cup at Royal Melbourne in 1988.

McCumber played in the tied Ryder Cup match at the Belfry in 1989. He and Mark Calcavecchia lost a fourball match narrowly to Nick Faldo and Ian Woosnam, when neither of the American pair managed to clear the water at the 18th; but he and Tom Kite played excellent golf to defeat Canizares and Langer in the second series of fourballs. McCumber had another tight game against Gordon Brand Jr in the singles but he scraped home at the final hole.

McCumber continues to play on the American tour and is also much involved in designing golf courses.

McGEE, JERRY

USA

Born: 21.7.43

Appearances: 1977

Record: P2 W1 L1 H0

During the late 1970s Jerry McGee was one of the most consistent players on the American scene. He won four events during the years from 1975 to 1979, including the Pensacola Open and the Philadelphia Classic, and a mark of his reliability was his performance in the 1976 season when he played in 33 events and only missed the cut in four of them.

He qualified for the 1977 Ryder Cup match at Lytham and, paired with Dave Stockton, fought back from two down with three holes to play to beat Neil Coles and Peter Dawson by one hole in the foursomes. McGee lost his singles to Peter Oosterhuis, but the Englishman was rarely beaten in Ryder Cup encounters.

MAHAFFEY, JOHN

USA

Born: 9.5.48

Appearances: 1979

Record: P3 W1 L2 H0

John Mahaffey has played on the American tour for over 20 years with mixed success. He won the Sahara Invitational early in his career, in 1973, and in 1975 lost a play-off for the US Open at Medinah. A year later triumph in the same event beckoned and then eluded him again as he was overtaken at the final holes by Jerry Pate. A succession of injuries interrupted his career but he came back in determined style to win the 1978 USPGA Championship at Oakmont and one other event. In the PGA he made up seven shots on Tom Watson during the final round and then beat him and Jerry Pate in a play-off.

Mahaffey was an automatic selection for the 1979 Ryder cup at The Greenbrier and lost both his opening matches, the fourball to the seasoned pair of Barnes and Gallacher and the foursomes to Lyle and Jacklin, who won four of the first five holes. But he won a very close singles match with Brian Barnes on the final green.

At the beginning of the Eighties Mahaffey defeated the most insidious of enemies, alcohol, and went on to win such prestigious events as the Kemper Open, Bob Hope Classic and the Texas Open and, in 1986, the Tournament Players Championship: Larry Mize, three ahead with four holes to play, suffered a minor collapse and Mahaffey won by a stroke.

Known as an exceptional striker of the ball, Mahaffey has also won the World Cup team title twice, with Andy North in 1978 and Hale Irwin in 1979, and the individual title.

MANERO, TONY

USA

Born: 4.4.05

Appearances: 1937

Record: P2 W1 L1 H0

Although described as an unexpected winner of the US Open at Baltimore in 1936, Tony Manero had a consistent record in tournaments. His best year was 1930 when he won the Glen Falls, Pasadena and Catalina Opens, and he was still playing tournament golf in the Fifties.

He won the US Open with a new record score of 282. 'Lighthorse Harry' Cooper was already in the clubhouse and being congratulated on his apparent winning score of 284 when Manero came in with a brilliant final round of 67 to take the title.

On his one appearance in the Ryder Cup in Britain, Tony Manero was described as a dapper little man with an engaging smile. He was a marvellous putter but took his time about it and was castigated as being 'insufferably slow'. This funereal pace was not helped by the appalling weather conditions on the second day at Southport, nor by the incompetent stewards who 'got in everyone's way with the utmost impartiality'. He and Ralph Guldahl beat Arthur Lacey and Bill Cox in the foursomes and on the second day, Manero was drawn against Henry Cotton, who beat him easily by five and three.

MANGRUM, LLOYD

USA

Born: 1.8.14

Appearances: 1947, 1949, 1951, 1953
Captain 1953

Record: P8 W6 L2 H0

With his trim moustache, centre-parted hair and a cigarette ever between his lips, Lloyd Mangrum might have understudied Clark Gable in some tale about a Mississippi riverboat gambler. Mangrum was a very tough and a very cool customer, who was never happier than when the stakes on the golf course were high.

He was born in Texas and played on the professional tour during the Depression days of the Thirties, when golfers were never entirely sure if the promised prize fund would materialise or not. Many of them, like Mangrum, made more money hustling bets on the course anyway. It was not until 1940 that he won his first event, the Thomasville Open, but he made a notable mark on the Masters tournament at Augusta. His first round of 64 was a record which, although eventually equalled by others, including Jack Nicklaus and Maurice Bembridge, stood for 46 years. Mangrum finished second to Jimmy Demaret but he was now established as a formidable tournament player.

He won another tournament in 1941 and three in the following year, and then went off to war. He was stationed in Britain for a time, took part in the Normandy landings, and was wounded twice in the 1945 Battle of the Bulge. The wounds were not too serious because, while recuperating, he won the GI Championship at St Andrews and the US Army Championship in Paris.

Mangrum's great strengths as a golfer were his uncanny accuracy around the greens and his ability to hole 'pressure putts'. In comparison, his long game was merely efficient but the sum of the parts added up to one of the most successful golfers ever seen on the American tour.

In 1946 Mangrum won his only major title, the US Open, after a play-off with Vic Ghezzi and Byron Nelson. They were still tied after 18 holes and the play-off went to a further round; Mangrum won by a single stroke. From 1947 to 1953 he won 28 tournaments, including the Los Angeles, Tucson, Western and Phoenix Opens. Seven events were won in 1948, including George May's World Championship of Golf, which carried a huge first prize. Mangrum caused a sensation in the latter event with a round of 63. He was in a play-off again in the 1950 US Open but was beaten by Ben Hogan. He was still playing on the American circuit in the early Sixties, although his last official victory was in the 1956 Los Angeles Open.

Mangrum made his debut in the 1947 Ryder Cup at Portland, Oregon, and played in every match up to 1953, when he was also the captain of the American team. He and Sam Snead were regarded as the American 'bankers' in the foursomes and they won three of their four matches by wide margins. The only exception was at Ganton in 1949 when Dick Burton and Arthur Lees had a tremendous battle with them and won a point for Britain on the 36th green. In the singles Mangrum won handsomely against Max Faulkner, Fred Daly and Harry Weetman but lost his last match at Wentworth in 1953, to the indomitable Eric Brown.

Lloyd Mangrum played on the American tour for over 30 years and registered nearly 40 official victories. He is still ranked in the USPGA's top ten golfers, which is the mark of his stature.

MARR, DAVE

USA

Born: 27.12.33

Appearances: 1965
Captain 1981

Record: P6 W4 L2 H0

Dave Marr's role as a commentator at the major American tournaments has kept him firmly in the public eye and it is surprising to note that the high points of his playing career were back in the Sixties.

He won the USPGA Championship in 1965 and his victory, allied to three others on the tour, made him the leading American player. He had won several tournaments in previous years and shown his class when he tied for second place with Jack Nicklaus in the 1964 Masters, which was won by Arnold Palmer.

Marr played only once in the Ryder Cup and must have wondered what had hit him as Dave Thomas and George Will started with three birdies against him and Arnold Palmer and finished them off clinically by six and five. The draw put the same pairs out again in the afternoon matches and Arnold Palmer, demonic in his intensity, pulled Marr along in his furious wake. The American pair had six 3s in a row from the second hole and went out in 30 strokes. They neatly reversed the morning's result.

Marr won again with Palmer in the next morning's fourball match, but they were defeated by Peter Alliss and Christy O'Connor in the afternoon. Marr made it a successful debut by winning both his singles, against Neil Coles and Bernard Hunt.

It was curious that Dave Marr made no other appearances for the USA but he was elected non-playing captain in 1981 at Walton Heath, when the American team had another trenchant victory.

Dave Marr (above) receives the trophy from the Duke of Kent in 1981

MARTIN, JIMMY

GB

Born: 27.7.24

Appearances: 1965

Record: P1 W0 L1 H0

The major victories of Jimmy Martin's career comprised the Piccadilly Tournament in 1964, the Carrols Open in 1968 and the Madrid Open in 1972. He represented Ireland in the World Cup on five occasions from 1962 to 1970.

Martin was a relatively short hitter, but he had a fine touch on and around the greens. This was not enough to withstand the very heavy guns of Julius Boros and Tony Lema in his one match in the Ryder Cup, at Birkdale in 1965. With Jimmy Hitchcock as a partner, their foursomes was lost by five and four.

MAXWELL, BILLY

USA

Born: 3.7.29

Appearances: 1963

Record: P4 W4 L0 H0

In 1951, at the age of 22, Billy Maxwell won the US Amateur title. He became a professional in 1954 and for a decade or so was among the leading money winners on the American tour. His best years were 1961 and 1962 when he won four tournaments, including the Palm Springs Classic and the Dallas Open, and he was second in the Carling Open. He was still a regular on the US tour in the Seventies and now plays on the Senior circuit.

Maxwell was a rather short hitter but he more than made up for it with his supremely accurate short irons and his superb putting. In his one Ryder Cup appearance he won both his fourball matches in the company of Billy Casper, his foursomes match with Bob Goalby and then defeated Christy O'Connor in the singles.

Billy Maxwell

MAYER, DICK

USA

Born: 29.8.24

Appearances: 1957

Record: P2 W1 L0 H1

Despite the American team's defeat by Britain at Lindrick in 1957, Dick Mayer did not lose a match, even if his half with Harry Bradshaw in the final singles was academic, as the tie had already been decided. But his play in the foursomes with Tommy Bolt had been brilliant. This pair covered the first 18 holes in 67 shots and then went to the turn in the afternoon round in 32 strokes. They finished Christy O'Connor and Eric Brown off soon afterwards.

Dick Mayer had a remarkable year in 1957 when he won the US Open after a play-off with Cary Middlecoff; he then won the Tam O'Shanter World Open. Such was the prize money provided by George May for the latter tournament that Mayer was the leading money winner on the tour by a long way.

Mayer's career was interrupted in 1969 by tendon trouble and a broken elbow and he was never quite as formidable a player again. Nevertheless, he picked up $50,000 for a hole in one at the Palm Springs Open in 1962 and two years later won the New Orleans Open.

MEHLHORN, WILLIAM

USA

Born: 1898

Appearances: 1927

Record: P2 W1 L1 H0

Bernard Darwin rather unkindly said that he looked like a hod carrier and nothing like a golfer; but Ben Hogan called him one of the finest players from tee to green that he had ever seen. Bill Mehlhorn was one of the foremost players in the USA during the Twenties when he won 20 tournaments, including the Western, San Jose, Westchester and Texas Opens. Sixteen of those victories were recorded in the years from 1926 to 1929. He finished fifth or better in the US Open five times and was the runner-up to Walter Hagen in the USPGA Championship of 1925.

In his only appearance in the Ryder Cup, in the inaugural match of 1927, he had a severe defeat with his friend Leo Diegel at the hands of the British foursomes combination of Aubrey Boomer and Charles Whitcombe. But, on the following day, he won a very close game, by one hole, over Archie Compston.

His nickname, 'Wild Bill', coined by Leo Diegel, did not imply an erratic temperament; rather it referred to his ability to string together an occasional run of remarkably low scores. As with most golfers, these runs happened when he was putting well, but Mehlhorn confessed that he was 'the world's worst putter' and at one stage he had a chronic attack of the yips. In one tournament his partner, Bobby Jones, watched with great embarrassment as Mehlhorn, a yard from the hole, putted off the green and into a bunker.

Bill Mehlhorn was a man of intelligence with decided views about the golf swing. Baseball was his first love and he compared the golf swing to swinging a baseball bat. It worked for him because he hit the golf ball great distances with a slow and easy rhythm. He experimented with the shape of his iron clubs and, in order to put more weight behind the ball, designed a shorter and stubbier blade. He had other accomplishments outside golf; for example, he was said to be a bridge player of the highest calibre.

MIDDLECOFF, CARY

USA

Born: 6.1.21

Appearances: 1953. 1955, 1959

Record: P6 W2 L3 H1

Although he qualified as a dentist, like his father and two uncles, Cary Middlecoff only practised his profession in the army, which he left in 1946. Perhaps that was a blessing because he was a nervous and fidgety man. Instead he became one of the most successful of American golfers.

Even as an amateur Middlecoff was able to win important titles; he beat all the professionals to win the 1945 North and South Open. He was honourable enough to decline a place in the American Walker Cup team for 1947 because he intended to become a professional, and so he did. It did not take him long to win his first major tournament, the US Open of 1949 at Medinah. After three rounds he had a lead of three strokes over Clayton Heafner and of six over Sam Snead. He could barely control his nerves and struggled to a final round of 75. He later claimed that, although he did not play well, he holed every putt of importance. It was good enough to win the title and was the start of a remarkable sequence of wins through to 1956. During those years, he won 32 tournaments and was always in the top ten money winners on the American tour.

Although Middlecoff's best effort in the USPGA Championship was to reach the semi-finals in 1954, he won the Masters in the following year by a record margin of seven shots from Ben Hogan. He won five other tournaments in 1955 and continued his brilliant run by winning the US Open again in 1956 at Oak Hill. He nearly retained the title at Inverness when he played two magnificent rounds of golf, two 68s on the final day, to force a tie with Dick Mayer.

Middlecoff was an extremely slow and deliberate player, partly because he was a great apostle of correct alignment and therefore fidgeted about until he felt just right. He also took an inordinate amount of time on the greens. As a protest, or as a piece of gamesmanship, Dick Mayer took a folding stool with him for the play-off. It worked because he beat Middlecoff by several shots.

Doctor Middlecoff (like the Italians, the Americans love a title) won his way into three Ryder Cup teams and made his debut at Wentworth in 1953. He and Walter Burkemo lost an unbearably tense foursomes to Harry Bradshaw and Fred Daly, who had to hole a four-foot putt on the final green for Britain's only victory on the first day. But Middlecoff easily took care of Max Faulkner in the singles. Two years later at Thunderbird Ranch he got his foursomes revenge on Bradshaw in company with Sam Snead, but lost another thriller, this time to John Jacobs who had to hole a very tricky putt on the last green.

His final appearance was in 1959, at Eldorado, when he and Sam Snead seemed to be heading for a defeat at the hands of Dave Thomas and Harry Weetman until the latter perpetrated a very ill-considered shot on the 36th hole and the Americans scrambled a half.

Middlecoff was quite a tall man with a distinctive style: a pronounced pause at the top of the swing enabled him to clear his left hip before he crunched strongly through the ball. He hit the ball a long way, especially off the tee. He won the last of his 39 tournaments in 1961 and retired from active tournament golf soon afterwards. He had problems with his back and was beginning to suffer the yips with his putter.

Middlecoff was a great golfer and had always been a most intelligent analyst of the golf swing. His contribution to the game continued, as an expert commentator for television, but more significantly as a writer. Two of his books, *The Golf Swing* and *Advanced Golf*, were notable contributions to the game's theory.

MILLER, JOHNNY

USA

Born: 29.4.47

Appearances: 1975, 1981

Record: P6 W2 L2 H2

During the middle years of the Seventies it seemed that Johnny Miller might set a new and astonishing level of golfing achievement. In 1974 he won the first three events on the American tour: the Bing Crosby Pro-Am, the Phoenix and the Tucson Opens. He went on to win eight tournaments in all and finished as the leader of the money list. Such a feat seems unattainable on the current American tour.

Miller had shown his pedigree as a golfer while still at Brigham Young University. In 1966 he was the leading amateur in the US Open when he ended in eighth place at the Olympic Club, San Francisco. Three years later he turned professional and won the southern Open in 1973 and was the runner-up in the Masters. His first major triumph was in the 1973 US Open, at Oakmont, when he followed a disappointing third round of 76 with a spectacular final round of 63. He began with four birdies and five more followed as he fired his iron shots with relentless accuracy into the yielding greens. He won the title by one shot as the likes of Weiskopf, Nicklaus, Trevino and Palmer were unable to match him.

Then came his brilliant year of 1974 and he began the next season in the same dazzling fashion. In the Phoenix Open all his rounds were under 70 and included one of 61; he won the event by 14 shots and was 24 under par. In the next tournament, the Tucson Open, he scored another 61 and won by nine shots; he was 25 shots under par. For a short while he lifted his golf to a different plane and he recalls the time as being almost a mystical experience. In that year he nearly added a second major title, at Augusta. The final two days saw an absorbing struggle with Tom Weiskopf and Jack Nicklaus but, despite Miller's closing rounds of 65 and 66, Nicklaus won the great prize.

Miller played in the Ryder Cup at Laurel Valley in 1975 and was unbeaten in his foursomes and fourball matches. But he was

unable to overcome Peter Oosterhuis in his singles, despite being two up after 11 holes. The Englishman reeled off six successive 3s to win the game by two holes.

Miller was to add to his tally of major championships in 1976 when he won the Open at Birkdale. After three rounds he was three strokes behind the young Severiano Ballesteros but had overtaken him after nine holes and eventually coasted placidly home to win by six shots. In the same year he won both the individual and the team title in the World Cup for the second time.

Johnny Miller was now at the height of his powers. He was tall and blond and slim, the archetypal tanned Californian (Miller called himself 'the original tour clone'); he rifled his shots at the flag with a flowing, upright and elegant swing. If he was earning vast amounts of money on the golf courses of the world, he was earning much more through endorsements and promotions: for example, he had a contract with Sears in the USA which guaranteed him around $1 million a year. It was said, perhaps apocryphally, that Miller had his own key on the Sears cash registers.

But suddenly the ability to win tournaments left Miller and it was not until 1980 that he won another event on the American tour. The cynics said that he had become too rich and comfortable, while Miller himself sought the answer by analysing his swing. In the past he had sometimes said that he got bored by too much golf, an easy remark to make when winning came so easily. Whatever happened, Miller's spark of genius never flared fully into life again, even though he won six more tournaments in the Eighties. His last victory was in the Pebble Beach Pro-Am in 1987.

He made one more appearance in the Ryder Cup, at Walton Heath in 1981. Although he and Tom Kite halved their fourball with Torrance and Clark, Miller lost his singles to Nick Faldo.

In the last couple of years Miller has become a noticeably candid television commentator for NBC; he also designs golf courses.

MILLS, PETER

GB

Born: 7.6.31

Appearances: 1957, 1959

Record: P1 W1 L0 H0

It was surprising that Peter Mills, the possessor of a superb golf swing, did not play more Ryder Cup games, and at one stage during the 1957 tie at Lindrick it seemed that he would not get to the first tee. His opponent, Ted Kroll, was taken ill but Dai Rees would not claim a walk-over (though entitled to do so) and Jack Burke, the American Captain, took his place. He had not only won the Masters and the USPGA Championship, but was undefeated in Ryder Cup matches.

Peter Mills was not the slightest overawed; he was five holes up at lunch and duly won a decisive victory by five and three. He won his place in the 1959 team but was unlucky enough to injure his back so badly during a practice round that he could not play.

Mills had several second places in tournaments in the 1950s and reached the semi-final of the PGA Matchplay Championship in 1956. His one major win was in the Bowmaker Tournament of 1958. Eventually Mills applied for and received reinstatement as an amateur.

MITCHELL, ABE

GB

Born: 19.1.87

Appearances: 1929, 1931, 1933

Record: P6 W4 L2 H0

It has been said of many golfers that he was 'the best never to win an Open Championship' but Abe Mitchell is the one of which it is true. He struck a golf ball as well as any of his contemporaries and did it with an utterly simple style. Henry Cotton referred to his 'casual yet masterly swing'; Mitchell had a short backswing and a limited follow-through but

Peter Mills

gave the ball a tremendously powerful hit by virtue of his huge and strong wrists and hands. Henry Longhurst admired him as no other golfer but recalled how the Cambridge golf team, of which he was captain, were nearly ruined by trying to copy his swing. In comparison their wrists were 'like matchsticks'.

Mitchell first came to notice in 1912 when he lost the final of the British Amateur Championship to the illustrious John Ball at Westwood Ho! He had a putt of just over a yard to win the title on the 36th green but missed it and finally succumbed at the second extra hole. Mitchell turned professional soon afterwards and was fourth in the Open in 1914.

When the Open Championship resumed in 1920 Mitchell led the field by six shots after two rounds. His great friend, George Duncan, told him that a couple of 75s would secure the championship, but Mitchell collapsed in the third round with a score of 84 and it was Duncan who triumphed. Bernard Darwin was to write later that if Mitchell had won that time he might have won again and again because 'he was a truly magnificent golfer, armed at all points.'

Mitchell cut an elegant figure in his tight-fitting tweed jacket, immaculately pressed plus-fours, tweed cap and beautifully polished brown shoes: he looked as if he were dressed for a day's shooting. Despite his failure to win an Open, his formidable powers as a matchplayer won him the British Matchplay Championship in 1919, 1920 and 1929.

He was to play a significant part in the history of the Ryder Cup. As an enthusiastic and very rich convert to golf, Samuel Ryder was able to employ Mitchell as his own personal golf professional. He paid him a huge salary for those days of nearly £1,000 a year and part of Ryder's thinking was that this would free him from the chores of a club professional's job and enable him to concentrate on winning tournaments – especially the Open.

In 1926 a match between British and American golf professionals was played at Wentworth. Abe Mitchell captained the British team and Ryder decided to put up a cup for a biennial match. The figure on the top of the cup was modelled on Mitchell.

It was ironic that Mitchell had to withdraw from the first

official match in 1927 because of an attack of appendicitis but he was back in the ranks for the 1929 tie at Moortown, under the leadership of George Duncan. He and Fred Robson were termed 'the grand old men' but they were too good for Gene Sarazen and Ed Dudley in the foursomes. In the singles Mitchell encountered Leo Diegel in all his brilliance; although he had a score of 70 in the morning round Mitchell was five holes down and could not recover.

In 1931 he and Robson won their foursomes at Scioto where the match was won by the Americans; but Mitchell won both his games in the very close tie at Southport in 1933. He and Arthur Havers beat Olin Dutra and Denny Shute in the foursomes and Mitchell was drawn against Dutra again in the singles. He was three down after nine holes, then won eight holes in a row and beat Dutra nine and eight.

Abe Mitchell was unquestionably one of the best golfers in the world and one of the most exciting to watch. Henry Longhurst recalled vividly how the sound of his club on a golf ball was different to that of any other golfer and how Mitchell 'hammered a course

into submission'. It is probable that he lacked the final ounce of devil, the 'killer instinct', to win an Open championship because he was a quiet and gentle man. But he will be remembered as one of the most glorious strikers of a golf ball in the game's history.

MIZE, LARRY

USA

Born: 23.9.58

Appearances: 1987

Record: P4 W1 L1 H2

Larry Mize was born just a short iron shot away from the gates of the Augusta National Golf Club and his middle name is Hogan, so perhaps the Fates had golfing glory in mind for him. It came at the US Masters in 1987 when he birdied the final hole to force a play-off against two giants of international golf, Severiano Ballesteros and Greg Norman. But it was the little-known American who won the great prize, by holing an immensely difficult chip shot of over 40 yards at the second extra hole.

Mize had joined the American tour in 1982 and won his first victory at the Memphis Classic in 1983. His next win was in the Masters and it ensured his selection for the Ryder Cup match in 1987, at Muirfield Village, Ohio.

Although the Americans were defeated, Mize played respectably to win two points out of four. He and Lanny Wadkins lost their opening foursomes, despite winning the first three holes, to Nick Faldo and Ian Woosnam; but he and Hal Sutton then halved their match with the same pair. Paired again with Sutton, he gained an unexpected victory over the formidable team of Ballesteros and Olazabal. Mize finished by halving his singles with Sam Torrance.

MOFFITT, RALPH

GB

Born: 18.9.32

Appearances: 1961

Record: P1 W0 L1 H0

Ralph Moffitt was a well-known figure in Midlands golf; he won the Midlands Assistants Championship several times and the Midlands Open in 1961 and 1964. In the major professional tournaments in the Sixties he was a perennial runner-up: on three occasions in the Dunlop Masters, in the PGA Close Championship and in the PGA Matchplay Tournament. He was capable of sustained runs of excellent scoring, as in 1961 when he played six successive tournament rounds of 67.

In his one Ryder Cup game, at Lytham in 1961, which was the year when the format was changed to matches over 18 holes, Moffitt was heavily defeated by the powerful Mike Souchak.

MONTGOMERIE COLIN

Europe

Born: 23.6.63

Appearances: 1991

Record: P3 W1 L1 H1

Colin Montgomerie was born into a golfing environment in Troon and had a distinguished career as an amateur. He played twice in the Walker Cup and the Eisenhower Trophy, won the Scottish Amateur Strokeplay Championship in 1985 and the Scottish Matchplay Championship two years later.

A tall and rather beefy man, Montgomerie has a powerful and natural swing. Rather than spending hours a day on the practice ground, Montgomerie confesses that he relies more on feel, on imagining how a shot should fly; he then lets his swing take over.

His first victory as a professional came in the 1989 Portuguese Open at Quinta do Lago, when he won by the remarkable margin of 11 shots. He played consistently well through the following year without winning a tournament and finished 14th in the Order of Merit. In 1991 an outright victory seemed as elusive as ever when he lost a play-off to Severiano Ballesteros in the PGA Championship and finished second behind Nick Faldo in the Irish Open. At last the well-merited victory was won in the Scandinavian Masters and his place in the Ryder Cup team for Kiawah Island was booked.

On the first morning Montgomerie was sent out in the foursomes with another newcomer, David Gilford, and they encountered two tough and battle-scarred veterans in Hale Irwin and Lanny Wadkins. The American pair recorded three birdies in the first three holes and cruised to victory. Montgomerie was not called to the colours again until the fourball matches on the Saturday afternoon when he and Bernhard Langer defeated Corey Pavin and Steve Pate.

Out in third position in the singles matches, Montgomerie was soon in trouble against Mark Calcavecchia, and was eventually four holes down with four to play. It seemed obvious to everyone that this was another American point in the bag. But the American's game collapsed in the most humiliating fashion as he dropped eight shots over the remaining four holes and allowed Montgomerie to steal a half. At the famous 17th hole, with the lake looming on the right, Calcavecchia, having seen his opponent's ball disappear into a watery grave, only had to find dry land to win. But he hit an abysmal shot into the water and then took three putts with his second ball. So, Montgomerie won a famous, or perhaps infamous, half.

There is no doubt that Colin Montgomerie has the skill to win many tournaments. Whether he has the temperament to win a major championship cannot yet be judged.

MORGAN, GIL

USA

Born: 25.9.46

Appearances: 1979, 1983

Record: P6 W1 L2 H3

Now in his 20th year on the US tour, Gil Morgan had his best years in 1978 when he won the Los Angeles Open and the World Series of Golf and was second on the money list, and 1983 when he won the first two events of the year, the Tucson Open and the Los Angeles Open.

Morgan finished his studies to qualify as an optometrist before joining the tour and has so far earned nearly $4 million.

His first appearance in the Ryder Cup, at The Greenbrier in 1979, was marred by trouble with his shoulder, although he and Lee Trevino halved a foursomes match with Brian Waites and Ken Brown. When the European player, Mark James, was declared unfit to play in the singles, Morgan was nominated to stand down from the American team and a nominal half was awarded to each side. In 1983, at the PGA National course, Morgan was fit enough to play four games and he and Lanny Wadkins demolished Sam Torrance and Canizares in a foursomes by seven and five. But Morgan lost his singles to Bernhard Langer.

His troublesome shoulder was operated upon in 1986 and he emphasised his complete return to form and fitness by winning the Kemper Open in 1990.

MURPHY, BOB

USA

Born: 14.2.43

Appearances: 1975

Record: P4 W2 L1 H1

A burly man who was often seen with a cigar between his lips, Bob Murphy won the US Amateur Championship in 1965, the first time that it was played as a strokeplay event. He represented America in the Walker Cup of 1967 and then became a professional. He won five tournaments, two of them in 1968 and the last, the Canadian Open, in 1986. His swing is notable for a remarkably slow takeaway and an almost agonising pause at the top; but it works well and he has a wonderfully sure putting stroke.

Murphy made his one Ryder Cup appearance during the American team's easy win at Laurel Valley in 1975. He partnered Jack Nicklaus in a halved fourball match against the formidable pairing of Brian Barnes and Bernard Gallacher and lost his foursomes, with Lee Trevino, to Jacklin and Huggett. However, he won both his singles, against Jacklin and Maurice Bembridge.

Bob Murphy (opposite)

N

NELSON, BYRON

USA

Born: 4.2.12

Appearances: 1937, 1947
Captain 1965

Record: P4 W3 L1 H0

Byron Nelson with Harry Weetman

It was a justifiable tribute to Byron Nelson that the golf ball testing machine used by the United States Golf Association was named 'Iron Byron' because, during 1945, Nelson came as close to mechanical perfection with his golf as has anyone, before or since.

Out of 31 tournaments, he won 18, 11 of them in succession; he was second in 7 events and never finished worse than ninth. He was approximately 320 under par and had a stroke average of 68.33. He had played with great success in the preceding year, when he had won eight events and had a stroke average of 69.67.

But Nelson was not satisfied. He felt that he had 'chipped poorly and hadn't concentrated hard enough' and that he could shave at least a shot a round off his scores. He did better than that and later confessed that there were times when he played 'almost in a trance'.

It was an astonishing sequence and he kept it going by winning another six tournaments in 1946. Some sceptics have denigrated his performance by claiming that the golfers could place their balls on the fairways ('winter rules') and that the standard of the opposition was poor because of the war (Nelson was not accepted in the US armed forces because of a blood disorder). But official records show that placing of the ball was only allowed in two events in 1945; and the presence of golfers such as Harold McSpaden, Henry Picard, Craig Wood, Denny Shute, Dutch Harrison and Johnny Bulla hardly constituted weak opposition. Above all, Sam Snead was around and won six events, as was Ben Hogan, who won five.

Byron Nelson was born in the same year and in the same place (Fort Worth, Texas) as Ben Hogan and they caddied together at Glen Garden Country Club. But Nelson's career came to an end before Hogan's had fully flowered. In 1937 Nelson won the Masters by making up six shots on Ralph Guldahl in two holes and in 1939 he won the US Open. He eventually beat Craig Wood in a play-off which went to two rounds (it was normally 18 holes) and he holed a 1-iron shot for an eagle at the 22nd hole. In 1942 he won the Masters again.

During a play-off with Ben Hogan he gained five shots on him in 11 holes (he was six under par for those holes) to win by one shot.

Nelson was a young golfer when steel shafts came into fashion and this forced a radical change in his method. Hickory shafts twisted during the swing and golfers had to manipulate their hands to square up the club face at impact. Steel shafts had much less torque and when Nelson took to them he found that he was hooking the ball violently. His solution was to move his body laterally and to drive his hands through the shot and keep them ahead of the ball. He was a tall man and because of the pronounced dip of his body the swing did not look graceful but he became supremely accurate. No one was able to hit the fairways so consistently from the tee and no one equalled his straightness with his irons.

This was the key to his brilliant years in the mid-Forties, but his efforts in those years seemed to burn him out. In 1946 he lost a play-off for the US Open with Lloyd Mangrum and Vic Ghezzi and had gone into virtual retirement by the end of the decade.

Nelson was also a formidable matchplayer and made his mark in the USPGA Championship. Between 1939 and 1945 he reached the final five times and won it in 1940 and 1945.

In the Ryder Cup, he lost one match, to Dai Rees in 1937, but more than got his revenge in 1947 when he beat Rees twice. Nelson was captain of the winning American team in 1965 at Birkdale.

He only graced the Open twice: in 1937 when he finished fifth at Carnoustie and in 1955 when he finished well down the field at St Andrews. But he went over to La Boulie for the French Open and won it. The golf writer, Pat Ward-Thomas, recalled that he had never seen such an exhibition of accurate golf: 'It was impossible to imagine iron shots of finer judgement and control'.

Byron Nelson was certainly one of the supreme golfers of his age and it is interesting to speculate how many more major tournaments he would have won if he had not retired so early. After his retirement he became a golf commentator with ABC Television and a notable teacher of the game. He has been a mentor to Tom Watson among others.

NELSON, LARRY

USA

Born: 10.9.47

Appearances: 1979, 1981, 1987

Record: P13 W9 L3 H1

Undramatic, steady, self effacing, consistent: these descriptions are usually applied to Larry Nelson, a man who had not touched a golf club until he was 21 years of age. He studied an instructional book, Hogan's *Modern Fundamentals of Golf*, and four years later was on the American tour.

It all sounds easy but Nelson makes the game look comparatively trouble-free and he made steady progress until he won his first tournament, the Inverarry Classic in 1979. He won the Western Open too and finished second in the money list.

He earned his Ryder Cup place at The Greenbrier in that year and showed what an accomplished player he had become. Nelson won five games out of five and Severiano Ballesteros, in particular, must have been sick of the sight of the quiet American, who defeated him four times, twice in the fourballs, once in the foursomes and again in the singles. Nelson played wonderful golf and his putting was outstanding. So it was two years later at Walton Health. Nelson holed an enormous putt on the final green to snatch a foursomes win (with Lee Trevino) against Langer and Pinero; and in his fourball match with Tom Kite, Nelson's birdies at the two final holes sank Sandy Lyle and Mark James. Nelson won his other two matches to accumulate nine straight wins.

He had not been idle on the American tour. In 1981 Nelson won the first of his three major championships, the USPGA, by four shots from Fuzzy Zoeller. Two years later his efficient golf brought him his great triumph, a victory in the US Open at Oakmont. A fine third round of 65 made it all possible and he fought off Tom Watson over the final holes. His score of 132 over the final two rounds is a record for the event. Nelson lay a little fallow thereafter, despite winning the Walt Disney World Golf Classic in 1984; but in 1987

Larry Nelson and Dave Marr in 1981

he won the USPGA Championship for the second time after a play-off with Lanny Wadkins.

Nelson's successes in the Ryder Cup were interrupted in 1987 at Muirfield Village. In partnership with Payne Stewart and then with Wadkins he lost two foursomes and one fourball, but halved his singles match with Bernhard Langer.

In 1991 Nelson finished 96th in the American money list but made a determined run in the US Open at Hazeltine. A final round of 68 put him into third place. Such is Nelson's consistency and his relish for the big occasions that it would be no surprise if he added to his tally of major championship victories.

NICHOLS, BOBBY

USA

Born: 14.4.36

Appearances: 1967

Record: P5 W4 L0 H1

After an appalling accident when he was in high school, Bobby Nichols was told that he would be lucky to walk again. But he confounded the doctors not only by recovering fully (though minus one kidney) but also by winning a football scholarship to a college in Texas.

He joined the professional tour in 1960 and had a brilliant year in 1962 when he won two events, was sixth in the USPGA Championship and third, behind Jack Nicklaus and Arnold Palmer, in the US Open.

Nichols reacted positively to the great occasions of golf and in his 20-year sojourn on the American tour, won such prestigious events as the Houston Classic, the Carling World Open, the Westchester Classic and the Canadian Open. In 1964 he won a major tournament, the USPGA Championship, by three shots from Nicklaus and Palmer, and was pipped by one shot in the 1967 Masters by his close friend Gay Brewer.

Nichols played wonderful golf in the 1967 Ryder Cup at the Champions Club in Houston. He won four and a half points out of five as the Americans inflicted a crushing defeat on the British. With Johnny Pott, he beat Bernard Hunt and Neil Coles twice, and Peter Alliss and Christy O'Connor once. Although Hunt got a half in the singles, Nichols beat O'Connor in the second series.

Bobby Nichols left the PGA tour to become the professional at Firestone and now plays on the Seniors circuit.

NICKLAUS, JACK

USA

Born: 21.2.40

Appearances: 1969, 1971, 1973, 1975, 1977, 1981
Captain 1983, 1987

Record: P28 W17 L8 H3

If the identity of the greatest golfer in the world can only be a matter for discussion, there is no doubt that Jack Nicklaus is the most successful player that the game has ever known. His victories in 18 major professional championships put him way beyond his nearest rivals; he has won 71 tournaments on the American tour; he has been the Australian Open champion on six occasions; he was a member of the victorious American team in the World Cup six times and was the individual winner three times. Perhaps the most telling statistic of all is his record in the four major championships between 1962 and 1986: 18 victories, 19 second places, 9 third places, and in the top ten on 70 occasions from 100 consecutive appearances.

Jack Nicklaus was born into a comfortable middle-class family; his father was a pharmacist, who encouraged him to play golf. He joined the Scioto Country Club, in Ohio, where he was taught by Jack Grout, his one and only teacher until his death in 1989. At the age of 13 Nicklaus went round Scioto in 69 shots; two years later Bobby Jones saw him play and described him as 'a new talent of the first magnitude'. At the age of 19 Nicklaus won the first of his two US Amateur championships and went on to play in the Walker Cup in 1959 and 1961. In 1960 he showed his aptitude for the great occasion by finishing second to Arnold Palmer at Cherry Hills in the US Open. It was clear that only the professional game could offer his extraordinary skills the required challenge and he joined the American circuit in 1962.

Nicklaus was blessed with enormous strength, concentrated in those areas essential to a golfer, the legs and the back. Jack Grout had taught him an admirably sound technique; the wide arc of his swing and his perfect footwork enabled him to release his enormous power. He was able to fly a golf ball huge distances and to reduce any golf-course to manageable proportions. A suitably impressed Bernard Darwin wrote: 'He gives the ball a blow like the kick of a mule'. Nicklaus was only an average performer with a wedge in his hands, but his putting has always been unrivalled for its consistency. Above all, he was the equal of Ben Hogan in his careful analysis of a championship course; nothing was left to chance.

It was a portent that Nicklaus's first victory as a professional was in the US Open of 1962 at Oakmont. It took a play-off against Arnold Palmer, and the key factor was Nicklaus's master of the slippery greens; he only took three putts once during the tournament.

This unexpected win, a rebuff to the people's champion, Palmer, triggered off their great rivalry which went on through the Sixties. It also triggered off some unseemly barracking of the young pretender. Certainly Nicklaus did not cut an especially attractive figure in his youth: he was tubby, had a crew-cut and his background was relatively privileged; but the attempts by Palmer's fans to put him off his game, their shouted references to him as 'Ohio Fats', only embarrassed Arnold Palmer. Nicklaus took it all in stoic silence; he never complained in public.

By 1966 Nicklaus had won 14 events on the American tour and, much more important to him, six major championships. His victory in the Open Championship at Muirfield gave him his first complete set (the Grand Slam) of the majors and he therefore joined the illustrious band of Gene Sarazen, Ben Hogan and Gary Player. In his second victory in the Masters, in 1965, Nicklaus set a new record for the championship of 271; he was nine shots ahead of his nearest challengers, Palmer and Player. Bobby Jones was moved to say that Nicklaus 'plays a game with which I am not familiar.' In the following year he became the first golfer to win the Masters in successive years, after a play-off with Tommy Jacobs and Gay Brewer.

Then Jack Nicklaus began his inexorable drive to win all four major titles again. In 1967 he took the US Open Championship for the second time. At Baltusrol, he set a new

record of 275 for the event and beat Palmer into second place. But he did not add to his tally of majors until the 1970 Open at St Andrews, where the unfortunate Doug Sanders missed a short putt on the final green to allow Nicklaus into a play-off. On the 18th tee of the play-off Nicklaus dramatically peeled off his sweater and hit his ball through the back of the green, about 350 yards away; he chipped back and holed the putt, to win by one shot.

Having won the USPGA Championship in 1971, Nicklaus began the following year by winning the Masters for the fourth time and the US Open at Pebble Beach. There was much speculation that the 'Golden Bear', as he was now dubbed, could become the first golfer to take all the four major professional championships in one year. But the third leg, the Open at Muirfield, just slipped away despite Nicklaus's brilliant last round of 66. He was briefly in the lead after a scorching first ten holes but Trevino's own brand of idiosyncratic brilliance finally won the day, just as it had when the two men played off for the US Open title at Merion in the previous year. Perhaps Nicklaus had been too cautious in the early rounds; it was one of his failings to be too calculating, to throttle back on his power in favour of safety. As Peter Dobereiner memorably put it: 'He plays with the timidity of a middle-aged spinster walking home through a town full of drunken sailors.'

Perhaps it was just as well for the morale of the British Ryder Cup teams that Nicklaus did not qualify for the match until 1969. Although he won his opening foursomes, with Dan Sikes, against Peter Butler and Bernard Hunt, he did not sparkle in his usual way; he lost his fourball match and his first singles against Tony Jacklin. But in his second singles, again in opposition to Jacklin, Nicklaus left his own singular mark on the history of the Ryder Cup. With the points equal and their match the last one on the course, the two great champions came to the final green. Their game was level and the result of the 1969 Ryder Cup rested on their shoulders. Jacklin left his first putt a couple of feet short of the hole, but Nicklaus, further away after too bold an approach, holed out bravely. With a gallant gesture, which encapsulated not only the spirit of the fixture but also Nicklaus's own sense of golfing honour, he conceded Jacklin's putt for a half and the match was tied for the first time.

Two years later the American team won the trophy at St Louis, where Nicklaus won five matches out of six. In 1973 at Muirfield his dominance continued as he won four and a half points out of six. It is foolish to write of Nicklaus as being in his prime; he had been in his prime since 1962 and was usually regarded as the favourite to win any important championship over the next two decades. In 1975 he added both the Masters and the USPGA Championships to his crowded prize cupboard. The Masters saw an intense battle between Nicklaus, Tom Weiskopf and Johnny Miller, but Nicklaus took a winning lead by a remarkable putt on the treacherous 16th green and jumped in the air in his excitement. Miller, playing behind Nicklaus, did not see the putt go in but later said, 'I found the bear prints on the green.'

In the Ryder Cup match of 1975 at Laurel Valley, easily won by the Americans, Nicklaus was undefeated in his first three matches. He then suffered an unexpected reverse at the hand of Brian Barnes in the first series of singles. The overall match had been won and lost by lunchtime and Nicklaus, intent both on revenge and on entertaining the crowd, arranged that he and Barnes should meet again. But the talented Englishman brought off a brilliant double by beating Nicklaus again. Barnes recalls how they talked mostly of their common interest, fishing, during the matches and how gracious Nicklaus was in defeat.

In 1977 at Lytham the Americans won the Cup yet again, and with great ease. For some time it had been apparent that the one-sidedness of the contests had led to a waning of interest in the fixture, especially in the USA. A Commonwealth team had been mooted, but Nicklaus, in discussions with Lord Derby, the President of the British PGA, lent his considerable weight to the concept of a European team. It became so in 1979 and it was ironic that Nicklaus was not a member of the opposing team. But he was one of the men who saved the Ryder Cup.

In 1977 Nicklaus had been involved, with Tom Watson, in one of the most exciting finishes ever seen in the Open Championship. At Turnberry they matched each other relentlessly for four days. With their third rounds of 65, they outdistanced all their challengers and dazzled the spectators yet again on the final day. Tom Watson was never in the lead until the 71st hole and then he clung on to win down the final hole, with a birdie of his own to match that of Nicklaus. But the latter bounced back in the following year to win the Open at St Andrews. It was his 15th

major championship and since 1962 he had always been in the top ten of the American money list; he has been the leader eight times and the runner-up five times.

By this time Nicklaus was regarded as one of the elder statesmen of world golf. He was no longer the fat kid who had knocked the crown rudely off the beloved Palmer's head. He had also softened his image in the early Seventies: he was slimmer and wore his hair long. Now that Tom Watson was treating him as he had treated Palmer, the fans transferred their adoration to Nicklaus.

In some quarters it was assumed that Nicklaus's expanding business activities, especially in golf course design, would reduce his enthusiasm for tournament golf. But no golfer has had such an intense will to win championships, especially the majors. In 1980, he won the

US Open at Baltusrol. It was his fourth victory and he began with a round of 63. A few months later he won the USPGA Championship at Oak Hill for the fifth time and thereby equalled Walter Hagen's record.

In 1981 Nicklaus reappeared at the Ryder Cup in one of the strongest of all American teams. He finished his playing career in the biennial fixture in great style with four wins from four matches, three of them in partnership with Tom Watson. It was inevitable that Nicklaus should captain the American team and he did so in 1983 and 1987. The narrowest of wins at the PGA National was followed by America's first home defeat, at Nicklaus's own course, Muirfield Village.

After Jack Nicklaus's victories in 1980 his tournament successes were meagre. Opinion was that Nicklaus was just marking time before one last foray on the Seniors tour. But he confounded the pundits once again at the 1986 Masters. With a dazzling final round of 65 he won his sixth green jacket. His play of the last ten holes, with seven birdies, was flawless. No one should bet against his winning another major championship, even in his fifties.

Jack Nicklaus has graced the game of golf for over three decades. It is unlikely that anyone will ever equal his success and only a few will attain his standard of sportsmanship and dignity.

NORTH, ANDY

USA

Born: 9.3.50

Appearances: 1985

Record: P3 W0 L3 H0

Andy North has the unusual distinction of having won the US Open twice out of a total of three victories on the American tour. His other win was in the Westchester Classic of 1977. The tall American from Wisconsin clearly has a liking for tough golf courses; when he won the 1978 US Open at Cherry Hills no player broke par; when he won again in 1985 at Oakland Hills North was the only man to do so. It is certain that he would have won many more events if he had not been plagued by injuries throughout his career.

North and John Mahaffey won the World Cup for the USA in 1978 but he did not make the Ryder Cup team until 1985. He started badly by losing both his fourball games, but seemed on the brink of redeeming himself in the singles when he was three holes up on Sam Torrance with eight to play.

But, on the 18th tee, Torrance had levelled the match and whereas he hit a scorching drive down the last fairway, North skyed his ball into the water. It fell to the Scotsman to hole the putt which brought the Ryder Cup back to Europe after 28 years. The scenes of jubilation must have made it all the harder to bear for Andy North.

O

O'CONNOR, CHRISTY

GB

Born: 21.12.24

Appearances: 1955, 1957, 1959, 1961, 1963, 1965, 1967, 1969, 1971, 1973

Record: P36 W11 L21 H4

There is no doubt that Christy O'Connor is one of the finest golfers to come out of Ireland; at his peak, in the Sixties, he was one of the pre-eminent players in Europe. He did not travel to Britain to play tournament golf until 1954 when he was nearly 30 years of age but he served notice of his great talent by taking Henry Cotton to the fifth extra hole of their semi-final in the Penfold tournament.

A year later O'Connor made his debut in the Ryder Cup at Thunderbird Ranch, in California. So began his unbroken sequence of ten appearances, which remains a record. He lost his match to Tommy Bolt in the singles but at Lindrick, in 1957, he played his full part in the famous victory. Although he and Eric Brown were undone by the brilliant golf of Dick Mayer and Tommy Bolt in the foursomes, O'Connor demolished Dow Finsterwald in the singles. After 18 holes, the match was level but the lunch must have revived the Irishman since he won six of the next eight holes and cruised on to victory by a 'dog licence'. Two years later, at Eldorado, he was to suffer the same fate at the hands of Art Wall, after he and Peter Alliss had beaten Wall and Ford in the foursomes. This was the start of a long partnership between O'Connor and Alliss. They played 12 matches together and, though their personalities were markedly different, made an excellent team. One of their successes, according to Alliss, was that they were both suspect on short putts and were therefore very careful not to leave each other putts of an awkward length.

In the late Fifties O'Connor won a long sequence of important events, including the Swallow-Penfold, the Dunlop Masters in 1956 and 1959, the PGA Matchplay Championship, the Daks and the Martini tournaments. He had the great ability to surge through the field and snatch victory with a low final round. In the 1956 Masters he made up six strokes on Eric Brown with a final round of 67 in a strong wind at Prestwick; in the same event in 1959, at Portmarnock, he saved the reputations of all the professionals by overtaking the amateur, Joe Carr, with a final round of 66.

O'Connor showed up strongly in the Open Championship. In 1958 at Lytham, he led the field after opening rounds of 67 and 68. Although he fell back in the third round, he recovered his position to such an extent that he judged that he needed a birdie three at the 72nd hole to win the championship. His tee shot landed in a bunker and he took five shots; a par four would have put him in the play-off with Peter Thomson and David Thomas. In 1961 he was equal third again and equal second in 1965. His record in the Open over the two decades from 1955 was more consistent than any golfer from the British Isles, in that he finished in the top 10 on 10 occasions and in the top 20 on 15 occasions.

The keystone of O'Connor's game was his smooth and rhythmic swing. He was often referred to as a natural golfer, but that beautifully free and uninhibited action had been ingrained by long hours of practice, often on the sands of his native Galway, during his youth. He was a powerful and attacking player who also had the ability to invent a whole range of different shots. Pat Ward-Thomas wrote of O'Connor's 'lovely, rounded movement, strong and yet graceful'. His one weakness was an occasional vulnerability with his putter, especially from short range.

The Ryder Cup matches of the Sixties brought only mixed success for O'Connor and no success at all for the British teams. In 1961, at Lytham, and two years later at East Lake, Atlanta, he won only two and a half points from nine games but, at Birkdale in 1965, he and Peter Alliss played some sterling golf and won three of their four outings together. Cyclical as golf usually is, they lost all three of their games together in Houston

in 1967 and O'Connor lost his singles to Bobby Nichols. But in the remarkable tied fixture at Birkdale two years later O'Connor played a vital part by winning two points out of four.

O'Connor had a very rewarding knack of winning the big money events: for example, he had won the Alcan tournament in 1968 and he demonstrated this ability yet agin in 1970 when he took the huge first prize of £25,000 in the John Player Classic. O'Connor was not perturbed by being chased all the way home on the final day by the US Open champion, Tony Jacklin.

In 1971, at Old Warson, St Louis, O'Connor was asked to partner Neil Coles in the opening foursomes match. Coles still remembers how he pressed the Irishman to decide who would hit the opening drive. Despite several attempts to force a decision the pair went to the first tee still undecided. To the amazement of their opponents, Billy Casper and Miller Barber, they proceeded to toss a coin. So much for tactics, but the British pair won the match.

O'Connor's tenth and final appearance was at Muirfield, in 1973, and once again he and Coles won their opening foursomes together, this time against Tom Weiskopf and Jesse Snead. O'Connor lost his next three games, including his singles against Snead on the final morning. He told his captain, Bernard Hunt, that he was too tired to play in the afternoon and settled down to a good lunch, helped on its way by a few glasses of red wine. But Hunt, mindful that the Americans only needed three more points from the afternoon's eight matches to win the Ryder Cup, prevailed upon O'Connor to turn out again. The captain reckoned that a well-lunched Christy O'Connor would be more than a match for any opponent. So it proved as, fortified by an occasional nip from the hip-flasks carried by his supporters, he forced a half against Tom Weiskopf, the Open champion of that year.

During his long career O'Connor won dozens of titles in Ireland and represented his country in the World Cup on 15 occasions between 1956 and 1975. In 1958, in the heat and the thin atmosphere of Mexico City, he and Harry Bradshaw won the team event. When O'Connor reached Seniors status he won the PGA Seniors title five times and the World Seniors event twice. His splendid swing stood the test of time and he is still the professional at Royal Dublin.

O'CONNOR JR CHRISTY

GB & Europe

Born: 19.8.48

Appearances: 1975, 1989

Record: P4 W1 L3 H0

A golfing apprenticeship in the long shadow of Ireland's greatest golfer, Christy O'Connor, might have adversely afflicted some men; but not Christy Jr, who pays tribute to the help he was given by his famous uncle, to whom he was an assistant at Royal Dublin. He became a good enough golfer to follow his uncle into the Ryder Cup team. Separated by 14 years, Christy O'Connor's two appearances could hardly have been more different: the dismal defeat by a wide margin at Laurel Valley in 1975, after decades without a win, and the dramatic tie at the Belfry in 1989, by which Europe retained the Cup.

O'Connor was an automatic choice for the Laurel valley encounter but lost both his matches. It was little wonder that he and Eammon Darcy made no impression on Lou Graham and Tom Weiskopf in their fourball game, since Weiskopf, with a wonderful burst of scoring, went to the turn in 30 shots. At the celebration dinner the jovial O'Connor entertained everyone by singing 'Danny Boy', at the special request of Lee Trevino.

That year had been one of O'Connor's best on the European circuit; he won the Irish Open and the Martini tournament. In 1985 his consistent play, which included third place in the Open

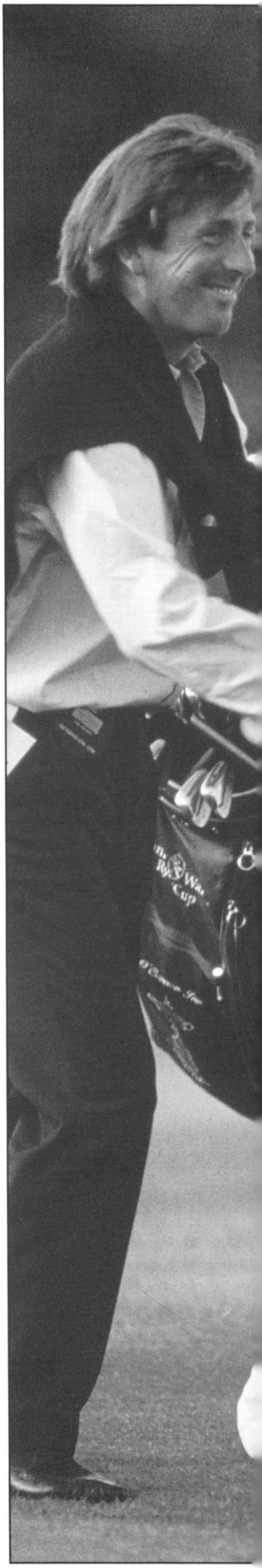

Christy O'Connor Jr acknowledges his win over Fred Couples in 1989 (left) and then sheds tears of joy.

at Royal St George's, took him to tenth place in the Ryder Cup points table, but the captain, Tony Jacklin, with the right to choose three out of the twelve players, overlooked him, to O'Connor's intense disappointment. All was forgiven and forgotten, however, when Jacklin did pick him for the 1989 match.

O'Connor and Ronan Rafferty lost their foursomes to Mark Calcavecchia and Ken Green and O'Connor was drawn in the singles to play the accomplished, long-hitting Fred Couples. With great determination he clung on to the American and they were level on the 18th tee. O'Connor's second shot across the water, played with a 2-iron to within a few feet of the flag, will never be forgotten as long as the Ryder Cup is recalled. It was a dazzling thrust which so discountenanced Couples that he pushed his 9-iron shot weakly to the right of the green. When he took three more shots to hole out the American conceded the match to O'Connor, who shed tears of understandable emotion.

O'Connor has spent over two decades on the European tour. Despite his popular win in the Irish Open, his five appearances in the World Cup for Ireland and his sparkling victory in the 1992 British Masters at Woburn, the personable Irishman will certainly best be remembered for that thrilling and vital shot to the 18th green at the Belfry.

O'LEARY, JOHN

GB

Born: 19.8.49

Appearances: 1975

Record: P4 W0 L4 H0

It was easy to pick out John O'Leary at the European tournaments in the 1970s. He was tall and good-looking, his long dark hair usually styled in an extravagant way and he had a good line in unusual clothes: one can remember a pair of trousers, one leg white and the other black.

While his appearance was striking, his golf, which sometimes promised so much, never really blossomed. He won the Sumrie Fourball Tournament with Jack Newton in 1975 and the Greater Manchester Open a year later, and in his home country he had a highly popular win in the Carrolls Irish Open in 1982. But his highest finish in the Order of Merit was in 16th place in 1976.

Although he lost all his matches at Laurel Valley in 1975 he encountered some fine American scoring along the way, notably from Lee Trevino and Hale Irwin in their fourball match. He lost his singles to Irwin when the tie had already been won by the Americans.

O'MEARA, MARK

USA

Born: 13.1.57

Appearances: 1985, 1989, 1991

Record: P8 W2 L5 H1

One cannot but warm to a man who treats the loss of a large quantity of money with equanimity. It happened to Mark O'Meara on a rough and windy practice day at the Open Championship at Royal Birkdale in 1991. As he opened his golf bag by the practice ground, great numbers of the folding stuff were whisked away on the wind. As the spectators set off in hot pursuit he told them not to bother. 'Easy come, easy go,' he said with a smile. There was some natural justice in his finishing third in the Open, after playing some sterling golf in tricky conditions. His reward was £55,000 which presumably covered his losses.

O'Meara's demeanour on the golf course is just as easy and charming, which perhaps explains his great consistency. In the last eight years he has never been out of the top 30 on the money list and has won seven tournaments. Although he won the US Amateur Championship in 1979, his best finishes in the major professional championships have all been in third place: in the Open in 1985 and 1991, and in the US Open in 1988.

O'Meara made his debut in the Ryder Cup at the Belfry in 1985 and lost his opening foursomes, in partnership with Curtis Strange, to Severiano Ballesteros and Manuel Pinero. However, he and Lanny Wadkins took their revenge on the Spaniards; with a better ball of 32 to the turn the Americans coasted to victory in the second series of fourballs. O'Meara lost to Howard Clark in the singles and, when he returned to the Belfry in 1989, lost both his matches. He and Tom Watson suffered a devastating attack from Ballesteros and Olazabal, who won the first five holes: Ballesteros then eagled the tenth hole and had three birdies in a row to finish the American pair off.

In the remarkable duel at Kiawah Island in 1991 O'Meara opened with a halved fourball match; but he and Paul Azinger demolished David Gilford and Nick Faldo, who appeared totally uninterested in the proceedings, by the dreaded 'dog licence' – seven and six. But O'Meara was fairly easily defeated by the newcomer, Paul Broadhurst, in the singles.

O'Meara has a stylish and versatile game, which includes a relaxed and effective putting stroke. Apart from his regular support of the Open he is prepared to travel outside America to play tournaments and has won events in Japan and Britain, as well as the Australian Masters. He started the 1992 season by winning the National Pro-Am at Pebble Beach for the third year running.

OLAZABAL, JOSE-MARIA

Europe

Born: 5.2.66

Appearances: 1987, 1989, 1991

Record: P15 W10 L3 H2

From an early age it was clear that Jose Maria Olazabal would have a career in golf. His home lay in the middle of the San Sebastian golf course in the Basque country of northern Spain and many of his family worked at the club. By the time he was 19 Olazabal had won a string of European amateur titles; in Britain he won the British Boys' Championship, the Amateur Championship and the British Youths' Championship, the first time such a feat had been achieved. It was already apparent that a great career in professional golf lay ahead.

Olazabal took the European circuit by storm in 1986, his first season. He won the Swiss Open and the Sanyo Open and finished second in the Order of Merit. It was an extraordinary debut and was founded on several virtues, in particular his unrivalled short game and his intense concentration. His second season was by no means as spectacular, but was sound enough to persuade Tony Jacklin to pick him as a wild card for the 1987 Ryder Cup match at Muirfield Village.

With great prescience the captain paired Olazabal with Severiano Ballesteros and they collected three points from their four matches. Olazabal had a nervous start in the foursomes against Payne Stewart and Larry Nelson but the senior partner rescued matters twice, with long shots of genius from bunkers at the tenth and at the final hole, to secure victory. The Spaniards lost their second fourball against Hall Sutton and Larry Mize, and Olazabal was defeated by Payne Stewart in his singles.

Olazabal found his best form again in 1988 when he finished third in the Order of Merit after winning the Belgian Open and the German Masters; in the following year he won the Tenerife and Dutch Opens and was the runner-up in the money list. In the Ryder Cup at the Belfry he was unbeaten; he and

Olazabal and Ballesteros toast Europe's 1987 victory

Ballesteros won three and a half points from their four matches and he gained his revenge on Payne Stewart in the singles. The Spanish pair were in imperious form in their fourball games; they won the first five holes against Tom Watson and Mark O'Meara and Ballesteros followed an eagle at the tenth hole with three birdies, to see the Americans off. They defeated Calcavecchia and Ken Green almost as comprehensively.

In 1990 Olazabal won the Benson & Hedges International and followed this by taking first prize in the Irish Open and the Lancome Trophy. But it was his performance in the World Series of Golf at the unrelentingly difficult Firestone course in America which proclaimed his arrival as a bright star of golf. Olazabal began with a round of 61 and added three further rounds of 67. It was an astounding display; he won by 12 shots, the biggest winning margin since the days of Johnny Miller, and Olazabal was 18 shots under par, whereas only three other players managed to score below par. Jack Nicklaus was moved to call him 'one of the most exciting talents in the world'.

The pundits are unanimous in their view that Olazabal will win not just one, but several major championships. His time nearly came at Augusta in 1991 when he was the joint leader as he stood on the 72nd tee. But a bogey five to Ian Woosnam's four sent him into a tie for second place. Although Olazabal finished seventh in the Order of Merit, his experiences at the Masters seemed to blight his season, such is the importance which he attaches to the blue riband events of golf.

Nevertheless, he arrived at Kiawah Island with all guns firing for the Ryder cup. Once again he and Ballesteros were unbeaten together and their fierce endeavour and unwavering will to win was a supreme example to the rest of the European team. In twelve matches together they have won nine times and only lost once. Olazabal ended with a narrow defeat in the singles by Paul Azinger but it was a fascinating battle played in the very best of spirits.

Olazabal began the 1992 season with victories in the Tenerife and the Mediterranean Opens and it is apparent that he has every quality that makes a great golfer. His long game is secure, his short game is remarkable and his putting is as accurate as anyone's. Ballesteros considers that he is the best putter in the world from ten feet and under. Above all, he has a remarkably sound mental approach to the game and a maturity beyond his years. For example, he shunned three of the very lucrative events which are now scheduled for the turn of the year (the Million Dollar Challenge in Sun City, the Johnnie Walker Championship in Jamaica and the Tournament of Champions in California) in favour of several weeks of relaxation with his family and friends.

Olazabal is wise enough not to chase every dollar; he is intent on chasing glory.

OLIVER, ED

USA

Born: 1916

Appearances: 1947, 1951, 1953

Record: P5 W3 L2 H0

With a nickname like 'Porky' you would expect a big and extrovert character and that was what Ed Oliver brought to the game. He was well under six feet tall but tipped the scales at well over 200 pounds. Not surprisingly, he had quite a brief backswing but propelled the ball great distances. The crowds loved him because he had the gift of making golf look easy and full of enjoyment.

Oliver was a player of considerable skill and he won many important events, including the Bing Crosby Invitational, and the Phoenix, Houston, Western and Texas Opens. But much more often he came second, especially in the major tournaments. In the 1946 US PGA Championship he beat Byron Nelson, then in his prime, but lost the final to Ben Hogan; he was second in the US Open of 1952 behind Julius Boros; and was second to Ben Hogan in the Masters of 1953. His most famous near-miss was in the 1940 US Open, when he started his final round early, along with 'Dutch' Harrison and Johnny Bulla, because of warnings of thunderstorms. Oliver came home with a 71, which tied him for first place with Gene Sarazen and Lawson Little, but he was disqualified.

In his Ryder Cup debut, at Portland in 1947 Oliver won both his matches, which included a crushing defeat of Henry Cotton and Arthur Lees by ten and nine. There was a reversal of fortune at Pinehurst in 1951 when he lost twice to Arthur Lees but 'Porky' Oliver went out in style, in the very close encounter at Wentworth in 1953, by beating Harry Weetman and Peter Alliss in the first foursomes game.

OOSTERHUIS, PETER

GB & Europe

Born: 3.5.48

Appearances: 1971, 1973, 1975, 1977, 1979, 1981

Record: P28 W14 L11 H3

During the early Seventies Peter Oosterhuis was one of the most successful golfers in Europe; from 1971 to 1974 he achieved the remarkable record of winning the Vardon Trophy (for the lowest stroke average) each year and he collected 19 tournament victories. After an excellent amateur career, in which he won the British Youths' Championship and played in the 1967 Walker Cup, Oosterhuis made an exceptionally assured transition to the professional game. His first tournament was the Natal Open and he finished in second place; in his first professional event in Britain, the Penfold, he reached sixth position. By the end of 1969 he was 16th in the Order of Merit and deservedly won Henry Cotton's 'Rookie of the Year' award.

In 1970 Oosterhuis got into his stride by winning the South African Open and he stepped up his pace a year later by winning three events in Europe and three more in southern Africa. He represented England in the World Cup and made his first appearance in the Ryder Cup.

At 6 feet 5 inches, Peter Oosterhuis had the problem which besets all tall golfers: how to get comfortable in the address position. He hardly seemed able to resolve the difficulty; he shuffled his feet about, gripped and re-gripped his club and looked about anxiously as if hoping that someone would suggest some easier activity for him. After several waggles, he would take quite a short swing and throw the clubhead at the ball. But his method worked very well, as his record showed, and when it went wrong his amazingly secure short game would invariably save him. Above all, the pleasant and well-mannered Oosterhuis had an intractable will to win which made him a feared opponent in matchplay, especially in the Ryder Cup. For many years he

seemed unbeatable in the singles, in which he collected six and half points out of nine games.

His opponents in these head-to-head battles included six US Open champions and he beat the legendary Arnold Palmer twice. An important factor in his success was that he relished the thought of taking on these great players.

Oosterhuis made his debut in 1971 in St Louis and had a dispiriting start. He and Peter Townsend played splendid golf but could not overcome the battle-hardened pair of Arnold Palmer and Gardner Dickinson. They lost both games narrowly and then Oosterhuis, partnered with Bernard Gallacher, lost again to Palmer and Dickinson. Nevertheless, he had begun his Ryder Cup career in great style by holing his first putt, one of about 20 yards, for a birdie. On the final day he showed his mettle by beating two Open champions, Gene Littler and Arnold Palmer, in the singles matches.

At Muirfield in 1973 Oosterhuis had an excellent Ryder Cup match, with four points won from six games. He and Tony Jacklin teamed up to good effect and won two and half points out of four. In the first series of singles Oosterhuis was drawn against Lee Trevino, who had informed his team-mates that if he did not beat the Englishman, he would 'kiss the American team's asses.' The match was halved and Trevino admits that there is a photograph in existence which shows the Americans, with their trousers around their ankles, waiting in vain for the bet to be honoured. Oosterhuis remembers that he let Trevino off the hook at the 17th hole when he hit his second shot, with a driver, into a bunker. In the afternoon Oosterhuis polished Arnold Palmer off by a score of four and two.

The years 1973 and 1974 were to be highly successful for Peter Oosterhuis. He won the French Open twice, the Italian Open, the Piccadilly and the PGA Championship. In South Africa he showed his matchplay skills by beating Harold Henning seven and six, and Bobby Cole seven and six on the way to the final of the 1973 Matchplay Championship, in which he beat Gary Player by six and five.

At the 1973 Masters tournament in Augusta he had led the field by three shots after three rounds but a pushed shot with a wooden club into the 15th green betrayed him and he ended in third place. In the Open at Lytham a year later he was the runner-up to Gary Player.

It was after the 1974 European season that Oosterhuis, mindful perhaps of Tony Jacklin's example before him, decided to seek the broader and potentially more profitable pastures of the USA. He was only in his mid-twenties and had a splendid tournament record, and it was a gamble well worth taking. But the expected breakthrough never happened. The nearest he came to a victory was in 1974 when he lost a play-off for the Monsanto Open and in the years up to 1981 he finished in the top 60 of the money list on only two occasions. Finally, in 1981, he won the Canadian Open but that was the extent of his success on the American tour.

In the meantime Oosterhuis continued to play a staunch part for Britain in the Ryder Cup. In the three encounters at Laurel Valley in 1975, Lytham in 1977 and The Greenbrier in 1979 he played 13 matches and won eight and a half points. It was only in the latter match that his unbeaten record in the singles was breached by Hubert Green. His final appearance was two years later, at Walton Heath, when he was one of captain John Jacobs' special selections. Unfortunately, he was out of form and lost all his three games.

Oosterhuis, as spirited as ever, soldiered on with the American tour but had declined to 188th position on the money list in 1986. He insists that his decision to storm the American golfing barricades in the Seventies was the correct one, even if, during his leaner times in the USA, he cast the occasional wistful eye towards the European tour.

In 1984 he became the director of golf at the Fosgate Country Club in New Jersey and, since 1991, has fulfilled the same function at the prestigious Riviera Golf and Country Club in Los Angeles.

P

PADGHAM, ALF

GB

Born: 2.7.06

Appearances: 1933, 1935, 1937

Record: P6 W0 L6 H0

Alf Padgham was a worthy winner of the 1936 Open Championship after his third place in 1934 and his second place a year later. He had to hole a putt of around 12 feet for a birdie at the 72nd hole to hold off Jimmy Adams, but Padgham had been putting well for most of the season and brilliantly at the Open. In the last round he had single putts on five of the last six greens. Bernard Darwin described some of his putts as 'indecent'.

Alf Padgham was what the Americans call a 'streak' putter, capable of brilliance or bathos. He had an ungainly style with a putter in his huge hands; he stood very upright, with his hands away from his body. He said that he pictured a putt just like a drive in miniature. It looked bizarre and was a marked contrast to the smooth rhythm of his upright, three-quarter swing. He was tall, wiry and athletic and hit the ball a long way, and he was notably accurate with his iron shots.

As well as his Open victory, he recorded other prestigious wins, including the PGA Matchplay event in 1931 and 1935 and the Irish, Dutch and German Opens.

Padgham did himself no justice in his three Ryder Cup matches and nearly all his defeats were by wide margins. In his first appearance, he and Alf Perry managed to fritter away a lunchtime lead of four holes and lost by one hole to Ed Dudley and Billy Burke. In the 1937 tie, when the Americans won on British soil for the first time, it was the popular opinion that Padgham should not have been selected. But he was the reigning Open champion, even if it was said that he had 'lost his game', possibly as a result of staleness after a trip to South Africa with a British team.

Padgham, as expected, played golf of very poor quality in losing the opening foursomes, with Henry Cotton, to Ed Dudley and Byron Nelson. The British captain, Charles Whitcombe, then compounded the problem by dropping himself in favour of Padgham, who was easily beaten in the first singles match by Ralph Guldahl.

PALMER, ARNOLD

USA

Born: 10.9.29

Appearances: 1961, 1963, 1965, 1967, 1971, 1973
Captain 1963, 1975

Record: P32 W22 L8 H2

Just as Walter Hagen elevated the profession of golf to a new plateau of earning power and social acceptability between the two world wars, so Arnold Palmer was the catalyst for an explosion of interest in the game in the Sixties. Television made golf much more accessible to the general public and Arnold Palmer's approach, uncompromising and heroic, full of risk and daring, was absolutely right for his time. His golf was the perfect antidote to the calculating approach of Ben Hogan and Peter Thomson; Palmer's philosophy was to attack on every occasion, to overcome every course with power and unrelenting aggression. If his ball landed in the rough it was not a matter for regret, but merely a chance to uproot a bush or two as the ball was thumped on to the green, usually to be followed by an improbable putt for a birdie. The crowds loved it; they warmed to the uncertainty inherent in Palmer's game; it was sporting theatre with a dashing hero who showed all the pleasure and the pain of the conflict. When he suffered, they suffered along with him; when he triumphed, they triumphed too. Pat Ward-Thomas wrote: 'The very nature of his golf suggests a man fighting to overcome great odds, a man unafraid of challenge'. It is no wonder that Henry Cotton described him as the most popular golfer of all time.

Palmer was taught to play golf by his father and announced himself by winning the US Amateur Championship in 1954. A year later he won his first professional tournament, the Canadian Open and was to win another 60 events over the next two decades. He won two more tournaments in 1956 but it was in the following year that he finished in fifth place on the money list and he remained in the top ten every year until 1972. He was the leading money winner four times and second on three occasions.

In 1958 Palmer won the first of his four Masters Championships at Augusta and his second victory, two years later, was achieved in the characteristically grand manner that symbolised his golf. Palmer had led the field after every round but, with two holes to play, he needed two birdies to overtake Ken Venturi. The putts went in and the green jacket was Palmer's once again. At the US Open a few months later at Cherry Hills, Palmer's charge to victory was even more dramatic. It seemed that all was lost after three rounds when he was seven strokes behind the leader, Mike Souchak. Made more fiercely intent by the remarks of a journalist friend, who told him over lunch that he had no chance of winning, Palmer drove his ball on to the green at the par-4 first hole and got a birdie; he chipped in at the second for a birdie; and had four more birdies as he raced to the turn in 30 shots. 'Arnie's Army', as his supporters were later dubbed, was now also on the charge and Palmer scored a 65 to win by two shots from a young amateur called Jack Nicklaus. It was an extraordinary victory which was the essence of Palmer's golf.

With two of the four major championships already won, Palmer was fired by the thought of equalling Ben Hogan's record of taking three majors in a single year. He made a valiant attempt to win the Open Championship at St Andrews but lost by one shot to the Australian, Kel Nagle. But his visit reinforced Palmer's respect for the traditions of the game, strongly imbued in him by his father, and he vowed to return until he won the oldest of the great championships. At the time the Open was in poor health. The leading Americans no longer supported it, as had Walter Hagen, Gene Sarazen and Bobby Jones between the wars and there were no great British players, such as Henry Cotton, to kindle the enthusiasm. But Arnold Palmer's dynamic presence did more than anything to restore the prestige of the championship, particularly since his example prompted other prominent American professionals to try their luck.

In 1961, in rough conditions at Birkdale, Palmer won his first Open Championship. Those who saw his second round, played in a gale strong enough to flatten

several marquees, recall it with awe. Only Palmer had the power to wrest birdies from three of the first six holes. At the 15th hole in the final round his ball was trapped under a bank in thick gorse and grass. Where a lesser mortal would have chipped out and settled for a dropped shot, Palmer thundered into the shot with a 6-iron and put his ball on the green. A plaque commemorates the stroke. Palmer won the championship by one shot from Dai Rees. A year later he retained the title at Troon in totally different conditions. The course was running so hard and fast that it was verging on the unplayable but Palmer blasted his shots down the burnished fairways and won by six shots from Kel Nagle, with the next men, Brian Huggett and Phil Rodgers, 13 strokes in arrears. Dai Rees wrote: 'I don't believe I shall ever see again such a display of attacking golf.'

Earlier that year Palmer had won the Masters for the second time, but had just failed to win the US Open at Oakmont. Jack Nicklaus beat him in a play off.

Palmer arrived on the Ryder Cup stage in 1961, at Lytham, and assumed his expected role. He was undefeated in his four games, and only Peter Alliss managed to force a half from him. The Englishman was to prove one of Palmer's toughest opponents since he beat him in their singles two years later at East Lake; but Palmer won four points out of a possible six and also captained the American team.

Arnold Palmer was now at the height of his powers and was the popular choice to win virtually every tournament in which he appeared. With the help of television, his characteristic gestures were familiar around the world: the cigarette flicked on to the ground; the hitch of the trousers; the mighty thrash through the ball with the right hand driving on down the line of the shot until the club was whirled into a variety of eccentric finishes; the knock-kneed stance as he sent one of his putts charging fearlessly at the hole. It was not elegant; Dan Jenkins wrote that Palmer 'hit the ball with all the finesse of a dock worker lifting a crate of auto parts'. But no golfer had ever brought such excitement and commitment to the game. He was Superman in a cashmere sweater. With all this, Palmer was friendly and engaging and showed endless patience in his dealings with his fans and with the media. With the help of an astute agent he laid the foundations of a significant business empire which prospers mightily to this day.

In 1963 Palmer lost a play-off for the US Open to Julius Boros but he won seven other events and led the money list. In the following year he reasserted himself at the Masters, which he won by six shots. Even though he was only in his mid-thirties, it was to be his last victory in a major championship. Palmer came close on several occasions; he was the runner-up in the

USPGA Championship on three occasions but was never able to complete the Grand Slam; he was second to Nicklaus in the Masters in 1965 and was the runner-up in the US Open in 1966 and 1967. Nevertheless, he won another 18 tournaments on the American tour and it was his putting that held him back in the major events: he was no longer able to ram so many long putts unerringly into the back of the hole.

The Open at the Olympic Club, San Francisco, in 1966 demonstrated how Palmer's do-or-die philosophy could misfire. With nine holes of the final round to play he was seven strokes clear of Billy Casper. Palmer probably had his eye on Ben Hogan's record US Open score of 276 and tried to force the pace too much. He frittered away his shots to such an extent that a play-off was required, which was won by Casper. In portentous style *Sports Illustrated* wrote of the result as 'one of the great debacles in modern times ... comparable to Liz Taylor's *Cleopatra*.' It wasn't as bad as that.

Palmer continued to make his biennial appearance in the Ryder Cup. At Birkdale in 1965 he and Dave Marr were totally outclassed in the opening foursomes by David Thomas and George Will, who won by six and five. The Americans spent their lunchtime on the practice ground, went to the turn in the afternoon in 30 shots, and neatly reversed the result against the same British pair. Two years later Palmer flew his own jet to Houston for the fixture and questioned the captain, Ben Hogan, about the advisability of using the smaller British ball in the match. The old maestro, as implacable as ever, told Palmer that he had not, as yet, been selected for any of Hogan's pairings. Palmer answered the rebuke with deeds; he won all five of his matches.

Palmer did not return to Ryder Cup duty until 1971, at St Louis, when his dominant form continued. He won both his foursomes and both his fourballs, three of them in harness with Gardner Dickinson. In their fourball game against Gallacher and Oosterhuis, controversy was stirred. At the short seventh hole, Palmer had hit a fine shot onto the green when Gallacher's caddie, greatly impressed, asked him what iron he had used. The question was an innocent one and was not made in the hearing of the British players. But it was reported to the officials as a breach of the rules, and the hole was awarded to the Americans. Gallacher believes that Dickinson claimed the hole, whereas Palmer did his best to have the technicality waived. Palmer was not such a force in the singles matches; he halved with the resilient Harry Bannerman and lost to Peter Oosterhuis, who beat him again at Muirfield in 1973. His final record in the Ryder Cup was formidable, with 22 wins and two halves in 32 matches. Palmer was also the non-playing captain of the Ryder Cup side in 1975 at Laurel Valley.

By the middle of the Seventies Arnold Palmer had won nearly 20 overseas events, to add to his tally of 61 on the American tour. He had won the World Cup team title six times in the Sixties and the individual title once. His appearances in Britain always attracted huge support and he won the World Matchplay Championship at Wentworth in 1964 and 1967. His victory in the PGA Championship in 1975, in the most testing conditions at Royal St George's, was greeted with delight. A few years later his presence on the American Seniors tour gave it the impetus it required; he won ten events, the last one in 1988.

If ever anyone had doubted Henry Cotton's description of Palmer as the most popular golfer in the world, they should have been at St Andrews in 1990. Thirty years after his first appearance, Palmer had decreed that this was to be his final foray in the Open Championship, the event which his presence had done so much to restore to its former prestige. His reception from the packed crowds was a moving and eloquent testimony to Arnold Palmer's standing as a modern sporting hero.

PALMER, JOHNNY

USA

Born: 3.7.18

Appearances: 1949

Record: P2 W0 L2 H0

Although the Americans won the Ryder Cup at Ganton in 1949, Johnny Palmer lost both his matches. He was the victim of Jimmy Adams and Max Faulkner in the foursomes and lost again to Adams in the singles.

Palmer was not a spectacular player, but he had an immaculate putting stroke and was one of the leading money winners in America during the late Forties and early Fifties. During those years, he won the Western, the Houston and the Canadian Opens, and the World Championship of Golf and was the runner-up to Sam Snead in the 1949 USPGA Championship.

PANTON, JOHN

GB

Born: 9.10.16

Appearances: 1951, 1953, 1961

Record: P5 W0 L5 H0

John Panton had a miserable time of it in the Ryder Cup. He had a disconcerting baptism in 1951, at Pinehurst, when he was drawn, with Jimmy Adams, to play the fearsome pair of Sam Snead and Lloyd Mangrum. There was no contest, and on the following day it was no surprise that Panton subsided to a heavy defeat by Skip Alexander.

Two years later, at Wentworth, he was paired with his fellow Scot, Eric Brown: in theory a formidable team. They came out of the hat against Snead and Mangrum again. It was an even worse defeat, as the British pair lost the first four holes and were seven down after nine holes. Panton won a place in the British side again in 1961 but in his only match, a foursomes, he and Bernard Hunt were heavily defeated by Arnold Palmer and Billy Casper.

Panton was a golfer of great ability and, with Eric Brown, he dominated Scottish golf through the Fifties and the early Sixties. He won the Scottish Professional Championship seven times and represented his country in the World Cup every year from 1955 to 1966. His most notable victory was in the *News of the World* Championship in 1956, and he went on to win the British Seniors Championship in 1967 and 1969. In the final of the World Seniors event of 1967, which was played on a matchplay basis between the respective champions of Britain and America, he faced his nemesis, Sam Snead, and beat him.

Panton had great control and accuracy with his long irons and was a fine improviser of shots. If his driving and his short-range putting were sometimes uncertain, nevertheless he had a golf swing that stood the test of time. At the 1970 Open at St Andrews, when he was aged 53, he recorded the lowest final round and finished in a tie for ninth position.

PARKS, SAM

US

Born: 23.7.09

Appearances: 1935

Record: P1 W0 L0 H1

He called himself the 'dark horse champion', and Sam Parks was regarded as a 20-to-1 outsider for the US Open Championship in 1935. But he knew the Oakmont course well – a tough one strewn with rutted bunkers. The greens were fast and so slippery that the Oakmont professional claimed that it was a course where even good putters worried about their second putt before they hit their first. Parks was the only player to break 300 and became the champion.

Parks had been taught golf by Gene Sarazen and was one of the leading players in the Pittsburgh University team. When he graduated in 1931, there were few jobs to be had in those years of depression after the Great Crash and he turned professional. His slow, controlled backswing made him a consistent player and he had high finishes in many tournaments. He was a methodical player, too, and was one of the first professionals to keep notes about the courses he played: which iron to hit from which point on the course, and how the grain ran on each green, for example. He was criticised by his contemporaries for slow play.

His only match in the Ryder Cup was at Ridgewood, New Jersey, in 1935 when the USA won by nine matches to three. He halved with Alf Perry, but had to hole out from 40 feet at the last to do so.

Parks's career as a professional golfer lasted no more than ten years. In 1942 he began work with US Steel and stayed with them for over 30 years.

PATE, JERRY

USA

Born: 16.9.53

Appearances: 1981

Record: P4 W2 L2 H0

Jerry Pate was blessed with one of the finest swings in golf. After a fine career as an amateur, during which he won the US Amateur Championship and played in the Walker Cup, he took the professional game by storm. Like Jack Nicklaus, with whom comparisons were inevitable, his first victory was in the US Open, in 1976 at Atlanta Athletic Club. He was only 22 years of age and followed this up by winning the Canadian Open with a final round of 63, a record for the event.

In his first year as a professional Pate finished tenth on the money list and was clearly destined to be the next superstar of golf. His achievements continued; in the following year he won the Southern and Phoenix Opens; the Southern Open again in 1978 and he lost a play-off for the USPGA Championship to John Mahaffey. Then came a gap without a victory, even if he was always among the first dozen in the money list. But in 1981 his classic swing won the Danny Thomas Memphis event; he celebrated by jumping into the lake by the clubhouse. His motive, apart from high spirits, was to show that 'golfers are human and the game is supposed to be fun.' There are a lot of professional golfers on both sides of the Atlantic who need to be reminded of that sentiment.

Pate easily qualified for the 1981 Ryder Cup team, judged to be one of the strongest American sides ever. The match was played at Walton Heath and in his first fourball match he was paired with Ben Crenshaw. They ran into a maelstrom of birdies from Sandy Lyle and Mark James, whose better ball was eight under par when the match ended on the 16th green.

At this point the burly figure of Lee Trevino intervened and he took Pate under his wing. Trevino said that the young American was the best player in the world 'from the shoulders down' and that Pate was to leave all the thinking to him and should merely go ahead and play the shots as instructed. It certainly worked: the American pair hammered Nick Faldo and Sam Torrance to the tune of seven and five in the second fourball series and then beat Torrance and Oosterhuis in the foursomes. Trevino later said: 'With my brains and his swing we were unbeatable. If I caddied for him, he'd never lose another tournament.' Without the benign influence of Trevino, Pate lost his singles game to Manuel Pinero, but the USA had by then retained the Ryder Cup.

In 1982 Pate's form did not waver. He finished equal third in the Masters and won the Tournament Players Championship at Sawgrass. Yet again he celebrated by hitting the water and this time took the designer of the course, Pete Dye, with him. Many of the golfers, who had found the course horribly difficult, were hoping that the water was very deep and that neither man could swim: especially Dye.

At the end of the season an injury to Pate's shoulder laid him low and, despite many operations, he has never been able to return successfully to tournament golf. It is a shame that golf has lost such a beautiful swing, and that Pate's iconoclastic sense of humour no longer enlivens the tournament scene.

Jerry Pate

PATE, STEVE

USA

Born: 26.5.61

Appearances: 1991

Record: P1 W0 L1 H0

Steve Pate had the great misfortune to suffer injury in a car accident on the way to a celebration dinner a couple of days before the Ryder Cup began. Although he played a fourball match, which he and Corey Pavin lost, he was clearly in pain and had to scratch from the singles. A nominal half was declared between him and the unfortunate David Gilford, who had to stand down from the European team.

Pate joined the US tour in 1985 and has won four tournaments, including the Honda Classic in 1991, his best year so far, during which he finished in sixth place on the money list with over $700,000.

PAVIN, COREY

USA

Born: 16.11.59

Appearances: 1991

Record: P3 W1 L2 H0

Corey Pavin started playing golf as a child and at the age of 17 won the Junior World Championship. He played in the 1981 Walker Cup, graduated to the European tour and won the German Open in 1983. In the following year, his first on the American circuit, he won the Houston Open and finished 18th on the money list. Since then he has won a further eight events and was the leading money winner in 1991.

Pavin is a very slender man with an unorthodox swing; he is a comparatively short hitter but more than compensates for this with his accuracy, his imaginative shot-making and his very sound putting. In 1991 he finished in the top ten in ten tournaments and only missed the cut once.

At Kiawah Island he and Mark Calcavecchia were easily dispatched in their foursomes by Mark James and Steve Richardson. In the fourballs he was paired with Steve Pate, who was clearly feeling the effects of an injury sustained in a car accident, and they lost to Langer and Montgomerie. But Pavin bounced back to win a crucial point in his singles against Richardson.

PEETE, CALVIN

USA

Born: 18.7.43

Appearances: 1983, 1985

Record: P7 W4 L2 H1

It is said that Calvin Peete, from a poor family, with 18 brothers and sisters, decided to become a professional golfer in the late Sixties when he learned how much Jack Nicklaus earned on the American tour each year. He fulfilled his ambition by joining the tour in the Seventies when he was over 30 years of age, but he did not make his mark until the following decade. He recorded twelve victories, four of which came in 1982, when he was also third in the USPGA Championship.

In the tense Ryder Cup encounter at the PGA National course in Florida, in 1983, Peete won his first game in concert with Tom Kite against Paul Way and Severiano Ballesteros. Although he lost a fourball match, he won a further one and a half points, including a narrow singles victory over Brian Waites. Despite his odd-looking swing (the result of a damaged left elbow), Peete is known as one of the most accurate players in golf and he won the Vardon Trophy for the lowest stroke average on the US tour in 1984 (70.56). Statistics, especially when applied to golf, can be very misleading but for ten years in succession, from 1981 to 1990, he was measured as the most accurate driver on the American tour.

In 1985 he won the Phoenix Open and the prestigious Tournament Players Championship and secured his place in the team to play Europe at the Belfry. His captain, Lee Trevino, paired him again with Tom Kite and rated them as his strongest foursomes pair. Although they opened with a win over Bernhard Langer and Nick Faldo, they were hammered by the Spanish combination of Canizares and Rivero. Peete got his revenge in the singles by beating Rivero but Europe won a great victory.

Calvin Peete

PERRY, ALF

GB

Born: 8.10.04

Appearances: 1933, 1935, 1937

Record: P4 W0 L3 H1

It was regarded as an unexpected victory when Alf Perry won the Open Championship at Muirfield in 1935. Most eyes were on the defending champion, Henry Cotton, and the Americans, Henry Picard and Lawson Little. Perry had a magnificent third round of 67, which tied the Open record for a single round, but began his final round with a chaotic six. Undaunted, he had a birdie at the second hole which seemed to quell his fears. He played with ever more confidence and even ventured to play a spoon (3-wood) shot from a bunker at the 14th hole. This was typical of his approach to the game; he never played safe, and, if he could see the pin, he went for it. He won the Open by four shots from Alf Padgham.

Contemporaries remarked on his inelegant swing and his eccentric grip with the right hand, but his action was sound enough and he had a splendid short game.

Perry's best result in the Ryder Cup was a half in 1935 with Sam Parks, who was the current US Open champion.

PICARD, HENRY

USA

Born: 28.11.07

Appearances: 1935, 1937

Record: P4 W3 L1 H0

Henry Picard won his first major tournament, the North and South Open, at the age of 27 but he made up for his comparatively late start by winning nearly 30 events in his career. They included the Masters in 1938 and the USPGA in the following year when he defeated Byron Nelson in the final. His *annus mirabilis* was 1939: he had five other tournament victories and was the leading money winner.

Picard's career fitted neatly between the retirement of Bobby Jones and the arrival of Hogan, Snead and Nelson. He took Bobby Jones as his model and possessed one of the finest swings in the game. It lasted, too. Although he went into virtual retirement in 1940, he played again in the USGPA Championship in 1950 and reached the semi-final.

In the Ryder Cup he won both his matches in 1935; in the next match he lost his foursomes narrowly to Percy Alliss and Dick Burton but won his singles against Arthur Lacey.

Picard won two major championships and swung a golf club as well as anyone in the game. He was also a generous and warm-hearted man, as Ben Hogan would testify. In 1937 Hogan, down to his last few dollars, was about to give up the so far unrewarding life of the itinerant golf professional. Picard persuaded him to carry on, with the promise of financial support if he needed it.

PINERO, MANUEL

Europe

Born: 1.9.52

Appearances: 1981, 1985

Record: P9 W6 L3 H0

Manuel Pinero has played on the European tour since 1971 and has won nine tournaments including three victories in the Madrid Open and two in the Swiss Open. He has also won the PGA Championship, and the Italian and European Opens. He has reached the top five in the Order of Merit on four occasions but has been much hampered in recent years by tendonitis in his wrist.

Pinero has a marvellous record in the Ryder Cup, with six wins out of nine games. He first played at Walton Heath in 1981 and partnered Bernhard Langer in two foursomes and one fourball match. They beat Raymond Floyd and Hale Irwin in the latter and Pinero halved his singles with Bruce Lietzke.

He and Severiano Ballesteros played a crucial part in the European victory at the Belfry in 1985. On the first day their two wins kept Europe in the hunt and, although they lost their fourball on the next morning, they bounced back to demolish Craig Stadler and Hal Sutton in the second series of foursomes. Full of confidence, Pinero was delighted to draw Lanny Wadkins, one of the doughtiest matchplayers in the game, in the top single on the final day. With birdies at the 10th, 11th and 15th holes he beat the American and gave Europe a fine start to the day.

PLATTS, LIONEL

GB

Born: 10.10.34

Appearances: 1965

Record: P5 W1 L2 H2

Rumour has it that Lionel Platts has won far more money in private golf matches for high stakes than he has ever won in official tournaments. Certainly, he was a splendid matchplayer, a golfer with an excellent swing and a supreme ability to hole 'the ones that count'.

Platts first came to notice by winning the Essex Open and the Essex Professional Championship several times in the early Sixties. He then won an unusual event at Turnberry in 1964, the Braemar 7-club Tournament. His best year was 1965 when he was equal first in the Swallow-Penfold event and reached the final of the British Matchplay Championship. On the way to the final he won four of his matches in extra time and only lost to Neil Coles at the 19th.

Platts had certainly earned his selection for the Ryder Cup of 1965 at Royal Birkdale, and he played with great courage to win two points out of a possible five. Although he narrowly lost his foursomes match, in partnership with Peter Butler, to Julius Boros and Tony Lema, he halved both his fourballs on the following day. It must be said that he and Butler lost a lead of four holes with four to play against Billy Casper and Gene Littler in the first series of fourballs; but in the second match against the same pair Platts got up and down in two shots from a bunker 70 yards distant from the 18th green to record another half point.

In the singles Julius Boros was too strong for Platts in the morning, but he bounced back in the afternoon to beat Tommy Jacobs by one hole – all in vain, because the USA had already won the tie.

Manuel Pinero (left)

POHL, DAN

USA

Born: 1.4.55

Appearances: 1987

Record: P3 W1 L2 H0

Dan Pohl had to overcome early failures on the American tour before he established himself in the Eighties. Although he qualified for the tour in 1978, his form was such that he had to re-qualify a year later. For several seasons he reached out but could not grasp a victory, most notably in the 1982 Masters when he lost a play-off to Craig Stadler.

Despite his short backswing, Pohl is one of the longest hitters on the tour and at last he gained his elusive first victory, in the Colonial National Invitation of 1986. As so often happens he had another win soon afterwards, in the World Series of Golf.

His debut in the 1987 Ryder Cup at Muirfield Village, when the European team won for the first time in the USA, was an unhappy one. Although he and Hal Sutton won their foursomes against Ken Brown and Bernhard Langer, that was his only success. He lost his fourball match and Howard Clark defeated him in the singles.

Since then Pohl's form has been patchy and in 1990 his career was interrupted by the need for surgery on a troublesome back. Nevertheless, he managed to finish in the top hundred on the tour in 1991.

POLLAND, EDDIE

GB

Born: 10.6.47

Appearances: 1973

Record: P2 W0 L2 H0

Born in Northern Ireland, Eddie Polland won several Irish tournaments during the 1970s and represented Ireland in the World Cup on six occasions. He won the Penfold in 1973, the PGA Matchplay Championship in 1975 and the Spanish Open a year later.

He was known as a good matchplayer but in his only Ryder Cup appearance, at Muirfield in 1973, he came out of the hat opposite three of the most accomplished golfers in the world. In the first series of foursomes (with Maurice Bembridge) he lost heavily to Nicklaus and Arnold Palmer; and in the fourballs (with Clive Clark) to Nicklaus and Tom Weiskopf.

POTT, JOHNNY

USA

Born: 6.11.35

Appearances: 1963, 1965, 1967

Record: P7 W5 L2 H0

In 1956, the year after he graduated from Louisiana State University, Johnny Pott became a professional golfer. He was a steady, rather than a brilliant player who was consistently in the money without ever threatening to win a major championship. His career on the American tour lasted into the early Seventies and he won five tournaments, including the Dallas Open and the American Golf Classic.

His debut in the Ryder Cup, in 1963 at East Lake, Atlanta, was a rather nervous one. He seemed to be overawed by his partner, Arnold Palmer, and they were easily beaten in the foursomes by two British newcomers, Brian Huggett and George Will. He lost again to Huggett in the singles but at least managed to win a point in the fourballs in partnership with the accomplished Tony Lema.

Pott was selected for the 1965 match at Birkdale but was unlucky enough to damage a muscle in his side and was unable to play. In 1967, however, at Houston, Pott took four points out of four. He and Bobby Nichols beat Hunt and Coles both in the foursomes and the fourballs, and Alliss and O'Connor in the second series of foursomes. Pott had no difficulty with George Will in his only singles match.

R

RAFFERTY, RONAN

Europe

Born: 13.1.64

Appearances: 1989

Record: P3 W1 L2 H0

Golf has dominated Ronan Rafferty's life since he first began to play at the age of 9. His handicap was scratch at 15, when he won the British Boys championship. Two years later he became the youngest golfer to play in the Walker Cup and turned professional soon after. A great future was predicted for the young Irishman and it was something of a setback when he failed to win his player's card at the qualifying school. But his performances on the Safari Circuit qualified him for the European tour.

For many years Rafferty found a tournament win in Europe to be elusive, although he won a number of overseas events: the Venezuelan, South Australian and New Zealand Opens, and the Australian Matchplay Championship. In 1989 he at last won his first European event, the Italian Open; he followed this with two more victories and came first in the Order of Merit.

His first appearance in the 1989 Ryder Cup was not auspicious; he lost both his foursomes games, one with Bernhard Langer and the other with Christy O'Connor Jr. But in the singles he won a vital point by his narrow victory over the Open champion, Mark Calcavecchia. The two golfers were level on the final tee but the American put both his first and his second ball into the water and conceded the game.

In 1990, Rafferty followed his previous splendid year by winning two more tournaments and finishing fifth in the Order of Merit. He and David Feherty represented Ireland in the World Cup and finished in second place. His progress in 1991 was dogged both by ill-judgement and by ill-luck. He walked out of the US Open halfway through the second round with an explanation that he was worried about his pregnant wife's sudden illness. His ill-luck was his withdrawal from the Open Championship because of a shoulder injury. He eventually finished 35th in the Order of Merit. But he demonstrated that his form had returned when, early in 1992, he won the first prize of over £100,000 in the Daiyko Cup at Palm Meadows in Australia; a few weeks later he won the Portuguese Open.

RAGAN, DAVE

USA

Born: 7.8.35

Appearances: 1963

Record: P4 W2 L1 H1

The pinnacle of Dave Ragan's career was reached in 1963 when he finished in second place behind Jack Nicklaus in the USPGA championship and was selected for the American Ryder Cup team. His first win on the American tour had come in 1959 and he was to have several more victories, including three in 1962. But his game declined from the middle of the Sixties, mainly because of eye trouble.

Ragan performed with success in the Ryder Cup encounter at Atlanta in 1963. He and Billy Casper won a foursomes match by one hole against Peter Alliss and Christy O'Connor, but he and Bob Goalby lost by the same margin to Neil Coles and O'Connor in a fourball. After a half in the second series of fourballs Ragan defeated Coles in his only singles game.

RANSOM, HENRY

USA

Born: 25.2.11

Appearances: 1951

Record: P1 W0 L1 H0

Henry Ransom played only one game in the Ryder Cup, at Pinehurst in 1951. Although the Americans won a convincing victory, he lost his foursomes, in partnership with 'Porky' Oliver, to Charlie Ward and Arthur Lees.

Like Ward, his adversary in that match, Henry Ransom had a fast swing but was capable of inspired bursts of scoring, as when he recorded eight birdies in the last eleven holes to win the Illinois PGA Tournament.

Ragan began his career as a club professional and did not join the American tour until he was in his thirties. He won around a dozen tournaments and had his best season in 1950, when he won George May's World Tournament and was equal fifth in the US Open.

RAY, TED

GB

Born: 28.3.77

Appearances: 1927
Captain 1927

Record: P2 W0 L2 H0

Ted Ray was a distinctive figure: large of physique and lumbering of gait, he dressed in a tweed suit with a baggy coat and a waistcoat, wore a trilby and was rarely seen without a pipe clenched in his mouth. He began his career when the Great Triumvirate of Harry Vardon, James Braid and J H Taylor dominated golf.

Ray was never able to win the prestigious British Matchplay Championship, although he reached the final in 1903, 1911 and 1912; he lost to Braid twice and to Vardon. However, he emerged from their shadows in 1912 when he won the Open Championship at Muirfield. He had previously finished in the top ten on seven occasions and began with a score of 71; he led all the way and finished in 295 shots, a championship record at Muirfield. He was the runner-up in the following year and also tied for the US Open with Vardon and the 19-year-old amateur, Francis Ouimet, who won a famous and unexpected victory in the play-off.

But Ray was eventually to gain his deserved triumph in America, when he won the Open at Inverness in 1920 by one shot from Harry Vardon. Ray's playing of the seventh, a dogleg hole of around 320 yards, was a crucial factor in his win. In each round his great power enabled him to cut the corner and score a birdie three. He nearly drove the

72nd hole too, but then played an indifferent pitch shot and a mediocre approach putt to leave himself a putt of just over a yard. He was then told that he needed to hole the putt to go one shot below Harry Vardon's total. The golf writer, O B Keeler, recalled that Ray handed his putter to his caddie, refilled his ever-present pipe, lit it and puffed away until it was going to his satisfaction and then, in tense silence, calmly holed out.

Ted Ray had an awkward style because he swayed markedly during his swing and swivelled his feet, but he gave the ball a tremendous clout. He occasionally perpetrated a disastrous shot but his recovery play was surpassed only by that of Walter Hagen and he had a superb touch on the greens. His game lasted remarkably well, primarily because his rhythm and timing were enduring gifts. Bernard Darwin wrote of him that he was 'ostensibly a rough-hewn, unpolished, unorthodox golfer but he had great strength and the invaluable gift of rhythm ... he had too a pretty, delicate touch around the green'.

He played in the first Ryder Cup match at Worcester, Massachusetts, in 1927 and had the captaincy thrust upon him when Abe Mitchell, the original choice, was taken ill. The British team were easily beaten, and after losing a close foursomes match to Hagen and Johnny Golden, Ray was heavily defeated by Leo Diegel in the singles.

Ray was one of the great British golfers and had the distinction, along with Harry Vardon and Tony Jacklin among British players, of winning both the British and the American Opens. After his Open win in 1912 he became the professional at Okhey and remained there until his retirement in 1941. The members no doubt benefitted from his friendly and forthright instruction, the key to which was the cry: 'Hit it harder, mate!'.

REES, DAVID JAMES

GB

Born: 31.3.13

Appearances: 1937, 1947, 1949, 1951, 1953, 1955, 1957, 1959, 1961
Captain 1955, 1957, 1959, 1961, 1967

Record: P18 W7 L10 H1

Very few players have given themselves with such ardour and determination to the British cause in the Ryder Cup as Dai Rees. His nine appearances as a player spanned a quarter of a century; he took on the extra burden of the captaincy in four of those encounters and was the non-playing captain in 1967.

The British win at Lindrick, in 1957, broke a sequence of American victories which had begun in 1935. It was very much a personal triumph for Dai Rees, founded as it was on those qualities of enormous enthusiasm and steely determination which he embodied both as golfer and captain.

Rees was the son of a club professional and from an early age was destined to follow a career in golf. He developed his own style, which mirrored his personality: his swing was free and uninhibited, fast and rhythmic. Though relatively small of stature, Rees was a powerful and naturally aggressive player with the highly important asset of self-belief. His two-handed grip was unusual but, despite this, his hands sat beautifully on the club. Above all, Rees was a magnificent putter, especially in his early days. He confessed that his purple patch with his putter 'lasted from 1933 to 1939'.

Rees first came to the fore in 1935 when he won the Assistants Championship and he established his golfing presence in the following year by winning the Matchplay Championship. He defeated Ernie Whitcombe in the final, despite being five holes in arrears with 14 to play, and this earned Rees his selection for the Ryder Cup match at Southport in 1937. Although Britain lost the match (their first defeat on home soil), he had a highly successful debut. He partnered the captain, Charles Whitcombe, in the foursomes and they drew the toughest of the American pairs, Gene Sarazen and Densmore Shute. Rees revelled in the occasion and played superbly all day, as he had to since his captain was more than a little wayward. The pairs were level as they played the 36th hole and the Americans were lucky to be allowed a free drop after Sarazen had hit their second shot through the green. Shute chipped dead for a par but Whitcombe putted up short and left Rees with a very unpleasant putt of around six feet to halve the match. With the great aplomb of a born matchplayer he knocked the British ball firmly into the hole. Rees drew the powerful Byron Nelson in the singles and beat him by three and one.

This early in his career Rees had demonstrated his penchant for the rough and tumble of matchplay and he was to win the Matchplay Championship again in 1938. He beat yet another Whitcombe: Eddie, who was the son of Rees's 1936 victim.

Rees had an equal facility for winning strokeplay events and his victories included the *News Chronicle*, Penfold, Dunlop Masters, Daks and Spalding tournaments. He also won the Open Championships of Ireland, Switzerland, Egypt and Belgium. But, although he came close on several occasions, he was not destined to win the most illustrious of all, the Open.

He finished equal second at St Andrews in 1939 and in the first championship after the war, staged again at St Andrews, he went into the final round level with Sam Snead, the eventual winner, but collapsed with a score of 80. In 1950, at Troon, he was in the lead after two rounds, still the joint leader after the third and went to the turn in 33 shots in the final round. But Rees did not sustain his effort and was passed by the winner, Bobby Locke, and by Roberto de Vicenzo.

Once again, in 1954 at Birkdale, Rees came close to winning the great event. At the final hole he struck a 4-iron superbly at the flag: too well because the ball finished through the back of the green and he took three more shots; Peter Thomson won by one shot. It was disappointment again at Birkdale in 1961. Rees had begun the final round with a seven, but finished in fine style with birdies at the 15th, 16th and 18th holes. He lost by one shot to Arnold Palmer.

If the final accolade of an Open Championship victory was not gained by Rees, he was

recognised as the foremost British golfer when Henry Cotton withdrew from tournament play in the early Fifties. He added to his tally of wins in the Matchplay championship in 1949 (when he beat Cotton in the final) and in 1950, and was a consistent winner of titles through the Fifties and early Sixties.

The Ryder Cup matches had been resumed in 1947 when the British were nearly whitewashed at Portland. However, the margin of defeat was far from humiliating at Ganton two years later, and, although Rees was not required to play in the foursomes, he had a rousing win in the singles. He scored a 65 in the morning and saw Bob Hamilton off by six and four.

In the next three Ryder Cups, Rees, along with the British team, tasted only defeat but it was noticeable that his results were usually close, such were his qualities as a matchplayer. For example, in the singles at Thunderbird Ranch in 1955, Rees was five down to Sam Snead at lunch but got back to just one down before his eventual defeat by three and one.

At Lindrick, in 1957, Rees and Ken Bousfield were the only British players to win a foursomes match. At three matches to one in arrears it seemed that a familiar story of American supremacy was unfolding. In his autobiography Rees told how he called a team meeting to discuss the selection for the singles on the morrow. Both Faulkner and Weetman had scored badly in their foursomes and volunteered to stand down, so the captain decided to send out the indomitable Eric Brown first, in the hope that he would draw Tommy Bolt and beat him. He was right in both assumptions. He had Peter Alliss, Ken Bousfield, himself and Bernard Hunt in the middle of the order and had an almost mystical faith that they would all deliver the points. Again Rees was right (only Alliss lost) and it was abundantly clear that his own opponent, Ed Furgol, stood no chance against such an incandescent will to win. Both Peter Mills and Christy O'Connor also had easy wins and the Ryder Cup had returned at last to British hands.

Even the Harry Weetman affair could not mar the tumult of congratulation which followed the victory. Despite his volunteering to stand down from the singles, Weetman later denounced Rees's decision and said he would never play under his leadership again. It all smacked of a misguided newspaper stunt, but Dai Rees had ascended to his own Ryder Cup pinnacle and was able to shrug off such minor irritations.

In 1959 the Americans won the Ryder Cup back and were not to relinquish it again until 1985. Dai Rees's final appearance as a player was at Lytham in 1961 when the format was changed to include two series of foursomes over 18 holes on the first day and two series of singles on the second day. This made the task of a playing captain, such as Rees, extremely difficult. The Americans kept the Cup but Rees, at the age of 49, went out on a resounding note with three wins out of four matches. He beat Jay Hebert and Doug Ford in the singles.

Dai Rees may have bowed out of the Ryder Cup as a player but his exploits on the golf course were far from finished. In 1967 he once again reached the final of the PGA Matchplay Championship, but lost to Peter Thomson. Two years later he was again the runner-up, at the age of 57 and 33 years after reaching his first final. In 1973, when past 60, he finished equal second in the Martini Tournament.

These results merely emphasised the durability of Dai Rees's game. Despite its rapid

tempo, he had a swing which was sound enough to last through 40 years of tournament play. His exemplary method was complemented by an enduring level of fitness and a devouring enthusiasm for the game. Whatever the difficulties or the setback, Rees would always bounce back, as eager for the fray as ever. His ability to find excuses for a bad shot were often amusing and sometimes irritating; he had much in common with the Wodehouse character who missed a short putt because of the 'uproar of butterflies in the adjoining meadows'. But this riveting self-confidence was an integral part of his strength. He was assertive, too, and perhaps not the most patient of men. Above all, he was lively and effervescent, always on the go, and a tireless advocate of the game he graced.

Many honours came his way. He was the BBC's *Sportsview* Personality of the Year, the captain of the PGA in 1967 and 1976 and the non-playing captain of the Ryder Cup team in 1967. He was also awarded the CBE for his services to golf.

REVOLTA, JOHN

USA

Born: 5.4.11

Appearances: 1935, 1937

Record: P3 W2 L1 H0

Johnny Revolta began his career in golf in the traditional way, as a caddie, and won the Wisconsin Caddies Championship at the age of 14.

His first professional victory of note was in the 1933 Miami Open and he showed his great ability in the following year when he won two more tournaments. He proved that he was a golfer of the highest class when he won the USPGA Championship in 1935. To achieve that he beat Walter Hagen in the first round and Tommy Armour in the final.

Revolta was characterised by contemporary writers as looking like a movie gangster, 'with a jaw like the prow of a battleship'. He had a rather unappealing style, as his swing began with a very straight take-away from the ball. But he had immense confidence and determination, based on a brilliant short game. Walter Hagen nominated him as one of the finest short iron players in golf.

Revolta's first outing in the Ryder Cup was with Henry Picard and they easily overcame Alf Padgham and Percy Alliss in the foursomes. Nevertheless, Revolta needed all his determination in his singles match with Reg Whitcombe. He was three down with nine holes to play but fought back to win. He only played once in the 1937 fixture at Southport; he and Picard were beaten by Percy Alliss and Dick Burton.

Revolta played on the American tour until the Fifties and won 18 tournaments, the last of which was the 1944 Texas Open.

RICHARDSON, STEVEN

Europe

Born: 24.7.66

Appearances: 1991

Record: P4 W2 L2 H0

Steven Richardson did not rush into the professional ranks. He represented England as an amateur, although he was not selected for the Walker Cup team in 1989. But he won the English Amateur Championship in that year and then turned professional at the age of 23. He made the transition to the professional game look easy and was 29th in the Order of Merit in his first season. His best tournament was the Volvo Masters, in which he tied for second place.

A splendidly successful start to the 1991 season virtually assured Richardson of a place in the Ryder Cup team. He won the Girona and Portuguese Opens and went on to have five other finishes in the top five. He showed his great ability and calm temperament to the full in the USPGA Championship at Crooked Stick where he tied for fifth position.

It was a measure of Richardson's ability that he was regarded as one of the key members of the European team at Kiawah Island. In his three outings, in partnership with Mark James, he more than justified the faith placed in him. The British pair demolished Mark Calcavecchia and Corey Pavin in the first series of fourballs; they lost by one hole to Calcavecchia and Payne Stewart in their foursomes, when Richardson missed the final putt; and then defeated Lanny Wadkins and Wayne Levi in another fourball match.

Several commentators thought that Richardson, with his great power, would prevail over Corey Pavin in their singles. But he lost a close match by two and one. It is certain however, that Steven Richardson has the raw talent to become one of the best players in the game.

RIVERO, JOSE

Europe

Born: 20.9.55

Appearances: 1985, 1987

Record: P5 W2 L3 H0

Jose Rivero must have golden memories of his two Ryder Cup matches, since the European team won both of them. In 1985 he was one of Tony Jacklin's special choices, since the captain remembered how Rivero had won the Laurence Batley tournament at the Belfry in the previous year. Rather oddly, Jacklin did not send him into battle until the fourth series, when he and Jose Maria Canizares trounced Tom Kite and Calvin Peete by seven and five. Peete got his revenge on Rivero in the singles but, by that time, Europe had already won back the Ryder Cup.

Two years later at Muirfield Village, Ohio, the European team recorded the first-ever Ryder Cup victory on American turf. Rivero and Gordon Brand started with a win over Ben Crenshaw and Scott Simpson but they were beaten in the foursomes and Simpson beat Rivero in the singles.

Rivero, who turned professional in 1973, has won only five European tournaments but has been remarkably consistent over the years. His earnings on the circuit are close to £1 million and he has played in the World Cup on four occasions; in 1984 he and Canizares won the team event.

ROBSON, FRED

GB

Born: 25.4.85

Appearances: 1927, 1929, 1931

Record: P6 W2 L4 H0

Fred Robson was the archetypal British professional golfer with a complete range of skills: as a player, club maker and teacher. As a player, he finished well up the field in the Open Championships of the 1920s:

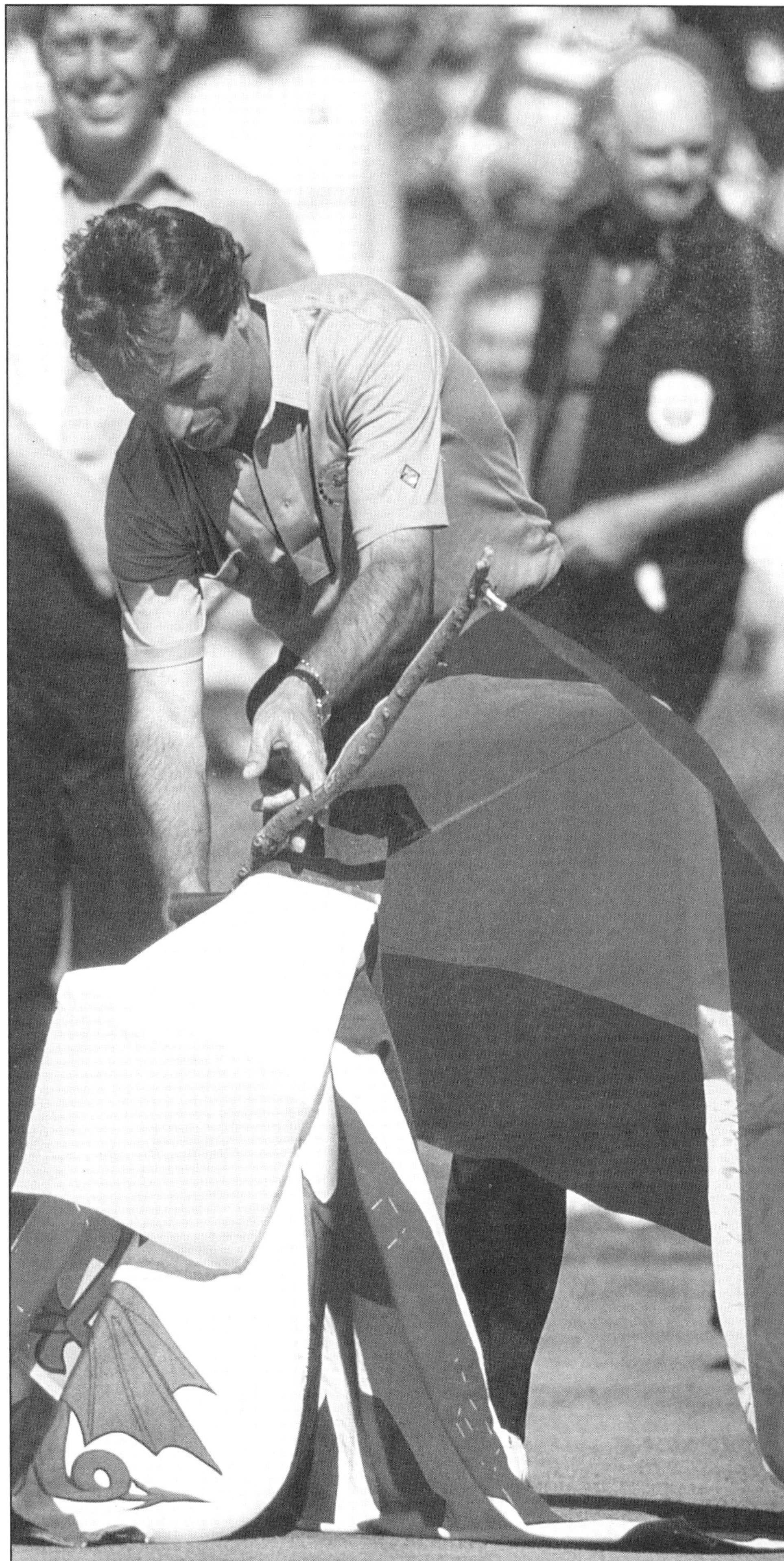

Jose Rivero, a member of two successful European teams

equal second (with Aubrey Boomer) behind Bobby Jones at St Andrews in 1927, equal fourth in the following year, and equal fourth again in 1930. At Cooden Beach and later at the Addington Club his skills as a club maker were much in demand and he was a distinguished teacher, who became the official coach to the Walker Cup team just after the war.

Robson played in the first Ryder Cup match in 1927 and lost both his matches; he and Ted Ray narrowly lost their foursomes to Walter Hagen and Johnny Golden and he was defeated by Al Watrous in the singles. But in 1929 and 1931 he teamed up with another 'grand old man', Abe Mitchell, and they won their foursomes on both occasions. Robson lost his singles matches, to Horton Smith at Moortown in 1929 and to Gene Sarazen at Scioto two years later.

RODRIGUEZ, JUAN

USA

Born: 23.10.35

Appearances: 1973

Record: P2 W0 L1 H1

Chi Chi Rodriguez has always been one of the extroverts of the American circuit, a joker with a series of routines. A small and slender man, a straw hat always on his head, he grins and dances his way down the fairways; if he holes a long putt, he waves his putter like a rapier and then sheathes it flamboyantly in his golf bag; if the putt goes in for a birdie, he drops his hat over the hole to make sure that the ball does not escape.

His antics amuse the fans but are sometimes too much for his playing partners. In the Kemper Open of 1970 Dave Hill, who was in contention for the title and whose temperament was brittle at the best of times, was definitely not amused. He had to be restrained from seeking what he regarded as just physical retribution at the end of the final round.

Rodriguez became a caddie at the Berwind Country Club in San Juan, Puerto Rico, at an early age and was playing to scratch or better by the time he was 15. Two years later he led the Puerto Rican Open at a late stage by six shots but managed to lose. Slight of figure, he learned to hit the ball a great distance by dint of a huge shoulder turn and a superb hand action.

Ed Dudley took him under his wing and Rodriguez achieved his breakthrough on the US tour in 1963 by winning the Denver Open.

A few days later his mentor, Ed Dudley, died. In the following year Rodriguez won the Western Open and eight major events during the years up to 1979, including the Texas Open, the Byron Nelson Golf Classic and the Greater Greensboro Open.

In 1973 he won selection for the Ryder Cup, but the bitter cold of Muirfield in late September was an alien setting for his golfing talents. He and Lou Graham got a half out of Tony Jacklin and Peter Oosterhuis in the first series of foursomes but they lost heavily to Maurice Bembridge and Brian Huggett – deservedly so, since they were many shots over par.

In the mid-Eighties Chi Chi Rodriguez became eligible for the Seniors tour and has since won dozens of tournaments and millions of dollars. He was the leading money winner in 1987; in 1991 he won four events and finished third in the money list with over $700,000.

ROGERS, BILL

USA

Born: 10.9.51

Appearances: 1981

Record: P4 W1 L2 H1

Bill Rogers, fair-haired and slight of frame, did not hit the ball far enough to be a great player but for a few years, at the beginning of the Eighties, his deft short game and secure putting stroke propelled him to the front rank of professional golf.

Rogers played in the Walker Cup in 1973 and became a professional a year later. His first victory in the USA was in the 1978 Bob Hope Classic, and he was so consistent in the following year that, despite not winning a tournament, he was in the first half-dozen in the money list. At the World Matchplay Championship at Wentworth, he played spirited golf to take first prize. In 1980 he did not win on the American tour but finished in the top 20 on the money list. The following year was to be his *annus mirabilis*.

He won the Heritage Classic and was second in the US Open at Merion. Rogers then went to Royal St George's for the Open Championship and won by four shots from Bernhard Langer. Later in the year he won the Suntory Open and the New South Wales and Australian Opens. Despite his brilliant form, Rogers did not fare so well at Walton Heath in the Ryder Cup that year. He and Bruce Lietzke lost their foursomes and fourball matches but, with Ray Floyd, he beat Sandy Lyle and Mark James in the second series of foursomes. In the singles he halved with Bernard Gallacher.

In 1982 Roger's form declined, although he finished equal third in the US Open at Pebble Beach. Despite a victory in 1983 Bill Rogers gradually withdrew from the tournament circuit.

ROSBURG, BOB

USA

Born: 21.10.26

Appearances: 1959

Record: P2 W2 L0 H0

The Open Champion of the 1860s, Willie Park, opined that 'a man who can putt is a match for anyone'. Bob Rosburg, whose game was firmly based on a wonderful putting stroke allied to highly intelligent course management, would have agreed with him.

Rosburg became a professional golfer in 1953 and won his first tournament, the Miami Open, in the next year. He played the US tour for 20 years and won his last tournament, the Bob Hope Classic, in 1972. His most successful year was 1959 when he won the USPGA Championship. In the final round he overcame a deficit of six strokes to put Doug Sanders and Jerry Barber into second place. He was also the runner-up in the US Open at Winged Foot. Ten years later he was to finish second again, in a tie with Deane Beman and Al Geiberger behind an obscure golfer called Orville Moody, who was said not to like practising and to have taken a two week break just before the championships. Rosburg had had a chance to tie with Moody but, unusually for him, missed a shortish putt on the 72nd green.

Even so, Rosburg secured his place in the 1959 Ryder Cup encounter at Eldorado and won both his matches at a canter. He and Mike Souchak were much too accomplished for Bernard Hunt and Eric Brown; they were six holes in front at lunchtime after scoring a 68. In the singles Rosburg dealt easily with Harry Weetman, just as the American team dealt easily with the British that year.

Rosburg was an intelligent and outspoken golfer. He served on the USPGA Committee from 1958 onwards and became its chairman. When he retired from the tour he turned his talents to commentating on the game for ABC Television. He still plays occasionally on the Seniors tour.

RUDOLPH, MASON

USA

Born: 23.5.34

Appearances: 1971

Record: P3 W1 L1 H1

Mason Rudolph represented the USA in the Walker Cup in 1957 and was undefeated. He became a professional a year later and played on the American tour until the middle of the Seventies. His five victories were spread from 1959 to 1970 and he was a highly consistent golfer: for example, in the mid-Sixties he won money in 52 tournaments in succession.

In his one Ryder Cup appearance, in 1971, in St Louis, he balanced his ledger exactly. With Lee Trevino as his partner he halved his foursomes against Brian Huggett and Tony Jacklin, who saved the game for Britain by chipping in at the final hole; Rudolph and Trevino beat Christy O'Connor and Brian Barnes in the fourballs; but Barnes exacted his revenge in the singles.

RUNYAN, PAUL

USA

Born: 12.7.08

Appearances: 1933, 1935

Record: P4 W2 L2 H0

The adage that a good big 'un will always beat a good little 'un was once again denied in the final of the 1938 USPGA Championship. Sam Snead was a 10-to-1 favourite to beat the diminutive Paul Runyan, who was often 60 or 70 yards behind 'Slammin' Sam off the tee. But whereas in the morning round Sam did not manage to birdie any of the par fives, easily in reach for him in two shots, Runyan birdied them all and eventually won by the resounding margin of eight and seven.

This was not Runyan's first victory in a major: he had won the same championship in 1934, when he was at his peak as a tournament player. From 1933 to 1936 he won 20 official PGA events in his grand total of 28, the last of which came in 1941.

Paul Runyan was the son of an Arkansas dairy farmer and he started his golf career in the traditional way, as a caddie. He was a small man with an unorthodox swing; to get more leverage he swayed back and then lunged through the ball. It looked unattractive but was highly effective. His short game, by dint of hard practice, was superb. He was unkindly dubbed 'Little Poison' because he was so deadly on and around the greens. He was also unusual in that he carried several wooden clubs in his bag, including three varieties of spoon (3-wood).

He lost both his matches in his first Ryder cup match in 1933, but evened things up in 1935. He and Horton Smith crushed Bill Cox and Edward Jarman by nine and eight, and Runyan easily defeated Dick Burton in the singles.

Runyan became an outstanding golf teacher and his playing career lasted longer than most, since he played Seniors golf with great success. He won the US Seniors in 1961 and the World Seniors title in the following year.

S

SANDERS, DOUG

USA

Born: 24.7.33

Appearances: 1967

Record: P5 W2 L3 H0

In 1970, at the traditional home of golf, St Andrews, Doug Sanders stood on the 72nd tee and knew that 'he only needed a par four to win the Open'. This is the stuff of dreams ... and nightmares.

Sanders had wanted to play in the Open enough to go through the unpleasant chore of pre-qualifying and had begun his fourth round in joint second place with Tony Jacklin and Jack Nicklaus, two strokes behind the leader, Lee Trevino. At the final hole Sanders hit a good drive, but pitched too strongly to the green and left himself quite a long putt. His nerves betrayed him as he putted up short and left himself with a downhill putt of just over a yard, with a left-to-right break. He settled over the shot and, just as he seemed ready, bent down and removed a speck of dirt from the line. In his commentary box Henry Longhurst murmured 'oh dear', as if he knew that Sanders would now miss his putt for the Open; so he did and in the play-off lost by one shot to Jack Nicklaus.

Doug Sanders was a very successful golfer on the American tour and won the Canadian Open while still an amateur in 1956. He turned professional soon after and won 20 tournaments during his career. His best years were in the Sixties; he won five events in 1961 and a total of 15 during the years from 1961 to 1967. He frequently threatened to win a major tournament. He was equal second in the USPGA Championship in 1959 and third in 1960 and 1961. He was equal second in the US Open in the latter year, at Oakland Hills and led the championship as he went into the final nine holes; but Gene Littler, with a run of birdies, overtook him. He also tied for second in the 1966 Open at Muirfield.

Sanders had a very unorthodox but highly effective swing, with a very short backswing and a follow-through that hardly seemed to travel above waist height; it was said that he could swing a club inside a telephone box. He had a very wide, stiff-legged stance and prefaced each shot with a series of waggles above the ball. Nevertheless, he hit the ball a long way with a strong flailing action and had a wonderful short game. Inevitably, his instructional book on the game was called *Compact Golf.*

Sanders was a popular figure on both sides of the Atlantic: a good-humoured man with a reputation for fast living and a taste for technicolour clothes, which stirred memories of Jimmy Demaret. Dave Marr described Sanders as 'looking like the aftermath of a direct hit on a pizza factory'.

He played in only one Ryder Cup match and won two matches out of five at Houston in 1967, but he lost both his singles matches to Neil Coles. Demaret was one of the owners of the Champions Club, where the match was played, and no doubt shared some sartorial insights with Sanders.

Doug Sanders played on the American tour through the Seventies and was a frequent visitor to Britain. When asked if he ever thought about the infamous missed putt in the 1970 Open, he replied that on some days whole minutes passed without its crossing his mind.

SARAZEN, GENE

USA

Born: 27.2.02

Appearances: 1927, 1929, 1931, 1933, 1935, 1937

Record: P12 W7 L2 H3

With seven victories in the major championships to his credit, Gene Sarazen must be judged one of the greatest of golfers. He was the first man to win all four majors: the Open, the US Open the USPGA Championship and the Masters. Only Ben Hogan, Jack Nicklaus and Gary Player have equalled that feat. In 1932 he won the Open championships of both Britain and the USA.

Sarazen's longevity as an active professional golfer also makes him a major figure in the game. He played in his first US Open in 1920 when Ted Ray (the winner) and Harry Vardon were still to the fore; and he made his last appearance in the Open Championship at Troon in 1973 when Tony Jacklin and Lee Trevino were at their peaks. At Troon, on the 50th anniversary of his first appearance in the Open, Sarazen holed in one at the famous eighth hole, the 'postage stamp', and then holed his bunker shot for a two in the second round. Thus he ended his career in the Open in brilliant style.

Sarazen might not have taken to golf if he had not been stricken in his youth by pleurisy and ordered by his doctor to get a job in the fresh air. He had been caddying since the age of 10 and became an assistant professional. He made a dazzling start to his career in 1922 by winning both the US Open and the USPGA Championship. His Open victory stirred a warm response from the American public for several reasons: he was very young (20) to achieve such success; he was of Italian descent; as a former caddie he was 'the people's champion'; and the domination of the event by British-born golfers had been breached.

Here began Sarazen's great rivalry with Walter Hagen, who won the British Open in 1922. A 'World Golf Championship' was arranged over 72 holes for a prize of $3,000. Sarazen won a narrow victory on the 70th hole and later that night was taken to hospital to have his appendix removed.

Sarazen was a tough customer: as he himself stressed, 'you had to be when you were Italian'. Small but muscular, with a cheerful look to him, his swing was typical of the man: simple, sturdy and without any frills at all. Hagen wrote that 'he was cocky and self-confident, but he had plenty of moxie and determination'. Their rivalry and friendship was to continue throughout their careers.

Sarazen won the USPGA Championship again in 1923, by beating Hagen in the final, but he was not to win another major championship for nine years. Hagen and Bobby Jones dominated golf on both sides of the Atlantic and Sarazen's experiments with his swing did not help him, although he continued to win tournaments, such as the Miami, Metropolitan and Long Island Opens, during those years.

In 1923, he visited Britain to play in the Open and won the North of England Championship *en route* to Troon. There, however, he caught the worst of the weather and failed, by one stroke, to qualify for the championship proper. To his great credit he told a sympathetic Bernard Darwin: 'I'll be back, even if I have to swim across'.

In his support of the British Open, he was as good as his word but, although he was runner-up to the inevitable Walter Hagen in 1928 at Sandwich, it was not until 1932 that the name of Sarazen was engraved on the famous old claret jug. In the care of Hagen's old caddie, Skip Daniels, Sarazen had a record score of 283 at Prince's to win by five shots from Macdonald Smith. His score was not surpassed until 1950. Bernard Darwin noticed how Sarazon's powerful swing 'just tears the ball through the wind as if it did not exist.'

Gene Sarazen's rehabilitation as a golfer had begun two years previously, when he won eight tournaments. It was the year after the Great Crash and he was one of many who needed some cash.

In 1932 he went on to win the US Open at Fresh Meadow, New York. He played the last 28 holes in a hundred strokes, which moved Bobby Jones to write: 'When the wand touches him ... when he is in the right mood, he is probably the greatest scorer in the game.' His closing round of 66 was the lowest last round by a champion until Arnold Palmer scored a 65 in 1960. In the following year he won the third of his USPGA Championships.

Gene Sarazen played in the inaugural Ryder Cup match and in every one up to the war. He had a remarkably successful record and his only two defeats were in 1929; he and Ed Dudley lost their foursomes against Abe Mitchell and Fred Robson and then lost by six and four to Archie Compston, who was in an irresistible mood. In the Ryder Cup he frequently showed his great powers of recovery, his ability to battle away in adversity. In his singles match against Charles Whitcombe in 1927 he was five down at one point but halved; in his foursomes in 1933 he and Hagen were four down with nine to play but they prised a half from Percy Alliss and Whitcombe.

Sarazen has left his mark on the development of golf clubs. Modern players would be lost without their sand wedges, and especially the professionals with their remarkable dexterity from bunkers. It is all owed to Gene Sarazen, who invented the broad-soled sand wedge in 1931 and perfected its use in the following year.

Sarazen is best remembered for his 'double eagle' or 'albatross' at the 15th hole of the final round of the 1935 Masters at Augusta. This is the tournament which began as a gathering for a few of Bobby Jones's friends and quickly attained the status of a major championship. As he surveyed his second shot to the par-five 15th, Sarazen knew that he needed three birdies from the remaining holes to tie with Craig Wood. His 4-wood to the green hardly wavered from the flag and he recorded an historic two. He made his pars on the three last holes and beat Wood in the play-off on the next day.

Sarazen continued to play on the American tour through the 1950s and was also the Seniors champion in 1954 and 1958. He also made his annual pilgrimages to the Open and to the Masters at Augusta. He will be remembered as one of the most successful golfers in the game's history. He was the James Cagney of the links, a pugnacious battler who brought an unparalleled zest to the game and brightened it with his own vivid flashes of genius.

Gene Sarazen

SCOTT, SYD

GB

Born: 20.12.13

Appearances: 1955

Record: P2 W0 L2 H0

With his smooth swing, Syd Scott was one of the most consistent British professionals of the 1950s. He won the German and Portuguese Opens and showed up well on occasion in the Open Championship. In 1954, at Birkdale, he finished equal second with Dai Rees and Bobby Locke, one stroke behind Peter Thomson; and in 1959 he was in fourth place behind Gary Player at Muirfield.

He made his Ryder Cup appearance in 1955, at Thunderbird Ranch, and lost both his games. He and Eric Brown were no match for Doug Ford and Ted Kroll in the foursomes and he was narrowly defeated by Chick Harbert in the singles.

Scott was a notable teacher of golf at Roehampton for many years.

SHUTE, DENSMORE

USA

Born: 25.10.04

Appearances: 1931. 1933, 1937

Record: P6 W2 L2 H2

Just as Bernhard Langer found himself, in 1991, in the unbearable position of having a putt on the final green to settle the fate of the Ryder Cup, so did Denny Shute in 1933 at Southport. With the match tied at five and a half points each, both Shute and Syd Easterbrook were on the final green in three shots. The British player putted and missed. Shute had one putt to win the Ryder Cup outright, two to ensure that America retained it through a draw or three to lose it.

The American captain, Walter Hagen, wrote that Shute was not aware of the overall situation, as a modern player would have been, and he wondered whether he should vacate his position alongside the Prince of Wales in the clubhouse to warn him; but Hagen felt that

Densmore Shute

he could not abandon his host. Shute putted boldly past the hole and missed the return and the Ryder Cup was Britain's by the narrowest of margins.

Langer bounced back from his ordeal in 1991 by winning his next tournament and so did Densmore Shute. At the Open at St Andrews he tied with Craig Wood and the beat him by several strokes in the play-off. Shute went on to win two more major titles, the USPGA Championships of 1936 and 1937. He tied for the US Open in 1939 with his old adversary, Craig Wood, and Byron Nelson, who won the play-off. In a career on the American tour which lasted for nearly 30 years Shute won 15 tournaments.

In his early days as a professional, Shute was a slight figure. Henry Cotton, who beat him in a challenge match over 72 holes at Walton Heath in 1937, noted his superb position at impact, with his shoulders still square to the ball but with his hips nearly turned to face the flag. He was known throughout his career as a superlative player with the long irons.

Despite his defeat by Cotton, Denny Shute was usually the 'form horse' in 72-hole challenge matches. He beat two reigning US Open champions over the distance: Johnny Goodman, the last amateur to win the title, in 1933 and Ralph Guldahl in 1937.

Shute's record in the Ryder Cup was also on the credit side with two wins, two losses and two halved matches. In his first game, in 1931, he and Walter Hagen defeated George Duncan and Arthur Havers by the extraordinary margin of ten and nine, and Shute beat Bert Hodson comfortably in the singles. In his final appearance, at Southport in 1937, Shute halved both his games.

SIKES, DAN

USA

Born: 7.12.30

Appearances: 1969

Record: P3 W2 L1 H0

Dan Sikes appeared in the nerve-wracking tie at Birkdale in 1969 and played two very tense matches with Jack Nicklaus as his partner. In the foursomes they got home by one hole against Peter Butler and Bernard Hunt but lost a fourball match by the same margin to Tony Jacklin and Neil Coles. Sikes went on to beat Neil Coles in the second series of singles.

Sikes became a professional rather late, when he had turned 30, but his first priority had been to finish his legal studies. He showed his calibre as a golfer by winning the US Amateur Public Links Championship in 1958 and turned professional two years later.

He played on the American tour until the late Seventies and won six events; his successes were concentrated in the years from 1963 to 1968 and included the Doral and Jacksonville Opens and the Philadelphia Golf Classic. Sikes was a very consistent player and a marvellous putter and, like Cary Middlecoff on whom he modelled himself, an acute analyst of the game.

SIMPSON, SCOTT

USA

Born: 17.9.55

Appearances: 1987

Record: P2 W1 L1 H0

Scott Simpson came off the college production line (in his case the University of Southern California) which manufactures solid and dependable golfers. Their swings are much the same, their physiques do not seem to vary much and, under those large visors, they appear equally anonymous.

Simpson turned professional in 1977 after playing in the Walker Cup. It took three attempts at the qualifying school before he gained access to the American tour but he won the Western Open in 1980. He later won the Greater Greensboro Open and the Westchester Classic but his great triumph was to take the US Open at the Olympic Club, San Francisco, in 1987 when he repulsed a last-round charge from Tom Watson with great resolution. With nine holes to go there were eight players within one shot of the lead but Simpson's successive birdies at the 14th, 15th, and 16th holes saw off his challengers.

In his Ryder Cup debut in 1987 at Muirfield Village, Ohio, he and Ben Crenshaw lost a fourball to Gordon Brand and Jose Rivero and he was not selected again until the singles matches in which he defeated Rivero.

SMITH, HORTON

USA

Born: 22.5.09

Appearances: 1929, 1931, 1933, 1935, 1937

Record: P4 W3 L0 H1

In 1928 a young man of only 20 years, tall, handsome and elegantly dressed, took the American professional golf scene by storm. Horton Smith won two tournaments in that year but in 1929 won eight events and finished second in six others.

On his first visit to America, Henry Cotton remarked that Smith, with a comparatively short, three-quarter swing, made the game look ridiculously easy. He was extremely accurate with all his shots and also hit the ball a great distance; not only that but he was a brilliant putter and Bernard Darwin reckoned him to be the best ever: 'a joy to watch, easy, elegant and of a horrid certainty'.

Walter Hagen was greatly impressed by the young Horton Smith and took him on a long tour of exhibition matches. Smith, who did not smoke or drink and believed whole-heartedly in an early-to-bed regime, must have made an incongruous travelling companion for the gregarious, party-loving Hagen.

Hagen also picked Smith for the Ryder Cup of 1929 at Moortown, Leeds. To the British eye he cut a boyish-looking, string-bean figure in his flat cap and grey sweater; and his leisurely swing and superb timing were greatly admired. Henry Longhurst saw him for the first time and wrote: 'His swing was smooth and slow and beautiful, and he putted like a violinist.' But the boy wonder encountered a major difficulty because his steel-shafted clubs, legal in the USA since 1926, were not so in Britain. He had to revert to hickory shafts, which was a radical change to force on any golfer. Such was Smith's great talent that, after a great deal of hard practice, he had little trouble in beating Fred Robson in the singles. He was much too long and accurate for Robson, who confessed that he had never met an opponent who made him feel so ineffectual.

Although Smith was selected for the next four Ryder Cup ties he only played three more matches. He beat Charlie Whitcombe in the singles in 1933, thrashed Bill Cox and Edward Jarman in the foursomes in 1935 and then halved his singles match with Cox in the same year.

In all, Horton Smith won 30 tournaments in his career, including the very first Masters Tournament at Augusta, in 1934, which he won again in 1936. Right up to the end of the Forties he was able to win tournaments; as in 1948 when he took the Michigan PGA Championship.

From 1952 to 1954 Smith was the President of the USPGA Tour committee. In the late Fifties he became seriously ill but recovered in fine style and received the Ben Hogan Award in 1961 for his fortitude.

Horton Smith, an elegant player

SMYTH, DES

Europe

Born: 12.2.53

Appearances: 1979, 1981

Record: P7 W2 L5 H0

Des Smyth's appearance in the Ryder Cup team of 1979 coincided with the inclusion for the first time of European players. It was an unhappy baptism for the engaging Irishman. In the second series of foursomes he was asked to partner Ken Brown, whose behaviour throughout the fixture was so bizarre that it attracted a fine of £1,000 and a year's ban from international team events. Brown made his lack of interest in the game and in his partner very plain and it was no surprise that Hale Irwin and Tom Kite beat the European pair by a 'dog licence' (seven and six). Smith was beaten by Irwin in the singles.

In 1981, at Walton Heath, Smyth fared rather better with a win, in partnership with Bernard Gallacher, over his old adversary, Irwin and Ray Floyd. In their afternoon fourball matches, he and Canizares trounced Bill Rogers and Bruce Lietzke by six and five. Normality was, however, imposed by the Americans on the next two days and Smyth lost his three games.

Des Smyth has won six events on the European tour. His best year was in 1988 when he finished seventh in the Order of Merit. He has represented Ireland five times in the World Cup and was a member of the Irish team which won the Dunhill Cup at St Andrews in 1988.

SNEAD, JESSE

USA

Born: 14.10.40

Appearances: 1971, 1973, 1975

Record: P11 W9 L2 H0

The nephew of the incomparable Sam Snead became a professional golfer in 1964, but did not win a tournament until 1972 when he came first in the Tucson Open and the Doral-Eastern Open. A tall, strong player, Snead won eight events on the American tour, including the San Diego and the Southern Opens. In 1987 he was still good enough to win the Westchester Classic.

He had a remarkable record in the Ryder Cup with nine wins from eleven games. In 1971, at the Old Warson Club in St Louis, he won all four of his matches, including a singles victory over Tony Jacklin. Two years later, at Muirfield, he lost his first game, a foursomes in partnership with Tom Weiskopf, but then won three points in a row, including singles defeats of Christy O'Connor and Brian Barnes. At Laurel Valley in 1975 he continued much as before with a victory in the foursomes and

Jesse Snead, nephew of the incomparable Sam

another in the fourballs, but he was beaten by Peter Oosterhuis in his final match.

As soon as he was eligible, Snead joined the American Seniors tour and in 1991 finished 19th in the Order of Merit with winnings of over $250,000.

SNEAD, SAMUEL JACKSON

USA

Born: 25.5.12

Appearances: 1939, 1947, 1949, 1951, 1953, 1955, 1959
Captain 1951, 1959, 1969

Record: P13 W10 L2 H1

The question of how many tournaments have been won by Sam Snead is a matter of some debate. The official American tour records quote 81 in the years from 1936 to 1965; the unofficial reckoning is put at around 135, including overseas victories. Snead himself claims that the grand total is roughly 165.

The debate is of academic interest only, because figures, however impressive, do no justice to the impact Sam Snead has had on golf. He was born in a remote part of Virginia, in the Back Creek Mountains and discovered the game through caddying. Not that his choice of sports was limited because he was an athlete of remarkable talent and was courted by several colleges for his potential as a baseball player and a footballer. He was blessed with great strength, a very supple and limber physique and the greatest athletic gift of all: natural timing.

Unknown except for a win in the West Virginia Closed Tournament in 1936, Snead burst on to the American professional stage in the following year. He won his second PGA event, the Oakland Open, with a score of 270. All his rounds were under par, an extraordinary feat for that time and he went on to win four more events that year and another eight in 1938.

It was not just the brilliance of his scoring which amazed his opponents and captivated the golf fans, it was his classic swing, fluent and unhurried, full of grace and power. When he was first seen in Britain, in the Ryder Cup of 1937, the illustrious writer, Bernard Darwin, wrote that Snead's swing 'brought tears of joy'. Gene Sarazen called him the finest natural swinger the game has ever known. His action was based on a fluid turn of the body, a full arc of the swing and unrivalled balance and control as he came into the ball. It looked so natural and effortless – 'as graceful as the spring of a cat' – because Snead was a superb athlete.

His swing has lasted longer than any golfer's. He won USPGA tournaments in four decades; in his fifties, he had high finishes in the USPGA Championship (sixth in 1966), the Masters (tenth in 1967) and the US Open (ninth in 1968); and as late as 1972 he was in contention in the Masters until near the end and was equal third in the 1974 USPGA Championship. In 1979 he became the first golfer to 'shoot his age' in an official PGA tour event with a round of 67 in the Quad Cities Open. He bettered this in the next round with a 66.

Sam Snead's most productive years were 1949 and 1950 when he had 17 victories, including the Masters and the USPGA Championship. A measure of his brilliance was his 1950 stroke average of 69.2 over 96 tournament rounds. He had already won the USPGA (in 1942) and was to do so again in 1951; and he won the Masters again in 1952 and 1954. In these years he and Ben Hogan ruled the golfing roost and it seemed that these major championships were their sole preserve. But there was one exception in Sam Snead's case: for all the beauty and fluency of his game, he could not win the US Open; indeed, he let the cup slip on a couple of occasions when it seemed to be in his grasp.

In 1937 Snead, after only seven professional tournaments, was the clear favourite to win the title. He had a splendid score of 283 at Oakland Hills, only to be beaten into second place by Ralph Guldahl, who had an eagle in his final round and scored 281, which stood as the US Open record until 1948. In 1939, at Philadelphia, he needed a par five at the 72nd hole to beat Byron Nelson. He was not aware of the other scores and thought he needed a birdie four. To compound his tension the spectators had flooded on to the 18th fairway and Snead had a wait of nearly 30 minutes while they were cleared. Disaster followed, as he took eight shots to finish behind Nelson, Craig Wood and Densmore Shute. In 1947 his birdie on the final hole forced a tie with Lew Worsham, but Snead lost the play-off by missing a tiny putt of about 30 inches on the 18th green. He was equal second in 1949 and the runner-up again in 1953 to Ben Hogan at Oakmont. But he seemed fated never to win his own country's Open championship and with every failure the mountain seemed more difficult to scale.

In contrast, he won the British Open at the second attempt, in 1946. He did not endear himself to the British public, jealous of their golfing traditions and suffering from the aftermath of war, when he was reported to have said, on seeing St Andrews from the window of his train: 'Say, that looks like an old abandoned golf-course. What did they call it?'. Walter Hagen, one of many great American players who had supported the Open, had urged him to make the trip, and so had the Wilson Golf Company which wanted Snead to put some promotion behind their equipment. He duly obliged but did not return until much later in his career. Snead had not been impressed by the golf-course, the food or the prize money; and certainly not by his caddie, who begged him to give him the ball with which he played the final round. It was something that the caddie 'would treasure all his life.' Snead gave it to him and later discovered that he had sold it at his local pub for £50.

Sam Snead has one of the best records in the Ryder Cup, with 10 wins from 13 matches. In 1937, he played only in the singles, in appalling conditions at Southport, and beat Dick Burton easily. Burton was known as one of the longest hitters in the game, but 'Slammin' Sam' was flying the ball past Burton's with the utmost ease. His only real falter in the matches was in 1953, at Wentworth, in a singles against Harry Weetman. The day before, Snead and Lloyd Mangrum had demolished Eric Brown and John Panton by eight and seven, and against Weetman he was four holes up at lunchtime and four up with six to play. It looked like a certain win for America until the finest swinger in golf had a sudden and inexplicable collapse. One observer said that Snead's swing looked as perfect as ever but the ball was sliced wildly a couple of times and then hooked. Weetman scented an amazing reversal of his drifting fortunes and won five holes in a row to take an unexpected point for Britain.

Snead won both his matches in 1955, was unbeaten in 1959 and was selected for the 1961 tie. He took some time off from the tour in the weeks before the Ryder Cup and played in a pro-am which conflicted with a regular PGA event. He had not sought permission and was suspended for six months by the USPGA. It was a harsh decision and the suspension was later reduced to 45 days, but Snead missed the Ryder Cup. Nevertheless, Snead and the PGA were to forgive each other in 1969 when he was appointed captain of the Ryder Cup team. This was the year of the famous tied match at Birkdale, when Jack Nicklaus, to his great credit, conceded a putt to Tony Jacklin on the final green. It was said that Snead, whose guiding principles were 'to keep close count of my nickels and dimes, stay away from whisky, and never concede a putt', was none too pleased with Nicklaus's action, honourable though it was.

Sam Snead arrived on the professional golf scene when interest in the game was on the wane. Bobby Jones had retired some years earlier and the stars of both Walter Hagen and Gene Sarazen were not shining so brightly. Then Sam Snead came out of the Virginian blue and within months was seen as the new wonder of American golf. He was a winner; he had power and grace; and, above all, he had a personality. He exploited a naive hillbilly approach to life and he quickly found himself a manager, Fred Corcoran, who was alive to all the possibilities. Between them they created the legend of the 'good ole country boy' who, barefoot, had wandered down from the Virginian hills and was going to take all those golfing sophisticates apart. And he was going to take their money, too, and keep it. Corcoran called Snead 'Daniel Boone with a driver' and made up all those tales about his meanness: 'Sam is the only man I know to make a million dollars and save two million'. Snead won a tournament near Detroit and his photograph was taken and sent by wire to New York, where it was printed. A few days later Corcoran showed it to Snead, who said: 'How could they get my picture in New York. I ain't never been there.'

Sam Snead

It was heady stuff and Snead kept on winning to bolster the legend. The only flaw that appeared in his game was his inability to hole short putts, and the dreaded 'yips' afflicted him as early as the late forties. His solution was to putt, croquet style, with his legs astride the line. The PGA banned this since it was not considered to be a 'golf stroke', so Snead began to putt in a peculiar 'side-saddle' stance, the putter outside the line of his body. It worked and lengthened his career to such an extent that he was still playing on the PGA tour in the mid-Seventies; in 1985 he played in 13 Seniors events and won money in all of them.

Sam Snead will rightly be regarded as the most natural of all golfers. There was a lazy beauty to his metronomic swing that propelled the ball huge distances. He was an intuitive golfer, not a strategist like Hogan or NIcklaus, and that was another reason why he enraptured golf fans all over the world.

Snead was usually the favourite golfer among his peers. Dave Marr rated him as ten out of ten in virtually every aspect of the game and Ben Crenshaw wrote that he 'plays the game the way it's supposed to be played – the way you dream about playing just once in your life'. The final words on Snead are best expressed by another supreme golfer, the Australian Peter Thomson: 'Like classic plays and symphonies, Sam Snead doesn't just belong to a generation. His mark will be left on golf into eternity'.

SNEED, ED

USA

Born: 6.8.44

Appearances: 1977

Record: P2 W1 L0 H1

A graduate of Ohio State University, like Jack Nicklaus and Tom Weiskopf, Sneed joined the American tour in 1968 and won his first tournament, the Kaiser Open, in 1973. His other three victories included the Houston Open in 1982. Sneed had a golden opportunity to win the Masters in 1979. He was three ahead of the field with three holes to play but managed to drop a shot to par at all of them. He lost the play-off to Fuzzy Zoeller.

He played two games in the Ryder Cup match at Royal Lytham in 1977 when the format was changed to comprise five foursomes on the opening day, five fourballs on the second day and ten singles on the final day. Sneed and Don January were let off the hook in the foursomes by Eammon Darcy and Tony Jacklin, who were two holes up with three to play. The American pair escaped with a half and Sneed and Lanny Wadkins beat Neil Coles and Peter Dawson in the fourball series.

SOUCHAK, MIKE

USA

Born: 10.5.27

Appearances: 1959, 1961

Record: P6 W5 L1 H0

Mike Souchak, who played football for Duke University, was a great chunk of a man and immensely strong. He had a lovely rhythmic swing and had the game to win a major championship, but the closest he ever came was in the US Open: he was equal third both at Winged Foot in 1959 and at Cherry Hills in the following year.

Nevertheless, he won 15 tournaments on the American tour and still holds the record for the lowest score in a PGA event: 257 (27 under par) in the Texas Open of 1955. In the process he scored the lowest-ever total for nine holes of 27 (since equalled by Andy North).

Souchak was an intimidating opponent in matchplay, as his Ryder Cup record shows. He won both his games at Eldorado in 1959 and his only defeat was in a foursomes at Lytham in 1961 when he and Bill Collins lost to Dai Rees and Ken Bousfield. In the singles he was far too strong for Ralph Moffitt and then beat Bernard Hunt in the afternoon.

Hunt more or less held him until the 11th hole which is a very long par five. Hunt recalled that he drove to the right to miss some cross bunkers but Souchak drove his ball right over the trouble. He turned to the American and said: 'You big ox, nobody else could get over the bunkers'. Souchak then picked Hunt up and carried him for several yards. Hunt reckoned that, from that moment, he had no chance of winning.

STADLER, CRAIG

USA

Born: 2.6.53

Appearances: 1983, 1985

Record: P8 W4 L2 H2

Craig Stadler has always stood out among the anonymous golfers churned out by the college production lines for use on the American tour. He is large and overweight and brand-new clothes seem to crumple and age as soon as they touch his frame. He has a thick walrus moustache, a sense of humour and an uncertain temperament. Above all, he is a powerful hitter with a marvellously adroit short game, and the golf fans warm to him.

Stadler was an accomplished amateur. He won the US Amateur Championship in 1973 and played in the Walker Cup two years later at St Andrews. He became a professional soon afterwards but found it hard going until he won two tournaments in 1980, the Bob Hope Desert Classic and the Greater Greensboro Open, and finished eighth in the money list. He won another event in the following year and this was the prelude to his brilliant 1982 season, during which he won four tournaments and was the leading money winner. As well as the Tucson Open, the Kemper Open and the World Series of Golf, he won his first major event, the Masters. After 11 holes of the final round at Augusta, he was five shots ahead of the field, but then tried hard to give the great prize away. He dropped four shots and found himself in a play-off with Dan Pohl; he won the title at the first extra hole.

In the 1983 Ryder Cup, at the PGA National course, Stadler won two points out of three. He and Lanny Wadkins were easily defeated by Nick Faldo and Bernhard Langer and only just managed a win against the lightweight European pair of Brian Waites and Ken Brown in their fourball. Stadler chipped in at the final hole to snatch a point. He defeated Ian Woosnam in the singles.

Stadler played consistent golf over the next two years and won one event, the Byron Nelson Classic. He took his place in the American team at the Belfry and teamed up with Hal Sutton to win a foursomes and halve a fourball match. On the morning of the second day Stadler joined Curtis Strange in a fourball against Langer and Lyle and they were two holes ahead with two to play. Lyle made a spectacular eagle at the 17th and, on the final green, Stadler had a putt of under two feet to halve the hole and win the match. With one of those inexplicable bangs on the funny bone in which the golfing Fates specialise, he missed it. With hindsight, it was clear that this was the turning-point of the whole fixture. The American team's heads drooped and they lost the afternoon foursomes series by three matches to one.

Stadler had a comparative slump over the next five years, even though he won nearly $1.5 million. In 1991, however, he came right back to form: he finished second in the money list and won the Tour Championship. His renaissance is good news for all golf enthusiasts who relish the colour be brings to the game.

STEWART, PAYNE

USA

Born: 30.1.57

Appearances: 1987, 1989, 1991

Record: P12 W5 L6 H1

Payne Stewart has one of the smoothest actions in golf, a blend of elegance and power that is certainly not matched by the outlandish clothes he wears, in the colours of the National Football League. But this eccentric attire cannot detract from his achievements on the golf course where he has won two major championships.

For some time it seemed that Stewart did not have the mental courage to win tournaments. After eight years on the American tour, despite his supreme talent, he had won only three events; he had come second so often that he was nicknamed 'Avis'. In 1986 he had finished third in the money list without winning a tournament. At last, in 1989, he won an important championship, the USPGA at Kemper Lakes. It is sometimes referred to as the event which Mike Reid lost, but Stewart won in fine style by playing the last nine holes in 31 strokes; and he had birdies at three of the last four holes. He finished second in the money list and third in the following year when he won both the Heritage Classic and the Byron Nelson Classic.

Stewart's debut in the Ryder Cup, in 1987 at Muirfield village, began inauspiciously with defeats in both his foursomes. First with Larry Nelson and then with Ben Crenshaw, he lost narrowly to Ballesteros and Olazabal. However, he won his fourball with Andy Bean and gained his revenge on Olazabal in the singles. Two years later Stewart gathered only one point from four games; in a fine foursomes match, he and Lanny Wadkins went round the Belfry in 68 shots to defeat Howard Clark and Mark James on the final green. But Stewart lost a vital singles match to Olazabal when he put his ball into the water from the 18th tee.

The early part of Stewart's 1991 season was blighted by a back injury but he surged back to win his second major

Payne Stewart

championship, the US Open, after a play-off with Scott Simpson. In the Ryder Cup at Kiawah Island he and Mark Calcavecchia forged a formidable partnership to win their two foursomes games. He and Fred Couples halved their fourball with Ballesteros and Olazabal, but he always trailed David Feherty in his singles and lost by two and one.

Stewart has the game to win many more major championships, including the Open. He has an excellent record, with several finishes in the top ten; for example, he was second at Royal St George's in 1985, third at Muirfield in 1987 and second again at St Andrews in 1990. His weight of shot and his ability to play inventive and subtle strokes give him the credentials to win the great championships.

STILL, KEN

USA

Born: 12.2.35

Appearances: 1969

Record: P3 L2 W1 H0

At one stage a career in baseball beckoned Ken Still but he elected to try the American golf tour in 1960. It was not until 1969 that he registered a victory, when he won the Florida Citrus Open and the Greater Milwaukee Open. His third and final win was in the Kaiser Open in the following year when he beat Lee Trevino and Bert Yancey in a play-off.

Perhaps the pressure of the Ryder Cup in 1969 was too much for Still, since he was the focal point of some unpleasant scenes. In a foursomes on the first morning he had to be asked by Maurice Bembridge, who was about to play a shot, to move out of his eye line and he reacted theatrically. Shortly afterwards Still attempted an explosion shot from a bunker and was silent when Lee Trevino, his partner, asked if the ball had hit him. Trevino told him to pick the ball up and conceded the hole. Bembridge and Gallacher won the game.

Matters deteriorated further when Still teamed up with the abrasive Dave Hill in a fourball match against Gallacher and Brian Huggett, both of whom were noted for their fiercely competitive instincts. On the first green Huggett had to ask Hill to keep still while he putted; and on the seventh green Still putted out of turn and, when taken to task by Gallacher, told him to 'have the hole and the Cup too'. A hole later the two captains, Eric Brown and Sam Snead, and the PGA President, Lord Derby, arrived to cool things down. It all seemed to spur Dave Hill on and he played superbly to win a point for the American team. Still played only one more game and lost a close singles match to Maurice Bembridge.

Still has played on the Seniors' tour in America since the mid-Eighties.

STOCKTON, DAVE

USA

Born: 2.11.41

Appearances: 1971, 1977
Captain 1991

Record: P5 W3 L1 H1

His father was a professional golfer and it was inevitable that Dave Stockton would follow suit. After attending the University of Southern California on a golf scholarship, Stockton joined the professional ranks in 1964 and went on to win ten tournaments. All his victories came between 1967 and 1976 and included two USPGA Championships. In 1970 he managed to stay ahead of Arnold Palmer and Bob Murphy to win by two shots at Southern Hill, Oklahoma; and in 1976 he holed a putt of over 12 feet to win by one stroke from Raymond Floyd and Don January.

Stockton was not an orthodox player and his swing was impaired by a back injury which he suffered while surfing at the age of 14. However, he was a very determined battler with a magical short game. He has confessed that his career was largely a triumph of mind over matter and that he was 'blessed with a short game most people would die for'. An example of his remarkable putting came in 1967 when, for ten successive rounds, he did not take more than 28 putts.

In his first match in the Ryder Cup, in St Louis in 1971, he was paired with Jack Nicklaus in a foursomes. The great man was apparently not amused at some of the spots on the Old Warson course into which Stockton hit their ball. They lost to Brian Huggett and Tony Jacklin. But that was Stockton's only defeat and he halved a singles with Bernard Gallacher, who was to be his opposing captain in 1991, and beat Peter Townsend. At Lytham in 1977 he won both his matches. In the foursomes he and Jerry McGee were two down with three to play against Neil Coles and Peter Dawson. But, in characteristically gritty style, Stockton holed long putts at the 16th and 17th holes to get back on level terms and a mistake by Coles on the 18th gave the Americans an unexpected point.

Stockton's all-American brand of determination was just right for the exacting task of the American captaincy in 1991. If the captain's enthusiasm was taken too far towards the bellicose by some members of his team (surely military-style forage caps have no place in a fixture which is meant to promote golf), it was perhaps understandable, since the Americans had not tasted success since 1983.

Dave Stockton played on the American tour until the latter part of the Eighties and intends to play on the lucrative Seniors tour.

STRANGE, CURTIS

USA

Born: 30.1.55

Appearances: 1983, 1985, 1987, 1989

Record: P17 W6 L9 H2

Only Tom Kite and Tom Watson have amassed more money on the American tour than Curtis Strange, who has won 17 events, including the Houston Open (twice), the Westchester Classic, the Canadian Open (twice), the World Series of Golf and the Nabisco Championship. In 1988 he became the first man to win over $1 million in a season. Strange, with his rather mechanical swing, made himself into one of the straightest and most consistent golfers in America. His intensity and his dedication brought him the nickname, 'The Grinder', and he once said of himself: 'My strength is that there aren't any major weaknesses'.

Strange was born into a golfing environment since his father was a professional who owned the White Sands Country Club in Virginia. After his father died of cancer, when Strange was only 14, he eventually found another mentor, Chandler Harper, and went to Arnold Palmer's university, Wake Forest, with a golf scholarship. Strange had a very successful career as an amateur, including selection for the Walker Cup of 1975, and he turned professional two years later. He endured a couple of lean years before he established himself; for example, in 1978 he played in 29 events and missed the cut in 14 of them. But his breakthrough came with a victory in the 1979 Pensacola Open. Thereafter, he was rarely out of the top ten in the money list and was number one in 1985, and 1988.

Strange made an inauspicious first appearance in the 1983 Ryder Cup at the PGA National course. Although he and Jay Hass beat Ken Brown and Brian Waites in their foursomes, he suffered two defeats at the hands of the youthful and inexperienced Paul Way. In partnership with Raymond Floyd, he lost this fourball to Ballesteros and Way and the latter also beat him in the singles. Two years later at the Belfry he fared somewhat better by winning two and a half points from four games.

Despite his superb record on the American tour, Strange found it difficult to maintain his form in the major championships. At the Masters in 1985 he seemed to put himself out of contention with a first round of 80, but, with rounds of 65 and 68 and an opening half on the final day of 32, Strange was in the lead by several shots. But he found water at the 13th and 15th holes and eventually finished in a tie for second place behind Bernhard Langer.

Strange was at last able to seize his opportunity in 1988 when he won the US Open at Brookline after a play-off with Nick Faldo. In the following year, at Oak Hill, he emulated Bobby Jones, Ralph Guldahl and Ben Hogan by retaining the title. In their endless quest for another golfing superstar the American media seized on Strange. He was referred to as the greatest golfer in the world, an absurd claim when measured against the incandescent talents of Ballesteros, for example.

Strange's consistency and stern determination ought to make him a Ryder Cup competitor of the highest calibre but his record is moderate. In the matches at Muirfield Village in 1987 and at the Belfry in 1989 he and Tom Kite, potentially a highly potent partnership, only won two and a half points from six outings; at Muirfield village, Strange also lost his singles to Ballesteros. Perhaps he was seen at his best when he played Woosnam in the final singles at the Belfry. On the 15th tee Strange was one down but showed his class by scoring three birdies in succession, to be one up with one hole to play. At the very dangerous 18th hole he hit a superb long iron to within a few feet of the pin to shut his opponent out and ensure that the Ryder Cup match was tied for only the second time in its history.

Strange has not won a tournament since the US Open in 1989, although he came close in the 1991 Doral Open when he lost a play-off to Rocco Mediate. But he has the skill and the determination to put that right.

Curtis Strange

SUTTON, HAL

USA

Born: 28.4.58

Appearances: 1985, 1987

Record: P9 W3 L3 H3

With a wealthy father to offer financial support, Hal Sutton toyed with the idea of remaining an amateur while still competing in the major professional tournaments. It was an unrealistic ambition and, after winning the US Amateur Championship in 1980 and playing twice in the Walker Cup, Sutton became a professional in 1981. In his first full season he won a tournament; and in 1983 he achieved a remarkable double with victories in the USPGA Championship and the Tournament Players Championship. He was the leading money winner and the pundits began to compare him to Jack Nicklaus: he was dubbed the 'Bear Apparent'. Although he has won five tournaments, Sutton has not lived up to that nickname.

His last tournament victory was in 1986, which was also the last time that he achieved a position in the top ten on the American tour.

He has played in two defeated American Ryder Cup teams. At the Belfry in 1985 he and Craig Stadler opened with a foursomes win over Howard Clark and Sam Torrance; they halved with Langer and Canizares and lost to Ballesteros and Pinero. Sutton did not endear himself to the British fans with his criticisms of their behaviour, especially since those criticisms came in the aftermath of a heavy defeat by Langer in the singles. Sutton fared a little better two years later when he won three points out of a possible five. His win in the second series of fourballs with Larry Mize, over Ballesteros and Olazabal, was particularly laudable since the American pair had a better ball of seven under par.

T

THOMAS, DAVID

GB

Born: 16.8.34

Appearances: 1959, 1963, 1965, 1967

Record: P18 W3 L10 H5

As a youth, David Thomas had already attracted attention; Pat Ward Thomas wrote about his enormous potential and Henry Cotton commented on Thomas's 'fabulous gift ... he could go through the ball in one piece with his driver and hit it miles'. Thomas, with his great physique and strength, could indeed hit the ball huge distances with his controlled and rhythmic swing and there seemed no limit to what he might achieve in golf.

At the 1958 Open, he faced his first great test as he played throughout the final day (36 holes were played at that time) with the international star of golf, Peter Thomson, who had already won the Open twice. Thomas's skill and resolution never wavered; both his driving and his long irons were magnificent. After 16 holes of the final round, he was one shot ahead of the brilliant Australian. Still only in his mid-twenties, Thomas was poised to grasp a great victory which would confirm his immense promise as a golfer.

At the penultimate hole, however, his swing tightened a shade and he scored a five to Thomson's four. They both registered par fours at the final hole and thus had to face each other in a play-off over 36 holes. Thomson was too consistent for the Welshman and won the title by a margin of four shots.

Nevertheless, the golfing horizon seemed to stretch out, wide and bright, for Dave Thomas. It could only be a matter of time before he won a major championship. But although he won many tournaments, including the Belgian, Dutch and French Opens, the Esso Golden, the PGA Matchplay Championship and the Penfold, only on one more occasion did he get close to winning the Open. At Muirfield in 1966 he had the lowest score over the final two founds but was beaten into second place by Jack Nicklaus.

In the Ryder Cup Thomas's great talent did not bring him the success that was anticipated. He made his debut in 1959 at Eldorado, California and, with Harry Weetman, should have won his foursomes against Sam Snead and Cary Middlecoff. The British pair were one up on the final tee and Snead's second shot deposited the American ball in the lake that guarded the green. Thomas had put Weetman miles down the middle of the fairway and all that was required was a quiet short iron to the edge of the lake, a pitch on to the green and two putts for a certain win. But Weetman seized a mid-iron and went for the green. The ball, with awful inevitability, ended in the water. Henry Longhurst was standing just behind Weetman and reported that he 'could hardly believe the evidence of my eyes'. It was inevitable, too, that the Americans would make a five to the British six and halve the match. P G Wodehouse's thump behind the ear with a sock filled with wet sand had been firmly administered by the golfing Fates.

Thomas was soundly beaten by Sam Snead in the singles and it was a long time before he registered a win. Although he managed two halved matches at East Lake in 1963, it was not until the fixture at Birkdale two years later that he notched a full point. This came in partnership with George Will and they dismissed Arnold Palmer and Dave Marr in the first series of foursomes to the humiliating tune of six and five. Marr was thoroughly demoralised as Thomas drove the ball 60 or more yards past him. In the afternoon, however, the same pairs were drawn together again and the Americans exacted their revenge.

Thomas's final Ryder Cup appearance was at Houston in 1967 and, as the British team sank to an overwhelming defeat, he kept his head nobly above the water with two wins in partnership with Tony Jacklin, two halved matches and only one defeat.

David Thomas's driving and long iron game could only be described as majestic, but he was never able to master the short game. However much he practised, and whatever the advice he took, he could not play those vital shots from within a hundred yards of the green. The irony was that he was such a long hitter that he was left more of those sort of shots to play than any of his contemporaries. If he had attained just an average proficiency with the wedge there is no doubt that Thomas would have won many more tournaments, including an Open or two.

He represented Wales in the World Cup on 11 occasions, but Thomas eventually withdrew from tournament golf to concentrate on his very successful business as a golf course designer.

TORRANCE, SAM

Europe

Born: 24.8.53

Appearances: 1981, 1983, 1985, 1987, 1989, 1991

Record: P21 W4 L12 H5

Sam Torrance's putt in the 1985 Ryder Cup match at the Belfry, whereby he beat Andy North on the 18th green and ensured Britain and Europe's first victory for 28 years, will remain etched on the memories of his supporters for many a day. He had fought hard to cut a three-hole deficit to the American Open champion, not least at the 17th hole where he was in heavy rough after his second shot; but he pitched close and won the hole to draw level. North's tension on the last tee made him sky his drive into water whereas Torrance hit a magnificent booming shot down the fairway. He thoroughly deserved his triumphal progress and his birdie putt from 15 feet was a fitting climax to the match.

For over two decades Torrance has been one of the great stalwarts of the European tour; it is calculated that during the years from 1972, his first full season, to 1982 he only missed two official tournaments, and then only because he broke a toe. His first important victories were in the Piccadilly Medal and the Martini tournaments in 1976, when he finished third in the Order of Merit. During the next 16 years he only once finished outside the top 25 and won over 20 events, including the Irish, Spanish, Portuguese, Italian and Colombian Opens and the Australian PGA Championship. He also represented Scotland in the World Cup on nine occasions.

Torrance has an excellent record and it is no surprise that such a busy golfer has won over £1.5 million. His swing, watched over by his father, Bob, a noted teacher, is a fine amalgam of power and fluency and he has long been judged one of the finest strikers in European golf. His putting, however, has frequently caused him problems, which became so severe in 1988 that he seriously considered abandoning tournament golf. He dropped to

51st in the Order of Merit but found his salvation in a putter with an elongated shaft. Whatever the aesthetic merits of the club (when asked if he had tried it, Arnold Palmer tersely replied 'only in the privacy of the bathroom') the broom handle putter saved Torrance's career. In 1989 he climbed back to 11th in the money list and in the following year signalled his complete recovery by winning the German Masters from Bernhard Langer and Ian Woosnam and finishing second in the Volvo Masters.

For such a wonderful striker of the ball Torrance's record in the Ryder Cup is mediocre. He made a dismal start in 1981 at Walton Heath when he won just half a point from four games; he opened his account two years later by beating Raymond Floyd and Bob Gilder in a foursomes, in partnership with Canizares. He also earned a valuable half against Tom Kite in the singles. In 1985 he had his great moments of glory but in the European victory at Muirfield Village in 1987 he contributed only half a point, from his singles encounter with Larry Mize. In the two matches at the Belfry and at Kiawah Island he won one and a half points from six outings.

No doubt Sam Torrance will play his usual full programme on the European tour during the next few years and will be a good bet to make the Ryder Cup team again.

TOWNSEND, PETER

GB

Born: 16.9.46

Appearances: 1969, 1971

Record: P11 W3 L8 H0

If a golfer ever looked bound for stardom it was Peter Townsend. He had a marvellous career as an amateur: in the Walker Cup in 1965 at Baltimore, when the match was tied, he won three points out of four. A year later he seemed to win everything, including the English Amateur Strokeplay Championship, the Lytham Trophy and the *Golf Illustrated* Gold Vase.

Above all, Townsend looked the part. He had a free-wheeling, uninhibited swing and a dashing outlook that signalled all-out attack. His professional career got off to a splendid start. In 1967 he won the Dutch Open and in the following year the PGA Close Championship and the Western Australian Open, and he was second to Gay Brewer in the Alcan Tournament.

Townsend won his way into the 1969 British team for Birkdale and was a natural partner for Tony Jacklin, the new Open champion. They had many similarities, both slim and dark and with enormous confidence in their abilities. In their foursomes against Dave Hill and Tommy Aaron they began with three birdies to go two up and, when they won on the 17th green, were seven under par. It was appropriate that Townsend finished the American pair off by hitting a 3-wood to six feet at the 17th and Jacklin holed out for an eagle. Their second match was much tougher, but they hung on against Billy Casper and Frank Beard to win by one hole. The captain, Eric Brown, split the successful pair up for the fourball matches on the next day and Townsend had his third win in succession, with Christy O'Connor against Dave Hill and Dale Douglass. Although he lost both his singles matches, Peter Townsend had made a splendid debut in the remarkable tied match.

In the next two years he won the Caracas Open and the Swiss Open and was selected for the 1971 match in St Louis. Although the British team did much better than expected, to lose by a margin of only five points, Townsend lost all six of his matches. In five of those matches, he faced either Jack Nicklaus or Arnold Palmer, and on one occasion they were paired together against Townsend and Harry Bannerman: it was the stiffest of golfing examinations.

Townsend won several tournaments in the Seventies, including the Irish Matchplay Championship, the Irish Dunlop tournament, the Caribbean Open and the Zambian Open. In 1983 he became the professional at Portmarnock and is now a director of the European tour.

TREVINO, LEE

USA

Born: 1.12.39

Appearances: 1969, 1971, 1973, 1975, 1979, 1981
Captain 1985

Record: P30 W17 L7 H6

A Mexican called Lee Buck Trevino arrived, unheralded, on the golfing scene in 1968. Tough and chunky, uninhibited and ebullient, he won the US Open at Oak Hill and put the fun back into golf. He had been noticed the year before when the Open was played at Baltusrol. Trevino could not afford the entrance fee but his wife scraped together enough money to pay his dues and he finished in fifth place behind luminaries like Jack Nicklaus, Arnold Palmer, Don January and Billy Casper. The experts said it was just a fluke; after all, Trevino had a swing that you would see any day on any golf range. He had a wide open stance, an out-to-in swing and made an ugly lunge through the ball.

Trevino certainly had a 'golf range swing' because that was where he had taught himself to play. It was remarkable that he ever picked up a golf club because he was born into extreme poverty. He never knew his father and was brought up by his mother and his grandfather in a four-roomed shack near Dallas. It had neither plumbing nor electricity and the kitchen had a dirt floor. His introduction to golf was as a caddie and he then worked as a greenkeeper at the Glen Lakes Club. His stint at a golf range was interrupted by four years' service in the Marine Corps, during which time he played a great deal of golf. But it was at the range that he perfected his own unique and very repetitive swing.

He became the professional at a public course, Tenison Park, and toughened his temperament in a hard school of hustlers and big-money matches. As Trevino later said: 'You don't know what pressure is until you play for five bucks with only two in your pocket'. He played for a great deal more than that and, with his gambler's instinct and inventive shot-making, would have been at home in any decade of golf; but especially in the Thirties when the bets between the players were usually bigger than the prize fund.

Trevino's place in the 1967 US Open gave him an entree to the tour and he eventually finished 45th on the money list and became 'rookie of the year'. Even when he won the Open in the following year at Oak Hill by four shots from Nicklaus, and became the first golfer to win the Championship with four rounds under 70, he was not taken seriously. Top golfers were conceived as being like Nicklaus: they were tall and reserved, had been to college and were carefully spoken. Trevino was not at all reserved: he rattled off his jokes, fast and loud; he chatted to everyone in sight, even to the spectators; and he clearly enjoyed his golf. He was a throwback to the days of Walter Hagen and he could not have arrived at a better time for golf.

Trevino followed his victory in the US Open by winning the Hawaiian Open and taking sixth place on the money list. During the next seven years he was always in the top ten and he won the Vardon Trophy for the season's best stroke average on four occasions: he won four more major championships and a string of other events on the American tour.

Trevino's successes were owed to an eminently sound and consistent swing. Until the early Sixties, he hit the ball from right to left and often produced a vicious hook. The scales fell from his eyes one day when he watched Ben Hogan on the practice ground; the great champion was fading his shots to the target with deadly accuracy and Trevino determined to emulate his technique. As he is fond of saying: 'You can talk to a fade but you can't talk to a hook'. He had other attributes essential to a great golfer: his extension through the ball, as he drove the club down the line towards the target, was unrivalled; above all, just like Nicklaus, he was an intelligent planner; his tactics for each course were carefully plotted in advance. The final links in the chain were his genius for inventing shots and his supreme accuracy. One of his toughest opponents in the Ryder Cup, Bernard Gallacher, said that he had never seen anyone 'pepper the flag with every club like Trevino.'

In his turn Trevino rated Gallacher as his most difficult opponent in the Ryder Cup fixtures; he was the only man who got the better of him. They first met at Birkdale in 1969, when Trevino won three and a half points out of five, but he and Ken Still lost their opening foursomes to Gallacher and Bembridge; and in the singles the young Scot beat him again. In 1971 in St Louis, Trevino only lost one match: a foursomes with Billy Casper against Gallacher and Oosterhuis. At Muirfield two years later he and Casper lost another foursomes game, to Gallacher again, in partnership with Brian Barnes. Trevino was unbeaten in his other five games. This was the occasion of Trevino's boast that, if he could not beat Peter Oosterhuis in the singles, he would 'kiss the asses of the American team.' He just scraped a half and it is said that a photograph exists which shows the team, their trousers around their ankles, waiting for the wager to be honoured.

In 1971 Lee Trevino showed the world that a great champion had taken centre stage. In the

space of a few weeks he won the US Open, the Canadian Open and the Open Championship. He had signalled his intent in his performances on the American tour in the preceding weeks: he had won the Tallahassee and the Memphis Opens and had a second and a third place in other events.

After four rounds of the US Open at Merion, Trevino was tied with the great Jack Nicklaus. On the first tee of the play-off on the next day Trevino broke the tension in a characteristic fashion by 'finding' a snake in his golf bag. It was a toy, and Trevino found Merion as harmless, as he scored a 68 to Nicklaus's 71 to win the title for the second time. The fans loved it and Trevino summed up a part of his appeal to them when he said: 'I represent the public golf-courses, the working man, the blue collar worker.' A week later he won the Canadian Open after another play-off, this time against Art Wall.

So Trevino arrived at Birkdale for the Open, which he had been well-placed to win at St Andrews the year before. A disappointing final round of 77 had dropped him into third place. With his ability to manoeuvre the ball and hit it low, Trevino had no fear of seaside golf and he endeared himself to the British by saying: 'I love this championship. I love the links courses, with the mist and the wind sweeping off the sea.' He won the title by one shot from Liang Huan Lu, the popular 'Mr Lu' of the politely doffed pork-pie hat, with Tony Jacklin in third place. Trevino had joined three other inimitable golfers, Bobby Jones, Gene Sarazen and Ben Hogan, in winning the two major Open Championships in the same year.

In 1972 he retained the Open Championship at Muirfield and broke Tony Jacklin's golfing heart in the process. At the close of the third round he produced some outrageous shots, including a holed bunker shot and a chip into the hole from off the green. At the 17th hole of the final round, whereas Jacklin was just short of the green after two thunderous shots, Trevino had hacked his way to the back of the green in four. It seemed all over until Trevino casually flicked his chip shot into the hole for a par five; it was inevitable that Jacklin would take three putts; and Trevino won the championship by one shot from Jack Nicklaus. 'God is a Mexican,' said Trevino. It is not reported what Jacklin said but he was never the same superlative player again.

In the next two years Trevino's game suffered from too many promotional commitments and too much hard living. He still managed to finish fourth on the money list in 1973 and again in 1974, when he won the USPGA championship at Shoal Creek, North Carolina. Once again Nicklaus was in second place.

The 1975 Ryder Cup match at Laurel Valley was won easily by the Americans; it was all over by lunchtime on the final day, with another eight singles to be played. Trevino relaxed at lunch with a few glasses of Rolling Rock beer but was called upon to play in the afternoon. He was certainly not at his sharpest against Norman Wood, especially after his captain, Arnold Palmer, gave him two more beers halfway through the match. Trevino lost on the 17th green.

Back trouble took its toll on Trevino during the next couple of years, partly as a result of his being struck by lightning at the 1975 Western Open. Although he won two events in the USA he did not qualify for the 1977 Ryder Cup, but he re-appeared at The Greenbrier two years later. He won two and a half points out of four but was again beaten by his nemesis, Bernard Gallacher; in partnership with Brian Barnes, the Scot beat Trevino and Fuzzy Zoeller in a fourball. At Walton Heath in 1981, however, Trevino won all his matches and was especially lethal in partnership with the talented Jerry Pate, whom he called 'the best player in the world from the shoulders down.' He told Pate that he would do the thinking for both of them. It worked: for example, the Americans thumped Nick Faldo and Sam Torrance to the tune of seven and five. Out first in the singles Trevino defeated Torrance in just over two hours and was back in the clubhouse, with a beer in his hand, before the last man, Jack Nicklaus began his match.

Trevino had another brilliant year in 1980 when he won the Tournament Players Championship, the Memphis Classic and the Texas Open; and he won the Tournament of Champions early in 1981. This was to be his last victory until 1984 when he dumbfounded everyone by winning the USPGA Championship for the second time, at the age of 45. At Shoal Creek he recorded four rounds under 70 to win by four shots from Lanny Wadkins.

Trevino has never threatened to win the fourth major championship, the Masters at Augusta. For many years he professed a genuine antipathy both to the course, which does not suit his game, and to the patrician attitudes of the organisers. He used to change in and out of his golf shoes in the car park. In recent years he has had some high finishes but it is probably too late, even for Trevino, to win the event and complete the grand slam of the major championships.

Trevino was not yet finished

with the Ryder Cup since he was appointed non-playing captain in 1985. This was the year that Europe regained the trophy for the first time since 1957 and Trevino's laid-back style of leadership attracted criticism.

In the latter part of the Eighties, Trevino turned to television as a commentator and also confessed that he could hardly wait to 'join the round bellies' on the Seniors tour and plunder their prize funds. That is exactly what he did. In his first year he won seven tournaments, was second in eight others and scampered away with over $1 million, more than the amount won by Greg Norman, who headed the money list on the USPGA tour. In 1991 he won over $700,000 and will add many more dollars to that total in the years to come.

Trevino has won 50 or more tournaments around the world, including six major championships. His charismatic personality and unparalleled shot-making talents have enlivened the golf scene wherever he has appeared. He is one of the most popular players ever to grace the fairways and one of the game's greatest champions.

TURNESA, JIM

USA

Born: 10.12.13

Appearances: 1953

Record: P1 W1 L0 H0

Jim was the sixth son of Vitale Turnesa, who fathered a remarkable golfing tribe: seven sons, of whom six became professionals. The seventh and youngest was William, who won the US Amateur Championship twice, the British Amateur once and captained the Walker Cup team in 1951.

Jim Turnesa was the most successful of the brothers, because he won a major championship, the USPGA, in 1952. When he won the 36th hole, it was the first time he was ahead of his opponent, Chick Harbert.

He had turned 40 when he made his one and only appearance in the Ryder Cup, but his victory in the singles over Peter Alliss in 1953 was a crucial one. It must have seemed to the spectators that each player was trying to give the game to his opponent. With Alliss one up in the 36 hole match, Turnesa hit a wild slice from the 16th tee (the 34th hole), but his ball hit a spectator, he saved his par and won the hole; Alliss drove out of bounds at the next; and Turnesa was deep in the trees at the 18th. But Alliss fluffed a pitch and missed a short putt and Turnesa had won a vital point for the USA.

TURNESA, JOE

USA

Born: 31.1.01

Appearances: 1927, 1929

Record: P4 W1 L2 H1

Known as the most relaxed and easy-going of the Turnesa family, Joe was the first to play the tour. In the heyday of Sarazen, Hagen, Tommy Armour, Leo Diegel and Bobby Jones, he won 14 events, including the Texas, Pennsylvania, Sacramento and Miami Opens.

He came very close to winning the US Open in 1926. At one stage in the final round he was leading Bobby Jones by four shots but underwent a minor collapse and lost by one shot. Joe's father, Vitale, kept his sense of proportion when he was told that his son was leading the Open. He said: 'Why shouldn't he? He's never done anything all his life but play golf.' In the next year's USPGA Championship he was leading Walter Hagen with a few holes to play but 'the Haig' came back at his opponent to record his fourth win in the event.

Joe Turnesa played in the first Ryder Cup in 1927 and, with Johnny Farrell, handed out a severe beating to George Duncan and Archie Compston, who were thought to be Britain's strongest pair. He lost his singles to George Duncan on the final green. Two years later Turnesa and Johnny Farrell halved their foursomes and Turnesa lost his singles to Aubrey Boomer.

V

VENTURI, KEN

USA

Born: 15.5.31

Appearances: 1965

Record: P4 W1 L3 H0

As a young man, Ken Venturi was probably the best amateur golfer in the world. Not surprisingly for a protege of Byron Nelson, his iron shots were superb and he played for the United States in the Walker Cup of 1953. In 1956, while still an amateur, he was within a couple of strokes of winning the Masters. After three rounds he led the field by four shots, but he subsided to a score of 80 in the final round to lose by one shot to Jack Burke.

Venturi turned professional soon after and won ten tournaments between 1957 and 1960. Once again, he suffered frustration in the Masters. In 1960 he had finished his final round and was already being congratulated on his victory when Arnold Palmer, in his inimitable way, birdied the last two holes and seized the crown.

For some time afterwards Venturi suffered a series of injuries which culminated in serious back trouble. He altered his swing to accommodate it and his golf became worse and worse. In 1964 his form was so bad that he had to seek exemptions to play and he had to pre-qualify for the US Open. As the final day began, when two rounds were played, the heat and humidity became intense. Venturi scored a 66 in the morning but was already near to collapse. With a doctor in attendance, he somehow lasted through the final round and scored a marvellous 70 to win by four shots. At last, he had won the major championship which he feared would be denied him for ever.

It was a victory attained through great mental courage but fate had another spiteful blow to deliver. Soon after, Venturi began to suffer circulatory problems in his hands and arms, which partly explained his lack of success in the 1965 Ryder Cup at Birkdale. In four matches he only recorded one win, with Tony Lema against Neil Coles and Bernard Hunt, which was hardly a true reflection of his great ability.

Venturi was to win one more tournament, in 1966, but eventually withdrew from competitive golf. He became an expert commentator for CBS Television and the teaching editor for *Golf* Magazine.

W

WADKINS, JERRY LANSTON

USA

Born: 4.12.49

Appearances: 1977, 1979, 1983, 1985, 1987, 1989, 1991

Record: P30 W18 L10 H2

The American Ryder Cup teams of the last 15 years have been fortunate to have one of the golfing world's toughest competitors, Lanny Wadkins, in their ranks. He is ever at his best in a crisis, as he showed during the nerve-wracking denouement of the 1983 match at PGA National: at the final hole of his singles against Canizares, he nearly holed his third shot; this ensured a birdie and the vital half point needed for the USA to retain the trophy.

Wadkins looks like a battler: there is a swagger about him; he swings the club fast and talks even faster. He would have made a wonderful partner for George Duncan, 'the galloping golfer'; they would have done 18 holes in less than an hour. Wadkins is known as a golfer to whom caution is a dirty word: he goes flat out on every shot. John Mahaffey said: 'You put a pin in the middle of a lake and Lanny will attack it'. The dark face of his character is seen when things go wrong and his frustration surfaces quickly. There are shadows of one of Dylan Thomas's characters in him: 'speaks rather fancy; truculent; plausible; a bit of a shower-off; plus-fours and no breakfast, you know ... a gabbing, ambitious, mock-tough, pretentious young man'.

Wadkins had a wonderful amateur career which culminated in 1970 with victories in the Western, Southern and US Amateur Championships. He played in the Walker Cup teams of 1969 and 1971 and showed his inexorable self confidence when he took on the professionals in the 1970 Heritage Classic and finished in second place. He joined the American tour in 1971 and in his second year finished tenth in the money list, after winning the Sahara Invitational. In 1973 he won two more events and was fifth in the money list. Some relatively fallow years ensued but in 1977 he won his first and only major, the USPGA Championship at Pebble Beach. Whereas Gene Littler dropped five shots in the last six holes, Wadkins recorded two eagles in his round and holed a slippery birdie putt of over six yards on the final green to force a play-off. He followed this success by winning the World Series of Golf at Firestone with a record score of 13 under par.

Wadkins's first two appearances in the Ryder Cup signalled his supreme competitive powers. He won all his three matches at Lytham in 1977 and he and Larry Nelson combined at The Greenbrier two years later to win four points out of four. They beat Ballesteros and Garrido three times. It took a doughty golfer like Bernard Gallacher to stop Wadkins; the Scot beat him by three and two in the singles.

In 1979 Wadkins won the Los Angeles Open and the prestigious Tournament Players Championship in rough and windy conditions at Sawgrass. He reappeared in the Ryder Cup in 1983 and won two full points as well as forcing a vital half in his singles against Canizares. Two years later, at the Belfry, he began with three wins but then lost his foursomes to Langer and Brown, who must have driven Wadkins to distraction with their slow play. The American was out first in the singles and lost to another highly combative player, Manuel Pinero.

Wadkins had won three events in 1985 and finished second in the money list. His consistent golf ensured his selection for the 1987 and 1989 Ryder cup sides but his results were moderate by his former standards, with only three points from eight games as the European team retained the trophy. But in 1991, at Kiawah Island, Wadkins played his full part in the American triumph. He was unbeaten until the second afternoon, when he and Wayne Levi lost their fourball to Mark James and Steven Richardson, but he defeated James easily in the singles.

In 1991 Wadkins won the Hawaiian Open and finished 12th on the money list. It is likely that he will be a prominent member of the American team at the Belfry in 1993 and, one day, will make as formidable a Ryder Cup captain as he is a player.

WAITES, BRIAN

Europe

Born: 1.3.40

Appearances: 1983

Record: P4 W1 L3 H0

The biggest win of Brian Waites's career came in the Tournament Players Championship in 1978, although he was much to the fore on the Safari Circuit in the Eighties and won several tournaments. Although he was a short hitter, Waites was a competent professional, a journeyman whose consistency justified his selection for England in the World Cup in 1980, 1982 and 1983.

In the latter year he earned selection for the Ryder Cup, when the team was chosen straight off the money list. The new captain, Tony Jacklin, was not permitted any special selections. In the match at the PGA National course in Florida the European team gave the Americans a real fright, but Brian Waites did not. although he and Ken Brown (summoned hastily from the practice ground at lunchtime when Bernard Gallacher and Sandy Lyle asked to be dropped from the afternoon fourball matches) beat Gil Morgan and Fuzzy Zoeller. Waites lost his next three matches.

Waites won the PGA Seniors in 1990 and again in the following year. His plans to play on the Seniors tour in the USA were disrupted by a serious car accident later that year.

WALL, ART

USA

Born: 25.11.23

Appearances: 1957, 1959, 1961

Record: P6 W4 L2 H0

The high point of Art Wall's career was his victory in the 1959 Masters when, at the beginning of the final round, he was six shots adrift of Stan Leonard and Arnold Palmer. He scored a wonderful 66, which included five birdies in the last six holes. He also won three other tournaments in that year.

Wall became a professional in 1949 after graduating from Duke University. His career had a long span; he won his last tournament, the Greater Milwaukee Open, in 1975 and played on for a few years thereafter. One can remember his appearing, towards the end of his career, in a televised series of matches, 'USA v The World'. He was unlucky enough to face Christy O'Connor on a links course in Britain on a day when the heavens opened and the wind howled. O'Connor loved every minute of it and turned in a score of under 70. Wall, a lugubrious figure with the rain dripping off him, clearly wished he was somewhere else, indoors by a roaring fire preferably, and just about broke 80.

Wall played one match at Lindrick in the 1957 Ryder Cup and he and Fred Hawkins were beaten in the foursomes by Dai Rees and Ken Bousfield. Two years later, at Eldorado, he and Doug Ford lost to O'Connor and Allis, but he at last earned a point with a decisive defeat of O'Connor. Wall won three points out of three in his final appearance in 1961 at Lytham. Two of the matches were decided on the final green. He and Jay

Hebert made a birdie, to beat Wall's old rivals, O'Connor and Alliss, in the foursomes; and in the singles he had a great contest with Harry Weetman. The British player covered the first nine holes in 33 strokes but was two down to Wall, who only needed 31 shots. Over the final nine holes Wall was just able to stay ahead to win by one hole.

Art Wall (Below)

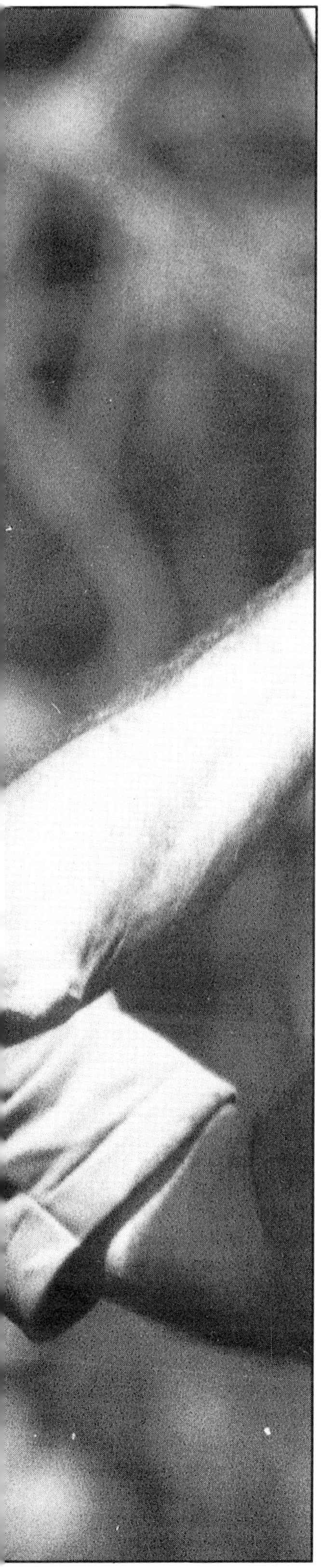

WARD, CHARLES

GB

Born: 16.9.11

Appearances: 1947, 1949, 1951

Record: P6 W1 L5 H0

The Second World War delayed Charlie Ward's full participation in professional golf but he more than made up for those lost years. He won 12 tournaments from the end of the war to 1951, including the Spalding tournament, the Dunlop Masters, the *Daily Mail* Tournament and the West Midland Open. He reached the semi-finals of the PGA Matchplay Championship in 1947 and 1949 and finished third in the Open Championship in 1948, at Muirfield, and in 1951 at Portrush. He won the Vardon Trophy for the best stroke average in 1948 and 1949 and was still winning tournaments in the late Fifties.

Charlie Ward was a golfer of considerable talent, despite his rather quick swing. He was not as powerful as many of his contemporaries but made up the difference by his remarkable skill near the green. He was also a very reliable putter, especially from medium and short range.

He had a very tough baptism in Ryder Cup golf at Portland, Oregon, in 1947 when the British team were heavily defeated. In the foursomes he and Fred Daly were six down at lunch to Sam Snead and Lloyd Mangrum and never recovered. Neither was Ward able to make much impression on the very powerful 'Porky' Oliver in the singles, despite some superb golf in the first nine holes after lunch which he covered in 34 strokes.

It was much the same two years later, at Ganton, when a run of birdies from Jimmy Demaret and Clayton Heafner in the afternoon sank Ward and Sam King. In the singles Ward drew Sam Snead and was only one hole down after 18 holes; but the great Snead moved into a higher gear after lunch and demolished him by 6 and 5.

In 1951, at Pinehurst, Ward at least won a match when he and Arthur Lees defeated 'Porky' Oliver and Henry Ransom. On the following day Ward had to confront the greatest golfer in the world, Ben Hogan. He reacted with typical determination and was only two down after 18 holes, despite Hogan's score of 67. In the afternoon, however, the implacable American edged away to win three and two.

Charlie Ward dominated professional events in the Midlands for two decades and was the professional at Little Aston for many years.

WATROUS, AL

USA

Born: 1.2.99

Appearances: 1927, 1929

Record: P3 W2 L1 H0

Al Watrous was on the receiving end of one of the most illustrious shots in the history of the Open Championship: it was played by Bobby Jones at the 17th hole of the final round at Lytham in 1926. The two players were drawn together and, although Watrous had been in the lead a couple of holes earlier, they were level on that tee. Watrous, a very accurate driver, put his ball safely down the right side of the fairway, whereas Jones hooked his ball into a bunker in the rough on the left. From there he hit an astonishing shot with his mashie-niblick (roughly a 4-iron in today's parlance) across the sandy wastes to the heart of the green. Watrous was on the green in two shots but, unnerved by Jones's audacity, he took three putts and let his opponent in for victory.

Watrous had a remarkably long career; he became a professional in 1920, was still playing on the American Seniors tour forty years later and was the Seniors champion three times during the Fifties. It is said that only Gene Sarazen has played in more PGA events. He won the Canadian Open in 1922 and was a steady winner through the Twenties and Thirties.

Al Watrous played in the forerunner of the Ryder Cup in 1926 and lost both his matches; but he reversed those results in the real thing in 1927, when he and Gene Sarazen beat Arthur Havers and Bert Jolly in a scrappy foursomes match. He also defeated Fred Robson in the singles. The British team reclaimed the Ryder Cup in 1929, at Moortown, when Watrous was beaten by the young Henry Cotton to give Britain the deciding point.

In addition to his long career as a tournament player, Watrous was the professional at Oakland Hills for nearly forty years. He was a fine teacher and as fascinated by the mechanics of the game. His enquiring mind prompted him to stand naked in front of a mirror and swing a golf club in order to see how the various muscles worked. Like Ben Hogan, he practised more than any of his contemporaries.

WATSON, TOM

USA

Born: 4.9.49

Appearances: 1977, 1981, 1983, 1989

Record: P15 W10 L4 H1

Between 1975 and 1984 Tom Watson was the most successful golfer in the game. He won eight major championships and 30 events on the American tour; he was never worse than 12th on the money list and was its leader on five occasions. Not only had Watson deposed the illustrious Jack Nicklaus as the monarch of world golf but he had also done so in a series of direct confrontations. In the 1977 Masters at Augusta, Watson responded to Nicklaus's superb final round of 66 with a score of 67 to win the title by two shots. A few months later the two men clashed at the Open Championship at Turnberry. In an absorbing struggle which was illuminated by some of the most brilliant golf ever seen in the tournament, Watson and Nicklaus matched each other for the first three rounds and left the rest of the field in their wake. In the final round Nicklaus was three strokes in the lead at one point, but Watson clawed his way back into the contest. His birdie at the 17th hole gave him the lead for the first time, and a 1-iron from the 18th tee, followed by a coruscating 7-iron to within a couple of feet of the hole, seemed to seal his triumph. But Nicklaus was not finished; it was typical of his unbending spirit that he holed a huge putt for a birdie on the final green. Watson rolled his short putt in for victory and set a new record score for the Open of 268. Such was the fierce splendour of the two Americans' golf that Hubert Green, in third place, was a distant ten shots adrift of Nicklaus.

Tom Watson had begun to play golf at an early age and was a scratch player as a teenager. He was intelligent enough to attend Stanford University and wise

enough to complete his degree in psychology. His first years on the American tour were not especially productive, but his breakthrough occurred in 1974 when he won the Western Open. At this stage of his career he was prone to dissipate promising positions in tournaments, especially in the major events. For example, poor final rounds in the US Opens of 1974 and 1975 ruined his chances. But his resolution never wavered in the Open Championship at Carnoustie in the latter year: tied with the Australian, Jack Newton, after four rounds, he won the play-off by a single shot.

If the following year was one of modest achievement by Watson's standards, 1977 saw his talent in full bloom. As well as winning the Masters and the Open he took first place in four other tournaments. Watson was to be the leading money winner on the American tour for four years in succession, with a phalanx of prestigious victories: the San Diego, Western and Tucson Opens, the Byron Nelson Golf Classic, the Tournament of Champions, the Hall of Fame Classic, the Los Angeles Open and the World Series of Golf.

Watson made his entry on to the Ryder Cup stage in 1977 and started with two decisive victories; with Jack Nicklaus he defeated Tommy Horton and Mark James in the foursomes and with Hubert Green he beat Horton and Brian Barnes in the fourballs. But, rather surprisingly, he suffered a reverse in the singles at the hands of the 20-year-old Nick Faldo. Two years later Watson was due to play in the fixture at The Greenbrier but withdrew on the eve of the opening matches because his wife was about to give birth to their first child. He returned to the fray in 1981, at Walton Heath, when he won his three games in partnership with Nicklaus but was beaten in the singles by Howard Clark.

In the Eighties Watson writ his name large on the history of the Open Championship. In 1980, at Muirfield, his third round of 64 paved the way for victory; two years later, at Troon, a steady performance gave him an advantage of one stroke over Peter Oosterhuis and Nick Price; and at Birkdale in 1983, Watson played the final hole with great confidence to win the illustrious trophy for the fifth time. His 2-iron into the 72nd green never wavered.

In 1981 Watson had won the

Masters for the second time, and once again Nicklaus had been relegated to second place. But Watson had never won his own country's Open title and he corrected this omission in 1982 at Pebble Beach. When Watson hit his 2-iron left of the green at the 71st hole, everyone, including the tournament leader, Jack Nicklaus, thought he had wrecked his chances. The hole was cut on a down slope, near the left edge of the green; it was thought that Watson would be lucky to get down in two more shots. But, with a stroke of genius, he holed his chip shot and went on to win the US Open by two strokes from Nicklaus. Tom Watson was now established as the dominant figure in championship golf.

The strengths of Watson's game were many; early in his career Henry Cotton had referred to him as 'the most complete of today's young players'. With his brisk and orthodox swing, he was a powerful striker of the ball, even if sometimes wayward from the tee. But Watson's short game was masterly and his putting fearless. A 'Watson par' became a byword in the game: the green was missed by 20 yards, the ball was pitched to eight feet and the putt was holed. If the quiet and unassuming Watson was never a great favourite of the spectators, like Palmer, Trevino and Ballesteros, he was admired for his great skill and for the intelligence and integrity which he focused on golf.

This was particularly so in Britain where Watson's professed love of links golf won him many fans. If he ever manages to win the Open for the sixth time and thereby to equal Harry Vardon's record it will be a very popular triumph. In 1984 at St Andrews, it seemed that the great day had arrived. But Watson's error at the 17th hole, the infamous 'road hole', enabled Ballesteros to win the championship. Watson hit his second shot with a 2-iron on to the road and took five strokes, whereas the Spaniard had a par four and then a birdie at the final hole to win by two shots. There was some consolation in that Tom Watson finished first in the money list in America in that year for the fifth time.

In 1983 he played with his usual verve in the Ryder Cup at the PGA National. He won four points from his five games and his only reverse was when he and Bob Gilder lost their foursomes to Ballesteros and Way. Watson beat Bernard Gallacher in the singles to secure the point that won the Ryder Cup for the American team.

It was in the middle of the Eighties that Watson's putting began to deteriorate. His aggressive style had been founded on his ability to hole the critical putts from around six feet but this knack deserted him. He found it increasingly difficult to get into contention in tournaments and his only win of consequence was the Nabisco Championship of 1987. But he was selected for the 1989 Ryder Cup at the Belfry. He and Chip Beck halved their foursomes against Ballesteros and Olazabal; but he and Mark O'Meara took a hiding in the fourballs (six and five) from the Spanish pair. To his credit, Watson bounced back to beat Sam Torrance in the singles, a point which helped the American team to tie the match as a whole.

In 1991 Watson began the final round of the Masters at Augusta one stroke behind Ian Woosnam. His eagles at the 13th and 15th holes more than made up for his earlier dropped shots and he was in a tie for the lead with Woosnam and Olazabal as he prepared to drive from the 18th tee. A disastrous shot into the trees on the right blighted Watson's chances and he finished in a tie for third place.

For a decade from the middle of the Seventies Tom Watson had shown himself to be one of the most formidable champions the game had seen. His triumphs were marked by a dignity and integrity which will be welcomed when he captains the American Ryder Cup team at the Belfry in 1993.

WAY, PAUL

Europe

Born: 12.3.63

Appearances: 1983, 1985

Record: P9 W6 L2 H1

If ever a golfer seemed destined to achieve greatness it was Paul Way. After a short but successful career as an amateur, when he won the English Open Amateur Strokeplay Championship and represented Britain in the Walker Cup, he won the Dutch Open in his first year on the professional circuit.

In 1983, at the age of 20,

Despite recent disappointments, Paul Way has a fine Ryder Cup record

Way won his place in the European team to play for the Ryder Cup at the PGA National course in Florida. It was an inspired tactic of the new captain, Tony Jacklin, to pair the tenderfoot Way with the experienced and dynamic Severiano Ballesteros. After losing their opening foursomes to Tom Kite and Calvin Peete, the Spaniard expressed his doubts, but these were allayed as the pair won two and a half points out of the next three. On an unbearably tense final day, Way defeated Curtis Strange but the Europeans lost the Cup by one point.

In that year Way finished eleventh in the Order of Merit and one place higher two years later when he won the PGA Championship. Once again he qualified for the Ryder Cup and played with great distinction. He and Ian Woosnam beat Fuzzy Zoeller and Hubert Green twice in the fourballs;in the second meeting the European pair were four up after five holes and never looked back. They lost their foursomes match to Peter Jacobsen and Curtis Strange, but Way beat the formidable Ray Floyd in the singles as the Europeans won a long-awaited victory.

In that year Way, partnered by Howard Clark, represented England in the World Cup and they finished in second place.

But 1985 proved to be the pinnacle of Paul Way's career and, apart from a victory in the 1987 European Open, he has struggled to make any further impact. Since 1985 his best position in the Order of Merit has been 57th, in 1991. Many other golfers have suffered such reversals of form and it is to be hoped that a golfer with such talent revives his career.

WEETMAN, HARRY

GB

Born: 25.10.20

Appearances: 1951, 1953, 1955, 1957, 1959, 1961, 1963
Captain 1965

Record: P15 W2 L11 H2

With his great golfing gifts, which were particularly suited to matchplay, it is surprising that Harry Weetman had such a poor record in the Ryder Cup. It is even odder when one considers his performances in the PGA Matchplay Championship. From 1951 to 1960 he reached the final five times and won it twice. His victory in 1951 was memorable since he beat Flory van Donck and Henry Cotton on the same day. He recovered from a position of two holes down to the great champion, Cotton, by covering twelve holes in seven under fours. It was wonderfully exciting golf and typical of Weetman.

Born in Shropshire, he had a physique that any fast bowler would have envied: a big, wide-shouldered frame underpinned by a massive pair of legs. With a huge pair of hands and long muscular arms into the bargain, Weetman was able to carry the ball great distances. Henry Cotton, as good a golfing observer as any, noted how he stayed behind the ball and hit past his body against a braced left side. His game through the green was all about power and on the golf course his whole mien was one of truculence and barely restrained aggression. Like the P G Wodehouse character, he 'never spared himself in his efforts to do the ball a violent injury'. But Weetman matched his strength with a remarkably adroit touch around the greens and he was as good a putter as anyone in Europe. His routine was unfussy and he gave his putts an easy and very crisp stroke.

His was beguiling golf to watch and especially entertaining for the spectators. Even if his rocketing drives ended in trouble his powers of recovery were

unrivalled. But because he hit the ball so hard, and was expected to, Weetman sometimes strained too much and was fallible off the tee. If he had reined in his power, as Sam Snead and Jack Nicklaus learned to do, he would undoubtedly have been an even more successful golfer.

Nevertheless, Weetman was one of the leading British golfers through the Fifties and early Sixties. Apart form his successes in the Matchplay Championship, he won the Dunlop Masters twice, the German Open and the Swallow-Penfold four times. He won the Vardon Trophy (for the lowest stroke average during a season) in 1952 and 1958 and represented England in the Canada Cup (World Cup) four times. But he made very little impact on the Open Championship: his best finish was equal fifth at St Andrews in 1955.

As the matchplay champion he was an automatic choice for the Ryder Cup in 1951, at Pinehurst, but he was heavily defeated by the steely Lloyd Mangrum in his singles. Two years later, in the very tight match at Wentworth, he and Peter Alliss should perhaps have scraped a half in their foursomes against Douglas and Oliver, but Weetman's errors down the 35th hole condemned them to defeat. However, he redeemed himself against Sam Snead, who was four holes ahead at lunch and in the same position with six holes to play. A combination of the American's errors and Weetman's superb golf saw him win five holes in a row and hold Snead off down the final hole for a remarkable victory.

The match at the Thunderbird Club in California went to the USA and Weetman lost both his matches but he was in the 1957 team at Lindrick under the captaincy of Dai Rees. However, Weetman's part in that famous victory was less than glorious. He and Max Faulkner played poor golf to lose their foursomes to Ted Kroll and Jack Burke and, at the team meeting that evening, they both agreed to stand down from the singles. In the short time that it took Rees to exchange his order of play with his opposing captain, Jackie Burke, Weetman had made a provocative statement to the Press: that he would never again play for a team captained by Dai Rees. It was the captain's opinion that the whole affair was orchestrated not by Weetman but by his 'associates' and family, especially by his wife, Freda. Unfortunately, the controversy detracted from the celebrations of victory which came on the morrow.

As a result, Harry Weetman was later suspended from PGA events for a year but the severe penalty was later moderated, partly through the intervention of Rees. All was forgiven and forgotten by 1959 when the British team, once again captained by Rees, travelled to the Eldorado Club, California. Weetman was paired in the foursomes with Dave Thomas, who hit the ball even further than his partner. On the 36th tee, they were one hole up on the formidable pair of Sam Snead and Cary Middlecoff, and, with the British ball a long way down the middle from a Thomas drive, 'Slammin' Sam' put the American ball into the lake which guarded the green. In effect, the Americans could do no better than a five, and a quietly hit short iron to the edge of the water, a pitch and two putts would assure Britain of one vital point. Without any forethought, Weetman seized a 5-iron and went for the green. With awful inevitability the ball went into the water; the British pair holed out in six strokes, but Snead sank a long putt to win the hole and scramble a half. It was an appalling error, even by a man like Weetman who was temperamentally unable to play safe. He was heavily defeated in the singles by Bob Rosburg.

At Lytham in 1961 he was once again the victim of unusual circumstances. He was only selected for the two singles matches, which were now played over 18 rather than 36 holes, and lost both narrowly. Against Doug Ford, he had a putt on the 18th green to win the match. He missed it, but also missed the putt back and lost the match. Against Art Wall, Weetman went to the turn in 33 strokes but was two down to his opponent, who clung on to win by one hole.

Weetman's final appearance was at East Lake, Atlanta, two years later when he played in five matches out of six. He only recorded one and a half points but managed to beat Julius Boros in the first of the singles. He was not yet through with the Ryder Cup and was the non-playing captain at Birkdale in 1965.

Weetman, because of the unpredictable power of his game, was a compelling presence on the golf course. The crowds warmed to him and he enlivened the golfing scene immensely. Despite his aggressive demeanour on the course there was a kind of bluff innocence to the man and he had a friendly and engaging manner away from the links. This made his death in a car accident in 1972 all the more tragic.

WEISKOPF, TOM

USA

Born: 9.11.42

Appearances: 1973, 1975

Record: P10 W7 L2 H1

Nearly all the elements required to make a great champion were present in Tom Weiskopf. He had a magnificent swing which was a majestic amalgam of power and orthodoxy. It was little wonder that he used to be called 'Long Tom', and he was also a superb putter. But he only won one major championship, the 1973 Open at Troon, and cannot be judged to have reached his real potential.

Perhaps Weiskopf did not take the game very seriously; Al Barkow wrote that he 'played often with the worried expression of an athlete who knows too much'. Perhaps he found it difficult to emerge from the considerable shadow of Jack Nicklaus, who had preceded him by a year or two at Ohio State University and was to some extent his mentor on the golfing scene. Certainly Weiskopf was never able to imitate Nicklaus's tunnel vision about winning tournaments, especially the majors.

Weiskopf also had a very brittle temperament: not for nothing was he called 'the Towering Inferno'. But he had an excellent record on the American tour with 15 victories, including the San Diego Open, the Kemper Open (twice), the Canadian Open (twice) and the Western Open. He was remarkably consistent too; in the decade from 1958, when he won his first event, he was always in the top 20 money winners and usually close to the top.

Weiskopf had an important victory at the close of 1972 when he defeated Lee Trevino in the final of the World Matchplay Championship at Wentworth. But the death of his father early in the following year seemed to jolt him into some self-examination and a realisation that an effortless style counts for nothing on the golf tour unless it brings victories too. In the space of about eight weeks he won five tournaments, including the Open at Troon.

If there had been any doubts

about Weiskopf's resolution, they were set aside by his play in Scotland. He led after each of the first two rounds and was drawn to play the third round with his nearest rival, Johnny Miller, who went to the turn in 32 shots, to take the lead. But Weiskopf made up three strokes in the second half to regain the lead and won the great prize on the following day by three shots. One remembers the quiet tones of the BBC commentator Henry Longhurst, as he referred to the winner's 'upright, soldierly bearing', and his wonderful swing.

Weiskopf came close to winning other major tournaments. He was third in the US Open at Oakmont in 1973, undone by the brilliance of Miller's final round of 63, and equal second in 1976 in Atlanta. In the Masters, he tied for second place on four occasions; but it was the last of these, in 1975, that caught and held the imagination. Weiskopf led the field at the start of the final round and played confident and relaxed golf. He said later that he had never doubted that he would win. But he three-putted the 16th green where Nicklaus, ahead of him, had scored a birdie two. At the final hole Weiskopf had a birdie putt of eight feet to force a play-off with Nicklaus but missed it on the right. The Golden Bear had won his fifth Masters in a dramatic finish.

Weiskopf played in the Ryder cup only on two occasions, at Muirfield in 1973 and at Laurel Valley two years later, although it is said that he refused a third invitation because he preferred to go on a hunting trip. He lost his first two matches, a foursomes and a fourball, but thereafter was undefeated in eight successive games, three of them in partnership with his mentor, Nicklaus. At Laurel Valley he had a perfect record: four wins in four matches.

Tom Weiskopf undoubtedly had the very highest credentials as a golfer and should have won many more tournaments, enough to put him among the front rank of champions. His failure to realise his potential does nothing to spoil the memory of one of the classic swings of modern golf.

He played on the American tour through the Eighties and his last victory was in the Western Open of 1982. No doubt Weiskopf could win a fortune or two on the Seniors tour, but he is currently building a reputation as a golf course designer.

WHITCOMBE, CHARLES

GB

Born: 1895

Appearances: 1927, 1929, 1931, 1933, 1935, 1937
Captain 1931, 1935, 1937

Record: P9 W3 L2 H4

Charles Whitcombe was the second of three brothers who were born to a Burnham gamekeeper and they learned their golf on the windswept shores of Somerset.

In Henry Cotton's opinion, Charles was the best of the brothers, a natural player who stepped up to the ball and hit it without any fuss, and usually down the middle. He beat Cotton twice in the final of the PGA Matchplay Championship, was third in the Open of 1935 and was the first holder of the Vardon Trophy in 1937.

Charles Whitcombe had a lengthy record in the Ryder Cup and in the first match in 1927 his lovely style made him instantly popular with the American spectators. Gene Sarazen later recalled how well he swung a golf club, and the two players halved their singles game, even though Whitcombe had been one down with one hole to play. In the 1929 tie he was unbeaten in his two games and heavily defeated Johnny Farrell in the singles.

He was a rather modest captain who dropped himself when he could have played to Britain's advantage. In 1935, when all three Whitcombes played, he excluded himself from the singles for the apparent reason that he felt three Whitcombes would be a little overwhelming; in 1937 he sent Alf Padgham, badly off his game, out first when he himself would certainly have done better. His record, with only two losses from nine matches, was formidable.

WHITCOMBE, ERNEST

GB

Born: 1890

Appearances: 1929, 1931, 1935

Record: P6 W1 L4 H1

After two rounds of the 1924 Open Championship, Ernie Whitcombe led the field by three strokes and was level with Walter Hagen with one round to play. He took 43 strokes to the turn in

The Whitcombe brothers: Reg, Ernie and Charles

the final round and finished second to the great American by one shot. It was his best finish in the Open, although he had the consolation of winning the PGA Championship in the same year. His other tournament wins included the Irish Open and the Dutch and the French Open Championships.

In the 1929 Ryder Cup match at Moortown he won half a point from his singles against Al Espinosa, but lost both his games two years later at Scioto. He gained his first full point in the 1935 match when he partnered his brother, Charles, to a win by one hole over Ed Dutra and Ky Laffoon – the only British success in the foursomes.

Ernest Whitcombe played with an unusual interlocking grip and, like his brother, was a natural swinger of the club, with a lovely feel for all the golf shots.

WHITCOMBE, REGINALD

GB

Born: 10.4.98

Appearances: 1935

Record: P1 W0 L1 H0

Reg Whitcombe was the youngest of the brothers and won tournaments on either side of the Second World War.

Some judges have termed him the least gifted of the Whitcombes, but in 1938 he immortalised their name by winning the Open. The final day brought immensely strong winds to Sandwich; the huge exhibition tent was in tatters and many of the stands were smashed to pieces: the wreckage reminded Henry Longhurst of Epsom Downs immediately after the Derby.

Only three players managed to break 80 twice on that final day and scores over 90 were common; so were four, five and even six putts per green. The wind was so strong that Alf Padgham drove the 11th green, 383 yards away, and made his two. It was a day made for a man of around 14 stones with a short and uncomplicated swing: Reg Whitcombe. He wrote an instructional book entitled *Golf's No Mystery* and to him it certainly was not.

In his only outing in the Ryder Cup, at Ridgewood New Jersey, in 1935, Whitcombe was defeated by Johnny Revolta in the singles.

WILL, GEORGE

GB

Born: 16.4.37

Appearances: 1963, 1965, 1967

Record: P15 W2 L11 H2

A tall, strong man with an excellent swing, George Will won only a couple of tournaments on the British circuit but earned his place in three Ryder Cup teams by his consistent play.

He made a splendid start, at East Lake in 1963, in company with another newcomer, Brian Huggett. They faced the legendary Arnold Palmer, partnered by a very nervous Johnny Pott, and won the opening foursomes by three and two. But Will lost his other three matches, including a singles against Palmer.

At Birkdale two years later he faced Palmer yet again in the foursomes, but he and Dave Thomas hammered him and Dave Marr by the resounding margin of six and five. The American pair spent the lunch hour on the practice ground and the draw for the second series of foursomes decreed the same match. This time, Palmer and Marr inflicted defeat on Will and Thomas by exactly the same margin. Though Will halved his singles match with Don January, he lost four other games and was similarly unsuccessful at Houston in 1967 with only half a point won out of a possible five. Once again Palmer played a notable role. He and Julius Boros were four down at the turn to Will and Hugh Boyle in the second series of fourballs, but they fought back to win by one hole.

WOOD, CRAIG

USA

Born: 18.11.01

Appearances: 1931, 1933, 1935

Record: P4 W1 L3 H0

It must have seemed to Craig Wood that he would be known as the eternal runner-up in major events, and a particularly unlucky one too. Like Tony Jacklin in the 1970's and Greg Norman in the 1980's, Wood invariably seemed to become the victim of someone else's unexpected brilliance. In the 1935 Masters Championship he looked a certainty to win, until Gene Sarazen holed out for his famous 'double eagle' two and then beat Wood in the play-off. In 1939 he lost another play-off, to Byron Nelson in the US Open; and Nelson holed a 1-iron for an eagle during the second round.

Wood's near-misses seemed to add up to an unfulfilled career: he tied with Densmore Shute on his first visit to Britain for the Open in 1933 and then lost the play-off; and he was second in the USPGA Championship and the Masters in the following year. But it all came right for him in 1941 when he won both the Masters and the US Open. In the Masters he began with a round of 66 and led all the way. In the Open he was troubled by back pain and played the tournament in a brace. In those days the last two rounds were played on the same day but such was his determination that he finished with a couple of 70s.

Craig Wood was a formidable golfer who hit the ball great distances in his younger days with a short flat swing, an action which he made more orthodox later in his career. He was also a brilliant putter. Sam Snead said, with some feeling, that Wood's putting made him green with envy. He became a professional in 1920 and had over 20 victories in America, including the Los Angeles, Pasadena, New Jersey and Canadian Opens. His last one was in 1944 but he played on until the end of the decade when he became the professional at Winged Foot.

His Ryder Cup record was rather unflattering: he won only

one game, against William Davies in 1933. His last match, against Percy Alliss at Ridgewood, New Jersey, in 1935, was a battle royal. Although Wood was three up at lunch, Alliss came back at him and eventually defeated him by one hole.

Craig Wood

WOOD, NORMAN

GB

Born: Born: 8.1.47

Appearances: 1975

Record: P3 W1 L2 H0

When he was selected for the fixture at Laurel Valley in 1975, Norman Wood had won nothing of note in Britain, although he was the champion of Italy in 1972 and had represented Scotland in the World Cup.

He lost his foursomes against Gene Littler and Hale Irwin and his fourball against Jack Nicklaus and Jesse Snead. It is noticeable that this little-known British professional was up against men who had won a number of major championships. Wood's predicament was a microcosm of the British teams' throughout the Seventies. In his singles he met yet another Open champion, Lee Trevino, and to his great credit beat him by two and one.

WORSHAM, LEW

USA

Born: 5.10.17

Appearances: 1947

Record: P2 W2 L0 H0

Lew Worsham was one of the first golf professionals to play his sport under the intrusive eye of the television cameras, which were used for the first time at a major championship in 1947, at the US Open. Everything rested on the final putts at the final hole of the play-off; Sam Snead missed his and Worsham holed his for victory. In 1953 he triumphed again in front of the cameras at the Tam O'Shanter event when he holed a wedge shot from about a hundred yards for an improbable eagle and victory over Chandler Harper. Jimmy Demaret was one of the commentators and, never at a loss, was heard to say: 'Well, I'll be goddamned, he sank it'.

Worsham had a perfect Ryder Cup record. He began with a sparkling win, with Ed Oliver, over Henry Cotton and Arthur Lees by ten and nine, and then beat Jimmy Adams in the singles. He continued to play tournament golf through the 1950's and became the professional at Oakmont.

WOOSNAM, IAN

Europe

Born: 2.3.58

Appearances: 1983, 1985, 1987, 1989, 1991

Record: P21 W8 L10 H3

Born in Shropshire of Welsh parents, Ian Woosnam is an archetypal battler, short in height but very long in aggression and determination. Despite his small stature he is one of the most powerful golfers in the world. He built up his exceptional strength while working on his father's farm in his youth, and his strong legs and brawny arms are the ideal attributes for a golfer.

Woosnam's determination to become a tournament golfer suffered many reverses. It took three visits to the qualifying school before he won enough money to keep his player's card; in those early days he shared a battered mobile caravan with other players and survived on baked beans and bacon sandwiches. He almost gave up his dream in favour of a club professional's job but finally tasted his first success in 1982 when he won the Swiss Open. In the same year he won the World Under-25 Championship and finished eighth in the Order of Merit. Since then, Woosnam has remained in the top ten and was the leader in 1987 and 1990.

If Woosnam made his initial breakthrough as a professional in 1982, he threw open the main gates in 1987. He began by winning the Jersey Open and the Madrid Open, won the Scottish Open by seven shots and then the Lancome Trophy. But his triumph in the World Matchplay Championship at Wentworth must have been especially sweet: he beat Faldo and Ballesteros in the initial rounds and then defeated Sandy Lyle in the final. In their amateur days in Shropshire, Lyle had always mastered Woosnam but at last the Welshman had taken revenge. To crown his year Woosnam went to the World Cup and won both the individual prize and the team event (with David Llewellyn).

By this time Woosnam was known as one of the best strikers of a golf ball in the game. His action is beautifully poised and rhythmic and Ballesteros has been heard to call it one of the best swings in golf. With his great strength Woosnam hits the ball vast distances and does so with effortless grace. It is no wonder that the galleries warm to him; apart from his power he is all bustle and aggression.

Woosnam had made a disappointing start to his Ryder Cup career in the desperately close affair at the PGA National in 1983. He won just half a point in a fourball partnership with Sam Torrance against Ben Crenshaw and Jerry Pate. His tally in the 1985 match at the Belfry was also modest; although he and Paul Way won their two fourball matches against Zoeller and Green, he lost his other two matches. Two years later at Muirfield village, however, Woosnam's partnership with Nick Faldo was a significant factor in Europe's first victory in America. They collected three and a half points from four games. Ian Woosnam played particularly well in the first foursomes; the British pair were four down to Lanny Wadkins and Larry Mize but recovered to win by two holes. When they met Tom Kite and Curtis Strange in the final series of fourballs Woosnam and Faldo were in imperious form and birdied the first five holes; they went to the turn with a better ball score of 29 and won easily.

The partnership with Faldo continued with great success at the Belfry in 1989, as they garnered two and a half points from their four matches. The only match they lost, to Paul Azinger and Chip Beck, was a feast of dazzling shots: when the Americans won on the 17th green, 18 birdies had been recorded.

By this time Woosnam had won several more important events, including the European Open, the PGA Championship and the Irish Open (twice). He also finished equal second in the US Open at Oak Hill and impressed the American spectators and critics with his powerful game. He had also improved his bank balance by winning the Million Dollar Challenge in Sun City in 1988; but to do so he had to forsake an appearance in the World Cup for Wales. His superb form continued in 1990 when he won four European tour events and the World Matchplay title for the second time.

Woosnam was certainly one of the best golfers in the world especially when he showed, by taking first place in the USF&G Classic, that he could win in America, too. But he suffered in comparison with players such as Ballesteros, Faldo and even Strange because he had not won a major Championship. He put this omission right at Augusta in 1991 when he won the Masters. On the tee of the final hole he was sharing first place with Tom Watson and Jose Maria Olazabal. He gambled successfully on being able to carry the bunker on the left side of the fairway; beyond, there was a flat area of ground which was part of the practice facilities. It was an intelligent tactic and Woosnam merely had to lob a short-iron on to the green. Nevertheless, he left himself a final putt of around eight feet to win his first major title: he stroked it beautifully into the hole.

Earlier in the round some of the American spectators had made the mistake of heckling Woosnam, but it only made him more determined to win: he was once described as 'Tom Thumb with two fingers up', an apt image.

In the Ryder Cup at Kiawah Island, Woosnam was thought to be one of Europe's strengths, but he was far from that with a disappointing tally of three defeats from four matches. His one success was with Paul Broadhurst when they defeated Azinger and Irwin in the second series of fourballs. He lost his singles to Chip Beck: it is extraordinary that Woosnam has lost all his singles games in the Ryder Cup.

Woosnam is a curious amalgam. On the one hand there is the busy and aggressive extrovert, pounding his shots with commanding strength and accuracy at the greens; on the other there is a petulant golfer who complains about his poor putting and sometimes chases appearance fees to the detriment of his golf. But Woosnam as a golfer is a delight to contemplate; he possesses one of the best actions ever seen, powerful and uncomplicated. Whenever he has doubts about his putting he should merely replay the video of the stroke with which he won the Masters with such aplomb.

PING

Z

ZOELLER, FRANK URBAN

USA

Born: 11.11.51

Appearances: 1979, 1983, 1985

Record: P10 W1 L8 H1

His carefree and engaging manner endears Fuzzy Zoeller to golfing galleries throughout the world. His very style of play makes the fans feel an affinity to him as he strolls up to the ball, addresses it with his hands very low and the toe of the club up in the air and casually wafts it away. This individual swing generates great power even though he has suffered from back trouble so severe that it necessitated an operation in 1984.

Zoeller joined the American tour in 1975 after graduating from the University of Houston. He made only $7,000 in that year but said that he spent at least five times that amount. His bank manager was probably relieved that he won his first victory in the following year at the Quad Cities Open. His score included a round of 63, during which he had birdies at each of the last eight holes. Three years later he won the San Diego Open and gained a place in the field for the Masters at Augusta. After three rounds he was six shots behind Ed Sneed and it was the latter's mistakes rather than any unwonted brilliance from Zoeller that brought the first sudden death play-off in the Masters. Tom Watson was also involved but Zoeller won the title at the second extra hole.

Zoeller, ninth in the money list, earned his place in the 1979 Ryder Cup match at The Greenbrier, West Virginia. It was not a successful beginning, since he lost four games out of five: his only victory was in a fourball with Lee Trevino against Ken Brown and Mark James.

He had two of his most successful seasons in 1983, when he won two tournaments and finished second in the money list, and 1984, when he won the US Open at Winged Foot. Once again he was involved in a play-off, this time with Greg Norman. When the latter holed a long putt on the 72nd hole, Zoeller who was waiting in the 18th fairway to play to the green, wrongly thought that it was for a birdie to give the Australian the lead. He underlined his sense of humour by grabbing a white towel from his golf bag and waving it in mock surrender. But there was no surrender on the following day as Zoeller won the 18 hole play-off by seven shots.

Zoeller continued to play with a lack of success in the Ryder Cup that was surprising for such a very talented golfer. In the Americans' last-ditch win at the PGA National course in 1983 he won only half a point, but that was in an absorbing battle with Severiano Ballesteros. Zoeller was suffering from a bad back and was at one stage three holes down to the Spaniard, but he came surging back to win four holes in a row. On the 18th tee the players were level and Ballesteros, in trouble off the tee, only got his half because of a shot of genius from a fairway bunker when he carried the ball about 240 yards to the side of the green. Two years later, at the Belfry, Zoeller lost three matches out of three.

He showed great determination on his return to golf after the surgery on his troublesome back. In 1985 he won the Bay Hill Classic and eventually finished 15th on the money list. He did even better in the following year, with three victories, but has not won since then. In 1991 he finished 42nd on the money list but has reduced his playing commitments in favour of other interests, including golf-course design. Wherever he plays Zoeller is a popular figure with his idiosyncratic style of play and good-humoured outlook; he is an essential antidote to the over-serious attitudes of so many of his fellow professional golfers.

LIST OF RESULTS

1927	WORCESTER, MASSACHUSETTS, 3–4 JUNE. CAPTAIN: E RAY (GB) W HAGEN (USA)	1927

USA 9½ GB 2½

GB		USA	
FOURSOMES	MATCHES		MATCHES
E. Ray & F Robson	0	W Hagen & J Golden (2 & 1)	1
G Duncan & A Compston	0	J Farrell & J. Ternesa (8 & 6)	1
A G Havers & H C Jolly	0	G Sarazen & A Watrous (3 & 2)	1
A Boomer & C A Whitcombe (7&5)	1	L Diegel & W Mehlhorn	0
	1		**3**
SINGLES			
A Compston	0	W Mehlhorn (1 hole)	1
A Boomer	0	J Farrell (5 & 4)	1
H C Jolly	0	J Golden (8 & 7)	1
E Ray	0	L Diegel (7 & 5)	1
C A Whitcombe (halved)	½	G Sarazen (halved)	½
A G Havers	0	W Hagen (2 & 1)	1
F Robson	0	A Watrous (3 & 2)	1
G Duncan (1 hole)	1	J Turnesa	0
	1½		**6½**

1929

MOORTOWN, LEEDS. 26–27 MAY.
CAPTAINS: G DUNCAN (GB), W HAGEN (USA)

GB 7 USA 5

GB	MATCHES	USA	MATCHES
FOURSOMES			
C A Whitcombe & A Compston (halved)	½	J Farrell & J Turnesa (halved)	½
A Boomer & G Duncan	0	L Diegel & A Espinosa (7 & 5)	1
A Mitchell & F Robson (2 & 1)	1	G Sarazen & E Dudley	0
E R Whitcombe & T H Cotton	0	J Golden & W Hagen (2 holes)	1
	1½		**2½**
SINGLES			
C A Whitcombe (8 & 6)	1	J Farrell	0
G Duncan (10 & 8)	1	W Hagen	0
A Mitchell	0	L Diegel (9 & 8)	1
A Compston (6 & 4)	1	G Sarazen	0
A Boomer (4 & 3)	1	J Turnesa	0
F Robson	0	H Smith (4 & 2)	1
T H Cotton (4 & 3)	1	A Watrous	0
E R Whitcombe (halved)	½	A Espinosa (halved)	½
	5½		**2½**

1931

SCIOTO, COLUMBUS, OHIO. 27–27 JUNE.
CAPTAINS: C A WHITCOMBE (GB), W HAGEN (USA)

USA 9 GB 3

GB	MATCHES	USA	MATCHES
FOURSOMES			
A Compston & W H Davies	0	G Sarazen & J Farrell (8 & 7)	1
G Duncan & A G Havers	0	W Hagen & D Shute (10 & 9)	1
A Mitchell & F Robson (3 & 1)	1	L Diegel & A Espinosa	0
S Easterbrook & E R Whitcombe	0	W Burke & W Cox (3 & 2)	1
	1		**3**
SINGLES			
A Compston	0	W Burke (7 & 6)	1
F Robson	0	G Sarazen (7 & 6)	1
W H Davies (4 & 3)	1	J Farrell	0
A Mitchell	0	W Cox (3 & 1)	1
C A Whitcombe	0	W Hagen (4 & 3)	1
B Hodson	0	D Shute (8 & 6)	1
E R Whitcombe	0	A Espinosa (2 & 1)	1
A G Havers (4 & 3)	1	C Wood	0
	2		**6**

1933

SOUTHPORT & AINSDALE, SOUTHPORT. 26–7 JUNE.
CAPTAINS: J H TAYLOR (GB), W HAGEN (USA)

GB 6½ USA 5½

GB	MATCHES	USA	MATCHES
FOURSOMES			
P Alliss & C A Whitcombe (halved)	½	G Sarazen & W Hagen (halved)	½
A Mitchell & A G Havers (3 & 2)	1	O Dutra & D Shute	0
W H Davies & S Easterbrook (1 hole)	1	C Wood & P Runyan	0
A H Padgham & A Perry	0	E Dudley & W Burke (1 hole)	1
	2½		**1½**
SINGLES			
A H Padgham	0	G Sarazen (6 & 4)	1
A Mitchell (9 & 8)	1	O Dutra	0
A J Lacey	0	W Hagen (2 & 1)	1
W H Davies	0	C Wood (4 & 3)	1
P Alliss (2 & 1)	1	P Runyan	0
A G Havers (4 & 3)	1	L Diegel	0
S Easterbrook (1 hole)	1	D Shute	0
C A Whitcombe	0	H Smith (2 & 1)	1
	4		**4**

1935

RIDGEWOOD, NEW JERSEY. 28–29 SEPTEMBER.
CAPTAINS C A WHITCOMBE (GB), W HAGEN (USA)

USA 9 GB 3

GB	MATCHES	USA	MATCHES
FOURSOMES			
A Perry & J Busson	0	G Sarazen & W Hagen (7 & 6)	1
A H Padgham & P Alliss	0	H Picard & J Revolta (6 & 5)	1
W J Cox & E W Jarman	0	P Runyan & H Smith (9 & 8)	1
C A Whitcombe & E R Whitcombe (1 hole)	1	O Dutra & K Laffoon	0
	1		**3**
SINGLES			
J Busson	0	G Sarazen (3 & 2)	1
R Burton	0	P Runyan (5 & 3)	1
R A Whitcombe	0	J Revolta (2 & 1)	1
A H Padgham	0	O Dutra (4 & 2)	1
P Alliss (1 hole)	1	C Wood	0
W J Cox (halved)	½	H Smith (halved)	½
E R Whitcombe	0	H Picard (3 & 2)	1
A Perry (halved)	½	S Parks (halved)	½
	2		**6**

1937

SOUTHPORT & AINSDALE, SOUTHPORT. 29–30 JUNE.
CAPTAINS C A WHITCOMBE (GB), W HAGEN (USA)

GB 4 USA 8

GB	MATCHES	USA	MATCHES
FOURSOMES			
A H Padgham & T H Cotton	0	E Dudley & B Nelson (4 & 2)	1
A J Lacey & W J Cox	0	R Guldahl & T Manero (2 & 1)	1
C A Whitcombe & D J Rees (halved)	½	G Sarazen & D Shute (halved)	½
P Alliss & R Burton (2 & 1)	1	H Picard & J Revolta	0
	1½		**2½**
SINGLES			
A H Padgham	0	R Guldahl (8 & 7)	1
S L King (halved)	½	D Shute (halved)	½
D J Rees (3 & 1)	1	B Nelson	0
T H Cotton (5 & 3)	1	T Manero	0
P Alliss	0	G Sarazen (1 hole)	1
R Burton	0	S Snead (5 & 4)	1
A Perry	0	E Dudley (2 & 1)	1
A J Lacey	0	H Picard (2 & 1)	1
	2½		**5½**

1947

PORTLAND, OREGON. 1–2 NOVEMBER.
CAPTAINS: H COTTON (GB), B HOGAN (USA)

USA 11 GB 1

GB	MATCHES	USA	MATCHES
FOURSOMES			
T H Cotton & A Lees	0	E Oliver & L Worsham (10 & 9)	1
F Daly & C H Ward	0	S Snead & L Mangrum (6 & 5)	1
J Adams & M Faulkner	0	B Hogan & J Demaret (2 holes)	1
D J Rees & S L King	0	B Nelson & H Barron (2 & 1)	1
	0		**4**
SINGLES			
F Daly	0	E J Harrison (5 & 4)	1
J Adams	0	L Worsham (3 & 2)	1
M Faulkner	0	L Mangrum (6 & 5)	1
C H Ward	0	E Oliver (4 & 3)	1
A Lees	0	B Nelson (2 & 1)	1
T H Cotton	0	S Snead (5 & 4)	1
D J Rees	0	J Demaret (3 & 2)	1
S L King (4 & 3)	1	H Keiser	0
	1		**7**

1949

GANTON, SCARBOROUGH. 16–17 SEPTEMBER.
CAPTAINS C A WHITCOMBE (GB), B HOGAN (USA)

GB 5 USA 7

GB		USA	
FOURSOMES	MATCHES		MATCHES
M Faulkner & J Adams (2 & 1)	1	D J Harrisson & J Palmer	0
F Daly & K Bousfield (4 & 2)	1	R Hamilton & S Alexander	0
C H Ward & S L King	0	J Demaret & C Heafner (4 & 3)	1
R Burton & A Lees (1 hole)	1	S Snead & L Mangrum	0
	3		**1**
SINGLES			
M Faulkner	0	E J Harrison (8 & 7)	1
J Adams (2 & 1)	1	J Palmer	0
C H Ward	0	S Snead (6 & 5)	1
D J Rees (6 & 4)	1	R Hamilton	0
R Burton	0	C Heafner (3 & 2)	1
S L King	0	C Harbert (4 & 3)	1
A Lees	0	J Demaret (7 & 6)	1
F Daly	0	L Mangrum (4 & 3)	1
	2		**6**

1951

PINEHURST, NORTH CAROLINA. 2–4 NOVEMBER.
CAPTAINS A J LACEY (GB), S SNEAD (USA)

USA 9½ GB 2½

GB		USA	
FOURSOMES	MATCHES		MATCHES
M Faulkner & D J Rees	0	C Heafner & J. Burke (5 & 3)	1
C H Ward & A Lees (2 & 1)	1	E Oliver & H Ransom	0
J Adams & J Panton	0	S Snead & L Mangrum (5 & 4)	1
F Daly & K Bousfield	0	B Hogan & J Demaret (5 & 4)	1
	1		**3**
SINGLES			
J Adams	0	J Burke (4 & 3)	1
D J Rees	0	J Demaret (2 holes)	1
F Daly (halved)	½	C Heafner (halved)	½
H Weetman	0	L Mangrum (6 & 5)	1
A Lees (2 & 1)	1	E Oliver	0
C H Ward	0	B Hogan (3 & 2)	1
J Panton	0	S Alexander (8 & 7)	1
M Faulkner	0	S Snead (4 & 3)	1
	1½		**6½**

1953

WENTWORTH, VIRGINIA WATER. 2–3 OCTOBER.
CAPTAINS: H COTTON (GB), L MANGRUM (USA)

GB 5½ USA 6½

GB		USA	
FOURSOMES	MATCHES		MATCHES
H Weetman & P Alliss	0	D Douglas & E Oliver (2 & 1)	1
E C Brown & J Panton	0	L Mangrum & S Snead (8 & 7)	1
J Adams & B J Hunt	0	T Kroll & J Burke (7 & 5)	1
F Daly & H Bradshaw (1 hole)	1	W Burkemo & C Middlecoff	0
	1		**3**
SINGLES			
D J Rees	0	J Burke (2 & 1)	1
F Daly (9 & 7)	1	T Kroll	0
E C Brown (2 holes)	1	L Mangrum	0
H Weetman (1 hole)	1	S Snead	0
M Faulkner	0	C Middlecoff (3 & 1)	1
P Allis	0	J Turnesa (1 hole)	1
B J Hunt (halved)	½	D Douglas (halved)	½
H Bradshaw (3 & 2)	1	F Haas	0
	4½		**3½**

1955

THUNDERBRID GOLF AND COUNTRY CLUB, CALIFORNIA. 6-7 NOVEMBER.
CAPTAINS: D J REES (GB), C HARBERT (USA)

USA 8 GB 4

GB		USA	
FOURSOMES	MATCHES		MATCHES
J Fallon & J R M Jacobs (1 hole)	1	C Harper & J Barber	0
E C Brown & S S Scott	0	D Ford & T Kroll (5 & 4)	1
A Lees & H Weetman	0	J Burke & T Bolt (1 hole)	1
H Bradshaw & D J Rees	0	S Snead & C Middlecoff (3 & 2)	1
	1		**3**
SINGLES			
C O'Connor	0	T Bolt (4 & 2)	1
S S Scott	0	C Harbert (3 & 2)	1
J R M Jacobs (1 hole)	1	C Middlecoff	0
D J Rees	0	S Snead (3 & 1)	1
A Lees (3 & 2)	1	M Furgol	0
E C Brown (3 & 2)	1	J Barber	0
H Bradshaw	0	J Burke (3 & 2)	1
H Weetman	0	D Ford (3 & 2)	1
	3		**5**

1957

LINKRICK GOLF CLUB, SHEFFIELD. 4–5 OCTOBER
CAPTAINS: D J REES (GB), J BURKE (USA)

1957

GB 7½ USA 4½

GB	MATCHES	USA	MATCHES
FOURSOMES			
P Allis & B J Hunt	0	D Ford & D Finsterwald (2 & 1)	1
K Bousfield & D J Rees (3 & 2)	1	A Wall & F Hawkins	0
M Faulkner & H Weetman	0	T Kroll & J Burke (4 & 3)	1
C O'Connor & E C Brown	0	R Mayer & T Bolt (7 & 5)	1
	1		**3**
SINGLES			
E C Brown (4 & 3)	1	T Bolt	0
R P Mills (5 & 3)	1	J Burke	0
P Allis	0	F Hawkins (2 & 1)	1
K Bousfield (4 & 3)	1	L Hebert	0
D J Rees (7 & 6)	1	E Furgol	0
B J Hunt (6 & 5)	1	D Ford	0
C O'Connor (7 & 6)	1	D Finsterwald	0
H Bradshaw (halved)	½	R Mayer (halved)	½
	6½		**1½**

1959

ELDORADO COUNTRY CLUB, CALIFORNIA. 6–7 NOVEMBER.
CAPTAINS: D J REES (GB), S SNEAD (USA)

1959

USA 8½ GB 3½

GB	MATCHES	USA	MATCHES
FOURSOMES			
B J Hunt & E C Brown	0	R Rosburg & M Souchak (5 & 4)	1
D J Rees & K Bousfield	0	J Boros & D Finsterwald (2 holes)	1
C O'Connor & P Alliss (3 & 2)	1	A Wall & D Ford	0
H Weetman & D C Thomas (halved)	½	S Snead & C Middlecoff (halved)	½
	1½		**2½**
SINGLES			
N V Drew (halved)	½	D Ford (halved)	½
K Bousfield	0	M Souchak (3 & 2)	1
H Weetman	0	R Rosburg (6 & 5)	1
D C Thomas	0	S Snead (6 & 5)	1
C O'Connor	0	A Wall (7 & 6)	1
D J Rees	0	D Finsterwald (1 hole)	1
P Alliss (halved)	½	J Hebert (halved)	½
E C Brown (4 & 3)	1	C Middlecoff	0
	2		**6**

GB 9½ USA 14½

GB		USA	
FOURSOMES (MORNING)	MATCHES		MATCHES
C O'Connor & P Alliss (4 & 3)	1	D Ford & G Littler	0
J Panton & B J Hunt	0	A Wall & J Hebert (4 & 3)	1
D J Rees & K Bousfield	0	W Casper & A Palmer (2 & 1)	1
T B Haliburton & N C Coles	0	W Collins & M Souchak (1 hole)	1
(AFTERNOON)			
C O'Connor & P Alliss	0	A Wall & J Hebert (1 hole)	1
J Panton & B J Hunt	0	W Casper & A Palmer (5 & 4)	1
D J Rees & K Bousfield (4 & 2)	1	W Collins & M Souchak	0
T B Haliburton & N C Coles	0	J Barber & D Finsterwald (1 hole)	1
	2		**6**
SINGLES (MORNING)			
H Weetman	0	D Ford (1 hole)	1
R L Moffitt	0	M Souchak (5 & 4)	1
P Alliss (halved)	½	A Palmer (halved)	½
K Bousfield	0	W Casper (5 & 3)	1
D J Rees (2 & 1)	1	J Hebert	0
N C Coles (halved)	½	G Littler (halved)	½
B J Hunt (5 & 4)	1	J Barber	0
C O'Connor	0	D Finsterwald (2 & 1)	1
(AFTERNOON)			
H Weetman	0	A Wall (1 hole)	1
P Alliss (3 & 2)	1	W Collins	0
B J Hunt	0	M Souchak (2 & 1)	1
T B Haliburton	0	A Palmer (2 & 1)	1
D J Rees (4 & 3)	1	D Ford	0
K Bousfield (1 hole)	1	J Barber	0
N C Coles (1 hole)	1	D Finsterwald	0
C O'Connor (halved)	½	G Littler (halved)	½
	7½		**8½**

USA 23 GB 9

GB	MATCHES	USA	MATCHES
FOURSOMES (MORNING)			
B Huggett & G Will (3 & 2)	1	A Palmer & J Pott	0
P Alliss & C O'Connor	0	W Casper & D Ragan (1 hole)	1
N C Coles & B J Hunt (halved)	½	J Boros & A Lema (halved)	½
D Thomas & H Weetman (halved)	½	G Littler & D Finsterwald (halved)	½
(AFTERNOON)			
D Thomas & H Weetman	0	W Maxwell & R Goalby (4 & 3)	1
B Huggett & G Will	0	A Palmer & W Casper (5 & 4)	1
N C Coles & G M Hunt	0	G Littler & D Finsterwald (2 & 1)	1
T B Haliburton & B J Hunt	0	J Boros & A Lema (1 hole)	1
	2		**6**
FOURBALLS (MORNING)			
B Huggett & D Thomas	0	A Palmer & D Finsterwald (5 & 4)	1
P Alliss & B J Hunt (halved)	½	G Littler & J Boros (halved)	½
H Weetman & G Will	0	W Casper & W Maxwell (3 & 2)	1
N C Coles & C O'Connor (1 hole)	1	R Goalby & D Ragan	0
(AFTERNOON)			
N C Coles & C O'Connor	0	A Palmer & D Finsterwald (3 & 2)	1
P Alliss & B J Hunt	0	A Lema & J Pott (1 hole)	1
T B Haliburton & G M Hunt	0	W Casper & W Maxwell (2 & 1)	1
B Huggett & D Thomas (halved)	½	R Goalby & D Ragan (halved)	½
	2		**6**
SINGLES (MORNING)			
G M Hunt	0	A Lema (5 & 3)	1
B Huggett (3 & 1)	1	J Pott	0
P Alliss (1 hole)	1	A Palmer	0
N C Coles (halved)	½	W Casper (halved)	½
D Thomas	0	R Goalby (3 & 2)	1
C O'Connor	0	G Littler (1 hole)	1
H Weetman (1 hole)	1	J Boros	0
B J Hunt (2 holes)	1	D Finsterwald	0
(AFTERNOON)			
G Will	0	A Palmer (3 & 2)	1
N C Coles	0	D Ragan (2 & 1)	1
P Alliss (halved)	½	A Lema (halved)	½
T B Haliburton	0	G Littler (6 & 5)	1
H Weetman	0	J Boros (2 & 1)	1
C O'Connor	0	W Maxwell (2 & 1)	1
D Thomas	0	D Finsterwald (4 & 3)	1
B J Hunt	0	R Goalby (2 & 1)	1
	5		**11**

GB 12½ USA 19½

GB	MATCHES	USA	MATCHES
FOURSOMES (MORNING)			
L Platts & P J Butler	0	J Boros & A Lema (1 hole)	1
D C Thomas & G Will (6 & 5)	1	A Palmer & D Marr	0
B J Hunt & N C Coles	0	W Casper & G Littler (2 & 1)	1
P Alliss & C O'Connor (5 & 4)	1	K Venturi & D January	0
(AFTERNOON)			
D C Thomas & G Will	0	A Palmer & D Marr (6 & 5)	1
P Alliss & C O'Connor (2 & 1)	1	W Casper & G Littler	0
J Martin & J Hitchcock	0	J Boros & A Lema (5 & 4)	1
B J Hunt and N C Coles (3 & 2)	1	K Venturi & D January	0
	4		**4**
FOURBALLS (MORNING)			
D C Thomas & G Will	0	D January & T Jacobs (1 hole)	1
L Platts & P J Butler (halved)	½	W Casper & G Littler (halved)	½
P Alliss & C O'Connor	0	A Palmer & D Marr (6 & 4)	1
B J Hunt & N C Coles (1 hole)	1	J Boros & A Lema	0
(AFTERNOON)			
P Alliss & C O'Connor (2 holes)	1	A Palmer & D Marr	0
D C Thomas & G Will	0	D January & T Jacobs (1 hole)	1
L Platts & P J Butler (halved)	½	W Casper & G Littler (halved)	½
B J Hunt & N C Coles	0	K Venturi & A Lema (1 hole)	1
	3		**5**
SINGLES (MORNING)			
J Hitchcock	0	A Palmer (3 & 2)	1
L Platts	0	J Boros (4 & 2)	1
P J Butler	0	A Lema (1 hole)	1
N C Coles	0	D Marr (2 holes)	1
B J Hunt (2 holes)	1	G Littler	0
D C Thomas	0	T Jacobs (2 & 1)	1
P Alliss (1 hole)	1	W Casper	0
G Will (halved)	½	D January (halved)	½
(AFTERNOON)			
C O'Connor	0	A Lema (6 & 4)	1
J Hitchcock	0	J Boros (2 & 1)	1
P J Butler	0	A Palmer (2 holes)	1
P Alliss (3 & 1)	1	K Venturi	0
N C Coles (3 & 2)	1	W Casper	0
G Will	0	G Littler (2 & 1)	1
B J Hunt	0	D Marr (1 hole)	1
L Platts (1 hole)	1	T Jacobs	0
	5½		**10½**

USA 23½ GB 8½

GB	MATCHES	USA	MATCHES
FOURSOMES (MORNING)			
B G C Huggett & G Will (halved)	½	W Casper & J Boros (halved)	½
P Alliss & C O'Connor	0	A Palmer & G Dickinson (2 & 1)	1
A Jacklin & D C Thomas (4 & 3)	1	D Sanders & G Brewer	0
B J Hunt & N C Coles	0	R Nichols & J Pott (6 & 5)	1
(AFTERNOON)			
B G C Huggett & G Will	0	W Casper & J Boros (1 hole)	1
M Gregson & H Boyle	0	G Dickinson & A Palmer (5 & 4)	1
A Jacklin & D C Thomas (3 & 2)	1	G Littler & A Geiberger	0
P Alliss & C O'Connor	0	R Nichols & J Pott (2 & 1)	1
	2½		**5½**
FOURBALLS (MORNING)			
P Alliss & C O'Connor	0	W Casper & G Brewer (3 & 2)	1
B J Hunt & N C Coles	0	R Nichols & J Pott (1 hole)	1
A Jacklin & D C Thomas	0	G Littler & A Geiberger (1 hole)	1
B G C Huggett & G Will	0	G Dickinson & D Sanders (3 & 2)	1
(AFTERNOON)			
B J Hunt & N C Coles	0	W Casper & G Brewer (5 & 3)	1
P Alliss & M Gregson	0	G Dickinson & D Sanders (3 & 2)	1
G Will & H Boyle	0	A Palmer & J Boros (1 hole)	1
A Jacklin & D C Thomas (halved)	½	G Littler & A Geiberger (halved)	½
	½		**7½**
SINGLES (MORNING)			
H Boyle	0	G Brewer (4 & 3)	1
P Alliss	0	W Casper (2 & 1)	1
A Jacklin	0	A Palmer (3 & 2)	1
B G C Huggett (1 hole)	1	J Boros	0
N C Coles (2 & 1)	1	D Sanders	0
M Gregson	0	A Geiberger (4 & 2)	1
D C Thomas (halved)	½	G Littler (halved)	½
B J Hunt (halved)	½	R Nichols (halved)	½
(AFTERNOON)			
B G C Huggett	0	A Palmer (5 & 3)	1
P Alliss (2 & 1)	1	G Brewer	0
A Jacklin	0	G Dickinson (3 & 2)	1
C O'Connor	0	R Nichols (3 & 2)	1
G Will	0	J Pott (3 & 1)	1
M Gregson	0	A Geiberger (2 & 1)	1
B J Hunt (halved)	½	J Boros (halved)	½
N C Coles (2 & 1)	1	D Sanders	0
	5½		**10½**

GB 16 USA 16

GB	MATCHES	USA	MATCHES
FOURSOMES (MORNING)			
N C Coles & B G C Huggett (3 & 2)	1	M Barber & R Floyd	0
R Gallacher & M Bembridge (2 & 1)	1	L Trevino & K Still	0
A Jacklin & P Townsend (3 & 1)	1	D Hill & T Aaron	0
C O'Connor & P Alliss (halved)	½	W Casper & F Beard (halved)	½
(AFTERNOON)			
N C Coles & B G C Huggett	0	D Hill & T Aaron (1 hole)	1
B Gallacher & M Bembridge	0	L Trevino & G Littler (1 hole)	1
A Jacklin & P Townsend (1 hole)	1	W Casper & F Beard	0
P J Butler & B J Hunt	0	J Nicklaus & D Sikes (1 hole)	1
	4½		**3½**
FOURBALLS (MORNING)			
C O'Connor & P Townsend (1 hole)	1	D Hill & D Douglass	0
B G C Huggett & G A Caygill (halved)	½	R Floyd & M Barber (halved)	½
B Barnes & P Alliss	0	L Trevino & G Littler (1 hole)	1
A Jacklin & N C Coles (1 hole)	1	J Nicklaus & D Sikes	0
(AFTERNOON)			
P J Butler & P Townsend	0	W Casper & F Beard (2 holes)	1
B G C Huggett & B Gallacher	0	D Hill & K Still (2 & 1)	1
M Bembridge & B J Hunt (halved)	½	T Aaron & R Floyd (halved)	½
A Jacklin & N C Coles (halved)	½	L Trevino & M Barber (halved)	½
	3½		**4½**
SINGLES (MORNING)			
P Alliss	0	L Trevino (2 & 1)	1
P Townsend	0	D Hill (5 & 4)	1
N C Coles (1 hole)	1	T Aaron	0
B Barnes	0	W Casper (1 hole)	1
C O'Connor (5 & 4)	1	F Beard	0
N Bembridge (1 hole)	1	K Still	0
P J Butler (1 hole)	1	R Floyd	0
A Jacklin (4 & 3)	1	J Nicklaus	0
(AFTERNOON)			
B Barnes	0	D Hill (4 & 2)	1
B Gallacher (4 & 3)	1	L Trevino	0
M Bembridge	0	M Barber (7 & 6)	1
P J Butler (3 & 2)	1	D Douglass	0
N C Coles	0	D Sikes (4 & 3)	1
C O'Connor	0	G Littler (2 & 1)	1
B G C Huggett (halved)	½	W Casper (halved)	½
A Jacklin (halved)	½	J Nicklaus (halved)	½
	8		**8**

USA 18½ GB 13½

GB		USA	
FOURSOMES (MORNING)	MATCHES		MATCHES
N C Coles & C O'Connor (2 & 1)	1	W Casper & M Barber	0
P Townsend & P Oosterhuis	0	A Palmer & G Dickinson (2 holes)	1
B G C Huggett & A Jacklin (3 & 2)	1	J Nicklaus & D Stockton	0
M Bembridge & P J Butler (1 hole)	1	C Coody & F Beard	0
(AFTERNOON)			
H Bannerman & B Gallacher (2 & 1)	1	W Casper & M Barber	0
P Townsend & P Oosterhuis	0	A Palmer & G Dickinson (1 hole)	1
B G C Huggett & A Jacklin (halved)	½	L Trevino & M Rudolph (halved)	½
M Bembridge & P J Butler	0	J Nicklaus & J C Snead (5 & 3)	1
	4½		**3½**
FOURBALLS (MORNING)			
C O'Connor & B Barnes	0	L Trevino & M Rudolph (2 & 1)	1
N C Coles & J Garner	0	F Beard & J C Snead (2 & 1)	1
P Oosterhuis & B Gallacher	0	A Palmer & G Dickinson (5 & 4)	1
P Townsend & H Bannerman	0	J Nicklaus & G Littler (2 & 1)	1
(AFTERNOON)			
B Gallacher & P Oosterhuis (1 hole)	1	L Trevino & W Casper	0
A Jacklin & B G C Huggett	0	G Littler & J C Snead (2 & 1)	1
P Townsend & H Bannerman	0	A Palmer & J Nicklaus (1 hole)	1
N C Coles & C O'Connor (halved)	½	C Coody & F Beard (halved)	½
	1½		**6½**
SINGLES (MORNING)			
A Jacklin	0	L Trevino (1 hole)	1
B Gallacher (halved)	½	D Stockton (halved)	½
B Barnes (1 hole)	1	M Rudolph	0
P Oosterhuis (4 & 3)	1	G Littler	0
P Townsend	0	J Nicklaus (3 & 2)	1
C O'Connor	0	G Dickinson (5 & 4)	1
H Bannerman (halved)	½	A Palmer (halved)	½
N C Coles (halved)	½	F Beard (halved)	½
(AFTERNOON)			
B G C Huggett	0	L Trevino (7 & 6)	1
A Jacklin	0	J C Snead (1 hole)	1
B Barnes (2 & 1)	1	M Barber	0
P Townsend	0	D Stockton (1 hole)	1
B Gallacher (2 & 1)	1	C Coody	0
N C Coles	0	J Nicklaus (5 & 3)	1
P Oosterhuis (3 & 2)	1	A Palmer	0
H Bannerman (2 & 1)	1	G Dickinson	0
	7½		**8½**

GB 13 USA 19

GB		USA	
FOURSOMES (MORNING)	MATCHES		MATCHES
B W Barnes & B J Gallacher (1 hole)	1	L Trevino & W J Casper	0
C O'Connor & N C Coles (3 & 2)	1	T Weiskopf & J C Snead	0
A Jacklin & P A Oosterhuis (halved)	½	J Rodriguez & L Graham (halved)	½
M E Bembridge & E Polland	0	J W Nicklaus & A Palmer (6 & 5)	1
FOURBALLS (AFTERNOON)			
B W Barnes & B J Gallacher (5 & 4)	1	T Aaron & G Brewer	0
M E Bembridge & B G C Huggett (3 & 1)	1	A Palmer & J W Nicklaus	0
A Jacklin & P A Oosterhuis (3 & 1)	1	T Weiskopf & W J Casper	0
N C Coles & C O'Connor	0	L Trevino & H Blancas (2 & 1)	1
	5½		**2½**
FOURSOMES (MORNING)			
B W Barnes & P J Butler	0	J W Nicklaus & T Weiskopf (1 hole)	1
P A Oosterhuis & A Jacklin (2 holes)	1	A Palmer & D Hill	0
M E Bembridge & B G C Huggett (5 & 4)	1	J Rodriguez & L Graham	0
N C Coles & C O'Connor	0	L Trevino & W J Casper (2 & 1)	1
FOURBALLS (AFTERNOON)			
B W Barnes & P J Butler	0	J C Snead & A Palmer (2 holes)	1
A Jacklin & P A Oosterhuis	0	G Brewer & W J Casper (3 & 2)	1
C Clark & E Polland	0	J W Nicklaus & T Weiskopf (3 & 2)	1
M E Bembridge & B G C Huggett (halved)	½	L Trevino & H Blancas (halved)	½
	2½		**5½**
SINGLES (MORNING)			
B W Barnes	0	W J Casper (2 & 1)	1
B J Gallacher	0	T Weiskopf (3 & 1)	1
P J Butler	0	H Blancas (5 & 4)	1
A Jacklin (3 & 1)	1	T Aaron	0
N C Coles (halved)	½	G Brewer (halved)	½
C O'Connor	0	J C Snead (1 hole)	1
M E Bembridge (halved)	½	J W Nicklaus (halved)	½
P A Oosterhuis (halved)	½	L Trevino (halved)	½
(AFTERNOON)			
B G C Huggett (4 & 2)	1	H Blancas	0
B W Barnes	0	J C Snead (3 & 1)	1
B J Gallacher	0	G Brewer (6 & 5)	1
A Jacklin	0	W J Casper (2 & 1)	1
N C Coles	0	L Trevino (6 & 5)	1
C O'Connor (halved)	½	T Weiskopf (halved)	½
M E Bembridge	0	J W Nicklaus (2 holes)	1
P A Oosterhuis (4 & 2)	1	A Palmer	0
	5		**11**

USA 21 GB 11

GB		USA	
FOURSOMES (MORNING)	MATCHES		MATCHES
B W Barnes & B J Gallacher	0	J W Nicklaus & T Weiskopf (5 & 4)	1
N Wood & M Bembridge	0	G Littler & H Irwin (4 & 3)	1
A Jacklin & P Oosterhuis	0	A Geiberger & J Miller (3 & 1)	1
T Horton & J O'Leary	0	L Trevino & J C Snead (2 & 1)	1
FOURBALLS (AFTERNOON)			
P Oosterhuis & A Jacklin (2 & 1)	1	W J Casper & R Floyd	0
E Darcy & C O'Connor, Jnr	0	T Weiskopf & L Graham (3 & 2)	1
B W Barnes & B J Gallacher (halved)	½	J W Nicklaus & R Murphy (halved)	½
T Horton & J O'Leary	0	L Trevino & H Irwin (2 & 1)	1
	1½		**6½**
FOURBALLS (MORNING)			
P Oosterhuis & A Jacklin (halved)	½	W J Casper & J Miller (halved)	½
T Horton & N Wood	0	J W Nicklaus & J C Snead (4 & 2)	1
B W Barnes & B J Gallacher	0	G Littler & L Graham (6 & 3)	1
E Darcy & G L Hunt (halved)	½	A Geiberger & L Graham (3 & 2)	1
FOURSOMES (AFTERNOON)			
A Jacklin & B W Barnes (3 & 2)	1	L Trevino & R Murphy	0
C O'Connor, Jnr & J O'Leary	0	T Weiskopf & J Miller (5 & 3)	1
P Oosterhuis & M Bembridge	0	H Irwin & W J Casper (3 & 2)	1
E Darcy & G L Hunt	0	A Geiberger & L Graham (3 & 2)	1
	2		**6**
SINGLES (MORNING)			
A Jacklin	0	R Murphy (2 & 1)	1
P Oosterhuis (2 holes)	1	J Miller	0
B J Gallacher (halved)	½	L Trevino (halved)	½
T Horton (halved)	½	H Irwin (halved)	½
B G C Huggett	0	G Littler (4 & 2)	1
E Darcy	0	W J Casper (3 & 2)	1
G L Hunt	0	T Weiskopf (5 & 3)	1
B W Barnes (4 & 2)	1	J W Nicklaus	0
(AFTERNOON)			
A Jacklin	0	R Floyd (1 hole)	1
P Oosterhuis (3 & 2)	1	J C Snead	0
B J Gallacher (halved)	½	A Geiberger (halved)	½
T Horton (2 & 1)	1	L Graham	0
J O'Leary	0	H Irwin (2 & 1)	1
M Bembridge	0	R Murphy (2 & 1)	1
N Wood (2 & 1)	1	L Trevino	0
B W Barnes (2 & 1)	1	J W Nicklaus	0
	7½		**8½**

GB 7½ USA 12½

GB	MATCHES	USA	MATCHES
FOURSOMES			
B J Gallacher & B W Barnes	0	L Wadkins & H Irwin (3 & 1)	1
N C Coles & P Dawson	0	D Stockton & J McGee (1 hole)	1
N Faldo & P Oosterhuis (2 & 1)	1	R Floyd & L Graham	0
E Darcy & A Jacklin (halved)	½	E Snead & D January (halved)	½
T Horton & M James	0	J W Nicklaus & T Watson (5 & 4)	1
	1½		**3½**
FOURBALLS			
B W Barnes & T Horton	0	T Watson & H Green (5 & 4)	1
N C Coles & P Dawson	0	E Sneed & L Wadkins (5 & 3)	1
N Faldo & P Oosterhuis (3 & 1)	1	J W Nicklaus & R Floyd	0
A Jacklin & E Darcy	0	D Hill & D Stockton (5 & 3)	1
M James & K Brown	0	H Irwin & L Graham (1 hole)	1
	1		**4**
SINGLES			
H Clark	0	L Wadkins (4 & 3)	1
N C Coles	0	L Graham (5 & 3)	1
P Dawson (5 & 4)	1	D January	0
B W Barnes (1 hole)	1	H Irwin	0
T Horton	0	D Hill (5 & 4)	1
B J Gallacher (1 hole)	1	N W Nicklaus	0
E Darcy	0	H Green (1 hole)	1
M James	0	R Floyd (2 & 1)	1
N Faldo (1 hole)	1	T Watson	0
P Oosterhuis (2 holes)	1	J McGee	0
	5		**5**

USA 17 Europe 11

Europe	MATCHES	USA	MATCHES
FOURBALLS (MORNING)			
A Garrido & S Ballesteros	0	L Wadkins & L Nelson (2 & 1)	1
K Brown & M James	0	L Trevino & F Zoeller (3 & 2)	1
P Oosterhuis & N Faldo	0	A Bean & L Elder (2 & 1)	1
B Gallacher & B Barnes (2 & 1)	1	H Irwin & J Mahaffey	0
FOURSOMES (AFTERNOON)			
K Brown & D Smyth	0	H Irwin & T Kite (7 & 6)	1
S Ballesteros & A Garrido (3 & 2)	1	F Zoeller & H Green	0
A Lyle & A Jacklin (halved)	½	L Trevino & G Morgan (halved)	½
B Gallacher & B Barnes	0	L Wadkins & L Nelson (4 & 3)	1
	2½		**5½**
FOURSOMES (MORNING)			
A Jacklin & A Lyle (5 & 4)	1	L Elder & J Mahaffey	0
N Faldo & P Oosterhuis (6 & 5)	1	A Bean & T Kite	0
B Gallacher & B Barnes (2 & 1)	1	F Zoeller & M Hayes	0
S Ballesteros & A Garrido	0	L Wadkins & L Nelson (3 & 2)	1
FOURBALLS (AFTERNOON)			
S Ballesteros & a Garrido	0	L Wadkins & L Nelson (5 & 4)	1
A Jacklin & A Lyle	0	H Irwin & T Kite (1 hole)	1
B Gallacher & B Barnes (3 & 2)	1	L Trevino & F Zoeller	0
N Faldo & P Oosterhuis (1 hole)	1	L Elder & M Hayes	0
	5		**3**
SINGLES (MORNING)			
B Gallacher	1	L Wadkins	0
S Ballesteros	0	L Nelson (3 & 2)	1
A Jacklin	0	T Kite (1 hole)	1
A Garrido	0	M Hayes (1 hole)	1
M King	0	A Bean (4 & 3)	1
B Barnes	0	J Mahaffey (1 hole)	1
(AFTERNOON)			
N Faldo (3 & 2)	1	L Elder	0
D Smyth	0	H Irwin (5 & 3)	1
P Oosterhuis	0	H Green (2 holes)	1
K Brown (1 hole)	1	F Zoeller	0
A Lyle	0	L Trevino (2 & 1)	1
M James (halved, match not played, injured)	½	G Morgan (halved, match not played)	½
	3½		**8½**

Europe 9½ USA 18½

Europe	MATCHES	USA	MATCHES
FOURSOMES (MORNING)			
B Langer & M Pinero	0	L Trevino & L Nelson (1 hole)	1
A Lyle & M James (2 & 1)	1	W Rogers & B Lietzke	0
B Gallacher & D Smyth (3 & 2)	1	H Irwin & R Floyd	0
P Oosterhuis & N Faldo	0	T Watson & J Nicklaus (4 & 3)	1
FOURBALLS (AFTERNOON)			
S Torrance & H Clark (halved)	½	T Kite & J Miller (halved)	½
A Lyle & M James (3 & 2)	1	B Crenshaw & J Pate	0
D Smyth & J-M Canizares (6 & 5)	1	W Rogers & B Lietzke	0
B Gallacher & E Darcy	0	H Irwin & R Floyd (2 & 1)	1
	4½		**3½**
FOURBALLS (MORNING)			
N Faldo & S Torrance	0	L Trevino & J Pate (7 & 5)	1
A Lyle & M James	0	L Nelson & T Kite (1 hole)	1
B Langer & M Pinero (2 & 1)	1	R Floyd & H Irwin	0
J-M Canizares & D Smyth	0	J Nicklaus & T Watson (3 & 2)	1
(AFTERNOON)			
P Oosterhuis & S Torrance	0	L Trevino & J Pate (2 & 1)	1
B Langer & M Pinero	0	J Nicklaus & T Watson (3 & 2)	1
A Lyle & M James	0	W Rogers & R Floyd (3 & 2)	1
D Smyth & B Gallacher	0	T Kite & L Nelson (3 & 2)	1
	1		**7**
SINGLES			
S Torrance	0	L Trevino (5 & 3)	1
A Lyle	0	T Kite (3 & 2)	1
B Gallacher (halved)	½	W Rogers (halved)	½
M James	0	L Nelson (2 holes)	1
D Smyth	0	B Crenshaw (6 & 4)	1
B Langer (halved)	½	B Lietzke (halved)	½
M Pinero (4 & 2)	1	J Pate	0
J-M Canizares	0	H Irwin (1 hole)	1
N Faldo (2 & 1)	1	J Miller	0
H Clark (4 & 3)	1	T Watson	0
P Oosterhuis	0	R Floyd (1 hole)	1
E Darcy	0	J Nicklaus (5 & 3)	1
	4		**8**

USA 14½ Europe 13 ½

Europe	MATCHES	USA	MATCHES
FOURSOMES (MORNING)			
B Gallacher & A Lyle	0	T Watson & B Crenshaw (5 & 4)	1
N Faldo & B Langer (4 & 2)	1	L Wadkins & C Stadler	0
J-M Canizares & S Torrance (4 & 3)	1	R Floyd & B Gilder	0
S Ballesteros & P Way	0	T Kite & C Peete (2 & 1)	1
FOURBALLS (AFTERNOON)			
B Waites & K Brown (2 & 1)	1	G Morgan & F Zoeller	0
N Faldo & B Langer	0	T Watson & J Haas (2 & 1)	1
S Ballesteros & P Way (1 hole)	1	R Floyd & C Strange	0
S Torrance & I Woosnam (halved)	½	B Crenshaw & C Peete (halved)	½
	4½		**3½**
FOURBALLS (MORNING)			
B Waites & K Brown	0	L Wadkins & C Stadler (1 hole)	1
N Faldo & B Langer (4 & 2)	1	B Crenshaw & C Peete	0
S Ballesteros & P Way (halved)	½	G Morgan & J Haas (halved)	½
S Torrance & I Woosnam	0	T Watson & B Gilder (5 & 4)	1
FOURSOMES (AFTERNOON)			
N Faldo & B Langer (3 & 2)	1	T Kite & R Floyd	0
S Torrance & J-M Canizares	0	G Morgan & L Wadkins (7 & 5)	1
S Ballesteros & P Way (2 & 1)	1	T Watson & B Gilder	0
B Waites & K Brown	0	J Haas & C Strange (3 & 2)	1
	3½		**4½**
SINGLES			
S Ballesteros (halved)	½	F Zoeller (halved)	½
N Faldo (2 & 1)	1	J Haas	0
B Langer (2 holes)	1	G Morgan	0
G J Brand	0	B Gilder (2 holes)	1
A Lyle	0	B Crenshaw (3 & 1)	1
B Waites	0	C Peete (1 hole)	1
P Way (2 & 1)	1	C Strange	0
S Torrance (halved)	½	T Kite (halved)	½
I Woosnam	0	C Stadler (3 & 2)	1
J-M Canizares (halved)	½	L Wadkins (halved)	½
K Brown (4 & 3)	1	R Floyd	0
B Gallacher	0	T Watson (2 & 1)	1
	5½		**6½**

Europe 16½ USA 11½

Europe	MATCHES	USA	MATCHES
FOURSOMES (MORNING)			
S Ballesteros & M Pinero (2 & 1)	1	C Strange & M O'Meara	0
B Langer & N Faldo	0	C Peete & T Kite (3 & 2)	1
A Lyle & K Brown	0	L Wadkins & R Floyd (4 & 3)	1
H Clark & S Torrance	0	C Stadler & H Sutton (3 & 2)	1
FOURBALLS (AFTERNOON)			
P Way & I Woosnam (1 hole)	1	F Zoeller & H Green	0
S Ballesteros & M Pinero (2 & 1)	1	A North & P Jacobsen	0
B Langer & J-M Canizares (halved)	½	C Stadler & H Sutton (halved)	½
S Torrance & H Clark	0	R Floyd & L Wadkins (1 hole)	1
	3½		**4½**
FOURBALLS (MORNING)			
S Torrance & H Clark (2 & 1)	1	T Kite & A North	0
P Way & I Woosnam (4 & 3)	1	H Green & F Zoeller	0
S Ballesteros & M Pinero	0	M O'Meara & L Wadkins (3 & 2)	1
B Langer & A Lyle (halved)	½	C Stadler & C Strange (halved)	½
FOURSOMES (AFTERNOON)			
J-M Canizares & J Rivero (7 & 5)	1	T Kite & C Peete	0
S Ballesteros & M Pinero (5 & 4)	1	C Stadler & H Sutton	0
P Way & I Woosnam	0	C Strange & P Jacobsen (4 & 2)	1
B Langer & K Brown (3 & 2)	1	R Floyd & L Wadkins	0
	5½		**2½**
SINGLES			
M Pinero (3 & 1)	1	L Wadkins	0
I Woosnam	0	C Stadler (2 & 1)	1
P Way (2 holes)	1	R Floyd	0
S Ballesteros (halved)	½	T Kite (halved)	½
A Lyle (3 & 2)	1	P Jacobsen	0
B Langer (5 & 4)	1	H Sutton	0
S Torrance (1 hole)	1	A North	0
H Clark (1 hole)	1	M O'Meara	0
J Rivero	0	C Peete (1 hole)	1
N Faldo	0	H Green (3 & 1)	1
J-M Canizares (2 holes)	1	F Zoeller	0
K Brown	0	C Strange (4 & 2)	1
	7½		**4½**

USA 13 Europe 15

Europe	MATCHES	USA	MATCHES
FOURSOMES (MORNING)			
S Torrance & H Clark	0	C Strange & T Kite (4 & 2)	1
K Brown & B Langer	0	H Sutton & D Pohl (2 & 1)	1
N Faldo & I Woosnam (2 holes)	1	L Wadkins & L Mize	0
S Ballesteros & J-M Olazabal (1 hole)	1	L Nelson & P Stewart	0
FOURBALLS (AFTERNOON)			
G Brand Jr & J Rivero (3 & 2)	1	B Crenshaw & S Simpson	0
A Lyle & B Langer (1 hole)	1	A Bean & M Calcavecchia	0
N Faldo & I Woosnam (2 & 1)	1	H Sutton & D Pohl	0
S Ballesteros & J-M Olazabal (2 & 1)	1	C Strange & T Kite	0
	6		**2**
FOURSOMES (MORNING)			
J Rivero & G Brand Jr	0	C Strange & T Kite (3 & 1)	1
N Faldo & I Woosnam (halved)	½	H Sutton & L Mize (halved)	½
A Lyle & B Langer (2 & 1)	1	L Wadkins & L Nelson	0
S Ballesteros & J-M Olazabal (1 hole)	1	B Crenshaw & P Stewart	0
FOURBALLS (AFTERNOON)			
N Faldo & I Woosnam (5 & 4)	1	C Strange & T Kite	0
E Darcy & G Brand Jr	0	A Bean & P Stewart (3 & 2)	1
S Ballesteros & J-M Olazabal	0	H Sutton & L Mize (2 & 1)	1
A Lyle & B Langer (1 hole)	1	L Wadkins & L Nelson	0
	4½		**3½**
SINGLES			
I Woosnam	0	A Bean (1 hole)	1
H Clark (1 hole)	1	D Pohl	0
S Torreance (halved)	½	L Mize (halved)	½
N Faldo	0	M Calcavecchia (1 hole)	1
J-M Olazabal	0	P Stewart (2 holes)	1
J Rivero	0	S Simpson (2 & 1)	1
A Lyle	0	T Kite (3 & 2)	1
E Darcy (1 hole)	1	B Crenshaw	0
B Langer (halved)	½	L Nelson (halved)	½
S Ballesteros (2 & 1)	1	C Strange	0
K Brown	0	L Wadkins (3 & 2)	1
G Brand Jr (halved)	½	H Sutton (halved)	½
	4½		**7½**

Europe 14 USA 14

Europe	MATCHES	USA	MATCHES
FOURSOMES (MORNING)			
N Faldo & I Woosnam (halved)	½	T Kite & C Strange (halved)	½
H Clark & M James	0	L Wadkins & P Stewart (1 hole)	1
S Ballesteros & J-M Olazabal (halved)	½	T Watson & C Beck (halved)	½
B Langer & R Rafferty	0	M Calcavecchia & K Green (2 & 1)	1
FOURBALLS (AFTERNOON)			
S Torrance & G Brand Jr (1 hole)	1	C Strange & P Azinger	0
H Clark & M James (3 & 2)	1	F Couples & L Wadkins	0
N Faldo & I Woosnam (1 hole)	1	M Calcavecchia & M McCumber	0
S Ballesteros & J-M Olazabal (6 & 5)	1	T Watson & M O'Meara	0
	5		**3**
FOURSOMES (MORNING)			
N Faldo & I Woosnam (3 & 2)	1	L Wadkins & P Stewart	0
G Brand & S Torrance	0	P Azinger & C Beck (4 & 3)	1
C O'Connor Jr & R Rafferty	0	M Calcavecchia & K Green (3 & 2)	1
S Ballesteros & J-M Olazabal (1 hole)	1	T Kite & C Strange	0
FOURBALLS (AFTERNOON)			
N Faldo & I Woosnam	0	P Azinger & C Beck (2 & 1)	1
J M Canizares & B Langer	0	T Kite & M McCumber (2 & 1)	1
H Clark & M James (1 hole)	1	P Stewart & C Strange	0
S Ballesteros & J-M Olazabal (4 & 2)	1	M Calcavecchia & K Green	0
	4		**4**
SINGLES			
S Ballesteros	0	P Azinger (1 hole)	1
B Langer	0	C Beck (3 & 1)	0
J-M Olazabal (1 hole)	1	P Stewart	0
R Rafferty (1 hole)	1	M Calcavecchia	0
H Clark	0	T Kite (8 & 7)	1
M James (3 & 2)	1	M O'Meara	0
C O'Connor (1 hole)	1	F Couples	0
J-M Canizares (1 hole)	1	K Green	0
G Brand	0	M McCumber (1 hole)	1
S Torrance	0	T Watson (3 & 1)	1
N Faldo	0	L Wadkins (1 hole)	1
I Woosnam	0	C Strange (1 hole)	1
	14		**14**

Europe 13 ½ USA 14 ½

Europe	MATCHES	USA	MATCHES
FOURSOMES (MORNING)			
S Ballesteros & J-M Olazabal (2 & 1)	1	P Azinger & C Beck	0
B Langer & M James	0	R Floyd & F Couples (2 & 1)	1
D Gilford & C Montgomerie	0	L Wadkins & H Irwin (4 & 2)	1
N Faldo & I Woosnam	0	P Stewart & M Calcavecchia (1 hole)	1
FOURBALLS (AFTERNOON)			
S Torrance & D Feherty (halved)	½	L Wadkins and M O'Meara (halved)	½
S Ballesteros & J-M Olazabal (2 & 1)	1	P Azinger & C Beck	0
S Richardson & M James (5 & 4)	1	C Pavin & M Calcavecchia	0
N Faldo & I Woosnam	0	R Floyd & F Couples (5 & 3)	1
	3½		**4½**
FOURSOMES (MORNING)			
S Torrance & D Feherty	0	L Wadkins & H Irwin (4 & 2)	1
S Richardson & M James	0	M Calcavvechia & P Stewart (1 hole)	1
N Faldo & D Gilford	0	P Azinger & M O'Meara (7 & 6)	1
S Ballesteros & J-M Olazabal (3 & 2)	1	R Floyd & F Couples	0
FOURBALLS (AFTERNOON)			
I Woosnam & P Broadhurst (2 & 1)	1	P Azinger & H Irwin	0
B Langer & P Broadhurst (2 & 1)	1	C Pavin & S Pate	0
M James & s Richardson (3 & 1)	1	L Wadkins & W Levi	0
S Ballesteros & J-M Olazabal (halved)	½	P Stewart & F Couples (halved)	½
	4½		**3½**
SINGLES			
N Faldo (2 holes)	1	R Floyd	0
D Feherty (2 & 1)	1	P Stewart	0
C Montgomerie (halved)	½	M Calcavecchia (halved)	½
J-M Olazabal	0	P Azinger (2 holes)	1
S Richardson	0	C Pavin (2 & 1)	1
S Ballesteros (3 & 2)	1	W Levi	0
I Woosnam	0	C Beck (3 & 1)	1
P Broadhurst (3 & 1)	1	M O'Meara	0
S Torrance	0	F Couples (3 & 2)	1
M James	0	L Wadkins (3 & 2)	1
B Langer (halved)	½	H Irwin (halved)	½
D Gilford (halved)	½	S Pate (halved)	½*
	5½		**6½**

*Match not contested; Pate injured.

BIBLIOGRAPHY

Alliss, Peter *Supreme Champions of Golf* (Willow, 1986)
Alliss, Peter *100 Greatest Golfers* (Macdonald, 1989)
Alliss, Peter (Editor) *Golf – A Way of Life* (Stanley Paul, 1988)
Aultman, Dick & Bowden, Ken *The Masters of Golf* (Stanley Paul, 1988)

Barkow, Al *Gettin' to the Dance Floor* (Heinemann, 1988)
Barkow, Al *The History of the PGA Tour* (Doubleday, 1989)
Bryan, Mike *Dogleg Madness* (Atlantic Monthly Press, 1988)

Campbell, Malcolm *Encyclopedia of Golf* (Dorling Kindersley, 1991)
Chieger, Bob & Sullivan, Pat *The Book of Golf Quotations* (Stanley Paul, 1987)
Cotton, Henry *This Game of Golf* (Country Life, 1948)
Cotton, Henry *Thanks for the Game* (Sidgwick & Jackson, 1980)

Darwin, Bernard *James Braid* (Batsford, 1991)
Demaret, Jimmy *My Partner, Ben Hogan* (Peter Davies, 1954)
Dobereiner, Peter *For The Love of Golf* (Stanley Paul, 1981)
Dobereiner, Peter *The Game with the Hole in It* (Faber, 1970)
Doust, Dudley & Sheldon, Phil *Seve* (Partridge Press, 1986)

Elliott, Alan & May, John Allan (Editors) *The Golf Monthly Illustrated History of Golf* (Hamlyn, 1990)

Gallacher, Bernard *Captain at Kiawah* (Chapmans, 1991)

Hagen, Walter *The Walter Hagen Story* (Heinemann, 1961)
Hobbs, Michael *The Ryder Cup* (Macdonald, 1989)
Hobbs, Michael (Editor) *The Golfer's Companion* (Macdonald, 1988)
Howell, Audrey *Harry Vardon* (Stanley Paul, 1991)

Jacklin, Tony *Jacklin* (Hodder & Stoughton, 1970)
Jenkins, Dan *The Dogged Victims of Inexorable Fate* (Simon & Schuster, 1990)

Keeler, O B & Rice, Grantland *The Bobby Jones Story* (Foulsham)

Lawrenson, Derek *The Ultimate Book of Golf* (Treasure Press, 1991)
Longhurst, Henry *Only on Saturdays* (Simon & Schuster, 1989)
Longhurst, Henry *The Essential Henry Longhurst* (Willow, 1988)
Longhurst, Henry *The Best of Henry Longhurst* (Collins, 1979)
Longhurst, Henry *Golf Mixture* (Werner Laurie, 1952)
Longhurst, Henry & Cousins, Geoffrey *The Ryder Cup 1965* (Stanley Paul, 1965)

McDonnell, Michael *The Complete Book of Golf* (Kingswood, 1985)
Morrison, Ian *Who's Who in Golf* (Hamlyn, 1988)

Peper, George (Editor) *Golf in America* (Abrams, 1988)
Plumridge, Chris *Golf Characters* (Stanley Paul, 1989)
Plumridge, Chris & Hopkins, John (Editors) *A Golfer's Companion* (W H Smith, 1990)

Rees, Dai *Thirty Years of Championship Golf* (Stanley Paul, 1968)
Rubenstein, Lorne *Links* (Stanley Paul, 1991)
Ryde, Peter (Editor) *Royal and Ancient Championship Records* (Royal & Ancient Golf Club, 1981)

St John, Lauren *Shooting at Clouds* (Mainstream, 1991)
Sarazen, Gene & Wind, Herbert Warren *Thirty Years of Championship Golf* (A & C Black, 1990)
Snead, Sam *Slammin' Sam* (Donald Fine, 1986)
Stanley, Louis T *A History of Golf* (Hamlyn, 1990)
Steel, Donald *Golf: Records, Facts & Champions* (Guinness, 1987)
Steel, Donald & Ryde, Peter *The Shell International Encyclopedia of Golf* (Ebury Press, 1975)

Trevino, Lee & Blair, Sam *Super Mex* (Stanley Paul, 1983)

Viney, Laurence *The Royal and Ancient Book of Golf Records* (Macmillan, 1991)

Wade, Don *And Then Jack Said to Arnie* (Contemporary Books, 1991)
Ward-Thomas, Pat *Masters of Golf* (Heinemann, 1961)
Wartman, William *Playing Through* (Mainstream, 1990)
Williams, Michael *The Official History of the Ryder Cup* (Stanley Paul, 1989)
Williams, Michael *The History of Golf* (Galley Press, 1988) *The Golfer's Handbook*